TRAILBREAKERS
Pioneering Alaska's Iditarod

*Blazing the Last Great Gold Rush Trail
In North America   1840 — 1930*

By Rod Perry

To Vance,

"Hold tight to the sled!"

Rod Perry

TRAILBREAKERS
Pioneering Alaska's Iditarod

By Rod Perry

"North! On North!" cry the most driven of the gold hunters

At the top of the continent lies an almost unknown land of limitless distances, great rivers, deadly rapids, foreboding mountains towering range beyond range, the whole savage country crouching in wait to devour even the bravest and best. They will penetrate its vastness and probe it for gold— or fill unmarked graves in the attempt.

Gold!

Fabulous discoveries   Magnetic place names
Yukon Territory — Alaska — the Klondike — Nome — Fairbanks

*A continent primed by economic depression
to catch gold fever is inflamed.
The most glorious gold stampedes ever known
electrify the world.*

Then on Christmas Day, 1908

**from the bottom of a twelve-foot-deep test hole
in remote, unknown Iditarod River Country
John Beaton calls the magical word up to William Dikeman.
Once more the irresistible cry rings out from the North,**

"Gold!"

The partners set off North America's last great gold rush.
Iditarod booms to become, briefly, Alaska's biggest city.

**Across the North, brawling cities, pulsing with energy,
bursting with riches, straining to thrive and grow...**

*But something holds them back,
restricting progress...*

Blazing the Last Great Gold Rush Trail!

WHEN ARCTIC TEMPERATURES FREEZE the Bering Sea and Yukon drainage, stopping navigation for seven to eight months yearly, cities of the gold country become cut off from the industrialized world. No city can thrive without supply, communication, and travel in and out for two-thirds of its year. They are desperate to connect to shipping that plies Alaska's more southern waters which remain ice-free year around.

Even more than the *distances* between cities and ice-free shipping, *topography* is the separating obstacle. For a thousand miles along Alaska's southern coast, North America's most daunting mountain ranges throw up an almost impenetrable barrier of massive crags and glaciers. In that entire length, searchers eventually discover but five hard-to-find chinks through its armor suitable for gold-rush-era passageways. The last found takes travelers through some of the most majestic mountain scenery in the world, crossing the Alaska Range near 20,320-foot-tall Mount McKinley. This spectacular cleft is named Rainy Pass. The trail over it to the goldfields of Iditarod and Nome becomes known as the Iditarod Trail.

In its golden era, legendary drivers and legendary dogs dare its miles and dangers and the trail itself becomes a trail of legend, this final, great gold rush trail.

Now journey as by dog team through the fabulous gold rushes of yesteryear, letting these pages impart to you an intimacy with how this historic trail of fame and glory burst to life, lived, faded—and lingered to live again.

ROD PERRY WRITES TRAILBREAKERS in two volumes which, respectively, chronicle the birth of the gold rush trail and the founding of the modern race.

Volume I takes readers back to the days of yesteryear. To serve the great human influx and the mining industry, vast numbers of men and amounts of mail, supplies, building materials and equipment must be brought in. Most come by water during the usual four or five ice-free months. Once the Bering Seacoast and rivers become ice locked, however, the only means of moving people, mail and freight in and out is over winter trails, mostly by dog team.

An important part of the story of the fabulous gold rushes of the North is the story of that transportation over the trail. Without winter movement, their discovery and development would have unfolded much differently.

During the harsh, sub-arctic winter, the towering bastions and deadly glaciers of the greatest mountains on the continent bar the way to interior gold for a thousand miles along the ice-free shipping waters around Alaska's southern coast. Only five rifts—just five cracks in the mountain fortress—provide useful corridors for moving men, freight, and mail into the heartland mining districts. The last one found, over Rainy Pass, is the most remote and most primitive, taking travelers and their loads through some of the wildest country and most majestic scenery on the continent on their way to the gold fields of Iditarod and Nome.

TRAILBREAKERS, Volume I chronicles the rich history of daring men and dynamic events that force the lock and break the silence of the unknown North. Gold rush leads to gold rush, trail leads to trail, until it culminates in the last, glorious, hell-bent-for-leather gold rush and the final great gold rush trail in North America.

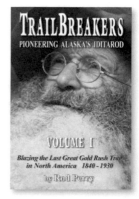

Trailbreakers, Volume I is the most-complete, most-accurate telling of how the fabled Iditarod Trail came to be. As it relates the 1840–1930 progression of events establishing the "Last Great Gold Rush Trail in North America," the book educates and corrects long-standing myths and misinformation that have grown up. It interests and entertains, filled as it is with humorous anecdotes and colorful gold rush tales. Anyone acquainted with Rod Perry as a raconteur knows he couldn't write history any other way.

TRAILBREAKERS, Volume II is the story of the founding of "The Last Great Race On Earth." By Rod Perry, a race pioneer who ran the first Iditarod Race, it is the most in-depth telling of **the most daring Iditarod adventure of all time.**

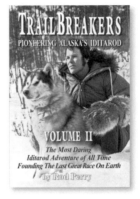

This volume:

- Includes never-before-told revelations surrounding the establishment of the event by an old insider.

- Blows away long-held myths and errors that have become imbedded in race lore.

- Draws from the only complete set of radio reports of the founding 1973 event.

- Tells little-known, incredible adventures and surprising details that were part and parcel of the wild and crazy, barely organized, absurd, glorious, trail-breaking running of first Iditarod Trail Sled Dog Race.

Turn to page 499 for more about
TRAILBREAKERS, Volume II

Books by Rod Perry may be purchased at
www.rodperry.com

TRAILBREAKERS

Pioneering Alaska's Iditarod

Volume I

Blazing the Last Great Gold Rush Trail in North America 1840 – 1930

By Rod Perry

TRAILBREAKERS
Pioneering Alaska's Iditarod
Volume I
Blazing the Last Great Gold Rush Trail in North America

ISBN 978-0-9823730-2-6

Library of Congress Control Number: 2013908036

520 pages

Early exploration history—Alaska and Yukon Territory

Early history of prospecting, discovery, gold rushes—Alaska and Yukon Territory

History of discovery, use, development of transportation corridors to gold strikes—
Alaska and Yukon Territory

Gold rush era dog team use—Alaska and Yukon Territory

Gold rush era stories—Alaska and Yukon Territory

Design and Layout: Molly Beich, Anchorage, Alaska

Cover: Daniel Quick

First Edition 2009
Revised Edition 2013

Dedication

———◆———

OUR POPULATION—probably in Alaska more than elsewhere—has individuals who, to use the words of the late Territorial Governor of Alaska Ernest Gruening, "are not wholly reconciled to the benefits of civilization—those who, while enjoying civilization's creature comforts, still hold a nostalgic longing for a vanished era in which men pitted themselves against nature's hazards and still yearn for the risks and challenges of an unspoiled wilderness."

That Gruening's words describe me may be attributed to the influence of my parents, both of whom were born shortly after the turn of the last century. My late mother, Eva Perry, grew up in a sod house on a land claim in New Mexico Territory when Pancho Villa was raiding nearby. Gilbert Perry, my late father, (whose picture graces this book cover) spent his early life on a homestead and trapline in the foothills of the Canadian Rockies where his family's closest neighbors and trapping partners were First Nations Canadians still living a semi-nomadic lifestyle. This book is dedicated to the memory of my parents.

TRAILBREAKERS

Acknowledgements

———◆———

I ENTHUSIASTICALLY THANK the following contributors to *TRAILBREAKERS*:

Foremost, my Creator and Lord, Jesus Christ who inspired me to write and blessed me with talent to spin a tale.

Larry and Pam Kaniut, my Alaska friends of longest standing, who, for more than thirty years, continued to believe I should write and never eased up on their urging.

Ingrid Sundstrom Lundegaard, whose expertise with words reflects a lifetime of professional editing, for her invaluable help with the first edition.

Marthy W. Johnson, editor of *TRAILBREAKERS* and author of the superb handbook for writers, *Write and Wrong*.

Daniel L. Quick, one of my oldest, truest friends, author of *The Kenai Canoe Trails: Alaska's Premier Hiking and Canoeing System*, creator of the *TRAILBREAKERS* covers.

Alan Perry, my brother, artist, partner in many adventures, Iditarod pioneer in his own right, and creator of the maps that are so instrumental in orienting the reader.

Chad and Jessie Chilstrom, friends and supporters extraordinaire whose untiring patience and cyber talents were desperately needed by an author just emerging—not very readily—from the Stone Age.

TRAILBREAKERS

Bob and Karen Byron, Rick and Jane Erickson, Clovis and Denise Marechal, Robert and Sandy Doran, Steve, Gwen and Lindsay Hufford, Fred Perry, Richard and Velma Perry, Speed and Evelyn Rasmussen, Irene DeLauney, Cliff Sisson, Richard and Lillian Person, Patty Parker, Ken Davis, Pat Nolde, and Dr. Frank and Sandi Moore for support that enabled production of *TRAILBREAKERS*.

Kevin Keeler, Iditarod National Historic Trail Administrator, BLM Anchorage Field Office, who provided invaluable historical resources.

Dr. J.P. Waller, a God-sent friend, professor of creative writing at Wayland Baptist University and University of Alaska at Anchorage who generously gave of his time and considerable talent to mentor and encourage me, pre-edit the work, supply changes in phraseology far beyond mere editing and suggest creation of the "voices" and other literary devices which so inject life-blood and orientation to this history.

The Beaton, Ramstad, and Szymanski families of Anchorage, Alaska, grandsons and granddaughters of John Beaton (co discoverer of Iditarod gold and a builder of Alaska) for their invaluable help regarding early Iditarod history and facts of John Beaton's life and times.

James A. McQuiston, biographer of his famous relative, Jack McQuesten, for generous donation of photographs from the McQuesten family collection.

My children, Jordan, Ethan, Levi, Laura, and Gabriel, who stir my heart to leave them a legacy. Lovingly, they assisted in the work and lent listening ears to my testing of wording and passages.

Finally, my gratitude embraces the love of my life, my wonderful wife, Karen, whose faith, patience and encouragement allow me to lose myself in far-off realms of sentences and paragraphs as well as broader visions beyond this book.

Table of Contents

Table of Maps

About the Author

Fat Albert and Rod Perry, "Nome or Buss"

ROD PERRY HAS RIDDEN a moose and nursed from one's udder, eats Eskimo delicacies such as oshok (walrus flipper buried in the frozen ground for a year to ferment), worked on a moose research project, made the motion picture *Sourdough*, the most widely viewed feature ever filmed in Alaska, and competed in the wild-and-crazy, loosely-organized, first Iditarod Trail Sled Dog Race. To read more about this Iditarod pioneer, turn to page 504.

Introduction

by Craig Medred, Outdoors Editor,
Anchorage Daily News

FOR AS LONG AS THERE HAS BEEN fur, gold, game and adventure to be found, Alaska has fueled dreams and crushed them. The land has made a few rich. It has sent far more home penniless and beaten. And it has forged in some others a strange fascination, a love almost, of what the north is, what it was, and what it yet might be. Rod Perry is of these.

There is old joke among them: "I'm a sourdough. Sour on the country, but without the dough to get out." The joke is not heard so much these days. The civilized parts of Alaska have become as politely Americanized as Seattle or Minneapolis. But the joke was once heard quite often, usually uttered by people you couldn't have paid enough to leave the country. Alaska grows on these people even as it pounds the snot out of them.

Perry knows of this. He is among that small group who once dreamed of winning the Iditarod Trail Sled Dog Race, though he'd probably deny that. Every Iditarod wannabe does.

The truth is different. Deep down, they all harbor the fantasy that somehow it might happen, that somehow by some freak accident they could win. It is a fantasy as old as Alaska.

The whalers, the trappers and especially the gold miners all flooded the country chasing the dream they would be the one to strike it rich, and they all knew full well how bad the odds were stacked against them.

When you read *TRAILBREAKERS*, you almost have to wonder if the supposed lust to profit off the bounty of the land wasn't more just an excuse for the adventure than anything else.

Too much of what so many did in those early years is like a grizzly bear excavating an entire mountain side in a futile effort to catch a tiny ground squirrel. Until you've witnessed this sort of behavior, or better yet lived it, it can be hard to fathom. Perry has lived some of it and well understands. He has sweated and grunted his way around Alaska. Anyone who does that develops a deep appreciation for the reality over the fiction.

As he notes: "Some modern writers claim that with the Nome Gold Rush beginning in 1898, and even more so with the 1906-1907 coming of mining to the Inland Empire, that mushers immediately commenced whizzing back and forth over the way through Rainy Pass.

"That could not be farther from the truth. Such writing demonstrates an absence of understanding of long-distance, wilderness dog team travel and Iditarod trail history. Unknowing writers just repeat what has been written by other unknowing writers, and so it goes back and back and back. To one who knows the subject, the constant errors in newspapers, magazines, books, brochures, tourist information, television and the internet stand out like the proverbial sore thumb."

It is time someone set the record straight. *TRAILBREAKERS* is a good first step, though much remains to be done. Too much of what is written about what goes on along the Iditarod Trail to this day is written by people clueless of what it is actually like out there. Perry is at the opposite end of that spectrum.

As a chronicler of the sweat, the struggles and the sheer bullheadedness of Alaska history, he is excellent.

This probably isn't so much a book about adventure, as it is a book about men who were by God determined to get from point A to point B for reasons often known only to themselves.

Their journeys became an adventure.

And the amazing thing is that people like this still exist in Alaska today. They are the best of the place and yet remain, at times, the hardest to understand.

Time changes everything and it changes nothing.

Preface

———◆———

by Rod Perry

Code of the Prospector

TO THE UTTERMOST, THEY ARE A WILD LOT, those who make up the intrepid vanguard that explores and moils the upper Yukon for gold during the two decades prior to the great turn-of-the-century gold rushes. Geologist Israel Russell, reporting for *National Geographic* in that day, describes the rabble:

> *My companions were rough and uncouth as men could well be. Their hair and beards had grown long, and their faces were tanned and weather-beaten by constant exposure. Their garments, then in the last stages of serviceability, had been made by those who wore them, from any material that chanced to be available, from buckskin and fur to flour-sacks, and had been repaired without regard to color or texture ... One not accustomed to the vicissitudes of exploration, coming suddenly on such a scene, would certainly believe he had stumbled on a band of the most desperate outlaws.*
>
> *They were a rough, hardy race, made up, it would seem, of representatives of nearly every nation on earth. Some are typical frontiersmen, dressed in buckskin, who are never at home except on the outskirts of civilization. Others were of doubtful character, and it is said are seldom known by their rightful names. The remote gulches of the Yukon country seem to offer safe asylums for men who are "wanted" in other districts. Despite the varied character of its inhabitants, this remote community is orderly and but few disturbances have been known.*

Many of the breed live unfettered by formal social contracts. Most hold a degree of anarchistic disregard toward written laws viewed as handicapping the most competent from making the North Country theirs. But rough, independent, and competitive as they are, their characters are marked by tolerance, honesty, and trust. The bearing of indescribable hardships inflicted by the isolation and harshness of the country produces the necessity to help and be helped. So these free spirits keep care of their kind and live by their own unwritten rules. None is more religiously held than their *Code of the Prospector*, also known as the *Law of the Miner*. Part of that code demands that you make the results of your prospecting known. Especially if you strike paydirt, loyalty to the brotherhood is expected; you are honor-bound to openly advance full information to others prospecting the surrounding country.

Now, in the waning days of fall, 1886, Howard Franklin—prospecting with Harry Madison—makes a rich strike on the Fortymile. This is not mere fine dust, but coarse gold—flakes and nuggets. It is the first such find in the Yukon Basin.

The cry issues forth up and down the great river. Within days every miner in the upper country has rushed to the new strike. Nearly every miner. Some are too far upstream to get the news and are going the wrong way. These are miners who have spent the summer scattered over the country upriver of the new strike, and are now getting out while the getting is good, pushing hard on their various 400- to 600-mile ascents of the river and mountains to beat freeze-up of the waterway and snows that will block the Chilkoot Pass.

Some of them are pulling out to avoid a repeat of seasons past, where those who wintered over barely scraped by on the edge of starvation. Others are going out to work for enough wages to fund a new grubstake to prospect next season. Yet others, after having failed to find paydirt—some after years of backbreaking toil and privation—have decided to turn their back on this harsh wilderness once and for all; enough is enough, they are quitting the country for good.

The Code dictates that word of Franklin's find be taken out to these gold hunters who have endured so much, paid their dues, and so deserve to be included. "Don't get left out; be first back over the pass next summer. Don't quit the country, we've found coarse gold on bedrock!"

Gone too, is Jack McQuesten, gone 1,600 miles down to the Yukon mouth to catch a late-sailing ship bound for San Francisco. Over the winter he will secure supplies and equipment to outfit the Yukon's miners for another year. Having left before Franklin's strike, he knows nothing of the discovery.

This portends disaster. His partner in their fur-trading and miner's-supply business, explorer and pioneer prospector Arthur Harper, is at once optimistic that Howard Franklin's find will trigger a major gold rush, yet fearful of the sure consequence of McQuesten's lack of information: a rush will bring far more people into the country than Jack will buy for.

Arthur Harper, this visionary who, with McQuesten, sees so much potential for the country and has worked so tirelessly for a decade to set up a support system for the benefit of the miners, sees missed profits for the partnership and lost productivity for the miners. But to this kindly man something looms of far greater concern: Harper foresees starvation.

Starvation—unless, across hundreds of miles of some of the harshest winter wilderness in the North, and thousands of miles by sea, he can somehow get word out to Jack McQuesten.

That year the Yukon had frozen early. It then broke up and ran unusually heavy in brash ice. Refreezing of the jumbled shards created a terribly jagged surface, making footing for traveling beyond difficult.

No one is a more experienced winter traveler than Arthur Harper. He fully realizes the ragged surface will slow progress. Even if the footing were perfect, he knows anyone who braves the hundreds of wilderness miles that are hard enough during summer will be in for a tremendous ordeal; no one yet has ever dared to go back up the Yukon and over the Coast Mountains via the Chilkoot Pass in winter. But taking all of this into account, even Harper could never have imagined the succession of utterly horrible conditions the North in all its fury will hurl against the two men who step forward to take the word out.

For days, unseasonably high temperatures create deadly thin ice and deep overflows. Suddenly, temperatures drop to forty to seventy degrees below zero. Blizzard winds shriek. Progress slows and food supplies dwindle. The North is pitiless; half a thousand miles of a trail so cruel must take its toll.

Now steamboat captain Tom Williams stumbles weakly toward the pass. Ahead, his valiant 18-year-old Indian trailmate Bob lurches along, barely able to break trail. They are laden with no more than the clothes on their backs and the packet sent by Harper. But for a little white flour they have been eating out of hand, their food is gone. Most of their dogs are gone and now their strength and endurance are all but gone.

It doesn't seem humanly possible that they can make it, but struggling on, nothing fueling them but sheer will, they near the pass. And then the snowstorm strikes. They are forced to dig in. While holed up in their snow cave, Williams' hands and feet freeze and the little endurance he had gives out.

Finally the storm abates. Emerging from their lair, Tom Williams can barely stand and make a little headway with Bob's support. Then he cannot manage even that. The debilitated Bob begins to carry Williams a few yards at a time between rests. They will not be able to last long this way, but on Bob's last reserves they lurch toward the summit.

Word to McQuesten must reach the outside world. And the *Code of the Prospector* drives them on.

———

Means for travel, transport and communications, cut and marked trails, a roadhouse infrastructure, the havens systematically spaced along the routes for support and supply of foot travelers, dog team transporters and mail carriers—those were some of the most dire needs during those primitive, early years of prospecting as well as in the years following the great gold finds of the Yukon District and Alaska. Their lack caused incredible want, hardship, inefficiency, and sometimes, excruciating, life-and-death ordeals.

The earliest explorers and prospectors pushed their way in and out of the country through virtually uninhabited, almost untracked wilderness. For sustenance they had to depend heavily on what they could kill and gather. Their travel during round trips of up to a thousand miles or more each summer coupled with the effort required to secure food took up a lot of time they could have more productively spent prospecting and mining.

A few began to stay year round. As small to medium-sized discoveries were made, the population slowly increased and mining villages and trading centers grew up. Riverboats on the Yukon, first one small one, next another, then one larger, and finally a growing little fleet serviced the river hamlets and posts during the brief ice-free season. Hardly anyone so much as considered taking on the backbreaking work and risking the life-threatening dangers of entering or leaving the country between freeze-up and breakup. That would have entailed a one-, two-, or even three-month-long trip of 500 to 900 miles. Those few who braved such a risky ordeal found it much like the one taken by Tom Williams and Bob. As lone travelers, they had the grueling task of breaking trail every foot of the way. They camped—often at far below zero or amidst fierce blizzards—wherever night overtook them. Absence of any source of resupply during the whole length of the trek necessitated absolute start-to-finish self-sufficiency, mandating that travelers had to take from the beginning supplies for the full journey. Starting out, such a load made up an almost impossible mountain for man and team to move. And in case of need or calamity, they had no help to turn to.

In the overall regional scope of things, during those earliest times prior to the great discoveries, lack of winter movement in and out of the gold country did not hold back progress much. The population was less than sparse. Resource development was minor relative to what would come later. So there was not yet a great volume of industry. Without that industry there was only infrequent demand for travel, freight, and communications in and out. And those who wintered over were typically men of the frontier, steel-tough sourdoughs used to coping with hardship, getting by on little, and not expecting much. They simply accepted that for most of the year their lot was an existence in a remote country almost sealed off from the outside world and its resources. An old axiom of the country went, "Blessed are they that expect little, for they shall not be disappointed."

But needs and expectations multiplied with the great turn-of-the-century gold rushes. Booming cities sprang up energized by business, industry, and all that maintaining a city infrastructure required. Of course, by careful planning, during summer stocks could be brought north from west coast ports by ocean-going ships. Transshipping loads at the Yukon mouth, shallow draft riverboats would then haul not just tons, but hundreds of tons at a time as far as almost two thousand miles upriver. It could then be stockpiled in company warehouses and prospectors' caches to last the long months between navigation seasons. Even so, vibrant cities serving up to as many as 40,000 or more in the Dawson area and perhaps 30,000 around Nome could not thrive while going two-thirds of their year without at least some incoming shipments of items of immediate need as well as back-and-forth movement of travelers and mail. Therefore, throughout the long winters, regular and efficient traffic by dog team and foot became vital.

Dog team and foot travel such as Tom Williams and Bob endured was a far cry from what the mining centers needed. In those primitive, pretrail days, mushers were challenged to the utmost to just make it through by the skin of their teeth. They had little capacity to carry anything for anyone else. A town of thousands doesn't gain much benefit from a lone musher's snail's pace or by his cargo, necessarily limited to the staggering loads of food and camp gear he and his team require to barely survive their personal passage.

Modern truckers freighting foods couldn't serve the needs of a nation if during cross-country hauls they had no roads to provide a fast surface, no way to refuel, and no rest stops. And what if they had to consume enroute all the food they were carrying just to survive until reaching their destination? For dog drivers of old to provide a flow adequate for the health and well-being of early northern business hubs and outlying areas they had to be able to travel and move payloads swiftly and efficiently. The supporting infrastructure of cut and marked winter trails and roadhouses for resupply and rest was of paramount importance.

TRAILBREAKERS, Volume I centers on the theme of Far North, gold-rush-era transportation—movement of men, supplies and mail. Though this work follows scores of rabbit trails—how can any storyteller resist the inclusion of such fabulous peripheral sagas and anecdotes as those which emanated out of the gold rush era?— this book keeps coming back on track, progressing toward creation of cut and marked trails with their support systems, as well as movement over those trails, especially by dog team. This is meant to be a fairly thorough treatment, so to shed enough light for the reader to gain a good understanding of how trail systems fit into the total picture, other transportation by water, wagon, and rail are part of the telling.

Of course, the bull's-eye objective of *TRAILBREAKERS*, Volume I is to provide a good account of how the old Iditarod Trail came to be and what its function was during the gold rush era. Because gold rush led to gold rush, one trail led to another. And because the Iditarod came near the end of the era, the larger history of all the major gold strikes and their transportation corridors during that most glorious, romantic time in northland history is necessary to digest if one is to gain a solid grasp of the subject.

Writers commonly try to cover Iditarod Trail and Nome trail history by diving immediately into writing about the Iditarod itself. In doing so, they shortchange the reader. By beginning in the middle of the story—actually, more toward the end, because the Iditarod was the last great gold rush trail—they fail to lay down a foundation upon which to solidly set their treatment of Iditarod history. By starting with Iditarod they completely leave out the heavy use of Nome's trail systems during Nome's peak that predated the Iditarod Trail by a decade. An adequate foundation must necessarily include prior gold rushes and their trails, other transportation methods and the evolution of the entire main trunkline transportation system of the Yukon Basin and Seward Peninsula.

Transportation methods, means, and routes—on the surface the subject sounds downright boring. However, the prospect of listening to a detailed account of a ten-mile hike may sound boring until you learn that the storyteller's particular ten miles are his final ten, dared solo and without oxygen, to the summit of Mount Everest.

The subject of this book is not about a stroll down some daisy-strewn lane in settled country and mild climes. No, within these pages we're talking about travel in the Old North leading up to, during, and immediately following the most fabulously adventuresome gold rushes the world has ever known. In that setting, transportation over the trail often meant using the age-old propulsion system of the Arctic and subarctic, the dog team. Dog team travel and other movement through the wilds of Arctic and subarctic Alaska and Yukon Territory often included death-defying, wild adventure, uncommon demonstrations of daring and courage, here and there spiked with tales so outlandish they take you to the outer fringe of belief.

TRAILBREAKERS, Volume I is one of the best general histories ever written about how the vast wilderness Interior of Alaska and adjacent Yukon Territory was entered, probed for wealth, and developed. Taking place as that exploration and development did, in the waning decades of a largely unmechanized North America, and especially in such a wild, uncivilized land so far removed from substantial influence of the industrial age, an indispensable role was played by the age-old transportation method of the north: marvelous, even heroic men driving magnificent dog teams. My friend, if such fodder for history livened with good story telling doesn't light your fire, your wood's wet.

Chapter 1

---◆---

An Old Album Speaks

Rod Perry: *As a young boy growing up in Oregon, I got to know Al and Alma Preston, a generation older than my father and mother, yet close friends. How close? When I was a baby, they appealed to my parents: "Would you consider giving Rod to us? You'd still be able to watch him grow up and you're young enough to have more children." Although the idea was naturally unthinkable to my folks, they felt honored.*

When I was about eight years old I became aware that whenever the weekly broadcasts of Sergeant Preston of the North West Mounted Police and his great lead dog, King, hit the airways, Al and Alma glued themselves to their radio. From the speakers Preston's urgent cry sounded out, "On, King, on, you great husky!" Ne'er-do-wells shuddered to hear the Sergeant's banal proclamation, "You're under arrest in the name of the crown! This case is closed." Years later, I understood that the attraction had nothing to do with the coincidence of a shared name; from those episodes the old couple received their weekly fix of reminiscence.

Later, I was to learn that Alma had eloped a few years after the great gold rushes with her first husband, Merrill Leonhardt, and shipped north to Seward, Alaska. There they were employed by "Colonel" Harry Revell, to whom the U.S. Postal Service had awarded the contract to run Seward-to-Nome mail over the Iditarod Trail. Working in Revell's dog-team transport business, Alma met many of the legendary dog drivers who covered the trails of Alaska and the Yukon. Perhaps realizing she was participating in history, she snapped pictures documenting her work—invaluable snapshots that she later assembled into a treasured album.

Merrill Leonhardt died in the devastating worldwide influenza epidemic of 1918 and was buried in Seward. Some years later, Alma

Alma in Seward

fell in love with and married Al Preston, a miner from Nome. And so, as I came to know them, they would mesmerize my family with gold-rush era anecdotes and tales of the old trail drawn from experience at both ends of the Iditarod.

Over time, as Al and Alma drew close to death, they offered everything they had to my parents. Almost everything. I was given the ancient album. There, inside the front cover and next to her memorabilia, Alma had lovingly affixed my portrait, taken when I was but six months old.

Today, a century after Alma began snapping her pictures of the "Colonel," his dogs, sleds, shelter cabins, and dog barns, Alaska Railroad construction, and the drivers and teams hauling U.S. mail coming through, and a half century after she first took me on a guided tour through her Iditarod photo record, I remember. Now, once more I open the old brown cover. As I thumb slowly through and savor aging images, the pages of the old album take me back yet once more to yesteryear. I fight to curb the emotions and choke back the lump in my throat as voices and images from a never-to-be repeated, glorious age I wish I, too, had seen, overtake my reverie.

Again, as I listen anew, the memory of her becomes so real that I smell the aromas that inevitably wafted from her kitchen, and I again hear not only her low, raspy voice but other voices brought to life through her well-told reminiscences. Drifting, I can listen to the give and take, ebb and flow of conversation . . . always I detect Alma's voice through the mix of the others. Her special way of speaking comes back as clearly as if she now sat near me patiently answering another of my persistent questions.

"Alma, how did the Iditarod gold rush and the Iditarod Trail come to be? The rush and trail couldn't have just materialized at once. Mr. Beaton and Mr. Dikeman did not just find gold at Iditarod out of the blue. The Iditarod Trail wasn't already there, was it? How did the Iditarod strike and the trail come to be?"

Alma Preston: "Rod, people are always asking me about Alaska, the great gold rushes and the Iditarod Trail. Of course there is a lot I can talk about with them but for quite a bit of it, I tell them, I can talk and talk, but if they don't get a pretty good grasp of the geography, they have no way to understand what I'm trying to explain.

"Privately, Rod, I sometimes wonder to myself as I answer their questions, 'Why am I going to the trouble, sir? Without at least a rudimentary idea of the lay of the land, oceans, rivers, mountains, and passes, I'm just beating my lips together for nothing; you won't get it anyway.'

"But I like them and enjoy talking about Alaska, the old trail and my wonderful sled dogs so I try to do the best I can. If they look interested enough, sometimes I get a paper and pencil and sketch.

"You would think that, among people interested in learning about Iditarod, if there existed a dominant trail system of the North, a great thoroughfare that bore huge traffic during the glory years of Nome's gold rush peak a decade before Iditarod, carried major Nome traffic even during Iditarod's heyday, and continued to serve Nome after Iditarod faded, you would think those interested people would certainly want to learn about it, wouldn't you? And you'd think historians would want to write about it. But when without that background historians begin with Iditarod, leaving out the background, and focus solely on Iditarod, they leave much of the Iditarod story out.

"Really, Rod, if people want to comprehend the Iditarod, and the other great trail systems used by Nome, I'll tell you this: No one can come close to understanding those histories in any depth as far as getting into the foundation of how it evolved, the background of how it all started, unless they understand the coastline and its mountains from clear down about Ketchikan or Wrangell all the way up and around to Cook Inlet. And the passes, especially the passes."

Chapter 2

The Great Mountain Barrier
A Tale of Five Passes

DURING SUMMER most turn-of-the-century Yukon District and northern Alaska gold finds were effectively served by water, being located either in country drained by the Yukon River system or on the Seward Peninsula, which extends into the Bering Sea north of the Yukon mouth. But northern waters run free but in summer, and summers that far north were short. For most of the year, the Yukon River lay locked in ice and the Arctic pack moved down to block Bering Sea shipping far south of the Yukon Delta. But while this on-again, off-again, now-open, now-closed access to shipping hampered development of the northern gold country, the influences of the Japan Current kept the ocean down along the Southeastern and Southcentral Alaska coastline free of ice, so shipping readily plied those waters summer and winter alike.

The obstacle to travel and transport between the southern ice-free bays and the northern Interior lay in the daunting fortress of mountain ranges thrown up between the sea and the goldfields: the towering crags of the great Coast, Saint Elias, Chugach, and Alaska ranges. Of the continent's fifteen highest mountains, The Saint Elias Range alone includes ten of them. These are not your garden-variety, weathered-down Appalachian Mountains, nor have these peaks attained their heights after a head start of rising from an already elevated plateau, like the Colorado Rockies. No, these ranges not only boast almost all of North America's loftiest peaks, but many rear their jagged summits far into the sky after rising virtually from the sea bed of the continental shelf, 1,000 feet below sea level.

The cataclysmic shocks of geologic past that upthrust the earth's crust into such heights rent great clefts between them. Through the

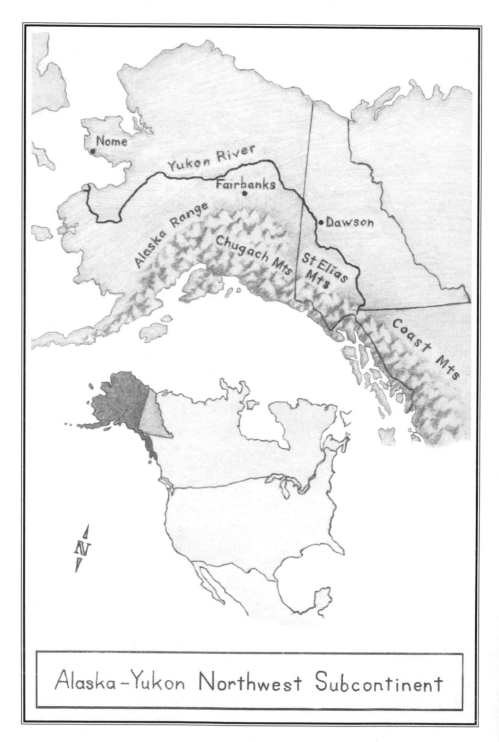

Alaska-Yukon Northwest Subcontinent

nearest range, these rifts present views of even more ominous mountains behind, and beyond them others, and others, mountain crowding mountain, precipice contesting precipice, rearing higher and higher, graying out into the uttermost distance, offering no hint of relief, only discouragement that pressed upon the hearts of even the brave. These interstices are not filled with grassy valleys and gentle waterways. No, between the ragged bastions flow treacherous rivers of half-mile-deep ice, ice split with deadly, shifting crevasses—many so deep as to be effectively termed bottomless—some gaping, but some hidden under thin coverings that wait to give way under the slightest footfall.

Anyone who would set forth to dare this harsh, inhospitable barrier had better be long on wilderness skills, endurance, heroic courage and a gambler's daring.

For a thousand miles the menacing battlements glower down upon the Inside Passage and Gulf of Alaska waters and guard the Interior and northern goldfields. A look at the map of the Alaskan coastline reveals that once you turn your back on the Stikine River, which begins in interior British Columbia, then cleaves through the Coast Mountains to empty into the Pacific near Wrangell in Southeastern Alaska, north and west the frowning crags, ice caps and glaciers yield only eight useable, ice-free breaks leading from the sea into the Interior. And of those eight, only five played important gold rush roles. A great part of the story of the opening and development of the North and of winter transportation between salt water and the goldfields could aptly be titled, *A Tale of Five Passes.*

If only the early goldseekers could find those narrow notches and broach the barricade, and if later developers could only tame them with their trails, roads or railroads, then almost all of the vast heartland of the entire northwest Yukon Territory-Alaska subcontinent would be open to development, most importantly the entire 327,000-square-mile drainage of the Yukon basin. That basin is 2,000 miles long and, in places, several hundred miles wide.

Not only would that vast heartland be opened, it would be available. In winter, although the everlasting subarctic cold hangs over the North like a cruel penalty, it would also transform the Yukon basin into a perfect platform for dog team travel. Frozen stream courses gift travelers with not only a clear path, but a gradient that is, practically speaking, level. In addition to the length of the Yukon (the trunk river), the lengths of its tributaries, the forks and branches of those tributaries, their feeder streams and the creeks that in turn feed them are virtually uncountable. These magnanimously handed early explorers and those who would follow thousands upon thousands of miles of white ribbons awaiting the stamp of snowshoes, the footfall of working huskies, and the glide of runners carrying men, supplies, and communications.

———◆——◆———

Alma Preston: "And Rod, that was not all. Once mushers had progressed all the way down to the Yukon mouth and had left behind the vast inland network of potential winter trails, they could travel the sea ice and shoreline margin south to the Alaska Peninsula or north to the Seward Peninsula (where Nome would spring up). They could continue farther north to Kotzebue Sound and yet even farther to the whaling station at Point Barrow. Beyond that northernmost outpost on Alaska's Arctic coast, the way was clear all the way to the Pole and beyond—if they could just get through the coastal mountain barrier to access it all.

"Rod, it was just incredible, a gift from a Creator who must hold a special love for prospectors. In summer, a portage of but thirty-two miles from salt water would deliver simple access to the second-longest navigable waterway in North America. It was floatable for over 2,100 miles top to bottom. That sequence, top to bottom, is the operative idea. Remember, the going wage for labor was only about two dollars a day. Gold seekers did not have to access the river from its mouth upstream. That would have necessitated use of a steamboat, costing thousands. No, it took almost no other resources than their own strength, wilderness skills, and the will to succeed. If men could just get through from the sea into the upper drainage of the Yukon they could fashion crude boats or cruder rafts from native materials and the power of the river would take them as far as they wished to drift.

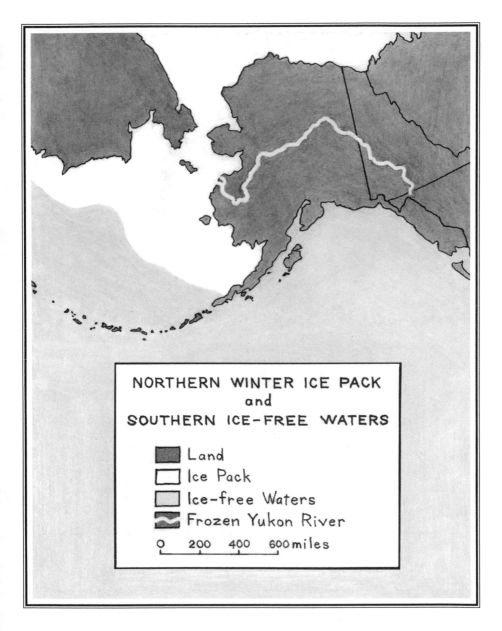

NORTHERN WINTER ICE PACK
and
SOUTHERN ICE-FREE WATERS

- Land
- Ice Pack
- Ice-free Waters
- Frozen Yukon River

0   200   400   600 miles

"Let me point out something that few notice, something about this remarkable river that adds wonderfully to its value. Most rivers, even the greatest rivers, have beginnings as mere trickles. They grow gradually to become a little creek. Then, typically, for some distance they course along while gathering enough small tributaries to form a

19

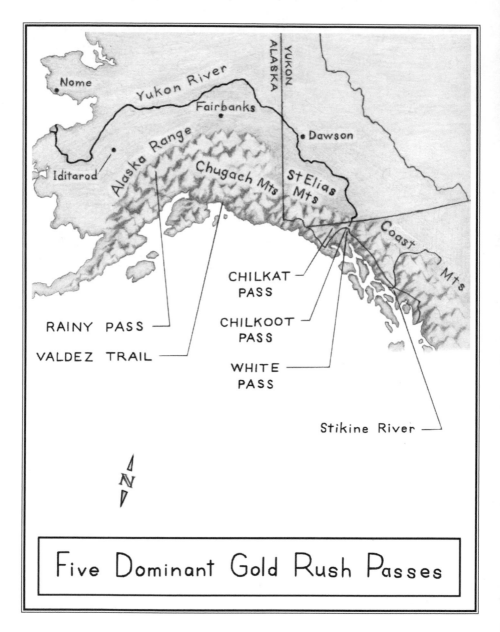

Five Dominant Gold Rush Passes

shallow river. On and on they run combining waters from other drainages. When the flow finally picks up enough feeder streams, perhaps a major fork, and maybe another small river or two, it finally becomes a river big enough to qualify as 'navigable.' Incredibly, the Yukon River is navigable within just 15 short miles from its origin above Lake Bennett. Think of it: a river 2,150 miles long of which 2,135 is navigable! Rod, that's about ninety-nine percent! I don't think any other river on earth that's anything near its length comes close to comparing. What a river, what a boon for the country it flows through, and what immeasurable worth in usefulness to its prospectors!

"So if prospectors could only find the ways to slip through the mountain barricade they could access the incredible length of the golden heartland's trails and waterways regardless of season."

———◆———◆———

The first of the eight rifts through the mountains beyond Wrangell—up the canyon of the swift Taku River near Juneau—was tried during gold rush times but was largely discarded. Gold seekers regarded it as a barely doable, but largely impractical route to reach the interior lake system draining into the upper Yukon River.

A triumvirate of passes—the second, third and fourth breaks north of the Stikine—issue from the head of Lynn Canal, some 100 miles north of Juneau. The southernmost of these three is the White Pass, separating salt water by only forty overland miles from Lake Bennett, which drains into the Yukon River. The great attraction to the White Pass was that, once gold seekers had hauled their gear and supplies to Yukon headwaters, they could let the river take over and do the work, floating their mountainous loads the hundreds of miles to the diggings.

The problem lay in that the valley of the pass was ballyhooed as a simple, steady grade to the summit, suitable not merely as a pack trail but offering possibilities for a wagon road. This gap did look deceptively easy at its beginnings at Skagway. But several miles inland the way grew into *The Path from Hell*. Quagmires, boulder fields, and precipices along the fiendish trail killed horses by so many thousands in the days of 1897–98 that it earned world fame as the *Dead Horse Trail*.

However, up the side of the valley that at first appraisal appeared the least accessible, the White Pass did offer possibilities for carving out a workable gradient. By taking creative engineering genius and almost superhuman construction effort to their extreme limits, the craggy, cliff-ridden side narrowly allowed a marvel of a railroad to be blasted through into the Upper Yukon. So immediate was the industrial and political pressure to force this supply line through that road builders started during the very height of the Klondike Gold

Prospectors Freight Loads Toward Chilkoot Pass

Alaska State Library Historical Collections, Charles Horton
Metcalf Collection, Charles H. Metcalf, ASL-P34-002

Rush frenzy and pushed rail over the summit within a year. Trains transported passengers and hauled freight and mail yearly totaling thousands of tons to where it could be boated downriver. That mass delivery turned the towns of Whitehorse and Dawson, Yukon Territory into transportation hubs that fed not only the immediate Klondike and other nearby Upper Yukon discoveries, but the distant strikes of Fairbanks—half a thousand miles away—and even Nome, the better part of two thousand miles west.

The storied Chilkoot Pass (the middle of the three Lynn Canal passes) courses parallel to the White Pass' and lies only a few miles north of it. The great appeal of the Chilkoot's was like that of the neighboring White—a short portage followed by a long float. Once its lofty summit was gained, not far over the crest nestles Lake Lindeman, a mere thirty-two trail miles from ocean waters. From there a short waterway led to Lake Bennett and the Yukon. However, those "mere thirty-two" would become fabled as the earth's *Cruelest Thirty-Two Miles*. The summit was so high and the climb at the final pitch so steep that it stymied crossing not only with beasts of burden, but even with hand-drawn sleds beyond a certain point. Strong, hardy men were reduced to having to break down their freight into light packs and make scores of spirit-breaking ascents.

This most famous of gold rush passes was the most heavily trodden route to the gold fields of the upper Yukon. However, as soon as builders established the nearby railroad over White Pass, use of the Chilkoot ceased.

Not far west of the Chilkoot Pass, beginning near the present town of Haines, the glaring mountains begrudgingly yield the third of the Lynn Canal triumvirate, the Chilkat Pass.

While the White and Chilkoot Passes carried stampeders by the tens of thousands, the Dalton Trail, which coursed the Chilkat route, received but a fraction of that traffic. The former two held the allure of only a short overland passage at the start after which wind and current would take over the work. However, the Chilkat Pass began with some 250 miles of overland travel. That absolutely necessitated the expensive use of large pack trains to haul gold seekers and their freight. The Dalton Trail met the Yukon far downriver from where the

White and Chilkoot Passes reached its headwaters. Dalton Trail users, starting their float so much closer to their destination, could take but reduced advantage of river power. Decades later, the quality of the route would be proven as a highway corridor. The builders of the scenic Haines Cutoff would use much of it to connect the Alaska Highway to the town of Haines on Lynn Canal.

Beyond the Chilkat Pass, the crags and peaks of the Fairweather and St. Elias ranges rear out of two-mile-high ice caps and glaciers to rend the clouds. Unbreachable, they bar the way for fully 350 miles farther north and west along the shelterless coast. A break is finally reached where the mighty Copper River irresistibly forces its way from the Interior through to the sea.

A river so large naturally offered hope of a major thoroughfare. Alas, the roiling swiftness and steep banks of the lower river thwarted upstream poling and tracking (towing by ropes walked upstream along the river edge.) Additionally, the course of the river upstream left stampeders too far from the goldfields. The Copper did not offer a very practical route.

Shipping must travel another hundred miles northwest of the Copper River to anchor at the beginning of the next ice-free break, the fourth up the coast from Wrangell, useful for heavy gold-rush-era access. There, at the east side of Prince William Sound, the harbor of Valdez marks the saltwater terminus of a route through the Chugach and Alaska ranges. This route saw heavy use first as a dog-team and pack-train trail, then as a road for horse-drawn sleighs, sledges, and wagons, and finally as the roadbed for the Richardson Highway serving Fairbanks. Many decades later, the corridor would be chosen to carry the Trans Alaska Oil Pipeline. Although a sleigh, sledge or wagon could not haul *hundreds of tons* of mail and freight at a time as could the White Pass and Yukon Railroad, those conveyances could at least bring it by the *ton* into Fairbanks. Because Fairbanks was closer to Nome by hundreds of miles than Dawson, much of Nome's winter traffic switched to the Valdez-Fairbanks Trail once it became useable.

As the coastline turns southwest, the port of Seward on Resurrection Bay (about 200 miles by water from Valdez) provides a jumping-off point for a route across the Kenai Peninsula, around

Turnagain Arm, across mouths of the Knik and Matanuska rivers, up the Susitna and Chulitna River valleys and through the Alaska Range by way of Broad Pass and the Nenana River Canyon to Fairbanks.

Unlike the aforementioned passes, this Seward-to-Fairbanks-via-Broad-Pass route was not used by stampeders to rush to a new gold strike or by transporters to supply one. Following well after the great Fairbanks gold discovery, builders planned and constructed it solely as a railroad route designed to open up the Interior and develop the territory. Everyone understood that Alaska's growth would continue to be inhibited until Fairbanks gained what Whitehorse and Dawson had when the White Pass and Yukon Route breached the mountain barrier. That is, Fairbanks desperately needed year-round, high-volume transport, connecting ocean shipping to the economic and political center in the Interior.

A half century after the Alaska Railroad began carrying freight in and out of the Interior, the George Parks Highway would be laid running generally parallel to the rails. With northern Alaska's only lasting railroad and a major highway over it, this seventh pass would eventually carry more traffic and tonnage than all the other passes combined.

To recap, of the seven gaps mentioned so far, the first pass, up the Taku River, the fifth pass up the Copper River, and seventh, through Broad Pass did not see major use as routes to the Interior during the gold rush era. Only the second, third, fourth and sixth so far in our survey, namely the White and Chilkoot passes and the Dalton and Valdez (later Richardson) trails provided heavily used gold-rush passageways.

There is yet another pass. It is the eighth gap, but only the fifth that could be considered a useful gold-rush supply and travel route. The last slip explorers examined through the thousand-odd miles of mountains and ice up the coast from Wrangell provided a distant way to reach the far northwestern goldfields of Nome and Iditarod. The ascent to its summit climbs through some of the most majestic mountain scenery in the world. It crosses the great Alaska Range not far from the mightiest mountain on the North American continent— 20,320-foot-tall Mount McKinley, which rises higher from its base elevation than any other mountain on earth. This spectacular pass is named Rainy Pass. The trail established over it became a trail of legend. It was known as the Iditarod Trail.

To gain understanding of how that storied trail came to be, we must go back, way back.

Chapter 3

---◆---

Gold Rush Spawns Gold Rush, Trail Leads to Trail

TO FULLY COMPREHEND the evolution of Nome's winter transportation situation a few years after the turn of the twentieth century, one must understand how the earliest traders and prospectors began almost 30 years earlier to force the Yukon's lock and pry open the northern Interior. Then one must comprehend the mining and prospecting booms and the resulting population explosions of Dawson, Yukon Territory, and Fairbanks—and the supply systems that developed to serve them.

Why is such comprehension necessary? Because early on, Nome's winter travel and mail and freight supply was so interwoven with and dependent upon those transportation systems developed to serve the great Klondike strike of the upper Yukon River in Yukon District, Canada, and the fabulously rich Fairbanks strike in the valley of Alaska's Tanana River.

Though Nome was dependent upon the transportation systems of those other towns and the Seward-to-Nome mail trail feasibility reconnaissance of 1908 delivered a discouraging report, Nomites continued to dream of a trail of their own. The Iditarod Trail, as it came to be called, grew out of those dreams. Because the Iditarod was originally Nome's idea, and Nome was so tightly linked by trail use to Dawson and Fairbanks, the story of the Iditarod Trail is inextricably joined to the rich and fabled history of gold discovery along the upper Yukon River and Fairbanks.

---•---

Rod Perry: *I once spent a week hunting with a man about whom another of the hunters in camp commented, "If all you need to know is what time it is and you ask Harley, he'll give you a dissertation about the evolution of telling time and a detailed explanation of how the clock was constructed!"*

The reader of this work, which explores the history of the gold-rush-era Iditarod Trail may wonder, upon finding so much space devoted to early exploration of the upper Yukon and the ensuing gold rushes it produced, if perhaps this tome was written by Harley himself. To the unknowledgeable who wish to remain that way or to those types who demand to cut to the chase, it may seem too unnecessarily roundabout to begin the Iditarod story so long ago and far away as the chronology of developments that took place many decades before the Iditarod strike and over 2,000 miles from Nome.

However, the patient, inquisitive reader may better understand Nome's early winter transportation desires and realities by examining the overall transportation picture leading up to the Iditarod Trail's establishment. Again, that is because the three great blockbuster gold rushes of the North—the Klondike, Nome, and Fairbanks—were so intermeshed not only by the routes that all these communities shared, but also by many of the same people who flowed over those common routes from one strike to another.

Following the 1867 purchase of Alaska from Russia, America's interest in her new acquisition faded. In 1880, fewer whites populated the territory than under Russian dominion. The post- Civil War years saw the nation swept up in a period of reconstruction and great industrial development. Vast regions west of the Mississippi that previously had been reachable only by wagon became available to development and commerce as transcontinental railroads opened the country. That simply flooded investors and developers with so much opportunity closer to home they had little reason to look farther— especially into far-separated, unfamiliar regions that were widely disparaged as the desolate Frozen North. Therefore, Alaska lay dormant for three decades, virtually forgotten by the American public and its government.

The famous geologist, explorer, and historian Alfred Hulse Brooks, for whom Alaska's Brooks Range is named, observed that the real development of Alaska began in1896, not with anything that happened in Alaska, but with the discovery of Klondike gold in the adjacent Canadian Yukon. Because the fabulous rush for riches so gripped world attention, and because the journey to the goldfields through such incredibly difficult wilderness was itself so overflowing with adventure and peril, a great part of the news was about the very getting there. The hordes who thronged into the largely unknown North usually found it necessary to cross some part of Alaska to reach the strike. Thus, gold-rush writing acquainted Americans with the possession they had almost totally ignored since its purchase from Russia three decades before. With the Klondike Gold Rush grabbing headlines and capturing national attention, America's last frontier began to occupy a new and important place in the country's collective thinking.

Moreover, Brooks pointed out that the discovery of gold at many Alaska locations was the direct result of a spill-over from the vast horde of gold seekers who had first flooded into the Klondike.

Additionally, other strikes may be attributed to explorations by prospectors who, though they did not take part in the Klondike rush, were pulled north to search areas far distant from Dawson (such as Nome, 1,400 miles away) by the sheer excitement first widely generated by the fabulous Canadian discovery, and by the widely held optimism the Klondike spread that all of Alaska held awaiting riches.

The 1908 Iditarod strike was the last of the series of four blockbuster discoveries that began with the Klondike.

<hr />

Alma Preston: "Alfred Brooks stopped overnight at our place at Mile Thirty-four and another time had a long layover with us waiting out a storm after we moved our operation up to Mile Fifty-four. Later, he corresponded with my former father-in-law. Though he was a giant as a geologist, explorer, and historian, he was so friendly and down-to-earth. You look at the tremendous hardships he endured on his explorations. Maybe that's what kept him so grounded and humble. How many people would sit down around the barrel stove and talk with you for hours—and on your level—who have one of the greatest mountain ranges on the continent named after them? Rod, even though you knew you were listening to someone who was very educated, sounding like a professor, he was just so warm and open around my former, late husband, Merrill, his dad, and me.

"Now if you're really interested in understanding from the ground up the evolution of how the Iditarod Trail came to be, listen carefully to what Alfred Brooks told us."

———————

Rod Perry: *In my mind's eye I see the great explorer, imagining him now as Alma described him then, larger than life in intellect, accomplishments, and renown, a veritable immortal, yet sitting there around the barrel stove, stocking feet propped up on a stove-door-size chunk of spruce in the round, in choke-bored Malones, suspenders down off his shoulders, shirted in a wool long-john top with several buttons undone at the neck, chair leaned back, hands clasped behind his neck, enjoying a break from the trail and a long visit with the Leonhardts.*

———————

Alfred Hulse Brooks: "I don't think anyone would argue that this is fact: If it had not been for the lure of the Klondike gold, the mineral wealth over here on the Alaska side would have stayed in the ground dormant for many years. Then Alaska would have remained a land of mystery to most Americans. They'd have just kept denigrating it as 'Seward's Icebox.'

"When the worldwide excitement caught up untold thousands of people it carried them northward into a virtually unknown land. The Russians, who had been there for over a hundred years, knew next to nothing about the Interior. Since we had done almost nothing officially in thirty years of ownership of our new possession and had

Alfred Hulse Brooks

UAF 1973-66-93, Archives and Manuscripts, Alaska and Polar Regions
Collections, University of Alaska Fairbanks

so few of our citizens even living along its outer coastline, much less within its vastness, we had only the vaguest ideas about what lay within Alaska's great, wild reaches until the Klondike discovery sent civilians pouring across its expanses.

———— ◆———◆ ————

Alma Preston: "Brooks was making a valid point about how unknown Alaska was both to our government and to our citizenry. To support his point, he could have mentioned one of Alaska's greatest feats of exploration, which actually took place in 1885, more than a decade before the Klondike, and one of the explorer's post exploration summary statements that said the same thing Brooks did.

"It was the astonishingly long expedition of Lieutenant Henry T. Allen of the Second United States Cavalry. In a single season, with less than a handful of men and almost no rations or equipment, almost starving the whole way, he explored three of Alaska's greatest rivers. (My, Rod, what a dedication to the performance of duty! No wonder he later became a general.) It wasn't that he was the first white to travel them—the earliest prospectors beat him. But their breed wasn't given to making careful maps or publishing reports."

"Lieutenant Allen commented in his official report, *It is a very remarkable fact that a region under a civilized government for more than a century should remain so completely unknown as the vast territory drained by the Copper, Tanana, and Koyukuk Rivers.*

"Rod, that's approximately 240,000 square miles."

Alfred Hulse Brooks: "It goes without saying that if it was unexplored, it was trail-less and roadless. Traveling the coastline was so treacherous, because it was not only rock-bound, it lacked charts and other navigation guides. Gold hunters packed across wild passes and boated down swift rivers, where the next bend might reveal an upcoming cataract. To make it worse, the new territory was almost totally lacking government or laws. I will tell you that it was during the Klondike rush—and not until then—that it dawned on our nation's leaders, its press, and our people, of the utter criminal folly of the United States' attitude of neglect toward its northernmost possession.

"With the huge rush to the Canadian Yukon, that population explosion absolutely necessitated the establishment of lines of transportation. How could a regional population of 40,000 or more get by, let alone flourish, had they not built a bustling riverboat system and constructed, first trails, and later railroads and wagon roads? All of it was brought about by Klondike gold. So although these mineral deposits belonged to Canada, Alaska benefited directly by their mining development. With the Klondike raising awareness, army posts were now established in Alaska. Laws were enacted. U.S. marshals were appointed, and commissioners. To begin its enormous task of detailed charting of the coastline, Congress finally funded the Coast Survey. It was like the nation was trying to admit its error of remaining blind for so long to the richness of the territory and make amends for the long neglect.

"I worked with the United States Geological Survey once they were ordered to begin exploring and studying Alaska's mineral resources. Washington became convinced of the need for a careful investigation of the fisheries, forests, and lands suitable for agriculture. One would indeed have to be blind not to see that Alaska's modern history truly begins with the Klondike discovery in the Canadian Yukon."

Alma Preston: "Brooks was ahead of his time. Rod, let's go over to the old folks' home. I want you to meet an old friend of Al's from Nome. Anton Radovitch went in over the Chilkoot in '94. He's one of many who hit all four of the big rushes up north, the Klondike, Nome, Fairbanks, and Iditarod, not to mention a number of the smaller ones. That gives him quite an encompassing perspective. He's spent most of his adult life standing bent over day after day working so many cold streams by summer, and so many winters thawing his way down to bedrock and drifting deep in frozen ground following pay streaks that he's just gnarled with arthritis. But he's a perky old character and he loves visitors. Especially if they come to talk about the old days. Of course, not many do down here so far from the North. They don't value what those old eyes of his have seen. If some writer wanted to plumb the depths of the history stored away in that ancient, gray head they'd have in their hands the material for quite a book. On the way home, Rod, I need to stop by the corner grocery up on Flag Street. You can pack my shopping bag for me."

Anton Radovitch: "Yessirree! Like a lot of others, I just seemed to miss it on the big stampedes. Got there a little late. Or rolled the dice and staked the wrong ground. Actually did better at some of the lesser discoveries. But let's say you're some wretched shovel stiff on the Klondike like me, just slaving to further the interests of some lucky El Dorado king who had happened to hit it big. One day you get an early tip from a guy who's just come up from someplace you never heard of he calls Nome. Way more'n a thousand miles away. What's a mere thousand miles or two when you're young and eager?

"You'd be a fool not to go. Nothing ventured, nothing gained.

"Worst can happen is you get a month's worth of exercise. When you roll in, if nothing good's left to stake, well, you've seen some new country. And you don't come out of the stampede any worse off than you were. You're back swinging a pick and wrestlin' wash boulders out of a sluice box for another lucky so and so. If that happened you'd be ready to do it again. The big strikes came one after another kind of overlapping each other about every two years at first. Got to where I'd just keep everything ready to throw an outfit together and be gone in a couple hours, brand-new shoes on my runners for slick going. Always kept a stash of money set aside and had it in my mind where I'd go to make an offer on a couple of good dogs on a moment's notice. If the rush was in winter and I didn't have to pull that hand sled by the back of my neck, but had a couple big striders, I could easy make forty miles a day jogging over a good trail. If I rushed off in summer, a couple of big dogs packing were worth everything. There was always a market for them once I got there.

"I tell you true, if you didn't come into the country before the big Klondike rush, you probably wouldn't have a clear, complete picture. Wouldn't have much of an idea of how the country was opened. How a few set it up for the rest of the miners to come in, stay, prospect, and mine. How that made it possible for the big Bonanza discovery on the Klondike. How the Klondike produced Nome and Fairbanks and how those two led to Iditarod. Yep, the whole progression's necessary to give a guy a complete understanding of the Iditarod rush and Iditarod Trail.

"I've seen many times that out bushwhacking in country you don't know, that sometimes you look over and see where you want to get to, but the clearest way isn't straight there. Often the shortest and best path across is the longest way around. You really want to understand how the Iditarod came to be? Start 60 years before and a couple thousand miles to the east."

———◆—————◆———

Rod Perry: *I sit looking out my window at the snow-burdened spruce and reflect on those words old Anton Radovitch spoke to me almost fifty years ago, "Often the best way across is the longest way around." Turn-of-the-century Nomites, desiring a short, direct connection to winter shipping but not knowing the topography and surface character of the landscape between Seward and Nome, and not understanding how the empty desolation lacking in human resources impacted practicability, might have wondered, and even impatiently chafed that the seemingly possible short trail directly to Seward was not put in. After all, the straight-line distance was known to be fewer than 600 miles. Likewise, an impatient reader of this history may wish that I would take a short, direct line to more quickly gain its destination—the Iditarod—just sticking to the bare bones, nuts and bolts of Iditarod Trail history and not heading down what they might consider side trails of peripheral information.*

Knowledgeable trail builders back in the day as well as today's knowing historians understand that neither the trail, if it is to be passable, nor the history of the trail, if it is to be informative, can take an arrow-straight line. Just as the old, historic Iditarod Trail took many twists and turns on its way to the gold fields, sometimes necessarily deviating many degrees from its general northwest direction to complete its course, and just as the modern Iditarod Sled Dog Race Trail deviates from the old route for various sound reasons—such as to bring numerous Native villages into the event, adding greatly to the richness of the spectacle—so this history takes twists and turns and side trails I deem essential to bring the reader to his Nome. And just as the trail does not start at Iditarod, but has to begin hundreds of miles far back to the southeast, this telling of the history must start much earlier in time than the gold strike at Iditarod, and start with events that led up to it over a thousand miles away to the southeast. Unlike followers of the trail in gold-rush days or the competitors in the modern race, readers of this book will find its long, roundabout path

Alma Ready to Head Out

will not make them trail-weary. The complete, meandering story is too rich, informative, adventurous, and sometimes rollicking.

I encourage you to don your parka, pull on your mukluks, jump onto my sled and travel with me start to finish, taking in all the interesting and informative twists and turns of the entire trail and enjoy learning about the evolution of gold-rush transportation. The result at trail's end is that you will step off the runner tails knowing more about the interesting old trail than you ever guessed existed.

36

Chapter 4

---◆---

First the Trapper, Then the Prospector

Alma Preston: "OK, Rod, if we're going to help people really understand Yukon and Alaska Trail progression leading up to the Iditarod Trail, you simply must begin by tracing the way the first gold hunters came into the country and how the succeeding gold rushes unfolded.

"Of course, in a land locked in ice most of the year, the transportation needs of the different gold towns demanded winter trails. All over the Yukon and Alaska, the progression of gold discoveries and evolution of trails were interrelated.

"Yes, you've got to go way back. How far, you ask? See this old man in the picture harnessing one of the Colonel's swing dogs? He was my late, first husband's dad. I sure loved Dad Leonhardt. Well, Dad knew François Xavier Mercier, who had been in charge of the Yukon District from the earliest days of the Alaska Commercial Company. François—or Franc— was physically impressive, standing head and shoulders above his fellows. His brother Moise (Moses) was put in charge of Fort Yukon when the U.S. government ran the Hudson's Bay Company out.

"François Mercier was born in 1838 in St. Paul l'Emmite, a small town northwest of Montreal. He was part of a prominent Quebec family descended from coureurs de bois that explored and pioneered the fur business of the upper Mississippi and western Canada. That breed thrived on hardship, deprivation, and adventure.

"His cousin Honoré Mercier was Prime Minister of Quebec from 1887 to 1891. His statue stands prominently in front of Quebec's Parliament Building. Another cousin was Joseph Royal. He was one of the true founders of western Canada. He held one high office after another. Royal served lieutenant governor of the North-West Territories

Leonhardt Family

from 1888 to 1893. Back then that included Manitoba, Saskatchewan, and Alberta, plus the Districts of the Yukon, Mackenzie, and much of the rest of the high Canadian North. François had four brothers, Eugène and Moise, and the two carriage makers, Felix and Joseph. I don't know if Dad ever told me his two sisters' names, but they were nuns and both superiors of their respective orders.

"But François felt the call of the frontier. He left home at eighteen for the fur business. He worked for the North West Company as a fur trader in the Dakotas and Montana for three years. After returning to Canada for a couple, he went to San Francisco. There he met some others who joined with him and formed the Pioneer Company to trade in the North. He was age thirty when Pioneer went to Alaska. They became the first American fur company to operate on the Yukon River.

"Though François began working in his teens, he had an outstanding education, only part of it formal. He had a wonderful library and had adopted a lifetime habit of reading in a chair by the fire during many winter hours spent at remote posts.

"I don't remember Dad telling me how he and Mr. Mercier first became acquainted way back in the early days. But after the trader retired to Montreal, Dad visited a time or two as his guest. Mr. Mercier became an avid traveler after he left the northern fur business. At least once he came back to Alaska. He was on his way into Siberia on a geographical society expedition, I think. He and Dad enjoyed a lengthy visit. After that the two corresponded a lot.

"He was quite a philosopher and a real student of history. Especially history of the fur trade. He'd get so animated while talking about it with Dad; his eyes would fairly dance. He knew a lot about prospecting history, too. Dad loved to pump the old agent for stories. Dad was a keen listener with an almost photographic memory; he just soaked it up. The two were really quite a pair to draw to. Raconteurs? I've never known their equal. Hearing Dad Leonhardt quote Mercier while imitating his Montreal French Canuck accent was like listening to Mercier himself. And listening to François Mercier was like listening to a polished lecturer—with a twist.

"I think Mr. Mercier had lived so much in books that his words flowed like you were reading one. But I must say, Rod, he had such a very distinctive way of expressing himself. He grew up bilingual and spoke impeccable English as well as French. If he wanted to, he could stay in the most perfect English, perfectly pronounced, and usually did during normal, careful conversation with English speakers. However, among his friends where he could relax and let down, once submersed fully into his stories he'd totally lose himself in the telling—it was almost like he took on another, rather magical identity. Then, speaking to us mostly in English, when he was really rolling along, he'd mix French words in singles and pairs so that he spoke in a wild amalgam. And he'd mix his pronounciations, sometimes sounding his letter "I" like a perfect English speaker, but the farther he'd get submerged into the telling, the more he'd mix in hees thees ees'es (his this is's). Additionally, he'd double up—repeating what he'd just said in one language with equivalent words in the other—and pop in these longer French phrases that made it sound like Mercier the pure

Frenchman was accenting or interjecting commentary on what Mercier the English-speaking French Canuck had just said.

"It's really hard to figure: was he was just losing himself in the telling and momentarily slipping partially back into his old tongue? Did he think the expressions added spice or punch to his story? Or was he perhaps toying with the mixture as some sort of storytelling device for his private enjoyment? Yet again, maybe he just liked to see the effect on his listener, particularly on Dad. For whatever reason, it sure gave Dad, who loved to try imitating the agent's French accent, a great tool for making his dramatizations of Mercier's stories come even more alive, and with humor. Dad could never sit down while doing Mercier. He did him maybe not absolutely perfectly, but enough that it wasn't hard to imagine that you were listening to the animated, energetic, tall Frenchman himself, pacing the floor right before you in the very room. Mimic copying original, Dad as François expressing himself with his hands and waving arms was every bit as captivating as the voice. I will try to do my best imitation for you—the verbal part, that is—of Dad Leonhardt's rendition."

François Mercier: "*Mon bien ami*, Monsieur Leonhardt, settle back please and I will give you a history of the forward wave of westward expansion over *le grand l'Amerique du Nord* (North America) and what drove it.

"As European *emigraeets* pushed their way westward across North America, men of steel spirit bent on discovery and acquisition traveled far ahead of even the earliest vanguard of settlers. Their goal? *Les bonnes affaires!* Profit! To harvest and extract the wealth of the continent. Of all of those rich land resources there for the taking, the quest for two theengs—fur and gold—lured men the farthest ahead.

"*Monsieur* must understand—the two enterprises affected the frontier differently.

"*Naturellement*, trapping was a rather solitary enterprise. It benefited from the country remaining wild and undeveloped, natural, a rather blank map. *Au contraire*, once gold and other minerals were found, they had to be mined. Mining required *the people, ees eet not so?*—and eendustry. That brought settlement and development much.

"*La avant guarde* was invariably the fur trapper, was eet not?"

———

Rod Perry: *A major reason the trapper and fur trader ranged far ahead of the prospector as civilization advanced west across North America was that as soon as the earliest European settlers set foot on the eastern shore, they stepped into a land rich in valuable fur bearers from Atlantic to Pacific, while—with notable exceptions in Virginia, the Carolinas and Georgia—few substantial finds of precious metals were made until they probed the western third of the continent some 225 years later. Therefore, trapping was established as a profession from the beginning, but prospecting as an occupation did not come into being until trappers had already ranged from shore to shore.*

———

François Mercier: "*Toujours, bien sur*—the trapper—had always ranged een front, but, when hats manufactured from the felted fur of the beaver set off a great fashion craze, demand and rocketing prices triggered an explosion een the North American fur trade beyond any other een history. *C'est vrai!* That birthed the wildest, most daring, most competent frontiersmen the nation had ever seen, the colorful Rocky Mountain fur trappers, the real *hommes de montagne*, the Mountain Men. *Magnifique!*

"As remarkable as the most famous woodsmen of the eastern frontier had been—such as the likes of Daniel Boone, Simon Kenton, George Rogers Clark and Louis Wetzel—their 1700s' probes and forays through the Appalachians went, at most, a few hundred miles west of the settled frontier. Een comparison, the distance covered by some of the expeditions of the Mountain Men measured een the thousands of miles. Jim Bridger, Tom Fitzpatrick, Jed Smith, Kit Carson, Joseph Walker and their contemporaries rode, explored, fought and trapped their way from the Mississippi to the Pacific.

Courageous! Such brave men! They would have gone farther west had they not run out of continent.

"But, *Monsieur*, they were not first by any means, *mais non!* North across the eenternational boundary line, nearing two centuries before Bridger and Fitzpatrick, and far more than a century before Boone and Kenton gained fame, *les valiantes* Radisson and Grossiliers and other *travaillers bien* made grand and daring explorations far to the north and west to the heart of the continent. Then following hard after, the great Hudson's Bay Company and their fierce competitors the North West Company began their relentless quest for the furs—pelts *marveilleuses*. Een doing so they formed a wedge of advancing Breetish ceevilization across Rupert's Land—western Canada. Systematically driving their eenterests west, they penetrated even to the Paceefic. They set up a great trading post network over the vast drainage of the Great River North, the Mackenzie.

"Eventually, the two great fur companies—rivals *fatals*—were forced by the crown to terminate hostilities, and simply merge under the name of "Hudson's Bay Company" the much older company. From the well-established posts on their northwestern Mackenzie-drainage frontier they looked even farther west—west toward the Russian–Alaska boundary, *a la fin de la terre*, at the end of the world.

"In 1839, Hudson's Bay Company fur trader-explorer John Bell bid *adieu* to Fort Good Hope on the Mackenzie, charged with finding an overland route to the Colville Rivière. *Ami*, she was not exactly a *voi-au-vent*—a flight of the wind—for Bell, oh *mais non!* Refusing defeat, after many attempts aborted battling ascension of the Peel and Rat *rivières* he finally ventured through an arctic gap een the northern continuation of the Rocky Mountains. Bell then passed down two *fleuves* that would become known as the Little Bell *Rivière* and Bell *Rivière*. Gaining the Porcupine *Rivière* by the latter, he would float eet *en route* to eets outflow eento the *Youcon Fleuve*. Thereby Bell became the first white person to see the upper *Youcon* and the first to reach eet from the east.

"In 1847 Alexander Murray of the Bay Company retraced Bell's route. *Monsieur*, pure and seemple, he went there *pour exploiter*—to poach, no less—upon the game preserves of the Russian Bear.

Eenvading Alaska he quietly established a Hudson's Bay Company (HBC) post, Fort Youcon (as Fort Yukon was known een the mid-1800s), near the *confluence* of the Porcupine and *Youcon rivières.*

"At first, *comme ci, comme ça*—the Bay Company desired to know, 'ees thees larger stream *la grande fleuve*, the great *rivière* 'Kvikhpak' of the Russians that empties eento the Bering Sea on Alaska's far west coast? Or,' they wondered, 'ees thees the Colville *Rivière* their own company explorers, Dease and Simpson, had found *en route* during exploration west of the Mackenzie delta ten years before?'

"What they felt sure of, *mon ami*, was that they had gone far enough west to be trespassing on Russian soil. *Mon Sa alors!* Many een the company knew that the eencredibly swift and far-reaching moccasin telegraph between native peoples would reveal their presence to Alaska's owners. *Lèse majesté!* But Fort Youcon lay way out at extreme fingertip reach, separated from the strong-arm might of the Russian American Company (RAC) seated een Sitka by thousands of *rivières* and sea miles and from *la force majeure* of the czar seated on hees throne half a world away. Should they be caught by the uneducated *hommes gauches* of the minor RAC outposts who might attempt *juste critique*, the Bay knew the crude RAC rank and file were not exactly *savants*. They reasoned they could, with *savoir-faire repartee*, feign ignorance and there would be no great repercussions. The lucrative trade would be worth eet as long as eet lasted."

Rod Perry: *Mercier's assessment that the low-born rabble commonly assigned to man the most remote Russian American Company posts were not exactly the sharpest knives in the drawer was quite probably generally accurate. Many were convicts sent from Siberia guilty of such crimes as theft, burglary, excessive drunkenness, and even manslaughter. They tended to drink hard and brawl at the slightest provocation. They trembled before superiors—who often ruled by the lash and other force. Then turning, they acted as despots to all below them. Commonly, they treated the Natives despicably.*

François Mercier: "Although HBC exploration and cartography had been responsible for filling een much of the *space blanc* on early maps of the remote north, the company carefully guarded what they knew about northeastern Alaska. By withholding all eenformation—oui, by making sure only *et Dieu sais*—God knew—about what they knew about thees country so far to the west of where they were supposed to be, they kept their presence from becoming widely known. And although during their almost 200 years een Canada 'the Great Company' had spared no effort—*rien*—when eet came to advancing eento new regions een pursuit of the fur, they halted at thees farthest-west location. By maintaining a buffer of several hundred miles they hoped to avert confrontation *et problèmes* with the Russian owners trading downstream. Eet was, as we say, *très sage!*

"The HBC continued to trade and feign *etant ignorant*. One of their men, James Anderson, carefully worded a *communiqué* to hees superiors that the HBC 'might not be particularly anxious about clearing up the doubt that exists regarding the position of thees fort.'"

Rod Perry: *During the first trading season at Fort Youcon the local Gwitch'in taunted Murray with reports of a large stock of Russian trade goods downstream at better prices and the threat of the Russians coming upstream with those goods.*

Though Murray hoped to avoid conflict, records show he prepared for its possibility. He stockaded his trading post as a fort. He did so not so much against Native threat as Russian. When finished, he said, "The Russians may advance when they d-----d please!"

François Mercier: "Russian America was *vraiment* a land of distances *magnifiques* and solitudes *dramatiques* that had seen little known, formal exploration. Eet was a wild region *sauvage*. During Russian dominion—as well as the earliest United States ownership which would begin een 1867—eet was almost universally *compris*, understood, among Americans and Canadians that Alaska and the Youcon District of North-West Territories was a vast wilderness wasteland, remote, empty, unexplored, uncharted, and largely undesirable. The Russian American Company had established a thin presence een a few locations een the Eenterior, trading and setting up a few churches along some of the major watersheds, most notably the Copper, Kuskokwim, and Youcon.

"Surely, the Russians had established a modest *commerce*, trade on the lower half of the Alaskan Youcon *Rivière* with a post at Nulato. Goods had to be transported thousands of miles across Russia, then *voyaged* by ship across the Bering Sea to even reach Redoubt St. Michel north of the Youcon delta. From that main coastal trading *dépot* everything that supplied Nulato had to be paddled downcoast to the delta and over 500 miles going *de plein fouet* against current and prevailing wind up the Youcon. *Difficile, Monsieur* Leonhardt, *si difficile!*

"Alternatively, they could boat everything up the coast to Unalakleet, *par travail gros* hand-carry the cargo eighty-five miles over the portage to Kaltag, then paddle the load thirty-five miles up the Youcon to Nulato. Profitwise, Monsieur, eet *est facile* to *comprendre* why they determined Nulato was their extreme leemit for supplying a post.

"However, they greatly desired to trade farther upstream. About 250 miles up the Youcon past Nulato lay one of the most strategic trading locations een the far Northwest.

"*Rivières*, as you know, are the natural trade and travel routes the world over. Where one of Alaska's longest rivières, the Tanana, flows eento the Youcon, the convergence of the two great currents forms a point on the upstream side of the *confluence*. The Natives' name for eet ees Nuchalawoyya, meaning 'where the great waters meet.'"

Rod Perry: *That was about as close as Monsieur Mercier came to phonetically reproducing the Native word for the point of land. Today's learned orthographers favor Noochuloghoyet. But in these pages we will* *allow Mercier and the other traders and miners to employ their own spellings of the place.*

———————◆———————

François Mercier: "There at the *confluence* of those *deux fleuves grands*, Natives of numerous tribes traditionally *rendez-vous* annually for trading and to *fêter—célébrer*—the return of spring. Such a *grande potpourri!* Han and *Loucheaux* (which English traders call the Gwitch'in) from 300 or 400 miles up the Youcon visited. Tananas from the 600-mile length of their *fleuve* came. Eet was not out of reach for a branch of the Ahatna from the Upper Nenana. People of Telida, Lake Minchumina, and other upper Kuskokwim villages often *portaged* either over their winter trail near the Cosna or down the Kantishna to get there. And Koyukons from down the Youcon canoed up.

"Now, *ami*, I do not want to present the eempression that thees traditional gathering drew many hundreds. Native populations een the Far North were sparse. And not all villages and camps could come *en bloc*. Some deed not travel every year. So eet was nothing on the scale of the old fur *rendez-vous* of the Mountain Men and the Native peoples *beaucoup* of the western United States. But for Alaska, you see, eet was a *milieu très signifique*.

"I haven't yet told of those from north of the Youcon. A long *portage* that ranged north–south *en route* the highlands between the Melozitna and Tozitna *rivières* came out on the north bank of the Youcon just downstream of the Tozi *confluence* and only about seventeen miles down*rivière* from the traditional Tanana-Youcon Native gathering place. Eet provided a link *très remarquable*. Eet had eets northern trailhead near where the Kanuti *Rivière* meets the *grande* Koyukuk *Rivière*. That ees close to the population hub of the Upper Koyukons. You might naturally expect only those Eendians to voyage over thees path. What you would *not* expect, however, *Monsieur*, ees that *portage* would also be used by Inupiat Eskimos! That people are usually thought of as people of the far seacoast, hundreds of miles from Nuchalawoyya, are they not? But they sometimes came over thees trail, too.

"You see, *Monsieur*, probably *vers les* the 1700s, emanating from far to the west, Eskimos of the Kobuk *Rivière* had advanced from their traditional lands and, een a continuation of age-old warfare, had pushed east over the divide eento Eendian country. By force they made the Upper Koyukons give ground and established an Inupiat population around the *confluence* of the Alatna and Koyukuk. And that just happens to be *exactement* where thees cutoff trailhead begeens.

"I say *cutoff trail.* Thees *portage* ees remarkable for another reason. People wanting to go between Alatna and the Tanana mouth by canoe would have to paddle about 650 combined Youcon and Koyukuk *fleuve* miles. And then turn around and paddle those miles back. Thirteen hundred miles. But *sans grosse difficulté*—with far less trouble—thees 120-mile shortcut connects the two points overland.

"Later I will tell you, *Monsieur* Leonhardt, why I point thees trail out." ~

<hr />

Rod Perry: *What is quite amazing is how contact and trade between Native populations spans many diverse peoples and interconnects over literally thousands of miles. To illustrate, the earliest Russian exploration of the lower and middle Yukon came about over plug tobacco. This lucrative trade item was reaching even the west coast of Alaska, flowing out of somewhere in the Interior. Where, they wanted to know, was it coming from? Had not the czar given the Russian American Company exclusive trade rights for all of Alaska? And now someone, somewhere, was encroaching, bypassing their system.*

Much later it became evident that it was flowing in from a thousand miles away to the east. It emanated from the faraway Hudson's Bay Company posts of Western Canada. Traded tribe to tribe, it worked its way over Rat Portage and down the Porcupine, into the upper Yukon. From there it spread up and down the great thoroughfare and throughout the vast Native trade network for hundreds of miles in all directions.

Considering that movement of tobacco, it should not be surprising that trade goods from Nuchalawoyya would find their way not only down the Youcon, but by either Indian or Eskimo carry across the cutoff into the upper Koyukuk, and over the divide into the Kobuk Inupiat Eskimo country. Down the Kobuk, it reached the coast at Kotzebue.

François Mercier: "Nuchalawoyya. *Vraiment, Monsieur* Leonhardt, what a good, strategic, lucrative position for a trading post! But een the days of canoe travel eet was almost proheebiteeve for the Russians to conseeder the up*rivière* paddle of over 200 miles from Nulato against the hard current and weend for even a brief, once-a-year *rendez-vous* to trade. Again for them, *si defficile!*

"As well, eet was almost proheebiteeve for the *habitants* of Hudson's Bay at Fort Youcon to conseeder the long dreeft down for, as you can eemagine, eet necesseetated the *gros* 350-mile paddle back up, of course against *la fleuve et le vent.* And trespassing every stroke, *Monsieur* Leonhardt, ees thees not so?

"Almost proheebiteeve, but not *absolument* proheebiteeve. But *Monsieur*, I am getting ahead of my chronology. We weell shortly come back to thees strategeec location, Nuchalawoyya, at the Tanana outflow. Now *mon ami*, let us descend to the southern half of our conteenent to peeck up our story.

"Prior to gold finds een the West, those een the East had been rather coeencidental, *accidentellement (par hazard).* That ees, they were usually made by people engaged een other theengs. But the 1848 California Gold Rush gave birth to *une race de gens nouvelle*— a new breed: the full-time prospector. Thereafter, most deescoveries were the result of their purposeful searches. The have-nots and latecomers to Sutter's Mill had spread out. Reech meeneral deposeets they found treeggered a succession of rushes across the western United States and north eento Breetish Columbia. Each new deescovery attracted more *intrépides* to devote themselves to full-time prospecting. These were men of extremely adventurous, eerrepressible *esprit*. They felt that, sooner or later, eef they only kept deeligently searching, they themselves would strike eet reech. *Oui*, they were *intrépides*.

"The attraction of the beaver and the marten pelts had been strong enough to draw men to the farthest reaches of the conteenent. But to come back to my point, *mon ami*, eet was as *rein* compared to the attraction produced by the lure of gold.

"Think about eet, *Monsieur* Leonhardt. Een eets economic development, society has decreed gold the standard of all value, has eet not? Alchemists strive to make eet. Misers gloat over eet. Abundance geeves eets owner standing, eenfluence, and power—*carte blanche.* Gold has captured and held the eemageenation, eenflamed the passions, and seized the very souls of men throughout all cultures, *milieux,* and ages. There ees sometheeng about the lustrous metal eetself that sets off an age-old fasceenation and lust. Eet goes far beyond the mere desire for *richesse* won een a twinkling. Eet ees, as I say, *comme un diable!* A devil! Eet sets off a craving as old as the race eetself, a pull that has been able to energize and moteevate to the extent of driving, even crazing, men to go to uneemaginable lengths. The glow of gold has been the catalyst starting untold wars.

"Gold prospectors met head-on the peetiless natural forces. No weelderness was too desolate, too *sauvage.* No mountain range was too formeedable. No *rivière* course was too dangerous. And no deestance was too daunting to deescourage the eendomitable gold hunters' search for the yellow metal. Neither hunger nor loneliness nor other privations, nothing could stop them. *Rien!* Nothing! When they struggled their way north een the summer heat, dense clouds of the most ravenous, blood-sucking eensects on God's earth could not drive them mad enough to deter them from their quest. Under the aurora borealis, weenter temperatures that plunged to 100 degrees below the frost point could not freeze out their hope fires of finding their own El Dorado. *Il était étonnant! Au contraire,* with each new deescovery amid varying geologeecal features these prospectors accumulated a more exact knowledge about what surface eendications might seegnal the presence of gold below.

"*Monsieur* Leonhardt, we've leeved among prospectors, you and I. We know the race well, do we not? I think you would vouchsafe with me thees: For the past two or three centuries the world's greatest explorers—leading the best private and government-equeepped expedeetions western ceeveelization has been able to muster—have streeven een vain to reach the North Pole, have they not? But, *mon ami,* eef there had been gold there, some pathetic, wretched, bedraggled, starving prospector would have sneeffed eet out and staked hees claim, would he not? And weethin a year there would be a booming polar ceety at the mines of borealis and *beaucoup, d' hommes*, thousands of the dreeven brotherhood fanning out from the top of the world looking for more.

"*Oui, oui, Monsieur,* I'll tell you *naturellment* that the frenzied rush for wealth across the West and Far North could not have been more *remarquable* had the only way to save the very eemmortal soul been to prospect and mine for gold."

Chapter 5

---◆---

Furs and Gold Open the Yukon Basin

WERE A RAVEN TO LIFT OFF from the tidal flats at the head of Southeastern Alaska's Lynn Canal, point his beak due east and catch a thermal updraft to carry him high above the intervening mountains, his flight would take him—in just fifteen miles—to a view looking down on the headwaters of not only one of the most famous, but one of the most remarkable rivers in the world.

One might assume that waters arising in such proximity to the Pacific would soon find their way to that close-by ocean. But no. As if above anything so ordinary and predictable, and as if disdaining to be defined as an indistinct, minor stream, finishing its course while still insignificantly small, it instead is seemingly determined to take charge of its own destiny, do something unique, and make a name for itself. So this unusual river immediately does an astonishing thing: it turns its back on the nearby Pacific and chooses a roundabout way to an entirely different, faraway sea.

The course it takes before it discharges its mighty flow into salt water is a path equal in distance to almost one-tenth of the entire girth of the globe. In doing so, it becomes the tenth-longest river in the world, the fourth-longest in North America. (Depending upon which headwater is chosen as its beginning it may be measured to rank third or fourth.)

The Yukon River does not gain its distinction as one of the world's foremost drainages based upon its length alone, but because of its volume: It drains some 327,000 square miles, the entire heartland of a vast subcontinent. Along its 2,100-mile course to the distant sea its swelling tide gathers numerous other mighty rivers, themselves hundreds of miles long. Some, most notably the Porcupine, Tanana,

51

Koyukuk, and Innoko, flow a great part of a thousand miles and drain basins vast in their own right.

As if controlling a guessing game and presenting deceptions to throw contestants off, it travels mostly north by northwestward along its 700-plus-mile length within Canada's Yukon Territory. After crossing the international boundary into Alaska, it continues that course another 250-plus miles as if it were heading for the Arctic Ocean. Just as it bisects the Arctic Circle and one is convinced—as were some early explorers—that its destination must surely be the polar sea just 300 miles farther north, it throws a curve: it turns abruptly west and southwest and does not deign to join even the salt water of its choosing until it has flowed another 1,200 miles across the Great Land. Then and only then does it finally submit its volume to the patiently waiting Bering Sea.

Fifteen miles as the raven flies, just a portage as a man walks of a mere thirty-two miles through the mountains from salt water, only that short distance to reach a passageway equal in length to one-tenth the circumference of the earth. Cleaving as it does through the heart of the Yukon Territory and Alaska, it presents access to most of the interior of that vast northwestern landmass as a navigable summer waterway and a frozen winter thoroughfare.

The great river has not only made a name for itself because of the length it achieves and the volume it gathers on its way to the sea. Among the rivers of the world, it is a river of preeminence, the ring of its name stands aside to no other. Throughout history, few of the earth's waterways have gathered such fame, been the scene of such adventure and kindled such imagination as this river of glory and romance—the Yukon, the legendary "Thoroughfare of the North."

***

François Mercier: "Een 1848, *comme je me rappelle*—as I recall— *oui*, eet was the year gold was deescovered een California and a year after Alexander Hunter Murray had pushed Hudson's Bay Company eenterests to the mouth of the Porcupine een Russian Alaska, the great deescoverer Robert Campbell repeated a route he had explored

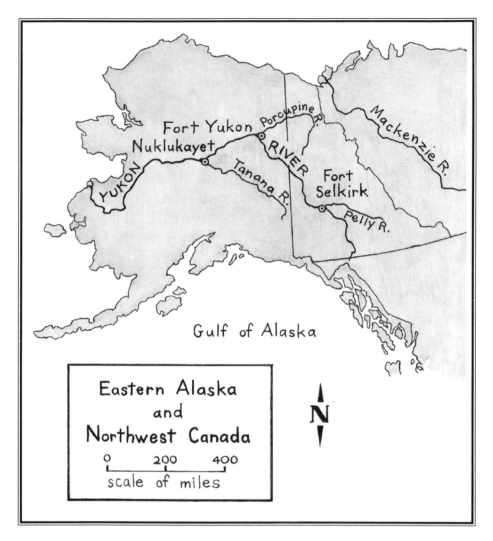

Eastern Alaska
and
Northwest Canada

0   200   400
scale of miles

een 1840. On a voyage *si difficile* he forced hees way up the dangerous, seven-hundred-mile-long Liard, ascended the Frances *Rivière* to Frances Lake—a beautiful sight—went up the Finlayson and portaged over to the Pelly. Then down the Pelly *Rivière* he drifted to the Youcon. There near the Pelly mouth, he estableeshed Fort Selkirk for the HBC. Located several hundred miles upstream from Fort Youcon, hees trading post stood about halfway between the Whitehorse Rapeeds and the mouth of the Klondike *Rivière*, Youcon Deestrict. Campbell peecked the most strategeec location for hundreds of miles.

Oh, I tell you, *Monsier* Leonhardt, eet was *c' était si bon! Loucheaux* from far to the north, and Han, from not so far north regularly made the trek south to the Pelly mouth. There they were joined by Northern and Southern Tutchone to *rendez-vous* een trade with the Tagish. All of those peoples were Athapaskans. The Tagish—Athapaskans, too— served as meeddlemen for Tlingit Eendian traders (an entirely different people) who brought goods over the mountains from the Alaska coast.

"A look at the map of the Southeast Alaska coastline shows that the Coast Mountains north and south of Juneau throw up an eemposing 200-mile-long barrier of ragged crags. *Il est comme un mur,* like a wall! To the south, thees dauntingly eenhospeetable wall begins near Wrangell, where the Stikine *Rivière*, from eets origin een Breetish Columbia, cuts through the range to salt water.

"The wall extends northward weethout offering practeecal *portage* through the peaks, ice caps and glaciers (deescounting the Taku River course as *eempracticable*) all the way to the head of Lynn Canal. There, *mon ami,* occurs an ice-free gap.

"That gap, eet happens—lies precisely at the point where the Youcon *Rivière* source and Paceefic are so close. How fortuitous! Eet also happens that the break through the mountains offers not one, but two useful passes *à terre*. Yet a third break and a third useful *portage* lies not far to the west.

"*Naturellement*, over the meellennia, the closest Natives, the Tlingit, had found and used the White Pass, the parallel Chilkoot Pass a few miles to the north, as well as the Chilkat Pass farther west. Alaska's warlike Tlingits, aggresseeve and domeeneering, tightly controlled a highly organized trading seestem that reached from their coastal veellages eenland to trade with the comparateevely mild and docile Athapaskans of the upper Youcon. The Tagish Eendians of the upper *rivière* were employed—actually almost enslaved—by the Tlingits as meeddlemen. On pain of death, the Tagish and other eenterior tribes, were forbeedden by their Tlingit *maîtres*—masters— to venture over the passes to the sea. *C'était mauvais, mon ami.* Eet was bad. Over time, the Tlingits had so eentermarried weeth the Tagish and were so commercially *en liaison* weeth them that the latter had left behind their Athapaskan language and spoke Tlingit.

"Each Tlingit chief had an exclusive trading partner, the chief of an Athapaskan group. The Tlingits took yearly—sometimes twice-yearly— trading *voyages* eento the Eenterior. They often lasted a month or more.

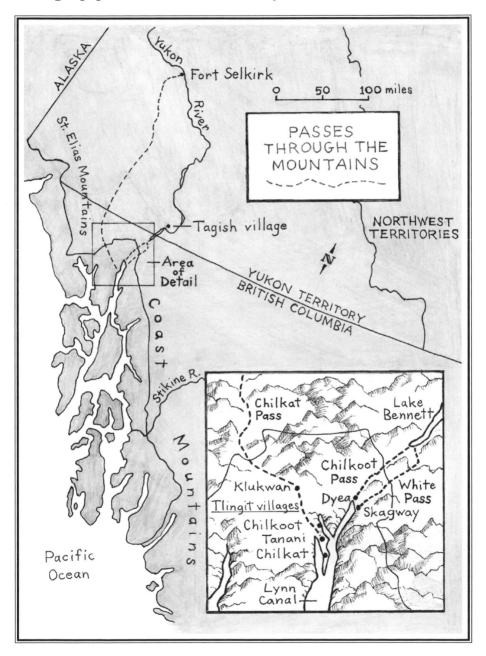

As many as one hundred *personnes* went. The coastal people were tremendous packers, *très, très* forts! Though one early explorer esteemated that the Native men averaged but 140 pounds een weight, each carried 100 to 130 pounds over the steep and precarious terrain. One was known to have shouldered some 160 pounds over the pass.

"A white trader of the day esteemated that the amount of trade goods carried eento the Eenterior yearly amounted to some eight *tonnes.* Oh, *Monsieur*, thees was serious commerce, trade *majeure*, was eet not?

"The jealously guarded passes were known as the Grease Trails. A primary trade item, carried eenland een sealskeen bladders, was oil rendered from the eulachon, or candlefeesh, a *petite*, smeltlike ocean feesh that enters coastal *rivières* to spawn. They are so oily that when dried they can be burned like a torch. Eenterior Athapaskans prized the oil—*un grand prix!*—as a delectable dietary enhancement and food preservateeve.

"Weeth the arrival of Europeans along the coast, the Tlingits became purveyors of the white man's trade goods. Their wealth and power over the people of the Eenterior grew even more. The Athapaskans, hunters and trappers *extraordinaires*, traded furs, hides, and copper nuggets een return.

"After estableeshing Fort Selkirk, Robert Campbell soon *comprendre* the Tlingits' trading and the Cheelkoot and Cheelkat passes.

"I will tell you, *mon ami*, that for the Hudson's Bay Company, getting goods eento Fort Selkirk and taking furs out was an eencredibly expensive, laborious ordeal. Between the time post supplies and trade goods left England, crossed the Atlantic, and were transported, toboggan to toboggan or canoe to canoe, post to post, from York Factory on Hudson's Bay thousands of overland and waterway miles across Canada, and the time the company's *voyageurs* and seamen had reversed that path taking furs back, een very extreme cases as long as seven long years could have been consumed een the turnaround to get Fort Selkirk furs to the London market.

"*Monsieur*, eef that deed not already render eet too economically eeneffeecient, Campbell had to compete at a deesadvantage with hees own company. The Tlingits also traffeecked een goods they procured from the Hudson's Bay Company trade steamer Beaver. That was the first motorized sheep to ply the northwest coast. They could procure HBC trade items, and een a few weeks or een some cases even *days* have them een the Upper Youcon at a fraction of the cost of moving those same goods eento Fort Selkirk over the cross-Canada route that Campbell was forced to employ.

"Campbell enthusiastically reported to HBC headquarters that the passes were short and might offer excellent prospects for supplying their westernmost posts from the Paceefic. *Quelle trouvaille!* What a find! He yearned to look over the routes to evaluate possibeelities.

"Een reply, Hudson's Bay Company governor George Simpson flatly rejected Campbell's request to explore eet: *Mais non, non! Probleme si mal!* 'That you suggest [breenging een trade goods] from Lynn's Canal, even eef practeecable, I could not recommend to the Council, as eef we obtained our supplies from thence, we should be opening a communeecation to the most valuable part of the Northern Department by wheech strangers might find their way theether. . . .'

"You see, too much general knowledge threatened their trade. The firm's most valued possession, *Monsieur* Leonhardt, was eets eenternal monopoly and unchallenged carte blanche control of the fur trade wherever they could maintain eet. The company deed not even heent that the pass exeested and successfully kept outsiders from believing that such a route could be found.

"As eet turned out, Campbell would not need to use the pass anyway. Angered about the eenterference with their trading monopoly among the northern Athapaskans, een 1852 a Chilkat war party of twenty braves marched *en bloc* een from the coast. Some theenk they came up the Valley of the Chilkat *Rivière* over their trade route that eentersected the Youcon at the Pelly mouth (later called the Dalton Trail). Regardless of the route used, when they arrived—*sacrebleu!*—een a *tour de force* they ran off the company traders, then plundered and burned Fort Selkirk!

"Campbell set off on one of the most astoneeshing overland treks een the annals of the North. Theenk of thees, *mon Monsieur* Leonhardt: the steel-weeled *explorateur*-trader traveled some 3,300 miles—over 2,000 miles of that deestance across the almost uneenhabited

Canadian subarctic by snowshoe een the dead of weenter. When he reached Lachine, Quebec he peteetioned HBC headquarters for permeession to rebeeld Fort Selkirk. But no. Unswayed by hees amazing loyalty and eencredible feat of endurance, offeecials—*pouf!*—flatly refused hees request. *Ainsi, si triste . . .* They *critiqued* the location as too *sauvage*, too remote to be profeetable, the route een and out too desolate and dangerous, and eets operation too compleecated to be conteenued. As eet turned out, Selkirk would not be rebeelt by the company for about eighty years.

"The Bay Company had found traces of gold along the upper Youcon. But, as was their habeet, they guarded that eenformation *complètement*, just as they guarded most topgrapheecal eenformation to keep their country private. They considered the fur trade far more lucrative.

"Eet ees believed that elsewhere een Alaska as early as 1804 the Russian American Company had found gold and suppressed the eenformation for identical reasons.

"The Epeescopal meessionary Rev. William West Kirkby arrived at Fort Youcon een 1861. Reverend Robert McDonald soon joined heem. The latter deescovered promeesing gold prospects on a treebutary of Birch Creek, probably Mastodon Creek. However, hees focus was on the souls, not gold. (Later he would become the Archdeacon of the Youcon.) Word of the reverend's deescovery did not gain wide circulation. I wonder, *mon ami,* could eet have posseebly been because conteenuation of the meessionaries' welcome at the Bay Company's post depended upon suppression of the eenformation? Whether or not, hees find was not followed up until some thirty years later. Then, the beeggest strikes along the Youcon to that date generated a gold rush *majeure* to the area. Preacher Creek was named een McDonald's honor. *Merveilleux!*

"Of course, as you might guess, *mon bon Monsieur* Leonhardt, long before thees time the *bidárshik* and hees *grand uprovalísha* of the Deestreect of St. Michel had learned of Fort Youcon. What, they wanted to know, deed the Breetishers have going way up there at the mouth of the Porcupine *Rivière*? So een the summer of 1860—some say 1863—the *bidárshik* charged one of hees Nulato agents to travel more than half a thousand miles upstream from Nulato to make a firsthand *reconnaissance*. Jolly leettle Russian-Spanish-Native Ivan Simonson Lukeen was the man chosen to make the solo paddle of many days. Arriving suddenly at Fort Youcon, the Creole spy, *soi-disant,* told the Bay Company men he had defected from the Russians. Confeedent een hees tale, they allowed heem to roam the grounds freely. After veesual eenspection, Lukeen returned downstream. Among hees assessments, he felt conveenced the Hudson's Bay post sat on Russian land.

"However, once he reported een at Redoubt St. Michel, the Russian American Company decided the HBC was working so deestantly upstream from Nulato, they would do nothing about eet. *Rien*. I theenk they may have conseedered eet beyond their capaceety to paddle 600 miles against the steeff current to not only drive the trespassers out but keep periodeecally going back to enforce that the English company deed not sneak back. As well, the grand *bidárshik* might have been preevy to the feeling of those higher up een the Russian American Company that Alaska was no longer profeetable enough and would be deefficult to hold on to and defend against American pioneering of the West.

"I previously told you, *Monsieur*, that we would come back to Nuchalawoyya. Now I will eenclude more about the Natives' tradeetional *rendez-vous* to trade and *célébrer* spreeng at the Tanana *Rivière's confluence* with the Youcon. I told you, as well, of the attraction thees *grand* yearly gathering worked on both the Hudson's Bay Company eentruding eellegally at Fort Youcon more than 350 miles above and the Russian American Company's rightfully operating at Nulato over 200 miles below.

"Long before, when Robert Campbell had sought permeession of HBC Governor Sir George Simpson to trade farther down*rivière,* Simpson had flatly denied the request, telling heem, '. . . Eet would be eempolitic . . . as eet would bring us eento competeetion weeth our Russian neighbors, weeth whom we are desirous of maintaining a good understanding.' Back een that day, the two titans, Simpson and Baron Von Wrangell, had just worked out a fragile truce at Hamburg. Now, though, Simpson's breelliant governorsheep and iron rule of forty years had just ended.

"Those een charge of the Bay's farthest northwest post must have felt some relaxing on their reins. Whatever the reasons, among the Breetish eenterlopers poaching up the *fleuve*, tempting prospects of trade *richesse* finally prevailed over heseetancy to push their fortune. Caution to the weends, een 1861 the Bay Company sent a trader and hired *Locheaux* down to the spreeng gathering. When I later got to know some of the Eendians who traditionally *rendez-voused* at the site they told me how surprised they were to look up and—*voilà!*—before them were the great, flat-bottomed *bateaux* of the Bay sweeping down powered by twelve oarsmen, each pulling a long sweep. They had never seen such mighty craft as those, forty feet long and nine abeam.

"Coeencidentally, that ees the very year the Russians at Nulato decided to push up*rivière* to the *rendez-vous*. Neither group, I theenk, knew of the other's plans.

"*Très facile,* Fort Youcon *bateaux* made their way down with leettle effort, just going weeth the current, sometimes hauling aloft a blanket to catch down*rivière* weends, *voyageurs bon vivants*. That put them at the trading grounds far een the lead. Oh, *Monsieur*, did they make a grand haul. Taking not only the bulk of the fur, they took the best, the prime pelts. Natives at the *rendez-vous* had long been eempressed weeth the quality of HBC guns, powder, shot and ball, tobacco, blankets, and tea, goods that had formerly reached them through trade with up*rivière* Han and *Loucheaux*. Now they were treated to a beegger volume free from so many meeddlemen.

"Meanwhile, *mon ami*, ice-out down at Nulato came later. Then, once the *fleuve* had cleared, the direction of travel for the Russians was up the *rivière*. *Vents*—weends—along the *grande rivière* can be fierce and the prevailing direction ees downstream. That combeenation of a late start and a hard, slow paddle against steeff current and weend put Russians at the *rendez-vous* well behind the Bay Company oarsmen. By the time Nulato bows touched een, the Bay *Loucheaux* were long gone, pulling uprivière with a cargo *si riche*. What leettle was left for the Russians was peecked over. And as the various people attending the *rendez-vous* compared wares, eet was plain that Russian goods as well as trade terms deed not compare well to those of the Hudson's Bay Company."

Rod Perry: *A good understanding of the difference between upstream and downstream travel over this stretch may be gained from the report of William Dall, who canoed that very section of the Yukon. Exclusive of rests, it took them twenty-seven days of the hardest labor to paddle from Nulato up to Fort Yukon. Turning around, Dall told that by tying the canoes together they could drift with the current day and night, sleeping when they wanted, not having to stop to camp. Embarking from Fort Yukon the morning of July 8, they arrived at Nulato the evening of 12 July.*

François Mercier: "The next year, 1862, the up*rivière* eentruders, weeth their past *success fou*, repeated the treeck. They even ventured farther downstream. Brazenly, the trespassers descended below Nuchalowyya to look over prospects all the way to the confluence with the Nowitna. Even having dropped down that much farther, because of their breakup timing and current and weend direction advantages, with the *crème de la crème—au revoir!*—they were still gone from the trading grounds and well away uprivière by the time the Russians arrived at the Tanana confluence. Eet was *déjà vu*. Again Alaska's offeecial owner got only the scrapings.

"Their trading presence on the meeddle Youcon and their spying foray farther upstream to Fort Youcon notweethstanding, weeth few exceptions Russian presence had been concentrated on the coast. Their North American empire was founded upon sea otter, fur seal, and other marine mammal pelts. Because of their theen eenland experience and their secrecy regarding what they deed know, what might lie throughout the vast, silent Eenterior could only be guessed by the Russians. And, as I have explained, *Monsieur*, the Hudson's Bay Company had their reasons for keeping eenformation about the Upper Youcon secret as well. *C' était inconnu.*"

"Seence Russian proprietors, weeth a heestory of over a century een Alaska, and Hudson's Bay eenterlopers, who had been here for decades, themselves deed not even know or kept secret about what they *deed* know about the Youcon Basin, well, *naturalment*, to Americans who had never veesited, the vast area was a great blank map, a meestery. They first gained widespread eenformation about the Youcon when een 1864 the Western Union Telegraph expedeetion organized a survey of the Russian Alaska section of a planned telegraph line that would circle the northern hemeesphere. The plan was to join North America, Russia, and Europe. Overland Telegraph scientists would veesit Fort Youcon, as had one of them—Robert Kennicott—some years *autre fois*, and would feel certain that the Bay Company was operating well west of Breetish territory. But the *groupe* were your United States ceetizens veesiting foreign territory. As guests having no vested eenterest, they exercised *savoir-faire.*

"Well, they abandoned the venture when, after a number of failures, the rival Transatlantic Cable was finally laid. But the United States benefeeted from the aborted try. They had gained offeecial access eento Russian Alaska because of the cooperative venture between governments. Expedeetion scientists Robert Kennicott and William H. Dall publeeshed een 1866 a report detailing resources of the Youkon *Rivière*. Their *voyage* began at the mouth and extended to Fort Youkon, where they *sojourned* with the Hudson's Bay traders. Dall described scores of plants and animals new to science. Though he, heemself did not collect or describe a specimen of the animal, subsequently the Dall sheep, *Ovis dalli,* would be named for heem.

"*Ainsi, mon ami,* een 1867, while een Nulato, Dall heard from a Russian-American offeecer that the United States had just purchased Alaska from Russia. Because both Russian and Breetish fur company secrecy had so effecteevely sealed off even the heent that gold had been deescovered weethin their realms, the United States had purchased Alaska largely for what was eveedent on the surface.

"Een 1857, when as a U.S. Senator William H. Seward first conseedered posseebeelities of purchasing Alaska, he saw whales, furs, and trade. But then came the deeversion of the Ceevil War. By the time Seward—by then U.S. Secretary of State—got back to theenking about Alaska, he saw a much beegger peecture. Now, *mon Monsieur* Leonhardt, Seward saw primarily not resources, but a Paceefic empire. He correctly analyzed that for a nominal fee he could secure the very key to the North Paceefic. He also saw that he could sandwich Breetish Columbia between Alaska and Washington Territory. He thought that might persuade the Breetish to eventually sell B.C. to the United States.

"Others, though, deed see a trio of resources I call Alaska's 'three Fs'—furs, feesheries, and forests. Your country's *vrai intelligentsia* probably suspected a land so vast had to contain meenerals as well. But they seemply had leettle idea what amazing, untold *richesse* lay underground.

"Eemmediately, for the sum of $350,000, paid een full een gold, the American firm of Hutchinson, Kohl & Company, wheech had been formed by seven men from various parts of the country, bought all the Russian America Company's sheeps, warehouses, and trading posts throughout Alaska. Though the eenventory was concentrated along Alaska's long coastline, the Russian company's posts on the Youcon— such as Redoubt St. Michel and Nulato—were part of the sale.

"I got the early jump on the fur trade competeetion een the vast Youcon *Rivière* drainage. Following hard after Alaska's U.S. purchase I formed the Pioneer Fur Company with three other French Canadians and a sailing captain, Elijah Smith. We brought our company to the Youcon een June of 1868. Mike LeBarge, for whom Lake LeBarge ees named, upon coming back from hees famous exploration of the upper Youcon for the Western Union Telegraph project, first joined with Hutchinson and Kohl, but queeckly queet them to join us een Pioneer. Other former telegraph employees joined us. As well, a few Russians who stayed on came aboard. We also drew away some Hundson's Bay employees.

"Eemmediately, for eets obvious strategic poseetion, I built the trading post I called Noukelakayet Station, a short deestance below where the Tozitna *Rivière* flows from the north eento the Youcon. That placed me about seventeen miles below Nuchalawoyya at the mouth of the Tanana, which joins the Youcon from the south. My post's poseetion was also close by that cutoff trail I spoke of earlier which leads from the Youcon *Rivière* over to the Upper Koyukuk. Another advantage was something Mr. William Dall mentioned een hees report. Packed on a bar at the Tozi mouth, leeterally hundreds of cords of dreeftwood lay, assembled and cured by nature and waiting close by the *fleuve*, easy to cut and load aboard for steamboat fuel.

"I no more than had the place up when, een 1869, Parrott & Company entered the field with their steamboat, a small stern-wheeler, *Yukon*. They established down*rivière* stations at Anvik and Nulato. Wanting to expand up*rivière,* they bought our Pioneer Company out, my post and all. Except for my brother Moise and me, the other Pioneer partners returned to San Franceesco. At that change of fortune, Moise *ventured* with Parrott, but *moi*—I signed on with Hutchinson and Kohl. To go head to head weeth Parrott I beelt Tanana Station a few miles closer to the Tanana mouth. As the company went through eemmediate changes I stayed on."

<hr />

Rod Perry: *The winter before, a company of American traders wintered at the Tanana mouth. One must wonder why the Russians had not long before taken such action since it would have been the only way to both gain a there-first timing advantage for trading and nab their illegal upstream competition in the act. (Neither William Dall nor François Mercier, two men who could have recorded this history, told whether this wintering group was the Pioneer Company. Neither was it set down whether they came up by canoe before ice-up or dog team over the ice.)*

Their wintering on-site positioned them to take part in the usual spring trade fair. When Fort Yukon's bateaus came sweeping down, expecting, no doubt, to have the action to themselves as usual, and a warm welcome, they arrived, instead, in second place and to a heated reception. The Americans met them head-on not only with indignation, but threats of force.

The Hudson's Bay traders, had, since the days of Fort Yukon founder Andrew Murray, anticipated such confrontation as inevitable, sooner-or-later. So, although they had long expected that it would be Russians jabbing the eventual accusing finger into their chests, they were well rehearsed when they found themselves caught in their poaching act instead by Yankees. The British company feigned ignorance.

The Americans then complained to Major General Henry W. Halleck, commander of the United States Army's Military Division of the Pacific.

The Hudson's Bay Company plead innocent to intent to trespass. They promised withdrawal from Fort Yukon if the U.S. could establish by astronomical observation that Fort Yukon was over the international boundary line. Halleck then directed the U.S. Army Corps of Engineers' Captain Charles Raymond and a small detachment to go find out.

When Raymond arrived at St. Michael he witnessed a historic first. On the deck of the ship Commodore was the fifty-foot sternwheeler, Yukon. *Fittingly, it was on July 4, 1869 that the* Yukon *entered the Yukon River mouth, the first steamer of many hundreds to come that would trade up and down the great thoroughfare's waters.*

———◆———

François Mercier: "Les Yankees *ambitieux* soon cast nationaleestic and profeet-seeking eyes at Hudson's Bay Company presence far up*rivière*. Een 1869, the *Yukon* headed upstream. Aboard was army engineer Charles Raymond and a few men of hees corps. When *en route* they got to Noukelakayet where my brother worked, Fredrick Smith, the Parrott supereentendent, took Moise on board. Also aboard was Ferdinand (or Fredrick) Westdahl. After steaming some 1,200 miles eastward from the sea, they tied up at Fort Youcon. Captain Raymond took hees readings to determeene the geographic poseetion. Having affirmed that the post was well west of the 141st mereedian, een a *tour de force*, Raymond ordered the fort's evacuation.

"*Adieu*. Down from the pole came the old *rouge*—red—ensign bearing een one corner the letters H.B.C., the banner so long well known across the northern tier of North America. *Bonjour!* Parrott and Company queeckly assumed ownersheep of the expropriated property. They placed Moise and Westdahl een charge. Of course, our Breetish *émigrés* were granted grace to move out and up the Porcupine een orderly fashion. 'Twas only *juste savoir-vivre*.

"*Brèvement, mon* dear *Monsieur*, between the departure of the Russians from their few posts on the lower and meeddle *rivière* and the expulsion of the trespassing Hudson's Bay Company from Fort Youcon, there exeested only a handful of white men along the entire 2,000-mile-plus course of the great Yukon *Rivière*. Een fact, *mon ami*, over the entire Yukon and Kuskokwim basins, and that ees most of the entire Eenterior, more than two-thirds of all of Alaska, at one time I knew there to be only thirty-four white men. And that eencluded Russians who had stayed. But few were on the Youcon; almost all were on the Kuskokwim.

"Een hees 'Report of a Reconnaissance of the Yukon River, Alaska Territory,' Raymond wrote, 'The Stars and Stripes now float at Fort Yukon. Anyone who desires to ees at leeberty to look for mines.' What he did not tell was that one of hees offeecers had already lost no time dabbling een that very opportunity. Weeth spare time while Raymond was engaged een hees offeecial beesiness, the man had privately panned a jar of sand and found a tantalizing amount of 'yellow material.' The offeecer kept the deescovery quiet. However, I will tell you, *Monsieur* Leonhardt, an observant Hudson's Bay trader at the fort did *tres certain* carefully note hees find. *Oui*, he deed. *Un cher ami* Frederick Harte, told me he later heard of eet from that Bay man's own leeps.

"The Americans eemmediately began spelling Youcon, *Yukon*. To not be at odds weeth the *mode du jour* and contreebute confusion, I followed.

"Hutchinson, Kohl & Company and Parrott & Company began talking. Both could see the futeelity of two companies competing and undercutting each other. Weeth the high cost of breenging goods so many thousands of miles from the source of supply, prices had to be kept up. The two companies agreed to merge, Parrott eento the much larger Hutchinson-Kohl. Upon amalgamation, een 1870 HK changed eets name to Alaska Commercial Company.

"Weeth our steamboat *Yukon*, we captured all the advantages of engine over paddle. No longer deed leemitations of canoe travel determine how far we could economeecally transport our supplies upstream against the hard current and weend. Now we could take goods upstream by the scores of *tonnes* and much more sweeftly, letting steam perform the *travail*. Almost the whole length of the *grande rivière* was ours to work effecteevely. Een 1866 a small sternwheeler had seen almost too-brief-to-mention serveece een support of the Russian-American Telegraph eenitiative. But our *Yukon* was the first steamer to regularly ply the *fleuve*.

"I eemmediately abandoned Tanana Station and dropped back down to my oreeginal Noukelakayet post beelt een 1868 near the Koyukuk Trail. And back near that eencomparable supply of firewood and steamboat fuel. When the new company put Moise een charge up at Fort Yukon and *moi* at Noukelakayet, *Monsieur* Leonhardt, the Upper Yukon fur trade was een the hands of the brothers Mercier.

"Offeecial artist for the Overland Telegraph Company Frederick Whymper was the first to publeesh mention of gold een the Yukon Valley. Een hees 1869 travel book on Alaska, Whymper reported that Hudson's Bay Company men had found "minute specks of gold" een the area of Fort Yukon." *Petit? Comme c'est drôle!*

"Then, *mon bon Monsieur* Leonhardt, een 1872, I became Alaska Commercial Company (ACC) general agent for their Yukon Deestrict. Based at St. Michel, I was charged to oversee *affaires* regarding estableeshment and supply for the nearby coast and entire Yukon Basin, about 400,000 square miles. We were spread so theen over two-thirds of all Alaska, I don't know, *mon ami*, eef you would call eet a trading empire, but as eet stood, we had a monopoly. I set out to keep eet that way eef I could."

<hr />

Alma Preston: "According to Dad Leinhart, François Mercier knew all the original Yukoners well, the two groups led by Harper and McQuesten that came into the country by way of the old trade route down the Porcupine. Ol' Franc thought very well of every one of those men. But his favorite was Frederick Harte, lifelong pal of Arthur Harper.

"Harte was just three years older than Mercier. Even though Fred held a degree in medicine from the University of Dublin, he had grown up the son of a dairy farmer, so his speech was colored like that of a man of the soil.

"Both Harte and Harper were Ulstermen, born in 1835 in County Antrim, Ireland. They had mined in California, and had joined in British Columbia's Frazier Canyon and Caribou rushes. Harte, too, knew his western and northern gold mining history and was highly interested in fur trade history. So he and Mercier really hit it off. They visited every chance they got. After Franc left the country, he and Harte corresponded.

"Remember that Dad had that steel-trap memory? I shouldn't even try to imitate Dad, (himself of German origin) trying to sound like a French Canuck mimicking an Irishman! [Alma laughs heartily.] But once François Mercier and Frederick Harte were sitting with a young writer sent north on his first assignment to collect stories for his magazine. Franc and Fred took such a liking to the boy. Poor fellow drowned later; it was said he walked too close to a high cutbank watching the dramatic spectacle of the river breaking up at iceout and the edge caved off with him. Maybe his notes went with him. I never heard of his work ever appearing in print. Anyway, here's how François quoted Fredrick to Dad, and told of Harte's and his explaining to the writer how prospecting came alongside the fur business to speed up opening the Upper Yukon."

———◆———

Frederick Harte: "M'lad, François, here, and I can tell you this is the way it started, can we not, Franc my friend? Both of us oldtimers, 'tis pleased we are and tip our hats respectfully for such a laddie as your father's fine son to get it down the way it happened. And sure you'll find it's worth goin' a mile o' ground to gain such a story as few have ever heard.

"I'm goin' to begin by tellin' you what notions and dreams drove the next pioneers here, the two groups of earliest gold hunters of which I was one. I go back to the 1860s while we're minin' in British Columbia. It still races my Gaelic blood when in my remembrance I return to the reasonin' and passions which consumed and inflamed us. Here's our excited thinkin', and even after all these years, when I put the come-hither on my memory, it fairly resonates like a grand poetic epic within my Irish soul.

"Gold! We know it lies within the structure o' the western mountain chain through the Americas from the Southern Andes up through our Rockies. We've dug it out of California, mined it from the Rocky Mountain West. The lure of yellow riches has compelled us to moil n' meddle the placers and lodes of British Columbia's Frasier, Caribou, and Cassiar. "Why stop here?" the most driven of us gold hunters reason, and we keep gazin' ever northward.

"But even among the most aggressive of our wanderin' breed's boldest searchers, the great, unknown north chills the heart; few seem willin' to test it. The vast, silent expanses are mostly a forebodin' mystery. All that has seeped out from scant reports of the few explorers is that it is a harsh, unforgivin' land of limitless distances, great rivers, deadly rapids, and loomin', forebodin' mountains towerin' range beyond range, the whole savage country crouchin' in wait to devour even the bravest and best. It remains almost unknown to even its English and Russian owners. They have hardly probed it.

"Now like a crack o' thunder out of a clear sky the incredible news bursts on us: Russia has just sold Alaska to the United States! As quickly as we sort out what that means, the potential just staggers us. Now, not just Canada's Yukon, but the entire northwest top of the continent is thrown open to our exploration and its wealth is made available to our own personal acquisition.

"Yet just the tiniest vanguard, only the most visionary and darin' of us set forth, turnin' our backs upon the last, wild fringes of the northern frontier, disappearin' toward the distant Arctic Ocean. We will penetrate the unknown and probe it for gold, or perhaps fill unmarked graves in the attempt.

"Faith, I think you see our excitement; does it begin to stir you, lad?

"Great mountain ranges almost completely wall off the way into the country, especially the way in from the Southeastern Alaska and Gulf of Alaska seacoasts. So it is by great good luck, and with us havin' only the barest ideas o' the geographical lay of northwestern North America, we forerunners decide upon a surprisin', roundabout path. The route takes us almost to the polar sea, the better part of a thousand miles farther than the way most would try. But those thousand miles bring us through the back door into the heart o' the gold country, takin' us completely *around* the Northern Rockies. That Irish luck saves us perhaps years of frustrated searchin' had we instead tried to find the few, thin breaks leadin' *through* the mountains from the southern, seaward side.

"We immediately find intriguin' traces o' gold, vindicatin' our expectations. As well, letters about our discoveries kindle bright fires of hope among the most intrepid of our brethren to the south who are first to learn of our success along the great and wonderful river we tell of.

"No matter how intriguin' the country seems, if others are to come and join us, the truth of it is, they need a shorter way in. But a more direct route is not so easily found. The coastal mountain fortress we circumvented yields but slight, hard-to-detect chinks in its armor. However, from inside information gleaned in bits and pieces from the native inhabitants, we find those cracks. Others enter the country to join our explorations. Small gold discoveries lead to the richest strikes on earth and the greatest, most glorious gold rushes the world has ever known.

"Efficient transportation by water is developed, but is useful only durin' the brief, four-to-five-month summer shippin' season. Most of the year arctic temperatures seize the North, squeezin' down or completely cuttin' off transportation and communication to the outside. Gold country is separated from the industrialized world, chokin' our development.

"Winter passageways must be found and developed if men, supplies and mail are to be moved in and out o' the golden heartland and the country is to grow to . . ."

———◆—◆———

François Mercier: *"Pardieu! Monsieur* Harte, *Monsieur* Harte, *halt, s'il vous plas't* stop. I request that you slow down. Your rendeetion waxes too vague and dramatic. There's a poetic beauty to your telling that I appreciate. But I know your story, do I not? So I can feell een all the blanks. *Mon ami,* eef thees gentlemen and hees readers are to gain any kind of true comprehension they must have your story *raconté*— recounted—een a more detailed and down-to-earth chronology. And, mon ami, try not to regress too much eento your old Irish tongue, like ees your *habitude* to lapse."

———◆—◆———

Frederick Harte: "Of course, of course, well so it is, François my friend. I get so overcome with the emotion and romance of it you'd think I was French. You're so well read you probably see ahead how what I'm sayin' will look in print. I just lose myself in the tellin' sometimes, prattlin' about the old days. I'll try to break with this lace-curtain Irish and get back into the goat-lipped Ulsterman that I truly am. Anyway, I'm glad you're here to rein me in. I'll start over. And thank you, son, for your forbearance. I'll begin anew, for surely tis a story that bears repeatin'.

"After California, prospectors had looked all over the American West. Followin' that, the main focus was north. Then, after the big placers of the Frazier, the Caribou, and the Cassiar in British Columbia had dropped off, some of us gold hunters like my pal Arthur Harper and me fixed our eye even farther, toward the subarctic and Arctic. For Art Harper especially, this was somethin' nearer to him than his shirt. He could not let go o' the idea that within all o' the great northern expanses that had never been prospected, there had to be the geological features we had learned were often gold-bearin'.

"I think he might have read of gold findin's in the Yukon Basin in Fredrick Wymper's travel book. I know he read the writin's of W.P. Blake because he showed them to me. Blake was an American geologist who went with a Russian expedition up the Stikine River in 1863. Everyone knew that the gold-bearin' zone stretched through the western mountains of both Americas north into British Columbia. Readin' Blake convinced us it would logically extend on north into the Canadian Yukon and Alaska.

"Then somehow Art got his hands on an Arrowsmith map. When it comes to a find, that took all the honors. You'd have thought he'd struck the mother lode! Let me explain. No one could match the likes of Aaron Arrowsmith as a commercial mapmaker; he was the finest of his day. He founded the Arrowsmith Map Company of London. After the Hudson's Bay Company let him into their archives of journals and surveys, he came out with his *Atlas of North America*. That was in 1775. President Jefferson himself used Arrowsmith plannin' Lewis and Clark's exploration. He gave the two a copy to carry.

Rod Perry: *The incomparable David Thompson (1770-1857) is recognized—for his extensive mapping of northwestern North America—as the foremost surveyor, cartographer, and geographer of his time. From England he immigrated at age 14 to Canada, there to serve as a Hudson's Bay Company apprentice. But in 1797 he went over to the rival North West Company. After bloodshed between the bitter competitors, the two companies were forced in 1821 to merge. Thereafter, the Hudson's Bay Company treated Thompson and his work with indifference. HBC Governor George Simpson later supplied Thompson's data to Aaron Arrowsmith. Although gained through wilderness exploration marked by untold hardship, peril, and deprivation—in the years 1792 and 1812 alone he traveled over fifty-five thousand miles—all the while driven by his vision and passion for his work and his work coated with his talent, David Thompson was given no credit for creation of much of the information that made the Arrowsmith's maps of our continent's northwest such priceless treasures to explorers and wilderness travelers.*

Frederick Harte: "For Art, it wasn't a case o' far-off gold glitterin' the brighter for the distance, but it just made sense. Studyin' Arrowsmith, Art reasoned it out this way: 'Fred,' he says, says he, 'tributaries of the Mackenzie contain areas known to bear gold. They head in the selfsame mountainous area the Yukon does. Now, I ask you, sure and does it not add up the Yukon should also hold deposits?' By the Hokey, a beguilin' concept it was and I fully agreed.

"Of course, Arthur could only dream of what might lie on the Russian side. He was brave and driven, but not enough to sup with the devil and dare the jaws o' the Russian Bear. Besides, he was no outlaw. At the same time, far northwestern Canada was big enough for Art without Alaska and he thought about it day and night.

"Then the United States bought Alaska from Russia in 1867. Now that whole land to the north suddenly became officially open to us.

As we prospected about B. C., Arthur went around, his two eyes leapin' in his head like flames. His talk with other gold hunters always turned to the Far North. Watchin' Art's effect on them, well, I wouldn't be puttin' a coward's name on them, I wouldn't, but I could see that few of even these men used to peril and hardship were darin' enough to plan seriously to head into that great unknown.

"Art Harper and the rest of us who were consumed enough to consider goin' north were next to the Indian as outdoorsmen. We redefined the word, *intrepid.* Like the earlier Mountain Men of the West, there was somethin'' in our way o' livin' we held precious beyond safety, gain, comfort, security, and the weal of family life. An unquenchable thirst to know what lay over the horizon drove us. We had unlimited confidence in our own strength, wits, and self-sufficiency. We'd shoulder our packs, leave the last supply source far behind, and not give it a second thought. No one I knew bested Art in these regards.

"Not us, but some of the other lads prospectin' British Columbia spilled over into Southeastern Alaska. The first gold they found was in 1871, small lodes around Sitka.

"People besides miners wouldn't think we could possibly communicate with each other scattered about a wilderness half as big as the United States. But there were enough of us bindlestiffs millin' around the wild country we could pass letters hand to hand or send forth spoken messages that, almost miraculously, connected more often than you'd think. The word went out and the Sitka finds drew a few score who used the old Russian capital as a base. From there, they began searchin' up and down the coastline.

"In 1872, while the coast was bein' prospected, we were pokin' around Peace River country inland. Art Harper just couldn't take it anymore. Far-off gold glitters brighter for the distance and he was just burstin' his britches to be done with mere blather and point our bows toward Polaris. He had me caught up in it, too. Well, you'll never plow a field by spadin' it over in your mind. Fortune favors the bold and brave; with no more than the britches on our backsides and our sparse outfits we had nothin' to loose by darin' the unknown, nothin' but our lives. We would cast our lots for the North and let our feet and paddles take us to where our hearts were; little did we know then that it would be a long and windin' life's road that had no turnin'. We found three other fine n' decent men staunch and maybe crazy enough to pitch in with us: George Finch, Andrus Kenseller, and Sam Wilkinson. They were tough and skillful. The lads would make a good team.

"Lookin' at Art's Arrowsmith, there seemed to be a logical route to the Yukon and we began headin' that way. As it turned out, if we'd only known the way we'd eventually take, we would have just kept to the way we were goin' and saved ourselves a lot of time and labor. You see, we were already travelin' the Peace in dug-out canoes we bought from the Indians. Instead of stayin' with it, descendin' to where it flowed into our eventual path, the Mackenzie, we struck off for Laird drainage and our intended route.

"Leavin' the Peace in the fall, up the Halfway River we went—so named because the mouth was half way between Rocky Mountain Portage and Fort Saint John. We had about a hundred miles upstream to go. We went as far as we could by water. Then when winter set in, we left the boats behind and built sleighs. Pullin' our supplies to the top o' the drainage, we then fought our way over a twenty-five-mile-long portage. Devil take it, it was hard as the very hob of hell goin' all the way across the height o' land over into the Liard Basin. With that long ordeal finally behind us, we pulled our sleighs about sixty miles down the Sikanni Chief River. There we quartered in our tents the rest o' the winter.

"The Laird River gets its name for the huge cottonwoods growin' in the basin. Some we found were five feet through and eighty or ninety feet to the first limb. The five of us spent the rest of the winter buildin' cottonwood dugouts. Then at ice-out we went down the Sikanni Chief and Fort Nelson rivers to the Nelson mouth at the Laird.

"There, in northeastern British Columbia we had a most surprisin' meetin'. We bumped square into another party of prospectors as crazed for the Far North as we were. Maybe that's why the good Lord cursed us with a blessin' and sent us this harrowin', roundabout, inefficient way instead of keepin' us on the Peace. Some members of our groups would have the pleasure of turnin' out lifelong friends and partners. Standin' there we could have never guessed that some would even figure prominently in history.

"Lad, you've heard of the notable Leroy Napoleon McQuesten? Aye, it is that same man who led the other group. Everyone called him Jack. With him was Alfred Mayo. An ex–circus acrobat and clown and great jokester, Al was. Kentucky born eleven years younger than Jack, since bein' discharged from the Civil War in about 1865 he'd been travelin' with McQuesten. 'No better trail companion ever noggin'd a tumpline or dipped a paddle,' McQuesten claimed. Jack was a big, burly man, powerful, over six feet and Al, in youth was short and wiry. These were real men, tremendous men. Like my friend Art Harper, they were of strong moral character, indomitable spirit. And like Art, they had a passion for the North that glowed like a peat fire and a vision that was broader and much longer in range than the rank-and-file gold hunter's. A third good man, James McKniff, completed their group."

———◆—◆———

Rod Perry: *Some of those adventurers were destined to become famous not only during their own time in the early development of the Yukon District and Alaska, but geographical place names and the contributions of their descendants will forever preserve their legacy.*

The descendants of Arthur Harper and Al Mayo remain especially numerous along the Alaskan Yukon. Archdeacon Hudson Stuck chose Arthur's son, Walter Harper, along with Harry Karstens, (the Seventy-Mile Kid) to join him on the first successful ascent of Mount McKinley. By the very fact that it was Stuck who had conceived and organized the expedition and chosen its members, he had every legitimate reason to stand on top first. But consistent with the character of the great churchman and adventurer, at the top he stepped back, thinking it appropriate that a Native Alaskan should be first to set foot on the summit.

Iditarod Race legend, the late Susan Butcher introduced the blood of Blackie, a prepotent male sled dog owned by racer Clyde Mayo of Rampart into her winning line.

———◆—◆———

François Mercier: "Jack McQuesten had been attracted to the West by the California gold rush, the same as Art Harper. And like Art, durin' the early 1860s, he prospected north into British Columbia. Jack hit the Frazer rush and the rush to the Finlay River later.

"After that he mainly trapped and fur-traded for almost a decade, some of that time for the Hudson's Bay Company. While workin' in the fur trade, he must have been intrigued by stories about the Pelly and Yukon rivers told by old Bay Company employees. Jack kept mullin' over his own conclusions, identical to those of Harper. He, too, thought that the mineralized zone of the western mountains surely must extend into the Upper Yukon and Russian America.

"It seems McQuesten's locations were so remote that it wasn't until 1871 that he found out that the United States had bought Alaska. And sure, that news excited him. That year he, Al, and I think McKniff had been winterin' on the headwaters of the Hay River, which feeds into Great Slave Lake, trappin' and operatin' as independent fur traders among the Dog Ribs or Yellowknives. They'd already prospected the entire length of the Peace River and found it wasn't worth a bob; all they got was so much savage amusement, a thousand miles of exercise. They kept thinkin' more n' more about the Yukon and finally decided to take the plunge. So they went down the Hay, through Great Slave and started up the Liard, plannin' same as us to go by way o' Frances Lake and the Pelly River to the Yukon.

"By the time they'd ascended about four hundred miles, as far as the Nelson mouth they could see that fightin' the progressively strengthenin' Liard current they'd never make Frances that fall. Jack thought it such good game country he called a halt and said to the lads, 'Let's winter over here, men, and live by our guns.' Besides, they'd been findin' wee traces of gold on the bars. It looked like it was gettin' better the farther upriver they went. It seemed prudent to the lads to catch the moments as they flew. Sure and they didn't want to pass anything up by bein' in too big a hurry.

"They built a cabin, then left on a three-week scoutin' trip to get acquainted with the country, lookin' around for food, fur, and inhabitants. Findin' the closest Indians, they traded with them for meat. (Word of that same tradin' must have traveled.) Back at the cabin they went to work buildin' snowshoes, a sleigh, and winter clothin'. They killed a couple moose and a very big bear. Confident now, they felt pretty well set to trap n' trade.

"First o' November, begorrah, but out o' the blue came the most revoltin' development. Three Hudson's Bay Company men showed up and lowered the boom on the lads' plans. They were straight up about their purpose; they'd been sent by the Chief Factor o' the region himself. Sent, they were, to keep Jack, Al, and James from trappin' n' tradin'. The Bay hated free traders and tried to run them off to keep them from disruptin' company relations with the Natives and abusin'

Leroy Napoleon ("Jack") McQuesten

Jim McQuiston Collection

them. You see, a lot of free traders were in it just for the short haul. They'd trade whiskey, which was the Indians' ruination. So faith, really, even a stepmother wouldn't blame the Factor for bein' on such guard.

"So the Bay men built a cabin almost atop Jack's camp. Bein' right there in each other's lap could have been untidy, but lucky thing, it turned out they all liked each other and visited back and forth.

"One o' the men was named Sibistone. He had been several years over on the Yukon and he painted the country as a gold hunter's and trapper's paradise. He was there when the steamer *Yukon* came up. He told Jack of Captain Raymond's officer findin' "something yellow" at Fort Yukon. Sibistone said the officer threw the stuff out so the men wouldn't see it. The officer told Sibistone that he'd never seen gold and didn't know what the yellow in his pan was. But Sibistone felt convinced by the way he acted in tryin' to hide what he'd found, it must have been gold. The officer breathed nary a word to the crew, fearin' they'd jump ship on their mission.

"Sibistone also said while he was at the post they'd catch a silver fox about every night at the water hole. And inside the stockade at Fort Yukon they commonly killed marten with a club. Just among themselves Jack, Al, and James were itchin' all the more to get to the Yukon. But outwardly, they stayed unemotional as bog men. Around Sibistone and the other Bay men next door they acted only mildly interested.

"Then Mr. McDougal, the HBC chief factor for the surroundin' region, put in his appearance. He's the one who'd sent Sibistone and the others to prevent Jack's group from trappin' n' tradin'. While they visited, talkin' in general of travels around the North, Jack, just sort of nonchalant, mentioned Sibistone's experiences on the Yukon. Mr. McDougal backed up everything Sibistone had told them about Fort Yukon and added to it. Seein' their possible interest as an answer to get them out of his hair, he made them a sweet proposition."

Chief Factor McDougal: "Now, i' thou'll nae trade amang the nearby Indians, and wad gie me thy word, McQuesten, I'll nae stand in the way o' thy trappin' i' trappin' only it will be. I' thee'll stick tae thy ain business and swear thy leal tae stay oot o' tradin' entirely, then ance spring brak's, i' ye hae gart a guid catch, I'll buy frae thee n' thee brithers a' thy winter's pelts."

Frederick Harte: "He had an even sweeter proposition I'll be gettin' to. Like I said, Jack's group had intended to follow the abandoned Bay Company route, the same one we figured to travel. Jack had probably heard the old canoemen talk about it. Off the Liard the route ascended the swift Frances River, to Frances Lake and up the Finlayson. Then they would portage to the Pelly River. The Pelly would take them down to the upper Yukon.

"But Chief Factor McDougal drummed it into their heads to give up on that route. While sure he wanted to be rid o' them, he didn't wish them early graves."

Chief Factor McDougal: "We invested a guid lot into establishing our posts at Frances Lake and Pelly Banks whare the pairtage trail frae Frances an' Finlayson fands the Pelly. And mair went intae setting up auld Robert Campbell's Fort Selkirk fast by the Pelly mouth. Why, then, mon, dost thou think the Bay ne'er flit tae rebuild bairned-out Selkirk? An' why dost thou think we finally just tairned our backs on the ither posts and abandoned thim? You think t'was because there was na fur there? Hoot, mon! there maud be fur, an' plenty o' it, else the company wad hae ne'er set up in those locations in the fairst place.

"I'll gar me sure I tauld thee sae thee ken, an' may that evil country be forever damned! Hell's Gate! Devil's Gorge! Rapids o' the Drown'd!

"I counsel thee, McQuesten, as I warn each mither's son tae take heed: The rairing Liard lap and flang a' men wham fand their lot tae paddle for the company amid that detestable rin's angry fyke! That rin's a vera fiend. In the years the company was abroad in those posts, eleven *voyageurs*—eleven!—an' every ane o' thim superb rivermen wham fear naether don, devil, or Dutchman—eleven o' thim drown'd, swallowed deep by the cursed Liard. Twa ware my freends an' a better mon than ither ne'er lifted a paddle. Thro these mony years as twad yisterday mony a nicht in the mirk I canst see their ghaist's cauld faces an', e'en yet, it bids bring a tear.

"The *Malevolent River* or *River of Malediction* auld Robbie Campbell called it, an' that be sooth. Three mair Bay brithers starved tae death, puir souls, along thy vera intended route, Mr. McQuesten. Now I've tauld thee, now thee ken. I would be laith tae see thee oot i' I dinna warn thee, for i' I did I'd expect tae hear the banshee's lonely croon an' backward cast my e'e intae the gloamin' fearin' thy stalkin' bogles. Dona go that way! I tell thee, mon, it's lang on mony dangers, it's tae difficult, an' sae drear, far frae supplies."

Frederick Harte: "Now havin' warned the lads fairly, Mr. McDougall first drove a hard bargain, tellin' them he'd take as many pelts as they could trap, but only if they'd accept payment almost two thousand miles away. Then he followed with a sweeter proposition than Jack and the others could have ever dreamed up."

Chief Factor McDougal: "I said eve I'd buy a' thy pelts, yet hear this: I'll pay thee naething fast by here at the hame sod. Thou canna come by thy lucre til far up at La Pierre House on the Porcupine. I'll weel provision thy lang trip, an' pledge thee'll fand a warm welcome at a' our posts o'er the auld trade route. We'll furninsh thee wi' Indian guides an' a guidly crew tae help thee pairtage frae Mackenzie waters o'er tae the Bell above the Porcupine. An' I'll send wi' thee a post that ance at La Pierre they'll throw in straucht lumber frae wham tae build a boat."

Frederick Harte: "You can see how highly he thought of Jack as an adversary! It could have well been that he thought if Jack took the Laird and saw how dangerous it was, he'd return and be in his hair again. Maybe he saw havin' them go the safe HBC trade route would be a surer way to guarantee his trip and see Jack's back once and for all.

"Well, those lads thought truly their ship had come in. The factor had greased the skids for them to do what they already planned on doin' with or without his boon: go to the Yukon. So they hit their traplines hard. At winter's close they had around four hundred marten.

"By the time we showed up, Jack, Al, and James McKniff were rollin' their bindles to take the trunk line north. The famous old HBC trade route went down the Liard, descended the great Mackenzie almost to its very mouth on the Arctic Ocean, ascended the Peel, traveled up Rat River, crossed over McDougall Pass, and took the Little Bell, Bell and Porcupine down to Fort Yukon. It was many hundreds of miles longer—really, maybe something around a thousand farther—but it was safe water the whole distance with several Bay posts along the way.

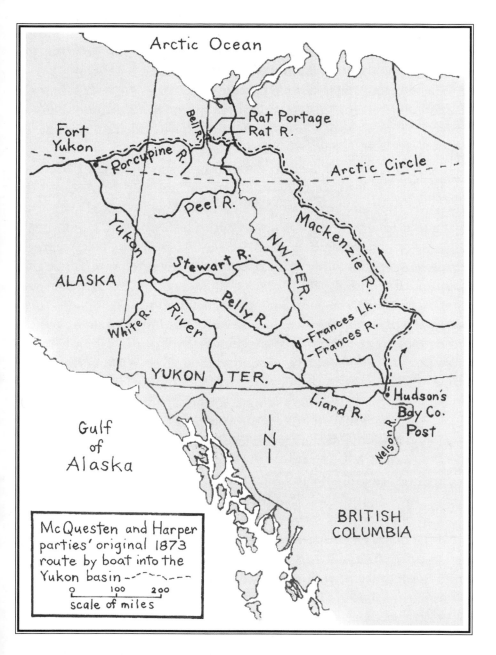

Arctic Ocean

Bell R.

Rat Portage
Rat R.

Fort
Yukon

Porcupine R.

Arctic Circle

Peel R.

Mackenzie R.

Yukon

NW. TER.

Stewart R.

ALASKA

White R.

River

Pelly R.

Frances Lk.
Frances R.

YUKON TER.

Liard R.

Hudson's
Bay Co.
Post

Nelson R.

Gulf
of
Alaska

N

BRITISH
COLUMBIA

McQuesten and Harper
parties' original 1873
route by boat into the
Yukon basin - - - - - - -

0   100   200

scale of miles

"That spring when we pulled into the Fort Nelson post the McQuesten party was just gettin' ready to take to the river. We had gone over and over Arrowsmith. It was clear the shortest way to the

81

Yukon was by the Liard, Frances, Finlayson, and Pelly. But sure it didn't take beatin' us with a shillelagh for the factor and McQuesten to change our thinkin'. We headed out the longer, safer way.

"May the good chief factor's troubles stay far apart as me dear old grandmother's teeth. His consideration merits my gratitude. If it was nay for the man's sage warnin', we might have added another seven to the Liard's grim rolls.

"Sam Wilkinson decided to stay and prospect the Liard. Then a few hundred miles downstream, when our flotilla drifted out of the Laird into the Mackenzie, McQuesten and Mayo departed. They had to make a long side trip of several hundred miles to finish some business at Fort Resolution on Great Slave Lake. That Jack, wherever he roamed he always had fur and trading business goin'. Since that would put them well behind, McKniff climbed out of their boat and went on with us. Our party again numbered five.

"The Mackenzie, 'the Great River North,' is indeed a great river. It drains most of the interior of western Canada, in fact more square miles than all of Alaska. The second longest river in North America it is, over 2,600 miles long measured from its Finlay River head to the Peace, down the Peace, across three hundred-mile-long Great Slave Lake, then down Slave's outlet, the Mackenzie proper. From the lake to its mouth on the Arctic Ocean the Mackenzie proper flows almost eleven hundred miles.

"In June and July it runs high carryin' lots of driftwood. We'd just pull up to a big uprooted tree, tie off, and build a fire on the swellin' at the roots. The river's three miles wide with few islands, so there was little chance of our tree hangin' up on a shoal. With the current makin' about four miles an hour and a pot of our stirabout simmerin' and another of tea, we were livin' like royal Turks. The very life o' O'Riley it was indeed. Just driftin' along sweet as you please day and night, leanin' back on the duffle, feet propped up, some o' the lads pullin' on their pipes, and pullin' on each other's legs, the blarney flyin' thick, fillin' the air so dense a starved no-see-um thinned down to skin 'n bones couldn't squeeze through sideways, watchin' the world go by, not a care on this green earth. Jack and Al traveled by the same method when they came along later.

"The HBC stations enroute treated us all nobly. The boat we left the Mackenzie with had a payload capacity of about two tons. It was easy at first travelin' up the Peel's almost slack water for twelve miles, then along the Husky Channel to the mouth o' the Rat River. But once we reached swift water on the Rat, even with help of enlisted Gwich'in it was all we could do to make headway up that racin' river. Day after day we waded and lined, first on one side, then bein' forced to the other. Mosquitoes? One slap on your shirt'd produce a hand covered in a gray, soupy pulp. Finally we reached McDougall Pass with its small lakes, four in a row. Then it was down the peaceful Little Bell to the Bell and on to La Pierre House. There James McKniff stayed behind to await Jack and Al.

"After months by river and portage, we came into Fort Yukon July 15, 1873. Begorrah, you could have knocked François' brother, Moise [Moses] over with a feather. Was he ever surprised and overjoyed when we four strange white men showed up!

"Jack and Al were trailin' us by four weeks. At Peel River they'd run into a man named George Nickolson. He'd been trappin' and prospectin' in the Mackenzie drainage for two years. He wanted to try the Yukon, so Jack invited him in. About July 20 they were ready to leave the Mackenzie. Like Chief Factor McDougal had guaranteed, the Bay Company sent a crew of Indians along to help. Their party lined and waded their canoes up the swift Rat, then left them near the summit. Just over the top, they reached the Little Bell River and built a raft. Down they floated to the Bell and on to La Pierre House. There, James McKniff was waitin' with the boat lumber the HBC agent had given him for Jack. After buildin' a boat and loadin' it with fourteen hundred pounds o' gear and supplies plus four dogs Jack had picked up—Jack had a thing about dogs—the four men pushed off. They pulled into Fort Yukon August 15, 1873. Jack told me when his lads reached the ACC station, Moses Mercier treated them like kings, just like he had us.

"Lad, let me give you a little insight into Jack McQuesten that otherwise wouldn't be apparent to you and your readers: that Jack looked upon his short pause at Fort Yukon as 'palatial' livin' gives a hint. What extreme hardship he must have willin'ly endured durin' the previous decade to follow the life he loved. Years later, he always remembered back to how particularly thankful he was when Moses—may peace and plenty be first to lift the latch on his door—spared them fifty pounds of flour. Seems Jack and Al had gone without a supply for two years. A further glimpse into the remoteness of the life he'd lived was that it was at Fort Yukon that Jack—and the rest of us, for that matter—first laid eyes on a repeatin' rifle.

"From the fur trade, McQuesten had a lot of experience with sled dogs. He planned to make good use of the four he brought with him.

"By the time Jack and Al and the lads got there, our bunch had been gone a couple weeks or more, buckin' the swift current up the Yukon, prospectin' along the way. We found fine gold on the lower reaches of a river we'd later name the Fortymile. We didn't prospect up that river further because local Indians warned of an impassable canyon upstream. Turned out to be blarney, there were rapids to be sure, but not nearly impassible. Indians we'd met at Fort Yukon had some copper nuggets they'd taken maybe four hundred miles up the Yukon. They said they got them on a big tributary river that turns the Yukon from runnin' clear to becomin' silty. Someone later named it the White River. We decided to turn from huntin' gold to a search for copper. We went up the White until the extremely swift current stopped us. In winter we forayed fifty or sixty miles up on the ice, pullin' sleds, just to look over the country. While we wintered over on the White we had plenty to eat, but it was almost straight moose.

"Before we left Fort Yukon, Andrus Kenseller had decided to winter with Jack's group. From advice of Mr. McDougal, backed up by hearin' around Fort Yukon about Reverend McDonald's gold find about a hundred miles downriver a dozen years before, their party went down the Yukon to the general vicinity of that vague discovery. They prospected a tributary, Beaver Creek. Findin' some fine gold on the bars, they readied for winter. Jack, Al, George, and Andrus built a snug cabin. O' course, they chinked the log walls with moss and topped it with a thick, sod roof. As was common in the earliest days, they used a sheet of ice for a window.

"They killed three moose, a fat bear which supplied gallons of grease, and lots of waterfowl before freeze-up. Jack said the whitefish they netted in the lake near camp were the biggest he'd ever seen, eight to twenty pounds. He later told me they'd fry themselves they were so fat; a pint or more of oil would come bubblin' out of each one while they sizzled. But that's about all they had, red meat, fowl and fish to fill them, fat and oil to keep them warm.

"They'd intended to spend the winter trappin' n' tradin' to make a new grubstake. But they found there was little fur in the vicinity and saw nary a single Indian. Jack and Al made one trip to Fort Yukon, snowshoein' back durin' bitter cold just after Christmas. Took them six days, and they stayed ten more until the cold broke. Moses again treated them like kings. They decided go back, abandon Beaver Creek, and bring the other boys and their outfits back up to Fort Yukon. Now they had a broken trail and made good time. It was a hundred down, a hundred up. On their last haul, Old White Eye, an Indian from Fort Yukon, came sixty miles down with his team bringin' a big sledload of meat for Jack's dogs and the men. By April 2 they finished all their transportin'.

"Jack and George Nickolson had to attend to some business with the Hudson's Bay Company. Wouldn't you know it—that's Jack and his business again. Immediately the two left on a forced march of four hundred miles to La Pierre House. As they snowshoed up the Porcupine they bucked extremely deep snow. Slowed, they ran out of food. They had to stop a few places to hunt rabbits. When they got there, who should they run into but their old friend Sibistone. Jack made fun of his gold and silver fox tall tales but let him off easy, admittin' 'twas only a stepmother would blame him. But ol' Sibistone insisted Jack simply hadn't looked in the right places.

"Jack and George turned about just in the nick o' time. They got back to Fort Yukon the very day—May 10—the ice went out. They shot a lot of geese waitin' for the river to clear. Then, with Moses in his boat, their group followed breakup downriver to the Alaska Commercial Company station near the mouth of the Tanana, hopin' to get supplies. None there, so they decided to continue with Moses when he went down to St. Michael.

"Our party followed the ice down from our winter of stayin' sated on moose up on the White. We drifted into Tanana on May 20. We were happy to see Jack's men there. Seein' no provisions, we decided to drop downriver too. Moses had a few days' business then started down. On the way the two groups compared first impressions and made plans. Toppin' all our lists was that we hoped to stock up on provisions and gear. With Tanana Station as thinly supplied as Fort Yukon, something needed to improve. It was no fault of Franc's and Moses'; how could they have guessed two groups of prospectors were going to come crashin' in unannounced? They were just stocked to trade with the local Indians, and barely that.

"The Alaska Commercial Company (ACC) had a virtual tradin' monopoly on the river. However, they hadn't done much except at Nukalayet to expand the Russian American and Hudson's Bay properties on the Yukon. Mainly they'd merely maintained the fur-tradin' operations about as they found them. Early on they had hired the Mercier brothers. Franc and Moses gave them experienced agents for a smooth transition from Russian ownership from the Tanana down and from the Hudson's Bay Company's former operation on the upper river."

———————

François Mercier: "*Mon ami*, Frederick, my brother Moise was elated when your Harper and McQuesten parties broke hees solitude. When you adventurers showed up at Fort Yukon he could scarcely believe hees eyes. You just seemed to have materialized from theen air. The last theeng we would have expected to appear up there was white men. Just before your arrival, only a half dozen or so whites populated the whole 2,100-mile-long *rivière*, none but Moise een the upper thousand. Moise and I really enjoyed the contact weeth our Native customers. But as anyone of any race and language weell tell you, after being separated a long time, conversing een your own heart language weeth your own people means so much.

"*Oui, oui, mon* Frederick, I know what you're about to eenterrupt and say. Before I let you break een with some of your Irish wise cracks aimed at my mother tongue and genetics, let me explain to thees gentleman that Engleesh has been my spoken second language from youth. Een my bush-bound state, when I looked up and saw Irish- and Engleeshmen, they were close enough.

"To conteenue, the only time all year we had been able to converse een English or French was when we took our leettle steamer *Yukon* on eets yearly run. At breakup we'd gather furs from the ACC's *rivière* posts as we went down to St. Michael. After loading up from company stocks, on our way back up the *rivière*, we'd supply our traders.

"Een addition to trade goods the Eendians wanted, what the company sent up the *rivière* was only enough to maintain the personnel that ran the posts. Eet had to last unteel next year's boat. So you can see, *monsieur*, that when *mon amis* Frederick and hees two prospecting parties suddenly blew een from out of nowhere we had almost notheeng to spare them."

———————————

Frederick Harte: "Lad, that's pertinent if your magazine readers are to understand our place in history. Our whole first year on the Yukon, all of us had lived the futility of bein' forced to focus a big part of our attention on roundin' up enough to keep the wolf from the door. It wasn't that we weren't accomplished at livin' off the land, it's just that it took valuable time; heaven's sake, the Indians were even better at it, and they spent most of their existence just scrapin' together enough to keep body and soul together. We sure hadn't come all the way to the Yukon just to practice skills as hunter-gatherers. We needed to train our time on prospectin', minin', and trappin'. We just simply had to do something to fix things.

"Prospectors, see, are like armies; they function on their bellies. The sword of famine is less sparin' than the bayonet. And we had to find a dependable source for more than merely *fillin'* our bellies. Health also must be paid its tithe. We needed feed of the right variety, too. Just like early sailors brought on scurvy and other ailments from poor diets, we knew a diet of straight fish and game would eventually run us to ground. All could see the futility of tryin' to work in a region where the sin of gluttony can be committed too rarely to count.

"If our groups as well as future prospectors were goin' to have any chance to find the minerals all of us—especially Art and Jack—were sure the country held, a more assured supply system was an absolute must. We determined a good retreat was better than a bad stand; with belts loosening and the memory of our last square growing ever fainter we decided to go out to the supply base and concentrate on settin' up a dependable source o' provisions.

"On June 4 we all clambered aboard Moses' boat to accompany him on his annual spring trip. He was bound for St. Michael. As we checked the ACC Tanana post on our way through we saw those shelves were pretty bare and continued downriver. June 20 we got to St. Michael. The redoubt's the old Russian fort and tradin' post not far north of the Yukon Delta. With U.S. takeover, it became the ACC distribution center on the Bering Sea. With Mr. François here, then headquarterin' out of the redoubt havin' charge o' the whole Yukon district, on June 25, 1874, McQuesten, Mayo, Nickolson, and I, Frederick Harte entered into an agreement with him to act as Alaska Commercial agents. That had a smack to it; we worked out a veritable franchise for the upper river.

"Down at the redoubt, Jack ran into an old acquaintance, Father Clut, a Catholic priest. The good Father pulled Franc aside and put a bug in his . . ."

———————◆—◆———————

François Mercier: "Please allow me to break een, Mr. Harte. Father Clut was like a dear father to me. He had come for a reconnaissance eento our Youcon country because of my correspondence weeth church heads I grew up under as a youth back een Montreal. The far Northwest, I had wreetten them, desperately needed Catholeec evangelizing.

"Therefore, when he told me I had really found a gem een Mr. McQuesten, I took eet as eef coming straight from the mouth of God. Father had known Jack from hee's fur business days een Canada's North-West Territories. Mr. McQuesten was not only a good trader, Father vouched, but wise, respected, well liked, and scrupulously honest.

"Father Clut's recommendation of Jack, as Mr. Harte would say, put a bee een my bonnet. I would seize the opportunity to expand afforded by the experience of Mr. McQuesten. I began developing plans to have Jack found and run a new trading operation about 350 miles up the *rivière* from Fort Yukon. But that arrangement would only be on the condeetion that Jack sell the company about one hundred marten and twenty beaver skeens he'd taken een trade with the Eendians, plus about $1,400 worth of the Hundson's Bay merchandise he'd brought down the Porcupine."

———————

Frederick Harte: "Thank you, François. At St. Michael we took on a load of supplies, all they could spare. The plan that first year was for me to learn the business by helpin' at Nulato. Al Mayo would break in by assistin' trader Napoleon Robert run Nuklukayet.

"Harper, George Finch, and James McKniff put together a separate supply to keep themselves prospectin'.

"With several small barges loaded with trade goods and supplies in tow, plus a whaleboat trailin' behind, on July 7 we started upstream. Pilotin' the *Yukon* was Tom Williams, who would later—God rest his brave soul—become famous. It was quite a sight to behold, the little stern-wheeler strainin' to move that train o' barges. We made only three miles an hour on the lower river. Mr. Forbes served as engineer and Mr. McIntire as cook. A big reason for such a full crew was that every ten hours or so, we'd have to pull up to a driftwood pile and all set to work cuttin' n' loadin' four cords o' fuel. Even with that many of us cuttin', carryin', and stackin', we averaged six hours a day takin' on fuel for the boiler.

"To establish tradin' relations, we put in at villages along the way. We dropped the first barge off at Anvik and the second off at Nulato. I stayed with it to help Mike Labarge run the fort there. He's the guy Lake Labarge is named for.

"Now I have somethin' mighty worth the tellin'. Just imagine with me that I had not debarked at Nulato but had still been aboard when the *Yukon* headed on up, breastin' the flow. Well it would have seemed to me that havin' rid ourselves of two barges we were in the process of freein' ourselves of our attachments and lightenin' up.

"Maybe I'd have felt like the guy who makes a practice of always carryin' a huge anvil around. Figures it helps him dam up a reserve of untapped speed. Says he, 'If I ever looks o'er me shoulder and spots a pack of wolves on me trail, by the very droppin' o' me anvil here, wi' nay burden I'll become light, nimble, and instantly blazin' fast.'

"Well, if I'd been in that train o' thinkin' I'd have been wrong as wrong can be. Because somewhere in the next few bends o' the river, a mist of Irish magic must've settled over the boat. While at the *Yukon's* next stop, Koyukuk Station, my lifelong friend, Arthur Harper, who I thought I knew so well, by all the goats in Kerry, he pulled a shenanigan that, when I afterward learn of it, completely surprises me. He's thirty-nine years old. I thought he was a confirmed bachelor. But something must've gotten into him. He spots a young Koyukon lassie. (I don't know, maybe I'd altogether missed noticin'; he could've already met her on our way downriver.) Her name's Seentahna, known also as Jenny Bosco. Only fourteen, she was. Anyways, almost faster than the human eye can follow what's happenin'—Tom Williams, he has the boiler fired up with a full head o' steam and needs to get goin'—in quick order Art checks around to find a little about her, asks her to marry him, arranges with her parents, holds the weddin' on the spot, loads her aboard, and steams away upriver with her.

"Now isn't that the wee knife! Even hearin' about it after the fact, it's all so quick it makes my head swirl. But between the time I learned of it and months later when I finally see Art and the missus, I'm recovered enough to heartfelt wish the happy couple that our Good Lord never close his fist too tightly above their household.

"We Irish have a reputation for carryin' an abidin' sense of tragedy which sustains us through temporary periods o' joy. Well, if I'd still been aboard after that first big jolt at Koyukuk, maybe I'd have suffered an impendin' sense o' dread. Whether or not, I'd have sure been in for another shock when next the *Yukon* stops.

"So I hear later, they no more than tie up at the village of Kokrines than Al Mayo adds to the load. Quick as a hiccup he finds and marries his own darlin' fourteen-year-old bride. His sweet colleen's Margaret, daughter of the big chief up near the Tanana mouth. She and the former Jenny Bosco—now the brand-new Mrs. Arthur Harper—are cousins.

"It doesn't end there. Jack McQuesten is not to be outdone. While still at Kokrines he puts the come-hither on his fourteen-year-old bride-to-be, the lady Katherine. She's home for the summer from the Russian Orthodox school at Russian Mission. Of Russian and

Indian parents, Katherine is some sonsy piece o' work. Not only is she fluent in the native Koyukon Athapaskan, she knows perfect Russian and can do OK in English. Of the three young girls, she's the only one with a whit of book-learnin' or exposure to Western culture. To the boat crew it's easy to see that Jack and Kate are instantly smitten with each other, but as it turns out they won't marry until she turns eighteen.

"No blarney, if I had still been on the boat, it's about this time I'd have been nervous as a long-tailed cat in a room full o' rockin' chairs, worried of lettin' my gaze bein' magnetized by some captivatin' river elf and bein' tied 'til death to the ball and chain. I'd have been thinkin' maybe I'd better seek hidin' somewhere belowdecks.

"When the *Yukon* pulls in at Nuklukayet, near the Tanana mouth they leave the third barge. That's where the newlywed Harpers and the rest had determined to prospect so they get off along with their outfits.

"Now look, lad, and leavin' all humor in our wake, sure I'm on the side o' the angels against the powers of darkness and I know marriage is the bone and sinew o' the country. I want to make something clear. And François, you can vouch for this too. To the unknowin', at first glance those unions might look like three lustful, wicked old scuts preyin' upon vulnerable young lassies—like maybe the kids were only goin' to get used by the blackguards and thrown away. If that's the thinkin', I want to snuff it right now. That was anythin' but the case. Each of the men was of absolutely sterlin' character, too high to consider such a vile, black-hearted thing. And the young ladies? Their people often had a short, brief lifespan. So they married in their early to mid-teens. There just weren't any left of the quality of those three young colleens after they were older than fourteen or fifteen.

"And I want to tell you something else, and François will back this up, too: Much credit for the successes o' the tradin' businesses eventually founded by Arthur Harper, Jack McQuesten, and Al Mayo would be readily given to the talent, hard work, and dedication o' their wives. They made faithful partners who'd mix the traders into the culture o' the river. They did that not only through their blood ties, but through their skills as translators and ambassadors. No man ever wore a scarf as warm as the arms o' those three good women around my dear friends' necks.

"Arthur's, George Finch's, and James McNiff's decision to prospect around Tanana was based on Napoleon Robert, the ACC trader at Nuklukayet, showin' them a lump o' quartz bearin' coarse gold. An Indian had given it to him. Said he took it from a mountain thirty miles downriver. So the lads outfitted and went to look for the location.

"It was not until a full month after leavin' St. Michael that on August 7 our good François, here, his illustrious crew and his great ship nosed up to the bank at Fort Yukon."

François Mercier: "After a few days' offloading Moise and hees Fort Yukon cargo, I got ready to conteenue our voyage. Andrus Kenseller had not taken the treep to the redoubt weeth the rest of us, but had stayed behind there at Fort Yukon. I hired heem to go down and help Mayo and Napoleon Robert at Noukelakayet Station. I told heem I would peeck heem up when the *Yukon* came back through.

"Pilot Tom Weelliams, hees crew, and I pointed the prow of the *Yukon enamont* on up the *rivière*. We carried Jack, three *tonnes* of beelding materials and supplies and hees new, eighteen-year-old helper Frank Banfield. *C'drait d'une importance historique.* That was heestoric—the first time a motorized vessel had plied the *fleuve* above the Porcupine. (I guess, looking back, everything we did was heestoric, was eet not, *mon* Frederick?)

"Also taken aboard at Fort Yukon was Catsah, Chief of Nuclaco, the Han village located near the mouth of the Tron-duick *Rivière*. The ten braves weeth heem swarmed aboard, too. I said earlier that when Father Clut eenformed me of Jack's character and skills, eet planted ideas een my mind. Now, een carrying out my plans for Jack, I was at the same time responding to the request of the chief. Catsah had some time before asked me to place an ACC post near hees village to save hees people the round treep of seven hundred miles to Fort Yukon. I also saw eet as good beesiness *stratégie*. We could keep furs of Nuclaco and a lot of other up*rivière* Han who leeved along the main *fleuve*, plus the furs of the Upper Tanana, from escaping farther up the *rivière* to the tradeetional Tlingit trading network. As well, I wanted to deescourage any new white traders that might come along from, as *mon ami* Frederick would say, 'leecking their chops', eyeeng the whole thousand miles of *rivière* above Fort Yukon as a wide-open opportunity free of competitors.

"Seence nobody had ever navigated that upper *fleuve*, we were delayed a lot, often going aground een shallows while trying to keep the channel. So eet took unteel the 20 of August, 1874 to get to where we wanted to go. Weeth eenput from Mr. McQuesten I peecked out a site seex miles downstream from the *confluence* of the Tron-duick *Rivière*. *Mon ami,* you and your readers now know eet as the Klondike. There we offloaded and began beelding the first of Jack's trading post/supply *dépots* on the Yukon *Rivière*. The good Tom Weelliams and the rest of the Yukon crew and I stayed two days to help clear the grounds. Then we left to peeck up Andrus Kenseller at Fort Yukon and take heem on down to Noukelakayet Station.

"That left Jack and young Banfield to erect the beeldings. The main beelding was almost twenty-five by thirty feet. A couple of smaller outbeeldings were put up a few feet away. They squared the logs on one side and joined the walls weeth dovetailed corners. The roof was poles overlaid weeth layers of birch bark and theeck sod on top for eensulation. The Han villagers were, *naturalment*, very excited to have an ACC station going up so close, so peetched right een. Jack hired some of them to help haul the logs, peel birchbark, breeng sod, and others to hunt and dry meat."

———————

Frederick Harte: "None of us engaged in our ACC work got to do any prospectin' that summer or fall. But it's never a delay to stop and sharpen the scythe. Surely and we gained a lot of ground to start a support for future prospectors. Those coming' along after us would be able to get out there and do their huntin' for gold instead o' food.

"Now lad, here's somethin' you should know that's important to the history o' the region. The rest of us would write a letter once in awhile.

But Harper and McQuesten were just tireless in promotin' the Yukon by tryin' to contact friends they'd prospected and mined with in British Columbia. They knew a lot o' their letters had very little chance of ever bringin' to bay the name on the envelope. The wanderin' prospector roamed remote country. Usually he traveled and worked with a partner or small band, but other times went alone. Sometimes, followin' some hunch, tip or rumor, he sure didn't want a crowd taggin' along. So here one day, gone the next, he often left no word where he was goin'. Good chance he didn't know himself. Or he'd change plans on the way. But Arthur and Jack never tired of castin' their bread upon the waters. Enough letters floatin' around out there and laws o' chance said some had to wash in on the right shores. That sounds like notes cast adrift in bottles, but it wasn't quite that chancy.

"When a letter did connect, recipients would talk with others about the information. Many of the earliest wave who would shortly push into the country would say their decision to prospect the Yukon Basin started with word spread throughout the goldfields by letters written in the very fist of Harper or McQuesten.

"One letter sent by Arthur Harper easily found its mark. That might be expected, sent, as it was, to a man with an established mailin' address. He was widely known professional minin' engineer, George Pilz. Some evidence of the high-quality content of the letter may be deduced. Based on Art's reasonin', thinkin' geologically that the region must hold great deposits, and his personal testimony about what evidence he and others were findin', that was enough for this highly regarded minin' expert. He later organized an expedition and came to see for himself.

"One thing Jack, Art, and Al wanted to find out for would-be Yukoners was how to get into the country by a shorter route than the roundabout way we took. Recall I said Jack had considerable time spent workin' for the Hudson's Bay. He was familiar with the tales floatin' within the company o' the foundin' and destruction of Fort Selkirk. He knew the Tlingits had marched in from the sea to burn out Campbell's competin' trading post. It only made sense they tracked in from their closest villages. Those were probably their sites at the head of Lynn Canal. Another thing, havin' a whole summer on the river in the company of Mr. Mercier, here, and his brother Moses, McQuesten had picked their brains for what they knew. Then when he built Fort Reliance and began talkin' to the nearby Han, they told of coastal Tlingit traders comin' over their trails through the mountains into the upper river.

"Now think of Jack imaginin' it from the Pacific side. We heard it was common knowledge over on the coast that the Tlingit villages north of Juneau were powerful through tradin'. Sure and they didn't get that way by limitin' themselves to tradin' between themselves. Or with their nearby coastal enemies, the Haida. Jack could have put two and two together. He and Art very well might have suggested in their letters that prospectors thinkin' about comin' in should investigate the country around the head of Lynn Canal for location of Native trade trails.

"It is very likely that as the Alaska Commercial Company's supply ship sailed for California after our visit to St. Michael, it carried many letters the two wrote while we steamed down river that first time. You can bet those letters were packed with valuable information. They probably got the blood stirrin' in many a gold seeker down south. As it turned out, they would play a big part in fosterin' not one, but many gold rushes. Enthusiasm, promotion, and information in the correspondence of Arthur and Jack would help open up and found the North Country.

"McQuesten named his station Fort Reliance. (Maybe fort is a wee bit pretentious, it didn't even have a stockade.) Because there were yet no other prospectors in the region and gold had not yet been discovered, and because of Jack's experience in the fur trade, he focused business entirely on the surest quick income, tradin' with the Indians for furs.

"One advancement that Jack brought in was a much heavier emphasis on the use of dogs for freightin' and travelin' than Natives of the upper river had used before. The early practice we saw when we arrived was the Native people usin' double-ended sleds pulled by their women. (The men weren't bein' lazy, mind you; when travelin' they ranged ahead and to the sides, scoutin' for game and stayin'

Fort Reliance, Reverend Sims Preaching
Jim McQuiston Collection

alert for enemies.) The Yukon Gwitch'in and Han were so poor they couldn't keep many dogs. Those they had were used more as pack dogs that could double as watchdogs. Among those who saw the advantage of adoptin' new ways it brought on big changes. They began raisin' enough dogs to build teams big enough to take over the pullin' from the women. When they increased the use of dogs to haul freight and run traplines, they could go farther and faster with bigger loads. That let them expand the range of their traplines so they caught more furs. More furs meant more wealth to keep bigger teams. That meant yet greater range and even more furs. The Indians of the region had before lived almost solely by subsistence with just a little tradin' as a supplement. Now they began relyin' more heavily upon trappin' n' tradin' as a means of gainin' their necessities."

François Mercier: "Let me step een here while you're on the subject of dogs. When Father Clut came to the Yukon at my behest to evaluate potential for *évangélizer* the Natives, he traveled three months and about 3,500 miles each way. Much of that was on foot and by canoe through the vilest condeetions. As I said, he was like a father to me, and I like a son to heem. One of my most treasured of all possessions ees a letter he sent that took more than a year to reach me. I have read eet so often I know eet line by line. He so admired two beetches owned by Moise that one part of the letter said,

> From Peel River I wrote to your brother Moise to send me two pups of Fortune or of Yukon. All the Fathers and Brothers of MacKenzie regret greatly that I deedn't breeng Fortune. Eef you send us thees breed of dogs, on which I am very keen, noteefy us by letter. The same eef you send a Fur Seal Hat."

Rod Perry: *It seems highly likely that for these dogs to have raised so much interest in the Mackenzie-based Oblate Fathers and Brothers there must have been something more unusual about "this breed of dogs" than being the familiar Porcupine River dogs, said to be a line of Mackenzie River Husky. La Pierre House, Rampart House (where the HBC had relocated up the Porcupine) and Fort Yukon had been heavily trafficked by HBC dog trains between the Mackenzie and Yukon as they brought in stock, took out furs, and moved personnel and communications back and forth. For decades there must have been a great mixing and movement of Mckenzie and Porcupine strains. So over on the Mackenzie where the Oblates dwelt, Porcupine dogs would probably not have been so commented upon and coveted.*

It is only conjecture, but my guess is that those dogs belonging to Moses Mercier were malemutes. The Merciers may well have brought such animals up from the coast. ACC ships plied the coast north St. Michael—malemute country—as part of their yearly sailing pattern and could have acquired select specimens. Beginning twenty years later, as many coastal malemutes as shippers were able to lay their hands on were boated into the Upper Yukon.

Frederick Harte: "That first winter at Reliance, Jack moved his entire stock of goods and took in a wonderful trade in furs. The ice went out May 10 and on the sixteenth he headed for Fort Yukon. After a few days there the two posts' men and furs started for St. Michael. Stoppin' at the Tanana post they found about three hundred Indians there tradin'. Arthur and his men were in from their prospectin'. He later told me they found gold in many places, but only in nonpayin' traces. They concluded the Indian's gold they had previously seen had probably come down with the ice from somewhere upstream. His crew was discouraged, and though Art was definitely not, even he decided he had to gain a more stable income than purely prospectin'. He decided to join in the tradin' business.

"So June of 1875 found a bunch of us down in St. Michael. After not findin' the gold they came for, Andrus Kenseller, George Finch, and George Nickolson left for San Francisco on the steamer *St. Paul.* May the road rise up to meet them, they'd been good partners all. There in St. Michael, Jack, Al Mayo and I were told the ACC had reorganized. They'd really shuffled around their business practices. The company would be henceforth leasin' their posts to independent fur traders to work on commission. McQuesten, Harper, and Mayo formed a partnership. The company gave Fort Yukon and everything upstream to them on a percentage.

"Our François, here, broke away from the ACC to build two tradin' centers for Western Fur and Tradin': another post at Nuklukayet and new tradin' station about one-fourth of the way from Fort Reliance to Fort Yukon. Our old friend Moses, Franc's brother, just bunched it and went back to Montreal, and I pray his home there will forever be too small to hold all his friends . . ."

François Mercier: "Frederick, *mon ami,* please allow me to again step eento your flow. I saw weeth a new company *une occasion lucrarive,* a lucrative chance. The Western Fur and Trading Company

(WF&T Co.) was just breaking eento the Yukon fur trade. They so needed someone of my experience they offered opportunity I couldn't turn down. Down at Noukelakayet I beelt still another trading post, my third there. I located eet between my first and Tanana Station, my second. Eet was the best constructed of the three.

"Een 1879 Western brought een the steamboat, *St. Michael.* Een 1880 I chose a location on the Yukon near *Gens de Fous* (you call David's Veellage) about eighty or ninety miles down*rivière* from Reliance. There I beelt a WF&T Co. station and commenced operating. By 1880 Western Fur and Trading had set up to compete head to head at most ACC locations. ACC had posts at Kotlik on the delta, Andreafsky, Russian Meession, Anvik, Nulato, Noukelakayet, and Fort Reliance. Fort Yukon had become unprofeetable so ACC suspended operations there.

"You know, all of us—Jack, Art, Al, you, Frederick, and I—had worked so closely together for so long, we conteenued friendly

The Remains of Fort Yukon. Arthur Harper center

Alaska State Library, Wickersham State Historic Site, Schiefflelin Brothers
Yukon River Prospecting Trip, Charles O. Farciot, P277-017-018

relationsheeps even as *compétiteurs*, did we not *mon* Frederick? But was that competeetion steeff! No one was making any money. Our Native customers knew they had us where they wanted us. They just went back and forth post to post and played us against each other.

"They'd get the same money for a smaller catch so their baseec needs were met weeth much less time and effort. Someone unfameeliar might eemagine that to be of great benefeet to them, but eet was not. Idleness ees the devil' tool, ees eet not? Weeth a lot less time spent out trappeeng, hunting, and feeshing the men spent a lot of time een the veellage *tower aux cartes,* gambleeng, making hootch, and drinkeeng. Weeth one company on the *rivière* we used to keep close control over how much sugar each family got, just enough for staple uses like *sucrer,* sweeteneeng, tea. But with the competeetion they came by a surplus that went far more eento *fermentation.*

"Eet really hurt to see thees degeneration. Weeth Father Clut I had baptized so many of them and for so long cared for them that many of their cheeldren conseedered me their godfather."

"Een 1881 I left the WF&T Company and took up again weeth Alaska Commercial. That left my post up near *Gens de Fous* abandoned. Eet was a strategic location so while trading on commeession for ACC I beelt a new station there. I called eet Fort Bell, honoring a company backer. Later the place became known as Belle Isle.'"

———

Rod Perry: *If Lieutenant Fredrick Schwatka's later description was accurate, he placed Belle Isle within the present townsite of Eagle, Alaska.*

———

François Mercier: "Then after the post I had beelt for Western Fur sat vacant a year, een 1882 Western sent John Bunyan up on the *St. Michael* and resumed trade there. Weeth both companies almost next door, competeetion was again so eentense weeth deeckering, *marchander,* so handy, that neither of us could turn much profit. Essentially, that was going on everywhere the two firms were located beside each other. Een the year 1883, Western *baissaient les bras,* they threw up their hands and sold out to Alaska Commercial. Again, ACC enjoyed a monopoly. But the Eendians of the country were not happy when prices shot back up. Word of their unrest even reached the U.S. meelitary. That would prompt the Schwatka expedeetion.

"Back een 1881 McQuesten and Mayo had become so conveenced the broad area of the upper Yukon held gold that while down at St. Michael they had a spirited conversation about eet weeth the officers of the ACC company steamsheep. When the *St. Paul* docked een San Franceesco the offeecers talked about eet to the press. Newspapers spread the news. The spreeng of 1882 three parties showed up. One, wheech came through St. Michael, prospected for seelver around Golovin Bay. Another was Ed Schefflin's party from Tombstone, Arizona. They brought their leettle steamboat, *New Racket* up and prospected country nearby the Tanana *confluence*. The other group came over the Cheelkoot Pass. They overweentered at Reliance, though I didn't know eet unteel April. Let me digress to tell about that.

New Racket *at St. Michael*

"On Easter Day, 1883 I was at my post at Belle Isle and went for a short *promenade*, a walk. I happened to look up*rivière* and saw four men snowshoeing toward me. At first I assumed they were either *Loucheaux* or Han, but as they drew closer I could tell by their motion they were white. That really took me aback. As far as I knew there were no other whites but our agents on the *rivière*. Eemagine my surprise and joy when they got close and two addressed me *en Français!* They turned out to be Joe Ladue and Jean Baptiste St. Louis. Their companions were George Spongeburgh, a Jew, and Piter Scofiel. After being confined een their small cabeen all weenter these four had decided to snowshoe eighty or ninety miles down the *rivière* just for a social call. Doing that, they became the first whites to enter Alaska by way of the Cheelkoot Pass and Upper Yukon. That deed not occur to us unteel later. At the time, we steell thought we had located Fort Reliance een Alaska, ees thees not so Frederick?

"After several days the others returned to Reliance, but Joe Ladue stayed on to prospect. I had showed heem a piece of gold-bearing quartz ore a Loucheaux had given me. I loaned Joe my dog team and set heem up with an *interprète*, to try to find the *Loucheaux*. Joe agreed to make me an equal partner eef he found a mine. Eemagine thees: for thousands of years these poor *Loucheaux* and Han had been barely staying alive on the edge of survival. As would be revealed, all that time these Eendians had been walking right over the very ground where only ten or twenty feet below were untold *richesse*. Well, Joe deedn't prospect long before eet came iceout. I had to go to St. Michael weeth the season's furs. On May 12 I began downstream. Joe went weeth me.

"Sir, eet's plain the trading landscape ees changing along the Yukon. Frederick and I see eet coming. We visualize the fur trade, een the not too deestant future, becoming secondary. Our trading company weell eventually focus on supplying the eencreasing number of miners. Between 1868 and 1882 not more than one hundred deefferent white men veesited the entire Yukon. But weeth that surge that began the year the first miners weentered at Reliance theengs greatly changed. Jack McQuesten welcomes eet. But mining breengs people and the fur eendustry works best een silent weelderness, so mining and trapping don't usually meex well. Don't get me wrong. I

*François Mercier (Petting Dog) and "Family" at One of
His Posts Near "Nuchalalwoyya" (Nuklukayet)*

Alaska State Library Historical Collections, Wickersham State Historic Site,
Schieffelin Brothers Yukon River Prospecting Trip, Charles O. Farciot, P277-017-037

like such frontiersmen. Among the miners, I have a lot of friends. But
I'm a fur man by very blood and soul, *monsieur,* from a long heritage
of *coureurs de bois,* fur business pioneers. I doubt I'm long for thees
trading beesiness the way eet's headed. I've been a fur trader working
among the Eendians since I broke eento the beesiness weeth the old
North West Company een Montana and South Dakota back een 1856
when I was eighteen. Eet just pulls at my heart; I hate to see the old
days pass."

Frederick Harte: "Thanks for addin' that, François. To wrap up the
history we were linin' out for your magazine, lad, I worked here and
there. When François jumped to Western Fur and Tradin', and Moise
having quit the country, that left Fort Yukon with no trader. So Jack
McQuesten took young Banfield and went down to be agent at Fort

Yukon. Arthur Harper having come aboard as a partner in the business, with Al Mayo he took over Fort Reliance for the next couple of years, but just as a summer enterprise. Each of those winters they'd drop down to the more well-appointed Fort Yukon to winter, the first with McQuesten. It was a treat for the young wives as well as for the three fast friends. The third year, Jack ran the company's Tanana post. Once he steamed way up the Tanana and traded with people who had never seen a white man. After a season at Tanana he returned to Fort Reliance. Jack operates it now year round. Art and Al spread out to other posts.

"Well, son, I hope that gives you enough for your magazine piece. If your readers are as interested in history o' the North as Franc and I are, and if they wonder how the country got opened up for the first prospectors, I think we pretty well covered it. By the way, you say you're going to be around for a few more days. If Mr. Mercier or I think of anything we should have included, we'll look you up."

———⬥———

Alfred Hulse Brooks: "François Mercier and the companies he had helped build had broken trail for the pioneers. During the next few years, with ACC support, Arthur Harper, Jack McQuesten, and to a somewhat lesser extent, Al Mayo would found a number of Yukon River trading posts. They responded to the supply needs of various gold strikes on one side of the international border or the other. Their enterprises stretched out over 800-odd river miles between the mouth of the Tanana and the mouth of the Pelly. It may be truly stated that without the foundational supply base these forerunning pioneers set in place to attract and support prospectors, none of the gold strikes of the Yukon Basin or Seward Peninsula would have happened as they did. Furthermore, this is important to understanding of Northland history: It is probable that the continent's far northwest would have lain dormant for decades into the 20th century without their efforts."

Chapter 6

---◆---

The Trickle Begins

Rod Perry: *We now drop back a few years to pick up part of the story that has been going on while the pioneer traders Mercier, McQuesten, Harper, and Mayo have been blazing trail in the Yukon Basin. While these forerunners have been laying down a support system ahead for them in the Interior, prospectors located along the thousand-mile-long Alaska coastline outside the great mountain barrier have not yet found a way to breach the seemingly impenetrable barricade to reach the Yukon. That is about to change.*

ACROSS THE RAGGED COAST MOUNTAINS from the *transmontaigne* area of the upper Yukon, in or about 1875 a daring prospector named C. George Holt furtively slipped into the dense forest at the end of saltwater on Lynn Canal. There he searched out the Tlingits' trail over the high Chilkoot Pass and penetrated the fastness of the upper Yukon. How he had acquired knowledge of the tribe's secret is lost to history. Whatever his source of information—some reports say he was guided by two Indians (if true, they must not have placed a very high value on their lives)—he gained the distinction of becoming the first white man known to gain the Interior from the Pacific by venturing across the pass.

Instead of following the watercourse far down the upper Yukon, Holt turned eastward at Marsh Lake, crossed the height of land and prospected the Hootalinqua (Teslin) River. It is likely that move which saved him from detection by Natives traveling their summer Yukon trade route. Though Holt's pack contained a small quantity of gold when he cautiously retraced his steps in the fall, his main triumph was going in, then making it back out without the knowledge of the Tlingits. Had he been caught in the act, the consequences would have no doubt been dire.

Holt came into Sitka, freely talked about his findings and encouraged others to duplicate his feat. He knew that since he had broadcast his accomplishment, the Chilkat Tlingits would double their watch. He would never be allowed back over their trail without military support. During the winter of 1875–76 it was said that he and the post commander formulated a plan to send an officer with him the next spring. However, the government withdrew U.S. troops from Sitka before the plan could be carried out. As far as is widely known, Holt never went back."

Rod Perry: *As he delivered Jack McQuesten to begin building Ft. Reliance, François Mercier heard from Chief Catsah that during the previous summer—1873—a white prospector had come over the pass and down the Yukon to the Little Salmon River. Because Mercier times receipt of that information to such a well-documented event—the August, 1874 founding of Fort Reliance—it firmly sets 1873 as the date of that prospector's reported penetration into the country. Years later, when Mercier wrote his recollections, the French Canuk said the lone prospector was "Slim Jeams Wioynn" (Slim Jim Wynn). However, because accepted word during those early years places Wynn elsewhere during 1873, it seems possible this man the Indians referred to could have been George Holt. Many early prospectors—who knew Wynn—held that no other prospector preceded Holt in penetrating the Upper Yukon. Additionally, it was thought by some that Holt may well have made more than one expedition in. With a firm date for both the reported early presence of someone on the Little Salmon (1873) and Holt going to the Hootalinqua (not the Little Salmon) during the summer immediately prior to meeting with the military the winter of 1875–1876, the time line allows Holt to have made two expeditions.*

This Ohio-born, redheaded Quaker, owning a volatile personality, did not emerge from all his experiences with Natives so successfully. Well after his foray(s) across the pass, in 1880 Holt appeared on the Yukon in the record of the Alaska Commercial Company. There he gained the distinction of shipping the first gold out of the Yukon Basin, two small nuggets obtained from a Tanana Native which he sent to St. Michael.

Next, Mr. Holt began operating the trading post, Nuchek (Port Etches)—Constantine Redoubt of the Russians—located about fifty miles off the Copper River mouth on Hitchinbrook Island. In 1882 he accompanied a band of Copper (Ahtna) Indians returning from trading, ascending to their village located where the Chitina River joins the Copper. Holt intended to conduct a search for rumored deposits of pure copper that, in 1867, officers of the Russian America Company had said lay in masses only about thirty miles up the Chitina. Prevented by injury from making a full exploration, he stayed in the village from spring through fall. Holt came away with the opinion that his hosts were treacherous, thieving, and dangerous. As would later become apparent, the Natives built up a violent dislike of Holt as well.

Through 1885 George Holt continued to trade from Nuchek.

According to the salvaged part of the journals of Sereberinikoff (a Russian America Company man sent in 1847 to explore the Copper, but who—along with two companions—had his head axed in by Ahtnas grown tired of being forced to tow the Russians while the explorers snoozed on their sleds) the far-ranging people of the Copper sometimes journeyed all the way to Upper Cook Inlet to trade. Sereberinikoff had written that from the Copper River, the Ahtnas ascended the tributary Tazlina River to Tazlina Lake. From there, a portage took them to the Matanuska River, which they followed down to the Inlet's Knik Arm, a twelve-day trip.

In 1885, as a couple of the Copper Natives visited the ACC store at Knik—later to be an important jumping-off point on the Iditarod Trail—who should they encounter but Holt. He now operated the company trading post on upper Cook Inlet, several hundred miles by water from Nuchek. Unhappily for Holt, one of the Ahtnas, still seething with old animosities, naturally became incensed when the hot-tempered Holt, following a trading disagreement, literally applied the boot, sending the man sprawling out of the door. Egged on over several days by a local Knik Indian (who served Alaska Commercial as an interpreter, but had a well-established reputation as a troublemaker) the Ahtna boiled over.

On December 19, 1895 he sent the trader the way of Sereberinikoff. Holt's remains were buried there at Knik, but five years later reinterred in Old American Cemetery in Kodiak. His headstone (featuring a wrong date of death) may be seen at the old burial ground on Mill Bay Road. So passed from this vale Mr. C. George Holt, first white man to have crossed the Chilkoot Pass into the Upper Yukon.

———◆———

Word circulated among west coast prospectors about Holt's Yukon headwaters findings. His access via the Chilkoot Pass may well have reached Harper and McQuesten. That would have provided information for them to add to their beckoning letters. Thoughts that Holt's successful passage could be duplicated increased the lure and led numerous prospectors to lay definite plans to enter the country.

Soon, George Finch (he of the original Arthur Harper party into the Yukon) somehow made it over the Chilkoot Pass and back. Here and there, a few others arrived in upper Lynn Canal, intending to make the trek. However, the watchful Tlingits, enforcing exclusive right of passage over the trade route they had considered their proprietary domain for hundreds of years, harshly thwarted all other attempts through the 1870s.

———◆———

Alfred Hulse Brooks: "Meanwhile, Harper, McQuesten, and Mayo, but especially the former two, continued in their unique partnership, each in his own way laying down a critical foundation for those who would follow."

———◆———

Frederick Harte: "Hello, lad. How are developments on your article? Mr. Mercier and I were discussin' our talk the other day. He reminded me o' somethin'. We can't let you go home to your magazine without it so we just had to run you to earth. Faith, but a man never had a truer, kinder friend than my lifelong pal, Arthur Harper. And sure I must suffer from a double dose of original sin and bring down a curse upon myself if I leave somethin' out Art should be credited with.

"Art had joined Jack McQuesten in the fur trade, but it was that creek swarming with nuggets as a granary with rats that occupied his thinkin'. Furs were to him merely a way to finance his next prospectin' trip. Truly, Art was the quintessential prospector. He just knew if he combed enough country he'd eventually make a big find. That confidence filled him and never died.

"On that first upriver trip we made after we came in in '73 we prospected some up the Stewart River. Now, he did not formally record his journeys, but through the followin' years I know Art made as many explorations as his tradin' business would allow. Some were short forays, but others were lengthy expeditions. On one of his long trips, in 1876 he prospected all the way to the head o' the Fortymile River. Sir, you might not be familiar with the map, but the Fortymile's well over a hundred miles long as the river flows. From there he portaged over to the Sixtymile and found color on his way back downstream to the Yukon. Several times he made lengthy trips into the Tanana country. On one such Tanana trip he entered the headwaters by goin' over the divide from the Fortymile. On a trip in 1878, he journeyed up the Tanana about 250 miles from its mouth in the company of Al Mayo.

"All those trips I mentioned? I didn't go into what he endured to work his way through. To those who know the nature o' that wild country, just thinkin' about it's enough, it is, to make a strong man shudder.

"Arthur Harper was first to find gold on the Stewart, the Fortymile, the Sixtymile, and the Tanana, includin' black sand and fine gold dust brought back from the vicinity o' the lower Chena River in about 1878. On the Sixtymile he did find bars containin' enough fine dust he thought it would pay. So he sent out for a tank of quicksilver to work it, but it didn't end up profitable. In all his prospectin', it seems Art was always in the field when luck was on the road and deposits worth minin' proved harder to find than a Scotsman's britches.

"No, let me correct that. He did make a rich strike one time, but lost it. I mean Art couldn't relocate it. In '78 or '79 he and an Englishman named Bates hired two Indians to help pack. They started in from David's Village. Bushwackin' they tramped from the Yukon over the height o' land to the headwaters o' the North Fork o' the Fortymile. While makin' a crossin', Bates—who had a sprained ankle—got swept off his feet and nearly drowned. While he dried his clothes and recovered, Al collected a sample o' very good-lookin' sand. The two continued over between Fortymile headwaters and the Upper Tanana.

"Because there was occasional traffic between the Han of the Upper Yukon with the Natives of the Upper Tanana—and even with the farther-away Ahtna of the Upper Copper—the two packers probably took Art and Bates into the Tanana by way of at least faint Native trails. Nevertheless, their cross-country journey from where the Yukon River crosses the International Boundary to the closest point on the Tanana River probably measured in the vicinity of two hundred tough miles. Once there they shot moose and got some Tananas to help build them a moosehide boat. Boat built, they made the extremely dangerous run through the rapids o' the upper river to reach safer waters they could float to the Tanana mouth.

"Later, when Bates had Art's sand-and-gold sample checked in San Francisco, Bates claimed it assayed $20,000 to the ton. Art went back the next year, but outgoin' river ice had so changed the bars he couldn't relocate the golden spot.

"So, for Art, himself, riches came not aye when sought. However, lad, it may be truly said, and my friend, François Mercier, here, will vouchsafe this as fact: Arthur Harper and no other should gain tribute as the chief pioneer discoverer o' gold in the Yukon Basin. 'Twas not for him I wouldn't have pointed my bow here back in '73 an there's nought I wouldn't do for the man. Of all the ships that sail the seas of life, the best ships are friendships. I've had grand ones, but, by the very gates of Heaven, like bell, book, and candle to my soul, two sit. One's Art, and I'll now lay credit on the other.

"I want to assemble together some of what we've been tellin' you and underline it just to make sure special credit gets placed where credit is due. My dear friend, Franc, here, is not expectin' this, but I want to firmly establish somethin' else. In the first fifteen years after U.S. purchase, it was Franc—this very grand doorfull of a man beside me, François Xavier Mercier—and no other, who was the dominant figure on the Yukon in the start-up of steamboat-supported tradin' companies.

"Franc was a founder o' the Pioneer Fur Company, the first U.S. company on the river. He headed up its field operation. Franc constructed the first U.S.-built tradin' post and ran it. When he and his partners sold their business to the second firm, Perrott & Company, he helped the third company, Hutchinson-Kohl, the biggest tradin' company of all, enter the Yukon River trade. It was Franc Mercier they leaned on to help gain them a competitive foothold. His expertise at directin' the competition was, to a great extent, what allowed Hutchinson-Kohl to so quickly gain the upper hand and push Parrott to merge with them. That amalgamation o' the two companies, Alaska Commercial Company, soon saw the advantages of placin' their entire Yukon Basin operation in his capable hands.

"We get a lot of credit for settin' things up for the gold hunters, but the work praises the man and Franc first set it up for us. By the time Jack, Al, Art, and the rest of us arrived in '73, François was already directin' the beginnin's of a firmly established tradin' monopoly over an area comprisin' two-thirds of all Alaska. He indeed laid down the well-founded base o' the Yukon drainage portion of a lastin' business empire.

"So, lad, as we wrap up our story of beginnin's o' the Yukon Basin's trappin' n' tradin' and gold huntin', I want to leave a firm statement: history should make sure François Mercier receives his due as the pioneer of all pioneers of American-based tradin' on the Yukon River. He's benefitted many and the grass on the road to Hell has grown long for the want of his use. I'd take it out, drawin' credit against my very soul if that's what it takes to render my fervent blessin' upon his seed, breed, and generation 'til the end o' time.

"As for me, myself, a narrow neck keeps the bottle from bein' emptied in one swig. No success has found me in large amounts. Human bein's tend to need the bitter with the sweet. But all in all, trouble has generally neglected me and many small satisfactions over the years have added up. So sure and my life's been full, and I've never rued the day I set my course north. Here on the Yukon I've savored much.

"Now lad, truth of it is, François and I are in your debt more for your listnin' than you are for our tellin'. It appears you've got a square head on your shoulders and the makin's of a good man yourself. I pray you use your talents well. May your fields be moistened by Heaven's own dew, and may the Good Lord take a likin' to you."

———— •—•—• ————

Alfred Hulse Brooks: "Regarding Arthur Harper, this is something most important for those prospectors who would follow: Harper pushed himself to his limits to explore distant, untouched, difficult country. His trips were invariably laborious in the extreme. They were often fraught with peril and deprivation. But they gave him an overall feel for the distribution of gold deposits and a general familiarity with the unmapped uplands and drainages of the central Yukon Basin. That knowledge he freely shared. Harper's discoveries and information led to the main strikes at Forty Mile—it was at his direction that Franklin and Madison prospected the Fortymile, which led to their big discovery—and the strikes, too, of the Sixtymile, Circle City, the Klondike and Fairbanks. Those rushes led, in turn, to all the noteworthy finds at other northern Alaska locations. Even Nome and Iditarod were tied to them.

"Being a geologist, I'll explain in layman's terms what Art and the other prospectors seek so diligently to find. They hunt for 'poor man's gold.' They don't have the wealth like Juneau's Treadwell to put together the huge camps that are veritable self-sufficient small towns, set up the giant machinery and hollow out whole mountains to develop lodes. What they're after is accessible, profitable concentrations where forces of nature have done most of the heavy lifting and processing. They comb the country for locations where upthrusting and working of the earth's crust in ages past has brought the gold-bearing quartz up from deep below. This was accomplished by buckling, folding, fracturing, melting, pulsating, grinding together, crumbling and erosion of the crust. Such actions had been hard at work on the living rock, separating the gold from the quartz. In essence, nature had been partly mining it for them.

"Prospectors must be sharp, analytical amateur geologists. Guessing what might have gone on in prior ages, they have to think below the surface. Where did ancient rivers flow? Where might newly freed gold have been carried into those ancient rivers and where might those rivers have taken it? Complicating it was that location of those ancient courses might have been well removed from present-day rivers. It could be higher along a valley hillside, usually marked by benches which are rather level terraces running along the hillside above the river. Or maybe the old bed is below the present stream level, covered by many feet of silt. Or, again, perhaps on the far side across a valley. Making the search harder was that later glaciation could have pushed the gold a distance from where the ancient stream had carried it. That would have redistributed and scattered the deposit.

"This placer gold is much better suited to the typical prospector. Free-spirited, individualistic, self-reliant, innovative, adaptive, they are, as well as restless and impatient of character. Theirs is a race long on physical strength, determination and willingness to work, but having an almost absolute absence of capital."

———————

While Arthur Harper, the prospector was the key discoverer, his faithful friend and longtime business associate, Jack McQuesten, was to play such an important role in the industrial development of the country that he would become known to history variously as the "Father of the Yukon," "Father of Alaska, "Father of the Country" and "Guardian Angel of the Miners." In the years following his initial prospecting upon his arrival on the Yukon, McQuesten seldom took part in the search for gold. Instead, as per the arrangement he made with Harper, he concentrated on providing a support base for his partner so that Harper could occasionally prospect for the group. He concentrated on the fur trade with the Athapaskans, the only viable source of income in the early days. His was the task of making yearly trips downriver with furs and bringing back supplies either from the

Kate McQuesten

Jim McQuiston Collection

ACC supply depot at St. Michael or company headquarters in San Francisco.

With families to raise and educate and with growing business interests as the partners spread out to more effectively capture the fur trade, it grew impractical even for Harper to be gone on numerous long prospecting trips. Like McQuesten, Harper—and Mayo, too—settled increasingly into management of their various trading and supply stations.

While the partners anchored their business in the fur trade, they never lost the vision that first attracted them to the North Country and viewed their fur business as a necessary means to an end, the end being gold.

Though McQuesten did not get to prospect much, that is not to say he did not search for gold at all. He prospected the Sixtymile River in 1877 and found gold on every bar. It wasn't in concentrations to entice him to mine, but enough, he figured, to provide a hard worker an average six to eight dollars a day. That anchored his confidence that somewhere in that area big finds would be made. Then in 1879, the year Harper found and lost his rich bar on the North Fork of the Fortymile, Jack, working far below on the main Fortymile River found gold, just not in paying quantity. He looked around behind Fort Reliance, a short few miles from the future Klondike strike, but came up with only traces. And he searched the Stewart and its tributary that now bears his name, the McQueston River.

To McQuesten and the others, the old steamer *Yukon* had always been a deathtrap. Jack felt the boiler was just an explosion waiting to happen. In 1879, down in San Francisco, shipwrights prefabricated a replacement. After disassembling it they sent the new riverboat north accompanied by four carpenters. And none too soon. The old boat was crushed by the ice during breakup. All of the ACC agents went down to St. Michael, pitched in helping the carpenters, and in short order the men had themselves a new, much larger and safer steamer. They named it *Yukon*, not very original, but they held their old boat in fond memory.

Out on the Southeast Alaska coast in 1880, a party of nineteen prospectors appealed to Commander Beardslee of the U.S.S. *Jamestown* stationed at Sitka to force open the Chilkoot Pass route. Seeing that the group was composed of serious, experienced men headed up by Edmund Bean, an old California Gold Rush prospector, the commander wrote a letter to the Chilkat chiefs. To deliver it, he dispatched a navy steam launch carrying two Indian interpreters backed up by eighteen armed officers and crew under the command of Lt. E.P. McClellan. Accompanied by the prospectors in their own boats, the navy steamed up Lynn Canal to the Chilkat village for a confrontation.

Commander Beardslee's persuasive letter writing and the skills of his interpreters changed the Tlingits' attitude about maintaining monopolistic dominion over the pass. Or perhaps it was the Gattling gun mounted on the bow. Whatever swayed the Tlingits, the meeting ended their several-hundred-year-long stranglehold on use of the pass. Ever commercially minded though, the tribe instantly adapted: they became packers for hire.

The expedition left the head of Lynn Canal May 20, 1880. Independently, Slim Jim Wynn and Johnny McKenzie followed the party a few days later.

On June 17 Bean wrote to Commander Beardslee and hired one of the Chilkat packers to deliver the letter. He told of being camped on a lakeshore over the pass and building boats.

By November 15 the party returned to Sitka. They reported having boated down the lake system and river to where the Holt's Hootalinqua—as the miners called the Teslin—flows in, then poling and prospecting their way up that river 200 miles. The party said they had found some gold, nothing outstanding. But, at least, they had verified Holt's route and opened it up. As well, they had substantiated his claims of gold to be found on the Hootalinqua.

That year, Jack McQuesten reported that eight men who had come over from Juneau ascended the Pelly hundreds of miles up to the old Hudson's Bay portage to Frances Lake. Rocking the bars, they had averaged about eight dollars a day. Might it be possible they were part of the large Bean group?

———————

Alfred Hulse Brooks: "I have said that Alaska owes credit for its modern history to the opening of the Canadian Yukon and the great rush to the Klondike. I must turn about and say that a much smaller, yet important part of that credit must be handed back to Alaska. First, the approach to the Chilkoot Pass begins in Alaska and it was due to Alaskan efforts that the Tlingits' deadly grip on its use was relaxed. Second, the same year the Bean Party went over the pass and back, two men based out of Sitka, Richard T. Harris and Joseph Juneau (nephew of the founder of Milwaukee, Wisconsin) made a rich strike at the present site of Juneau, Alaska. By the way, that strike occurred on 17 August. Coincidentally, that is the same day of the year when, sixteen years later gold would be found on the Klondike. The pair's findings led to the establishment of the incredibly rich Alaska-Juneau Mine. The discovery of a gold-bearing quartz ledge across the channel from the present site of Juneau by French Pete in about 1881 and its sale for a pittance to John Tredwell, led to the development of the wonderful Glory Hole of the Treadwell Mine.

"As I've explained, placer, or free gold, is what most prospectors seek because it can usually be mined with no more than a pick, shovel, and a strong back. Hardrock mining is altogether different. The gold lies within the solid rock. Miners must tunnel into a mountain or dig deep open pits to get at gold-bearing ore. The ore is then pulverized with big machinery to separate gold from rock. Often tons must be crushed for each ounce of gold.

"The nature of the lode-mining effort around Juneau necessitated enormous capital investment. It took machinery, the employment of large numbers of miners and support staff, and the establishment of well-built, permanent company mining camps to house and feed the men so work could go on regardless of season. These great camps were destined to play an important part in the opening of the Canadian and Alaskan Yukon Basin. They not only drew miners from throughout the West, they formed a strategic staging base from which a few of the more intrepid could set forth on their long expeditions over the Chilkoot Pass. (I should add a subnote, here. Maybe a man had to be braver just to stay and work in these Juneau mines. They had the reputation among the miners of a man injured severely or killed every day.)

"After working the winter in the Juneau or Tredwell mine, some of the hardiest, most adventurous prospectors boated north a hundred miles to the head of Lynn Canal and crossed the pass. In the Interior, they built boats or rafts from native timber, drifted, sailed and rowed down the Yukon several hundred miles, prospected all summer, then traveled back upstream through fall, retreating to beat the onset of winter, returning to the haven of the Juneau or Treadwell mine. (Let me comment here that few have the background to even imagine the details of the toilsome journey of hundreds of painfully won miles back against the swift flow of the Yukon.) At the mines they could count on rehiring to labor another winter. There, at the very doorway to the Interior, they could stay warm and well-fed and earn enough to outfit for a further go at the Yukon. Had they not been able to rely upon this nearby support base for security and replenishment, the initial trickle of gold seekers heading over the pass each summer would have remained just that for many more years: a mere trickle."

———◆——◆———

In 1881, four men who crossed the Chilkoot Pass became the first to find gold in actual paying quantities in the Interior. They noted at least some color on every bar they tried for 200 miles up a Yukon tributary, the Big Salmon River. Enthusiastically, they reported that some bars not only paid, but paid well.

At first, it was but an almost unnoticed trickle of gold seekers who crested the pass. But the silence of the little-known Yukon began to break. Year by year, a few more arrived. About fifty would come over each year from 1881 to 1883, and seventy-five the following year. Most would descend the Yukon to the mouths of the Pelly and Teslin rivers, then prospect up those tributaries. In 1886, on bars along the Stewart River and along the Yukon on bars 27 miles below the mouth of the Teslin River, finds of encouraging colors would make them major points of activity.

Miners named those bars 27 miles below the Teslin mouth "Cassiar Bars." British Columbia's Cassiar Gold Rush had served as a perfect training academy for Yukon miners. Reaching the Cassiar had necessitated packing tools, camp gear, and provisions 150 miles over the mountains. Life that far from the nearest supply base sharpened their skills at securing much of their sustenance from the land. Men learned to erect snug shelters and grew practiced at daily living and working through cold winters. They became adapted to short working seasons. Though numerous Cassiar prospectors came into the Yukon as the Cassiar wound down in the late 1870s, almost total depletion of those British Columbia placers by 1884 would cause nearly complete evacuation. Many headed for the Yukon.

The model Holt and Bean set in the mid-1870s, that of only supplying and outfitting for the brief summer season, but not to winter over, was followed by the rest of the early-day Yukoners. Until 1882 the unbroken pattern was to beat a retreat at season's end. It wasn't so much that they were afraid to face the cruel winters of the Upper Yukon, which receive some of North America's lowest temperatures. They were just learning gradually that the country held enough gold to make a much more expensive and lengthy commitment worth mounting. So not having yet dedicated themselves to that extent, from the farthest reaches of their midsummer explorations they would use late summer and fall to get back across the Coast Mountains before the fall storm season set in. The heavy coastal precipitation would not take long to bury the mountain trail beneath not just a few inches, but many feet of snow. Retreating prospectors knew they dared not dawdle, for to let the pass become impassable ahead of them would be to die trapped in the Interior, provisionless. Wintering back on salt water meant physical survival as well as replenishment of resources.

That prevailing practice had dictated a timely start back. Because most of them had boated up Lynn Canal, packed over the mountains, floated down the Yukon, and worked their way into the country fully 400 to 700 miles from Juneau, the way back involved long days of arduous, upstream going *for many weeks*. No lying there snug in the blanket; it was up in the pitch blackness, a hurried fire and breakfast, then at the first hint of light it was back bent to the pole or line, or paddles or oars in full stroke.

Where they could, the retreating prospectors bucked the current by "tracking." The process involved several men pulling the boat upstream by a long line attached to the bow while a man in the boat steered the craft away from shore. Their boats were not only crafted of green (heavy!) lumber, but not being painted, they remained saturated (heavier!). But as much as they favored tracking, much of the way the banks were not conducive: too much brush and downed timber on top of the banks or the banks too high; below the banks, too much downed timber and sweepers slanting down into the water from above. In other locations, deep water next to the bank and other obstacles too greatly complicated the way.

Therefore, the men gained much headway by laboriously poling against the flow. Hour after hour, day after day, week in, week out, a man jammed his spike-pointed pole into the bottom at a slight rearward angle and, maintaining a constant thrust, shoved to move the boat forward. Pulling his pole, he would take another bite and repeat.

So they could reach bottom they had to keep to the shallows. On the bends this usually required working the bar side (inside the bend). That was, as well, the side featuring the slowest-moving current, often slack water, perhaps even a back current running their way. If the miners saw they were coming up on a cutbank (outside of the bend) they would cross the swift river to the bar side. Endlessly poling, sometimes losing ground in the many crossings and recrossings, these retreating miners made as few as seven or eight miles daily in the toughest going and but twenty where it was better.

Once they reached the lake system they sailed, rowed, or poled the edges to the head of navigation. Probably securing them high and dry for the following year, they left their boats. Shouldering their packs, they climbed the Chilkoot Pass and descended to the head of Lynn Canal. Then it was row or sail, playing wind and each outgoing tide, the hundred miles back to Juneau.

The Yukon Interior offered these earliest prospectors a May-through-September season. May and early June had always been largely consumed by packing their heavy outfits in across the mountains, perhaps taking several relays, building boats, and working themselves into the locations where they would prospect. The distance they had penetrated into the country determined the date in August they had to start back. That gave them as few as two months in the middle to practice the very object of their whole yearly endeavor. It goes without saying that initial lack of familiarity with the country and what it held forced the earliest adventurers to do it that way in the beginning. But it was highly inefficient."

Rod Perry: *The number of relays these men took to cross the mountains was far fewer than what would be required of the 98ers of the future Klondike rush. There were no Mounties—as there would be in '98—enforcing that each man take in a ton of gear and supplies to last a year. And the early Yukoners, far, far exceeded that of the average 98er in the areas of physical strength and competence at making pack-content choices, not to mention skill at traveling and living off the country.*

Alfred Hulse Brooks: "It was in 1882 when the first of those prospectors venturing in from Juneau over the Chilkoot pushed their way far enough north to take advantage of the beginnings of the infrastructure, meager though it was, that Harper and McQuesten—and Mayo to a lesser extent—had, through a decade of hard labors, been establishing for them. They would find the beginnings of a Yukon riverboat service. Fort Reliance, though thinly provisioned, served as a supply hub and winter quarters. Just as important was the vast body of information about the country related to topography, traveling and prospecting conditions and subsistence tips the men had to offer.

"By sheer dint of their own vision and almost unaided effort, these pioneers had opened up the Yukon drainage to the prospector. Therefore, much of the later development of Alaska and the Yukon must be considered to stand upon their shoulders."

⬥———⬥———⬥

Rod Perry: *On August 5, 1882 Jack McQuesten found himself surprised by the sight of three white prospectors arriving at Fort Reliance. One can imagine their prior hail from well upriver—the customary silence-shattering rifle shots fired into the air—alerting Reliance of their approach. And McQuesten can be envisioned dropping whatever he was doing, hurrying out to the bank. At a glance, by their craft, load and motion, even at a distance he would have seen they were white men. And he would have surely been surprised! Waving a greeting, he would have watched them, wondering, as they drifted down on the post.*

Now Jack, catching their thrown bowline, snubs them off. The stern swings around to bring the craft broadside to the bank. The inside chine of their greatly-burdened boat grounds in the shallows. The arrivals spring from gunwales to shore. As the men exchange handshakes and greetings Jack must be eager to discover who these unique men will turn out to be and to learn of their plans.

⬥———⬥———⬥

Simultaneously, Jack McQuesten and the Yukon Basin were experiencing three historic watersheds. First, these were the first white men, apart from the original Harper-McQuesten parties or trading company personnel, to visit Fort Reliance in the eight years of its existence.

Second, they were coming down from upstream. That meant they had come over from the coast. From George Holt's furtive foray(s) almost a decade before until this moment, of all who had crested the pass to prospect none but these men had ever dared extend downriver so far.

Third, it was August. That meant it was high time for the miners working farthest downstream to be about leaning into their poles against the mighty Yukon flow, certainly not risking trapping themselves by drifting farther downriver. That is, if they planned to make it back to Juneau before the pass snowed in. Obviously, then, these were the first prospectors to venture over from Lynn Canal who planned to winter in the Upper Yukon.

The vanguard was French Canadian Joe Ladue, John They, and John Rogers. Superbly prepared, they arrived with provisions for two years. After settling in, the prospectors voiced eagerness to test the country. Jack, just as eager to encourage them, took them by steamboat up to the Sixtymile River on a short prospecting trip. They found very encouraging traces about 15 miles below Miller Creek, a tributary that would later become a major gold producer. Burning a hole down, they made 10 feet in only three days, but when the hole flooded out they headed back down to Reliance."

———————

Rod Perry: *That trip infused Joe Ladue with a confidence and enthusiasm about Sixtymile country that would never leave him.*

Enthusiasm as well as industry marked the man in everything he did. Harper and McQuesten would in the future partner with him in business. Ladue would go on to fame and fortune as not only founder of Dawson, but owner of the very ground he established the town upon.

———————

The men had barely returned to Reliance when another group of adventurers drifted down. They, too, came to hole up for the winter at McQuesten's haven almost 700 miles from Juneau. Included in their number was Captain William Moore, who would go on to found Skagway, Alaska, and partners Howard Franklin and Harry Madison, whose discovery of gold up the Fortymile River would lead to the town of Forty Mile springing up at that river's mouth on the Yukon.

Two of the others, Frank Densmore and Thomas Boswell, were destined as well to play important roles in the development of the North Country. Densmore would lead a long exploration in 1889 by way of the Tanana and Kantishna rivers and Lake Minchumina to the North Fork of the Kuskokwim, then down that tributary to the main Kuskokwim. Magnificent views of the huge mountain they passed so impressed Densmore, and he talked about the great peak so often to so many, that for a decade the miners of the Yukon Basin called it Densmore's Mountain. The greatest mountain on the continent would later be tagged by newcomer William Dickey with the name which stuck, Mount McKinley.

Thomas Boswell became a codiscoverer of the most paying location of bar gold on the Stewart, gold deposits on the Cassiar Bars, below the mouth of the Teslin River, and became one of the first to prospect the Koyukuk.

Plainly, this was no ordinary band of prospectors.

What gave these two groups knowledge of the fort's existence and the confidence to commit their well-being to pushing farther down the Yukon to winter there? It must almost be a foregone conclusion that it was either correspondence from Harper and McQuesten or the word spread by a San Francisco newspaper after officers of the ACC ship *St. Paul* related to newsmen their St. Michael conversation the previous fall with Jack McQuesten and Al Mayo.

The trailing group brought adequate outfits, though did not come nearly so heavily supplied as the first group. However, McQuesten had stocked the fort well. That year he had flour aplenty and other staples, enough to help feed all the new arrivals into the following summer. The men built cabins and prepared to settle in. They must have either laid in a good supply of fish, caribou, and moose or bought it from the nearby Han.

The local Han Athapaskans favored the nearby Thron-diuck (later known as the Klondike) Valley as a moose-hunting ground. At one time during the winter when the miners needed to restock their larders, Joe Ladue and a few of the others set up a camp from which to hunt moose at a location where a little side stream flowed into Rabbit Creek, an indistinct-looking Thron-diuck tributary. Little could they have dreamed that they were camped over not just a fortune, but an incredibly vast fortune. Rabbit Creek and the side stream would later be renamed Bonanza Creek and El Dorado Creek, respectively. The junction would become known as the world-famous "Grand Forks." But in their day as they hunted meat, the nondescript geological features of the valleys did nothing to arouse interest in the men, superb gold hunters though they were. None of them ever returned to prospect it.

Jack McQuesten thoroughly enjoyed the winter. It was the first time since he came back to Fort Reliance that he had men to converse with whose natural tongue was English. Finer times were never spanned by a rafter. The prospectors spent most of their evenings gathered at his main building visiting and playing cards. As the men talked and planned they foresaw that more and more prospectors would eventually come and gold would sooner or later be found. Addressing that both the Canadian Upper Yukon and Alaska were located so far from their seats of government, they knew they would have to be a law unto themselves. So during those long winter evenings, by flickering candle light these eleven men, most not even citizens of the country they were wintering and largely prospecting in, bent to the task of establishing an orderly set of rules by which mining claims could be staked, recorded, worked, transferred, and ownership maintained. Out of their cooperative camaraderie they also laid the groundwork that winter for what would grow into the fraternal brotherhood, *Yukon Order of Pioneers*. They elected Jack McQuesten chief administrator and recorder for the mining district as well as the first president of the brotherhood.

In April, having learned from McQuesten that another white man operated a trading post downstream, four of the men strapped on webs, shouldered their packs, and snowshoed eighty or more miles down the Yukon to pay a social call on François Mercier.

The most important feature of their pioneering winter at Reliance was the example they set for others to follow. They showed the great advantage of remaining in the country over winter so that the entire five-month prospecting season could be devoted to hunting and mining gold instead of wasting half the time making the arduous, yearly, thousand-plus-mile round trip. Their other noteworthy demonstration was that McQuesten could be depended upon to supply them, at the least partially, once they made it as far as his post. As the word about their overwintering circulated their pattern began to be duplicated by increasing numbers.

Furthermore, they demonstrated confidence that the Yukon Basin held rich gold deposits worth the commitment of more than a short summer foray. Optimism was growing that Yukon prospecting and mining could become a self-sustaining, full-time enterprise. Men were gaining confidence that they could live year round in the country, able to pay their way from what gold they could find. It looked like they would no longer necessarily be bound by the prior common pattern of having to fund their outfitting through outside winter employment.

***

Rod Perry: *That winter of 1882 was a turning point for Harper, McQuesten and Mayo's operations, as well as for the opening and future development of the Yukon Basin. The traders had been on the upper Yukon the better part of a decade "going before, preparing the way in the wilderness." From 1882 on, the rate of arrival of men dedicating themselves to at least a year in the country would pick up momentum.*

Chapter 7

———◆———

Free Spirits in a Realm of Their Own

Rod Perry: *Ottawa and Washington knew little about and seemed to virtually ignore their holdings so distantly removed from the two seats of government. Conversely, the pioneer prospectors who roamed the Far Northwest between 1873 and the early 1890s were typically an independent lot that embraced the separation. In the midst of an entire subcontinent that was indeed a single, incredibly immense, seemingly boundless wilderness undivided by any identifiable national boundary, where prospectors migrated back and forth freely and where they were almost unrestricted by formal laws and social conventions, it is not difficult to see why the early prospectors—many of whom tended to be borderline anarchistic—not only tended to think of the Yukon and Alaska as a rather single country, but as their proprietary, common domain to have and hold together.*

In their fanatical search for gold, they faced in common almost unimaginable hardships and isolation. Their shared causes and needs made these individualistic, self-reliant, libertarian-type men socially dependant and bonded them into a brotherhood exceedingly more loyal to their own peripatetic fraternity and the communal, independent ethic which they developed than to distant absentee governments.

———◆———

THE UNITED STATES PURCHASE OF ALASKA from Russia in 1867 generated an immediate flurry of heated argument over whether the purchase spearheaded by Lincoln's Secretary of State William H. Seward had merit or not. Pundits' and political adversaries' scathing criticisms called it, "Seward's Icebox" and "Seward's Folly." But when the contention wound down, the far-off new possession at the distant northwest corner of the continent became largely forgotten by the media and general public. Washington D.C. largely forgot about it as well. There at the close of the Civil War, the attention of government focused on the great task of reconstructing the South. Not wanting the bother, politicians passed off administration of Alaska first to the U.S. Army, next to the U.S. Customs Service, then to the U.S. Navy.

Looking back, perhaps political and military indifference should not be surprising when far closer to home in many parts of the still Wild West the federal government was too weak to keep control.

One incident at Sitka in 1879 provides a good example of federal lack and indifference. After a brief presence stationed at Sitka, the U.S. Navy pulled out. That left not one iota of governmental presence to watch over the entire body of Alaska. Feeling in peril when the Tlingits threatened to break out in hostilities, Sitka's non-native inhabitants sent a hurried message south pleading with *the British in Victoria, British Columbia* to come protect them!

What little attention was paid and what thin, sporadic governmental presence was established during that time only touched the coast. But within the great Interior—most of the land mass of Alaska—the only federal action to amount to anything was a single, brief military mission just after purchase. That was the quick trip up the Yukon to run British interlopers back over the international boundary to their own side. Though the lifting of the Stars and Stripes over Fort Yukon was a necessary gesture, Washington would do nothing else to bolster its authority over that huge wilderness for another quarter century.

So there it sat from 1867 well into the 1890s, owned by the United States, but largely apolitical. The oceanic gap and a foreign country in between detached the new possession physically from the contiguous states. Even when that gap was crossed by ship and Alaska's coast was gained (a coastline totaling more miles than that of the rest of the United States combined) from its shoreline the almost impenetrable mountain fortress barred entry and the great distances into Alaska's Interior kept the Yukon Basin far out of sight. White presence was so thin and activity so quiet that nothing that went on inside escaped the remoteness and barriers or traveled the distances to make the slightest ripple in the national awareness. With their possession so far removed and asleep way up there in the frozen north, there were other things to occupy the national attention and caring.

Over Alaska's border to the east, neighboring Canada, for some of the same reasons and a few of their own, regarded their far Yukon District of the North-West Territories the same way: out of sight and mind. Looking from Ottawa, Yukon District was distanced from the seat of government by the extreme diagonal width of their nation. Viewed the other way, from the heart of the Yukon looking toward Ottawa, it was first separated by a thousand miles of deep wilderness which included the Rocky Mountains, next by another thousand characterized as barely settled, then by the third thousand of settled, but mostly rural country until the big population centers of the east were neared. Due south it was spaced from the nearest Canadian population of any appreciable size by a thousand miles of range after range of rugged mountains. Ottawa, like Washington, considered their far northwest remote, insignificant, irrelevant, and worthy of ignoring as the landscape on the back side of the moon, suitable, as Voltaire had deemed it, "only for barbarians, bears, and beavers."

The great Alaska-Yukon subcontinent, most particularly its interior vastness, lay almost unexplored by civilized man. Needless to say, the 141st parallel, which divided the two countries, was significant only to the two national seats of government thousands of miles to the east. With not even a surveyed line running between, much less a visible swath of demarcation, to the earliest white entrees the boundary was only an abstract concept. If even that. Practically, the 141st was no more meaningful or restraining to them than it had been for the aboriginal inhabitants who for millennia had freely wandered back and forth over it knowing nothing of imperialistic takeovers by the world's great powers or of the concept of longitude.

This governmental vacuum, so far beyond the thinnest edges of even rough frontier society, so lacking in strictures or bounds, and situated in such an almost limitless wilderness, would have been magnetic enough to have pulled north many of the borderline anarchists and free-spirited adventurers who found their way there even if the political isolation and endless silent spaces had been the only attractants. However, when the lure of gold was added, the appeal to their opportunistic natures made the far northwest corner of the continent irresistible.

Into this great emptiness they came, the pathfinders. They were dog-poor immigrants, this motley assortment of loners, frontier adventurers, former Indian fighters and Civil War veterans, bringing with them or finding upon arrival almost too few resources to qualify. Four characteristics of the country demanded cooperation among them: the great distances, extreme isolation, formidable topography, and harsh climate. Men of numerous nationalities, some formally schooled, some hardly able to read and write, some pious, some irreverent, and differing in innumerable other major and minor ways got along in almost unbroken harmony.

In the absence of formal laws, law enforcement, and social restrictions these men, many of them considered misfits, outcasts, oddballs and eccentrics back in more polite societies, formed their own social order. They were separated so far from any power holding jurisdiction over them they ran the country as they saw the need. They set rules of conduct and business, and meted out justice suited to their own collective interests.

They lived by the *Code of the Prospector,* otherwise known as the *Law of the Miner.* It was a rudimentary set of unwritten rules, in essence: Respect others and appraise them as you see them. Be who you seem to be on the outside. Judge men by their conduct. Be open and honest in your dealings. Exercise tolerance. Trust others. Share without reservation. They summed up their modus operandi as, "Do as you would be done by."

The miners' meeting, the tool of the anarchistic democracy they established, was sparingly used because the few white men in the country largely knew each other and life in such a harsh environment almost perfectly weeded out those who did not fit in. But when the miners were forced to settle conflicts, their process was egalitarian—fair, fast, and efficient. Though carrying no political force or influence officially recognized outside their own domain, their *Miners' Law* provided the bare necessary structure, not only all they required, but about all they could tolerate.

Actually, in the almost total absence of any other law and order, the U.S. government, if and when they found out about them, did tend to accept miners' meeting verdicts as lawful. When bartender Jim Chronister killed troublemaker Jim Washburn in self-defense, he immediately offered himself up for his case to be decided before a miners meeting. It took the assemblage 20 minutes to acquit the defendant. When specifics were sent to Washington, D.C., the process and verdict were confirmed.

Involved with such intensity and ardor in their individual enterprises, struggling and clawing in an environment so merciless, all were constantly aware of how close they lived to the edge of existence. Where life often hung by a thread and a man depended upon finding food and gear where he had stationed them, robbing another's cache almost never happened. However, when it did, it was counted a crime worthy of capital punishment.

One prospector caught in the deed during winter was put on trial and sentenced to the maximum. But because all would have had to put their hand to the rope, the court turned to other means of carrying out the sentence. They asked him if he would rather shoot himself or walk out. Walking out meant starting then and there with no supplies other than some camp gear and the clothes on his back. "Out" meant banishment. Out of the country, never to return. Out the treacherous 600 miles up the Yukon and over the blizzard-oppressed mountains to the coast.

He was last seen by a group of miners who were overwintering far upriver. Amazingly, the outcast had made it 350 miles and was still going. Puzzled by why he would attempt such a trip alone, and with no provisions, they extended to him the warmth of their camp and a little dried salmon. When this later came to light and the region's prospectors discussed it, all agreed that had the man made it all the way out to the coast they would have heard about it.

Much later, an Irishman and a Dane were caught stealing. Anticipating the consequences, the Irishman shot himself. Fifty lashes with a one-half-inch rope (probably soaked) was the Dane's sentence. They tied the offender standing belly to a post, stripped to the waist. Lashes began to fall as Billy Onions, a mighty, left-handed mule skinner lay the hemp to him. At lash number fifteen, one of the witnesses with medical training implored them to stop the terrible strikes. He assessed the Dane as already half dead. The men cut him loose, but he was forced to head for the coast next day. Provisionless, he staggered along with a large sign bound to him reading, "thief."

In a wilderness so void of evident national boundaries, this shifting, wandering mishmash of nationalities demonstrated more allegiance to one another than to their nations of origin. Though the rest of the world recognized Canada and the United States as official owners of the land, to a degree, the prospector inhabitants thought of the seemingly limitless interior of the Yukon District and Alaska as a combined realm over which they held more of a legitimate, proprietary claim than did those absentee seats of power which obviously thought little and cared less about their remote holdings and the seemingly few and insignificant goings-on within them.

This rough, intrepid lot were indeed heroes born of heroic times, although their heroism was quiet. No grand send-offs trumpeted their goings out, no heroes' welcome celebrated their homecomings. It probably never so much as entered the mind of even the foremost of them, but these motley prospectors, and the fur traders who preceded them were performing as crucial tools in the hands of destiny, laying the farthest northwestern foundations of North America's two nations.

Had they not been so willing to expend their all, and such impulsive gamblers, so reckless and ready to cast their fate to the winds, they would never have come to discover the gleaming lure that would win the northwest subcontinent. Citizens of reserve and caution who pause long to consider consequences are not of the stuff to win empires.

Chapter 8

───◆───

Hard Life in a Harsh Land

Rod Perry: *Alma's husband, former Nome miner Al Preston, knew many of the old-time dog punchers from the upper country because many of them migrated among all the big strikes. Although like most miners, Al was too occupied with mining to keep a team, he loved dogs and life on the trail. He spent a lot of time in the company of the drivers when errands and business took him into town from his claim.*

One of the drivers was famous early Yukon Basin sourdough Ben Atwater. He had first explored and prospected the Upper Yukon, then later worked throughout Alaska. During the great Klondike Rush, between September 1898 and January 1899, Americans in Canada's Dawson got almost no postal service. Bags of U.S. mail stacked up in such mountains in Juneau and Skagway they had to develop mail service, and fast. Atwater secured one of the earliest, if not the earliest contract to haul mail by dog team from Skagway over White Pass to Dawson. Almost immediately his contract was extended to move mail to Nome. His route totaled 2,300 miles each way. Ben Atwater later became oft seen around Fairbanks and hit many other strikes, including Iditarod.

I knew his grandson, the late Ted Atwater of Willow. Ted was a close friend of my friends Mike Lee and his former wife Carolyn, who introduced me to mushing dogs. Ted was a wonderful sled builder, crafting one from native birch for Mike. He made another for Tom Mercer to take on the first Iditarod Race. In the picture on the cover of this book, the old sourdough (my late father, Gil Perry) wears the hat given him by Ted Atwater.

My dear friend, the late Hazel Menke (aunt of Iditarod Race pioneer musher Ken Chase of Anvik) told me one of her memories of the 1920s or early 1930s was seeing the venerable old sourdough Ben Atwater, himself, come drifting down the Yukon on a log raft and tie up at Holy Cross.

To my memory comes Al, a person as familiar and dear to me as Alma. The voice I hear carries the same affection as Alma's, but with an edge to it, and deep. Al's conversation in his flinty bass drifts back to me. "

———————————

Al Preston: "Rod, I knew Old Ben Atwater, alright. He came in over the pass so early he was one of the first prospectors into the upper country. Later he became a famous mail runner. His retriever-malemute crosses were the fastest mail team anyone had ever seen. He used Yukon sleds so there was nowhere to ride. Tough as whang leather. Hand on the gee pole, he could jog all day long, forty, fifty miles or farther. Didn't matter to Old Ben. You'd know him as far as you could see him by his great, black beard. Many years after he made his way into the Upper Yukon he looked back on the difficulty and painted a good picture about how it was."

———————————

Old Ben Atwater: "Yeah, Al, I been up here since way before Heck was a pup, prob'ly somewhere between an eternity and two forevers. In fact, the spring I first humped a pack in over the pass, I think God had just turned four.

"Arduous hardly describes our prospecting expeditions into the Yukon and back out. From Juneau, sometimes we went maybe 1,400 miles before we got back. We only had about five months to do it.

"Looks to me like those writers and historians back in America tend to live in the city library. Probably expire up here pretty quick. Ever since the gold rushes made big news people want to read about us. So the writers sit back there trying to pass themselves off as authorities on the North. Might be great at driving their desk and handling a typewriter, but couldn't drive a dog team and handle a sled any more than the man in the moon. Far's I can see, couldn't tell one end of an axe or paddle from the other and wouldn't know a tumpline or gee pole from Adam's off ox.

Ben Atwater, Mail Carrier, with His Dogsled Team, ca. 1898
University of Washington Libraries, Special Collections, Hegg052

"Maybe I shouldn't be so critical. And I 'spose they do the best they can. Al, you and I know you can't look at even the best map and have so much as an inkling. They'd never guess unless they've been here. And even then they couldn't begin to imagine 'cause their type only visits the safest part of the frontier. Prob'ly hold close to the settlements where others could save them from effects of their mistakes. Or keep their distance, just observing from the deck of a riverboat. Even if they got out and muddied their boots they wouldn't know. Not unless they did it same ways as we did. And for as long in time and as far as our trips were. Pretty plain those librarians never traveled on their own on foot or by river up north themselves. So they just don't have any personal experience to even guess what we had to do. Or how tough it was for us to get around in the old days.

"Readers down in civilization don't know enough about it to know the writers don't know anything. So they don't know the writers are leaving anything out. I shake my head at most of their naiveté. While it might rile me, I mostly shrug it off. But Al, the particular ones that made me work my grinders were the so-and-sos during the big rushes who published worthless rags titled like, 'Definitive Guidebook to Alaska and the Yukon.' Just for the lucre they passed themselves off as authorities on the North. How to get here, what to take, what to expect, where to look. Professed to know everything, even though they never revealed how they came by such intimate wisdom. A lot of their advice wasn't worth a cold half-pinch of last year's bear scat.

"Wouldn't have been so bad if the new stampeders had any background to wise up that they'd spent their hard-earned on such barnyard leavings. But they took it as gospel. Suckered in a lot of gullible newcomers who trusted they had a corner on the straight, inside dope. Main sin was sending ignorant folks over the most tomfool routes to reach the diggings. Crazy-dangerous, ill-conceived routes like over the Valdez Glacier. Ushered lot of good, honest citizens direct to their deaths. I imagine a passel of those publishers are sizzling right now or soon will be, roasting for the utter, despicable sin of it.

"Some were so dishonest it should have been evident they were just peddling material for which the bull had no further use. But a lot of stampeders were so naïve. Others were so gold-crazed they threw out their brains. I saw where you could pay for some person who claimed to be a clairvoyant to—from several thousand miles away—to pinpoint for you where riches were. People payin' him didn't ask why, if he knew so much, he didn't just go fill bags with all those millions himself. Or maybe not charge an initial fee, but just send his clients out in return for guaranteed shares. Then there seemed to be a land-office business going with all kinds of confidence men selling secret maps to lost mines. People buying such drivel deserve to be taken.

"Oh, yea, then there were the types selling gold-digging machines. And cure-all patent medicines and magic elixirs to keep you healthy and shoveling gold into your pokes. One I saw advertised said it contained, 'all the known and unknown vitamins.'

"But back to those pencil pushers, take any of them, honest or dishonest, and they can't begin to imagine the distances and emptiness. Alaska's about one-fifth the size of the whole blame United

States. Drop a map of Alaska overtop a map of the States and it reaches Pacific to Atlantic and goes Canada to Arkansas top to bottom. The Yukon Basin's more than half of it. Add Canada's Yukon District to it and it makes that giant northwest wilderness about maybe a third the size of the U.S.

"Now, Al, how do you think one of those hapless pseudo-experts would react if he was snatched up and had his chair-softened posterior plunked down in the middle of the thousands of square miles of silence? One thing I know, he'd never been so alone and vulnerable. The immensity and farness would instantly terrify him. The poor devil's knees would start knocking like an engine set to throw a rod. The chattering of his teeth would sound like castanets. Look in his countenance, white as a sheet, eyes wide, face like two pee holes in the snow. Wagh! If he commences to snivel, whimpers'd prob'ly draw every predator for miles, wolf packs and bears lickin' their chops, shoving and jostling for the claim of him.

"They got no idea of the conditions so don't fill their readers in. Without knowing about details, they write about us going here and there such that their readers imagine going from Chilkoot Pass to Dawson and Dawson to Fort Yukon is like going from their town to the next one down the road. Well, maybe up here it is the next settlement. But there's no road, not even a trail. And almost no habitation in the deadly space between. And it's as far to get there as crossing two of their medium-sized states.

"Now say one of 'em even had it enter his mind to tell about a cross-country tramp, maybe from Eagle to Tanana headwaters. Or write about walking on foot several score leagues along a river. One thing, they don't imagine the effect it has that right underground a foot or two is the everlasting ice. We don't get that much rain and snowfall in the Interior. But what we do get, the rain and meltwater can't soak in. It just can't percolate down and leave us be. The surface cover that insulates the permafrost in summer, a lot of it's tundra and muskegs with spongy moss you sink into every step. Eats up your energy worse'n hoofing through soft sand.

"Some of that cover's the infernal tussocks. During creation, God musta left that part to Satan. They're straight from hell, mixed dead and live grass and dirt that form matted, clumped, unstable sod towers one or two feet tall. They grow so crowded together, leaves barely room between to fit your boot. You've got to choose . . . try to balance wobbling your way on the unsteady tops, or pick your way down among 'em. If you take the going down in the soggy in-betweens, your steps are at odd intervals all uneven in length. Toe way in, splay way out, most steps you can't even get your foot down pointing your boots straight ahead. And most every move requires lifting your foot high over a tussock. You're not careful, every other step you'll stumble or trip and go down. Maddening enough to make the very Pope himself foam at the mouth. Many times you got no choice, but we try to avoid 'em like the plague. Especially when you're grunting along, breaking your sorry back under a debilitating load.

"Don't even enter the minds of most historians to try to fill in their readers about the spirit-breaking labor. The packs we humped around were staggering. Food staples, clothing, simple shelter, hunting and fishing gear, and boat building, camp and prospecting tools. Quite a ditty bag of possibles, too. I'd start with over 120 pounds most times, sometimes way more. Up mountains so steep sometimes you could nearly reach out and touch the upslope ahead. In valleys bogged by that moss and tussock footing I just mentioned. Endless tangles of crisscrossed downed timber, alder thickets, willow brush, and young birch growing thick as hair on a dog's back. Hardly thrash your way through. Wrings the gumption right out of you. Along the rivers, feeders to ford and flooded banks, inlets, beaver swamps, side channels, and ox bows you got to wade or circle around. Every mile's hard-won, legs numb from all the wading, a man-eating battleground.

"Yeah, they got no idea how much harder going by shank's mare in the Yukon and Alaska is than where they live. Maybe one of those soft, city-bound, pencil-necked types has tried enough foot travel to amount to something. I doubt many of those'd be strong enough, but maybe the rare one's bushwhacked a ways with no trail in forest farther south. That country's almost sure to be a stroll in the park held up to the same number of Yukon or Alaska miles. Al, you know exactly what I'm talking about.

"Those historians that write about our prospecting expeditions up or down a river never mention something major that almost always went along with water travel: first we had to build a boat. If the library guy does mention it, he doesn't put in what that takes.

"And he wouldn't have the foggiest about setting up an armstrong sawmill—a sawpit for whipsawing boards from rough logs. Fact, most wouldn't know a whipsaw from a two-man misery whip. Huh! And the logs aren't always very good. Sometimes they're small, or knotty. But you got to have a boat so you take whatever the country gives.

"Man on the scaffold pulls up, man in the pit pulls down. Stroke by stroke, terribly hard and pure misery. Every minute your motions and body heat draw mosquitoes, no-see-ums and black flies by the thousands, maybe millions. The man on the scaffold works like a dog hauling the saw up. And he's mostly responsible to stay to the line snapped with a stringload of soot. But I'd rather man the upstroke any day. The pitchy sawdust that showers down is torture. It's itchy and sticks to your sweating body. And it blinds the eyes of the man in the pit as he looks up to help keep the cut running true. Takes about a week for a couple of experienced men to build a boat, longer if the logs are small and knotty.

"I'll tell you, whipsawing lumber's the greatest test of a friendship known to mankind. A pair of angels fresh arrived, sent straight down from Heaven assigned to help you, put 'em on opposite ends of a whipsaw and before the first board's finished they'd be fighting like two lynx chucked in a gunnysack.

"Nope, and those scribblers never poled a heavy, 20- to 28-foot-long boat made of rough, unplaned, water-soaked green lumber upstream against a swift current day after day. They wouldn't know that time and again you come to currents too swift to pole and too deep to wade. There you're forced to track it up, hauling, leaning hard into the towline, trying to keep it tight while battling your way beside the stream. You're fighting the unending trees, down timber, brush, sweepers, inlets, and swamps along the uneven bank.

If one of those typewriter jockeys had tasted even a mile of it, he'd be convinced we're all liars to claim we've done it thousands. So he just mentions in passing the expedition went up such and such a river. Then like as not he merely says we left one river and crossed a divide to follow another. Al, you ever see him include the first boat we'd built and all the blood, sweat, and tears that went into it had to be waved goodbye? Or see him explain when we got to the next drainage, another sawpit had to be set up, a new pile of lumber had to be whipsawed and we had to go through the torture all over again?

"Al, you and I know travel in the North Country was just hellacious, soul-eroding work.

"Those who're used to tying on the nosebag at the first pang of hunger would gain a whole new experience when maybe months at a stretch your belly's so intimate with your backbone you're afraid they might permanently fuse. All the old-timers up here have spent long periods stretching supplies. Dried fruit for breakfast, water for lunch, and swell up for supper pretty much typifies the routine.

"Most folks out in America are used to a fresh change of lily-sweet clothes every day. Well, in the bush we wear our skin like bark on a tree. A sourdough can't rate the rank 'til he can jump his sox three times. Let stockins outta sight after peeling 'em off and you get to worrying they'll walk over the ridge on their own.

"Now we haven't even touched on the peril and risk, have we? And we pretty much stuck to what they leave out about summer going. We haven't even mentioned what they're not clued to about winter. The country lays down its own climatic terms in a long list. And they know nothing about coping. Some mighta come up for a peek in summer. But they couldn't guess what it's like to live where it sinks down cold enough it changes a cup of boiling coffee tossed into the air into frozen vapor, freezes the fire right off the end of a lit match, and on a still night standing outside your cabin you can hear the smoke rising from your chimney. Yea, we won't even start talking about winter, my friend, that's a whole huge, 'nother volume.

"But we can't leave off summer vicissitudes without cussing those infernal vampires. God left that part of creation to the devil, too. I've seen those blood-sucking hordes of hell crush strong men, just break them down weeping from exhaustion due to lack of rest. Oppression's drove some to insanity and even suicide."

Al Preston: "Old Ben used to tell about awakening one morning to a whispered voice that told him he was not alone. Opening one eye barely a slit, he saw a huge mosquito, gloating over him like the devil over a fat friar. Hunkering there licking his chops, the fiend was mumbling to himself, 'No, better eat him here; if I haul him back to the swamp the big ones'll take him away from me.'

"Seriously, Rod, folks Outside can't imagine clouds of vicious insects actually thick enough to darken the air around you. Numbers not even a physicist could comprehend. Each one has a diabolical little heart and a single-minded purpose. I've never known anyone who wrote about experiences in the north who didn't spend a lot of ink on the incredible multitudes and ferocity and never-ending depredations of them.

"One time up in Woodchopper country a guy fell in with me going the same way. While we shared a fire to boil tea he started scribbling in this journal. When I asked about it, he allowed he might turn it into a book if he ever made it back out. I politely asked if he'd mind sharing what he was writing. He said glad to; reading out loud helped him test his wording, and sometimes others offered something he could use. So when he read the section, it was about those hordes of hell Ben mentioned. After we talked about it he put in a couple of my phrases. He said he wouldn't mind if I copied down that page. I saved it because he worded things way better than I could:

"'No attempt at description of the torment inflicted by these thorns in the flesh and predators of the soul could exaggerate their wickedness. The most creative tortures of the Spanish Inquisition pale by comparison. Men must exhaust all effort to shield against them devouring the body and grinding down the nerves. We suffer untold cruelties from their venomous onslaughts, no matter how we array against them. A strong wind bringing relief is an answer to fervent, tearful prayer. As God's great gift, fall's first hard freeze seems like the gentlest caress of Nature, though we well know that it signals the beginning of months of Arctic temperatures and may be the lead-in to a winter of starvation.'"

IN THE YUKON AND ALASKA, fiendish clouds of blood-sucking insects billowed out of the vegetation at every footstep. They'd follow along in black swarms so dense that any encounter suffered in the "South 48" may be dismissed with a wave of the hand as comparatively insignificant. Many ranked mosquitoes, black flies, no-see-ums, and horse flies the worst obstacle of all. Remember, modern repellents were not yet available.

At their thickest, they were almost impossible to cope with. Pack horses were often covered with canvas sheets and their nostrils had to be periodically cleaned to keep them breathing clearly. After several horses on one expedition drowned in a river trying to escape the hordes, the men kept smudge fires burning when they camped for the night so the horses could gain relief. Then the animals grew so thin and weak refusing to leave the smoke to graze that some had to be shot. Some of the early prospectors reported their head nets becoming so covered with insects seeking entry they could hardly breathe. Not a few who had previously conquered all other hardships gave up the country, driven raving mad by the onslaught of the diminutive tyrants that pressed them with no respite day and night.

Famed biologist William Dall wrote about the phenomenon this way: " . . . mosquitos were like smoke in the air. Thousands might be killed before their eyes, yet the survivors sounded their trumpets and carried on the war. A blanket offered them no impediment; buckskin alone defied their art. At meal times, forced to remove our nets, we sat nearly stifled by the smoke, and, emerging for a breath of fresh air, received no mercy. My companions' hands, between sunburn and mosquitos, were nearly raw, and I can well conceive that a man without a net, in one of these marshes, would soon die from nervous exhaustion. The mosquitos drive the moose, deer, and bear into the river, and all nature rejoices when the end of July comes and their reign is at an end."

Some early prospectors rubbed on a mixture of bear grease, tar, and tobacco juice. Others tried to make sure they carried head nets. But beyond that, they accepted that torments from insects were part of their assigned existence even with the best expedition planning.

What they could try to avoid by careful preparation was mal-nourishment and starvation. Before gold hunters began to depend on restocking at the downriver ACC stations, the best-planned expeditions followed the Edmund Bean group example and hired Chilkat packers. When business was brisk, not only the Tlingit men, but women and children got in on the freighting business. They charged $12 to $13 a hundred to carry loads over the pass. Employment of such a human pack train allowed gold hunters to bring across the pass in two days a supply of staples to last all summer.

———————◆———————

Al Preston: "Funny thing, Rod, after listening to him grouse about the hardness of it all, you'd think someone like Old Ben hated the country so much he couldn't wait to escape. But like many, he held so tight to his love for the savage beauty, individual independence, adventure, desire for exclusive domain, and anticipation about what lay around the next bend in the river, it swung the dial way over on the side of the North.

"Thinking of that crusty old sourdough brought something to mind. Let me clarify something for you. Nobody hardly wrote about the North until the great gold rushes captured the attention of the world. So a lot of people hold the popular misconception that the great strikes just materialized in the late 1890s overnight. They hardly think of the search as something that had been hard underway for almost a quarter century.

"Another thing: without the writers' knowing there's any distinction, they give the public the perception that people participating in the Klondike Rush of '97—'98 were great frontiersmen, no different in wilderness skills than the earlier prospectors, just a bigger wave of the same.

"Well, I gotta tell you, there was a huge world of difference. First, the hardships the Ninety-eighters faced were only modest compared to what confronted men who came in from the early '70s through late '80s. Even the early '90s were way harder than the later Klondike miners had it. Then there was no comparing the skills at living and traveling in the wild between the old sourdoughs and most of those who came in later during the Klondike and other big rushes. Day and night between the two; no comparison at all. The Ninety-eighters just made all the news and got their pictures snapped.

"Let me ask you, if your canoe upset, you lost everything but your knife and the clothes on your back, and you're trapped in a great wilderness too big to escape, would you rather depend on the Ninety-eighter who resigned as mayor of Seattle to join the rush to the Klondike? Or would you rather choose for your survival partner old Yukoner Nick Goff, who'd heard of them, but had never seen a railroad because he'd always pushed on ahead of their coming? (Ol' Nick used to say, "Towns? I ain't got much use fer 'em. All's I kin see they're good fer's gittin' drunk, gittin' reoutfitted, 'n gittin' the blazes out of!")

"Those earliest gold hunters who came in over the Chilkoot before '97, were, almost to a man, experienced, professional prospectors. They were hardened outdoorsmen out of the mold of Old Ben Atwater and Nick Goff, themselves. They knew what to take and what to leave out. They never left out essentials. But at the same time you'd never see them packing one thing they didn't really need. Unless they hired Tlingit packers they could have never carried enough staples over the pass to keep them four or five months of a prospecting expedition. So they had to be good at finding fish and game to make up a lot of their diet. The ones who decided to overwinter were sure of their ability to field anything the country might throw at them. They had to be quick on their feet and nimble-minded at survival.

"The earliest into the country had to improvise in many ways. Some improvisations exhibited a lot of creative thought. For instance, Jack McQuesten invented an ingenious thermometer that was widely used throughout the region. It consisted of a row of vials or bottles mounted on a rack. The first contained quicksilver, the next Jamaica Ginger Extract, the third coal oil and the fourth Perry Davis Pain Killer. The four congealed in that order every ten degrees Fahrenheit from minus 40 to minus 70. When Pain Killer went past merely congealing and crystallized the men knew it had to be minus 75 degrees or lower. The wide saying around the country was that a man thinking of traveling left without giving it a second thought at frozen quicksilver. At Extract he took some caution. He didn't even possess the sense God gave a spruce burl if he didn't pause to mull over the risk at kerosene. Then if it sank down to Pain Killer, even the daftest fool dived back into his cabin and stoked a big fire.

Old Ben Atwater: "Another example of how we got by was our making 'bone butter.' All the old sourdoughs made it 'cause one of the things we missed most was butter. (Fact, we almost hung one man caught stealing Art Harper's whole stock of butter, but banished him on a death march out of the country instead.)

"Bone butter: You cut several sets of caribou antlers into ten-inch pieces. Boil 'em in a large cauldron for two nights and a day. Remove the bones and cool the liquid. Wait for it to set up on the surface and you can lift a couple of inches of butter off the top. Then add salt to your taste; the saltier, the longer it'll stay fresh in warm weather. It'll be white instead of yellow. And don't expect it to taste quite the same. But after bein' in the upper country long enough you'll think it's just as good as sweet cream butter. Only trouble, it takes a lot of valuable time.

"No man could stay in the country without being able to throw up a fast log cabin. 'Course, some were better craftsmen than others. Lots were never meant to last longer than a winter. To make 'em easy to heat we kept 'em small. Men built all dimensions, but around twelve by fourteen was probably most common for a group of up to four. And just over head-high, with low, small doors with moosehide hinges, and only one window. Our sod roofs were notoriously drippy in summer rains, but they were warm in winter. Men that were more skillful took a few extra pains in their joinery of the logwork. And those that did a good job chinking kept lots of heat from escaping out the walls.

"If you built nearby a source for good, big rocks, especially flat ones, and there was clay to be had, a Russian furnace could be laid up in the center of the floor. We sawed out carefully dimensioned sheets of ice at the first of the winter when it was just the right thickness. Kept a stack for window panes. You could gauge how warm a man built his cabin by a combination of how much firewood he had to cut, and how often he had to replace his window. I figured I'd done a good job insulating if my window had to be renewed once a week. Some new comers I knew said their digs were so cold one sheet lasted 'til spring. Later, the trading companies started bringing in mullioned windows, sheet-iron stoves, and stovepipe.

"Speaking of windows, folks farther south can't imagine how valuable light would be during a long, dark winter. They never experienced darkness eighteen hours a day. And that's in the brightest spot outside. A lot of days so cold you have to keep close to the fire in the dim of the inside of your cabin. Then, one of the most valuable commodities to a man's a good supply of candles. You got a lot of 'em in a camp where nobody else has any, either you can trade for almost anything, or you'll have a constant flow of visitors. Sitting in darkness all winter's surefire to inflict a man with raging cabin fever.

When we didn't have candles, we made Yukon lamps. They were twisted cotton poked down through the neck of a bottle filled with rendered grease. Bear or beaver worked good, or bacon grease, but you had no light when you didn't keep the bottle hot. And it was smoky as a demon's lair. Hacking and wheezing and our eyes always watering, but a willing trade-off to keep from going stark raving bug-house for lack of light.

"The nearest professional medical and dental help was one or two months' travel away. That is, in summer. And only if traveling conditions were good. Also, only if the poor devil seeking help was in condition to make good time. In winter nobody but the most fit could possibly survive the trip. Even in the peak of health it was a huge risk. Every man on a winter expedition out had to be able to pull his own weight. Stretched a healthy man to limits of human endurance just to get himself through without someone hanging on him.

"So we doctored ourselves and each other. One time hauling the Nome mail, down near the Melozi I swung in to the cabin of an old Creole who'd been a trader back in Russian days. He was over ninety so we used to check up when we went through. The chimney was smoking, but when I hallooed the cabin I didn't hear a reply. I went in. The old man lay there on a bed he'd fixed arm's length from the stove and by a big pile of ready firewood. Also had stocked some food and water right there in reach. Took only a glance to see he'd prepared to be stuck there. He was drained and shaking, pale as death, drenched in sweat and could only talk in a weak voice. Seems I got there a little late to help. He'd just finished struggling all day before he finally got his own broken arm set.

"Sometimes one of us needed something on the order of a major amputation. Say the removal of a gangrenous leg. If you're fortunate enough, you might find some old coot up the crick to perform it. If the patient (victim) was really lucky, the enlisted sawbones might even bring a fairly clean crosscut saw. And maybe even a jug of his own proprietary stupor enducer: Yukon Fog, 160 proof.

"Al, I'll tell you a story of life in the early days in the upper country. The event was pretty famous among us sourdoughs. A well-known old prospector friend suffered such severe toothaches the pain drove him stark raving enough to jerk all his own teeth. Once healed up, he got tuckered of having to cut each and every bite into tiny tidbits then work and work, mouthful by mouthful, gumming his chuck forever before swallowing. Said it took him so long to eat, by the time he finished one meal, he'd got so hungry just by the very eating he felt famished enough to start the next. Impatient, he turned to his miner's ingenuity.

"Now quite a few bears were working the blueberries on the slopes above the bar he was rocking. Selecting one he calculated just the right size, he plugged it. From that bruin's pearly gnashers he fabricated what had to be one of the most remarkable sets of dentures ever created. Featured incisors, canines, molars, the works.

"Anxious to try out his new choppers he set about testing his workmanship. Turned upon the very donor. Ate that bear with its own teeth!"

Chapter 9

———◆———

The Trickle Becomes a Stream

SIMULTANEOUS TO THE FIRST GROUPS' OVERWINTERING at Fort Reliance that year of 1882-1883, wintering near the Tanana mouth was a party headed by Ed Sheiffelin, the wealthy discoverer of the rich mines of Tombstone, Arizona. A group had prospected 200 miles up the Stewart the year before, found good prospects, and got a report out to Sheiffelin. His expedition was the first prospecting venture in the Yukon Basin in which significant capital was invested. As deck cargo on a ship he had chartered, his 12-by-40-foot steamer, *New Racket*, had been brought to the Yukon. The party had used it in their summer-fall prospecting venture in the vicinities of the Tanana mouth and Ramparts on the Yukon. When Sheiffelin and his men folded their venture, the newly reorganized partnership of McQuesten, Harper, and Mayo was there to buy the boat. Scheiffelin sold to them, hand-delivered there on the Yukon, cheaper than it would have cost to buy it in San Francisco.

The good fortune that had the partners stationed at Tanana was born of adversity. That fall, which was the fall after the ten—some accounts say twelve—miners wintered over with Jack McQuesten, the supply chain failed. All but Joe Ladue and Charlie Powell were forced to buck the current of the Yukon several hundred miles and go back out over the Chilkoot to winter. McQuesten's steamer had broken down, rendering Fort Reliance provisionless. Four other miners who had come in from Juneau and successfully prospected the Stewart River dropped down to Fort Reliance, expecting to winter there. Instead, they found it abandoned. Everyone had descended to the mouth of the Tanana where there was food.

During the cutthroat years when ACC and Western Fur and Trading Company had gone at each other in a profitless, last-man-standing Pyrrhic war, the only economic beneficiaries had been their customers, mostly Natives. When ACC bought out Western, the furs-for-goods exchange rate that had so recently been so extremely favorable to the locals on the Yukon disappeared. Not being aware of what had been going on in San Francisco boardrooms and knowing nothing of corporate profits and losses, but only knowing that suddenly and without warning their pelts would buy them only a significantly reduced amount of flour, tea, tobacco, and the all-important sugar(!), the people of the river were shocked and resentful.

Word of their anger reached General Nelson A. Miles. As commander of the U.S. Army's Department of the Columbia, which watched over the northwest coast, he coveted northern extension of his jurisdiction. Such an opportunity as afforded by this Alaskan unrest he quickly recognized and seized. In 1883, despite opposition from Washington, D.C., and the refusal of the War Department to sanction it, Miles dispatched First Lieutenant Fredrick Schwatka into the Upper Yukon on a broad-spectrum geographical, ethnological, economic, and military fact-finding mission. Not only did Schwatka's superiors send him off without bothering to secure higher approval up the Army chain of command, they sent the military expedition into a foreign country without that government's permission or even notification. The lieutenant and his party of six men slipped away on his quickly convened, clandestine reconnaissance, in his later words, "like a thief in the night."

At the head of Lynn Canal, Schwatka was fortunate to encounter the superintendent of a nearby salmon cannery. The man briefed the lieutenant on the packing abilities of the Chilkats and recommended what to pay them. Sixty of the ever commercially minded Chilkats not only freighted the gear for the expedition over the steep pass, the sure-footed, bull-strong Natives even piggy-backed the explorers themselves during their fording of the Taiya River.

———◆—◆———

Frederick Harte: "Arthur Harper met Lieutenant Schwatka as he and his men rafted into Art's tradin' station. Later he got hold of a couple copies of the lieutenant's reports. Another year, the two met again. Here's a little of what I remember from readin' the report and from what Art told me the man said; I can hear Schwatka . . ."

———— ◆—●— ——◆— ————

Lieutenant Fredrick Schwatka: "That portage over the pass was indeed a steep climb. But Mr. Harper, compared to battling 2,100 miles or so upstream to accomplish such a survey as we made, well, that mere thirty-two miles was mere trivia. When I reached the Yukon so close to its source and found that it lay so near to the Pacific, I was just dumbfounded. Dumbfounded that U.S. government mapmakers had been so inaccurate in their placement of the river's headwaters. To show our disgust my men used the maps for target practice.

"It truly amazed me that my top-to-bottom route to look over the Yukon had not been discovered and taken by earlier explorers. No wonder the Yukon had not been formally surveyed. Before steamboats arrived on the river, starting from the mouth would have meant poling and paddling and fighting the current, like I said, 2,100 miles. That struggle would have consumed a whole season, maybe even two seasons of the hardest labor. All to get to where our packers took us in only two days. Mr. Harper, in the times before your resupply posts they would have had to hunt and fish along the way. And once they reached the upper waters, not knowing there was a short trail out to saltwater and only about 850 miles through a protected, inter-island passage back to Seattle they would have had to float the 2,100 miles back down to the mouth and sail maybe 2,700 miles of treacherous, open ocean. All because they hadn't any idea of this short pass."

———— ◆—●— ——◆— ————

Frederick Harte: "Now I'll quote from Schwatka's report:

Why this route had not been picked out long ago by some explorer, who could thereby traverse the whole river in a single summer instead of combating its swift current from its mouth, seems singular, and can only be explained by supposing that those who would place sufficient reliance on the Indian reports to put in their maps the gross inaccuracies that fill even our Government charts of the Yukon's source, would be very likely to place reliance on the same Indians; and these from time immemorial, have united in pronouncing this part of the river unavailable even by canoes, filled as it is with rapids, whirlpools, and cascades.

"You know, one thing bothered us old-timers about Schwatka: Proud as a white-washed pig, the man took lots of our old place-names and put his own new ones on them. It was like he thought the country had never been discovered until he showed up.

"Now I know some might rightly bring up that we ourselves disregarded a lot of Native place-names that had stood almost since Adam. But our renamin' was mostly practical. The Natives tended to name places and land features describin' the nature o' the place like, 'Where the Muddy Water Flows Into the Clear River With Fish in It.' Or describin' something the people did there like 'Ridge Where We Spear Caribou.' It sometimes took whole a string of compound words too long to easily spit out. Often they were too tough to get our tongues around. So it just made sense for efficiency's sake, to tack on our own names we could remember, pronounce, utter quickly and have room on a map to write.

"But back to Schwatka's names; funny thing, the foreign nation he had no permission to enter on a military mission, I'll be hanged if they didn't let some of his names officially stick.

"He said as he and his men drifted downriver, he was impressed that so much more prospectin' and minin' activity was goin' on along the upper Yukon than he expected. Addin' to the activity he mentioned seeing the *New Racket* headin' upstream. Jack McQuesten told me later that he pulled over and visited with Schwatka as they were passin' each other. Jack was pilotin' the steamer the partners had recently bought from Ed Sheiffelin. After runnin' the *New Racket* down to St. Michael and takin' on cargo, he headed upriver with thirty tons of tools, gear and supplies for the miners on the Cassiar bars."

Rod Perry: *That passage upriver piloting the New Racket happened to be McQuesten's first haul dedicated largely to the outfitting and supplying of the growing number of prospectors working the upper river. Closing in on their first decade in the Yukon, the partners' enterprise had before concentrated almost solely on the Native fur trade.*

Lieutenant Fredrick Schwatka: "Our expedition accomplished the first complete survey of the third-largest river of our country. We did it, as I stated in my report, with 'far less money in our hands to conduct it through its long journey than was afterward appropriated by Congress to publish its report.' Both the official and popular reports of our expedition were published in 1885. It became the first widespread mention of the Yukon and its resources to reach the American press. Mine was, as far as I know, the first published description of the crossing of the Perrier Pass."

Rod Perry: *That was one Schwatka renaming that didn't stick; Chilkoot Pass remained Chilkoot Pass.*

In the fall of 1884 Jack McQuesten made the first of what would become many trips to Alaska Commercial Company headquarters in San Francisco. Speaking to the ACC board of directors, he tried to persuade them that the nature of the demand on the Yukon was changing. Whereas from their earliest days their entire Yukon thrust had been aimed at the Native fur trade, demand for goods was becoming dominated by prospectors and miners. Until recently, ACC had dealt mainly in flour, sugar, tea, and tobacco. There had been nothing like tools or boots or general gear for the miners. Yes, he had taken one load of thirty tons of mining supplies up to the Stewart miners the year before, but that was a drop in the bucket to what was needed. Prospectors were not only arriving in increasing numbers, many were staying year around. Even more would come, he told them, if the miners could depend on ACC to adequately stock supplies geared to their needs. If the company did not respond, competitors could be expected to move in to fill the void.

The board did not look favorably on McQuesten's ideas. Like the Hudson's Bay Company, they considered themselves a strictly fur trading business. However, it was so plain to Jack how his future bread would be buttered that he privately decided to form a new firm. Soon after the board meeting, word reached ACC heads that Jack McQuesten was in Portland talking with potential backers. Still not wishing to engage in mining supply, but knowing the treasure they had in McQuesten, they wired him asking that he return to San Francisco to help them plan changes in their business focus.

Though ACC agreed to significantly step up supply of the mining industry, the feeling grew along the river that the company either just plain disliked prospectors or thought it not worth the effort to send them quality food and equipment. Miners commonly found their only choice was to buy spoiled or degraded staples or go without. Bacon regularly came in 3-foot-long slabs, yellow with spoilage. A purchase of beans included paying for weight of the plentiful gravel in the bag. Dried fruit was commonly coated in green mold. It was not unusual to find that the rice had been wetted in the bag and formed into clumps. Likewise, the flour had often been soaked, sometimes in salt water during the sea voyage, and sometimes alternately resoaked and dried, even heated, until the contents of the 50-pound bags fused rock hard. One miner reported having to take an axe to the flour. Cutting through the hard, thick exterior, green and yellow with mold, he said they counted themselves lucky if they could get fifteen pounds of uncontaminated, hard lumps in the middle. Before using it, they first broke up the lumps with a hammer then rubbed it forcefully through a sieve. As bad as it all was, the men were often forced to eat the worst of it, mold, contamination, and all. McQuesten could do nothing about the quality, he could only sell supplies in the state they arrived. It would not improve until competition arrived on the river.

Frederick Harte: "Hunger's a good sauce, but a man's sensibilities and stomach have their limits. We hated to be the purveyors of such a sorry excuse for sustenance, but didn't have much stroke in the seat of power down in Frisco. What did change things was our competition moving in, when the black and red of the balance sheet spoke to them. ACC was forced to reduce prices and increase quality."

As prospectors increased in number, McQuesten and Harper tried not to just respond to that demand, but stay one jump ahead of it. In the Yukon Basin every major gold discovery lay relatively close to the big river or one of its navigable tributaries. That enabled them to efficiently ship the miners' needs from San Francisco to St. Michael, then by river boat up to supply centers. From those points miners or hired dog team freighters could distribute it farther out to individual cabins and claims.

Alfred Hulse Brooks: "The traders differed from many who would eventually come in to compete for the Yukoner's dollar. While most of the prospectors were so focused on their own searching and digging they could not see much else, McQuesten, Harper, and, to an extent, Mayo had a much broader view. They had been up and down the river for years. They knew the entire country. Being experienced prospectors themselves gave them the advantage of being able to step back, study the big picture, and make sagacious predictions regarding where the best chances lay for someone to make the next strike. They often backed prospectors, grubstaking them to investigate country they thought held promise. However, beyond any thought of their own financial benefit, the partners, especially Jack McQuesten, gained the well-loved reputation of never turning away a hard-working explorer who had come up short in his search for gold. He was, indeed, the veritable guardian angel of the prospector. Often, McQuesten sacrificed personally to help miners down on their luck. Other companies that would soon arrive typically resisted such investing in futures. They firmly demanded cash on the barrelhead for all purchases.

"McQuesten had another practice that endeared him to the miners. During the early years, a severe shortage of provisions seemed to be the order of things every winter. He instituted a personal policy of apportioning his limited supplies equally. Financial standing had no bearing. One fall when supplies were thin the joke went up and down the river that each man's share came to two bags of flour and instructions detailing a new way to catch rabbits! When things got that tight, many men would leave the country by way of the Chilkoot or St. Michael in the fall, returning the following summer."

Yukon Pioneers Pose Around Russian Cannons at St. Michael, 1885
Middle row, left to right: Al Mayo (third), Joe Ladue, Francois Mercier,
and Grigory Kokrine stand side by side. Back row: Arthur Harper
and Howard Franklin stand second and fourth, respectively.

Alaska State Library Historical Collections, Wickersham State Historic Site,
Schieffelin Brothers Yukon River Prospecting Trip, Charles O. Farciot, P277-017-003

Chapter 10

Prelude Strikes Set the Stage

CHARLEY FARCIOT, the only member of the Scheiffelin party to stay, canoed 150 miles up the Stewart River in 1884, the first to prospect that far up the big tributary. Then in 1885 several developments took place that would spur an influx of prospectors. Tom Boswell, Charley Powell, Frank Mondffalt and two French Canadians, Bertrand and Caselais found fine gold at the rate of $30 to $100 a day there on the Stewart. According to François Mercier, when Mr. Bertrand later visited him in Montreal he told Mercier that prospectors in his group had averaged about $5,000-$6,000 yearly in the years 1883-1886 mostly on the Stewart River bars. Also in 1885 the Cassiar Bars rewarded miners with good results. Miners were beginning to make some serious money. In 1885 Jack McQuesten ascended the Stewart and its tributary which would later be named the McQuesten River, to look over mining prospects. As many as 75 to 110 miners ended the season on the Stewart. Additionally, 1885 was the year Schwatka's expedition report was published.

One prospector who was lured north in early 1885 was George Washington Carmack. He crossed the Chilkoot Pass and descended the Yukon to about Miles Canyon. Without an outfit to winter over, he retreated that fall. The following spring, while at the Healy and Wilson Post at Dyea he met Tagish Athapaskans, Skookum Jim and his cousin, Tagish (later, Dawson) Charlie. The three hired out to pack prospectors' supplies across the pass. Over the summer, George and the two became fast friends. The white man was so drawn to Tagish culture that, at the invitation of his partners, he began to live in their Yukon headwaters village, Carcross. George married one of Skookum Jim's sisters, whom he called Kate. Some reports say he had married another another of Jim's sisters first, and when she died, following the Tagish custom, George took Kate to wife.

Carmack's first notable find, probably aided by his relatives' intimate knowledge of the country, was a major coal deposit. He attempted to develop a mine, building a cabin that became a trading post. Years later, it grew into the Yukon River settlement that now bears his name.

Sixteen stayed at Fort Reliance the winter of 1885-1886, but all thoughts were on the Stewart. (Miners overwintering on Stewart headwaters stuck close to their fires through the coldest month the upper Yukon had yet recorded. On January 4 the temperature was said to hit eighty below. The month average was minus fifty-six. Steve Custer badly froze a foot and had to have a few toes lopped off.)

The Reliance miners, itching to get at the Stewart, traveled with Jack's dog team all the way up to the Stewart Falls in April, prospecting along the way. In response to the more than 100 miners working the Stewart and vicinity, with the coming of spring, Alfred Harper and Jack McQuesten disassembled Fort Reliance for its logs, and as the river opened took most of them up the Yukon and reassembled them as their new trading post at the Stewart confluence. McQuesten named the place Fort Nelson for his friend, famed naturalist Edward H. Nelson (incidentally, the same individual for whom Alaska's Nelson Island was named).

The Schwatka publicity as well as reports that seeped out telling of gold on the Stewart brought over 200 prospectors across the Chilkoot Pass in 1886. About $100,000 in gold was taken by miners scattered along the Stewart and bars of the upper Yukon that season.

Simultaneously, that season of 1886 saw two prospectors diligently searching the country in a gold hunt that would significantly change the region. Between ice-out and freeze-up partners Howard Franklin and Harry Madison covered a lot of ground. First, they retraced an expedition McQuesten had undertaken the year before, prospecting the Stewart (all the way to the falls) and McQuesten rivers as far as they could pole. That examination of the country up-and downstream approached four hundred miles' length. Looking for something better, they heeded the advice of Arthur Harper and drifted from the Stewart

120 miles down the Yukon to the Fortymile River. Turning into the mouth, the gold hunters began methodically testing likely-looking bars and structures along the watercourse.

As Franklin and Madison worked their way upstream, McQuesten took a late boat out to San Francisco to procure goods for the trading and supply operation. Then, in the waning days of fall, twenty-five miles up the Fortymile, across the boundary line in Alaska, Franklin—assisted by Madison—struck gold. Soon following their strike, Franklin made another, on an upstream tributary, Franklin Creek which flows into the South Fork of the Fortymile. "

—————◆————◆—————

Rod Perry: *Franklin was a professional land planner. He created the first city plat for Juneau, Alaska. A street there is named Howard Franklin Street in his honor.*

—————◆————◆—————

Before Franklin and Madison's discoveries, prospecting along the Yukon had been limited to the search for gold-bearing bars where the force of the current and the yearly cataclysm of spring ice breakup tended to stir fine gold up from deeper deposits. Therefore, previous gold production had only been in dust form. Franklin's find of a continuous bedrock paystreak was a first for the region and the coarse gold it yielded suddenly revolutionized the way prospectors sought and mined gold in the Yukon basin. The miners found that Fortymile gold lay close to the surface on most of the claims. That gave them quick returns for their labors.

When Franklin and Madison came boating back up the Yukon to Fort Nelson and reported their strike, almost to a man the Stewart River miners who had stayed to overwinter stampeded to the exciting new site. McQuesten and Harper's new post was almost literally in business one day, out of business the next, left virtually devoid of customers as quickly as word spread up the Stewart and to other nearby digs.

The myriad forks and tributary creeks of the Fortymile River are located in Alaska, but the river (originally estimated to be about forty miles downstream from Fort Reliance) flows into the Yukon just east of the international boundary. At the confluence, miners, racing to beat winter, quickly threw up beginnings of the town of Forty Mile, Yukon District. One notable encampment was crudely cobbled together on a nearby island, inhabited by a motley group. Having only a few candles, to preserve sanity they occupied themselves during the long, dark winter by trying to outdo one another in the telling of stories, taking their art to rare heights. Other prospectors tramped between mainland settlement and island all winter to listen in. The site became renowned as "Sixteen Liars Island."

Harper would have to wait until spring ice-out to move operations down to the new townsite. In the meantime, dog teams kept the trail hard-beaten, hauling his supplies down from the Stewart to the miners.

Arthur Harper read Franklin's discovery of coarse gold as a clue that a lode must be nearby. If his hunch proved true, it would draw far more miners to the area than he and Jack McQuesten had planned for prior to the latter's departure on his buying trip. And if that came about, development of the strike would be restricted by lack of supplies to keep the miners working. As well, the partners would miss profits. However, those predictions paled next to the most dire consequence Harper foresaw. That was the very real potential that a food shortage the following year could be life-threatening.

Harper decided that he must try to get word out to his partner. Additionally, he felt duty-bound to follow the Code of the Prospectors and communicate the news to as many as 200 Yukon regulars who had been diligently exploring the country but had left well before the strike to make it over the pass before winter closed it off. Many were wintering around Juneau. Numerous others were thought to be in locations where they could be reached by letter. Steamboat captain Tom Williams, accompanied by an eighteen-year-old Native boy the miners called Indian Bob, responded to Harper's call to carry a packet containing news of the strike some 600 miles to Lynn Canal. Once there, they were to devise some way to forward it to McQuesten.

The whole country knew the trip would be extremely hazardous. Everyone was aware there existed no known precedent of anyone daring to cross the Chilkoot Pass in midwinter. A mere handful of miles above the coast where rain is a byword, fall and early winter are the wettest seasons. Rain at sea level falls as snow in the mountains. The pass becomes swiftly buried many feet deep. Adding to the peril was that Williams' primary experience was as a riverman; he was neither an experienced dog driver nor winter traveler. But even the savvy sourdoughs who watched him leave could not have predicted the extent of the terrible trail conditions Williams and Bob would encounter: half a thousand miles of utter hell, but without the benefit of the heat.

It was December 1, 1886 when the men pulled out of Fort Nelson driving a few dogs pulling gear and supplies. The river surface had frozen into an unusually jagged and jumbled surface, the result of freezing seasonally early, briefly breaking up to run heavily in brash ice, then refreezing into a several-hundred-mile-long jumble of ragged shards. The men were slowed from the start.

Near the end of the second week, at Rink Rapids their sled was severely damaged, forcing a stop to recondition it. While they were halted the rain set in. Rain? This was supposed to be winter in the Yukon Interior. It developed into the warmest early winter weather in memory. The warm spell dragged on and on. Water covered the ice, not just a skim on the surface here and there, but much of the river ice became covered well up on the dogs' legs.

This thinned the ice from the top as the swollen river simultaneously ate away from below. Bob broke through into water over his head on 17 December. One of them broke through the following day and again the day after that. Each time it was in deep water well over their heads. Miraculously, in every occurrence they were able to get out before being swept under the ice and without the other man or the team and sled breaking through. Finally the river started to break up, then jam, damming the flow, in some places backing the water up very deeply for long distances. At one point they had to leave the river and slash through brush two miles to work their way around a section too deep for the dogs to wade. The wet conditions were hard on the dogs' feet.

The difficult going exhausted the team. On December 22 they made but nine miles. The slow going caused rations to dwindle.

Then it looked as if their luck might change. The travelers encountered a group of miners who had been working upstream bars and were waiting out winter in their riverside camp. As the men fed Williams and Bob, the messengers fed the camp details of the Fortymile strike. The miners reprovisioned the two with what amount they could spare, added their own letters to the packet, and wished them godspeed.

The news bearers pushed on while temperatures remained above freezing. The entire middle of the river became open, leaving only shelf ice on the sides for a traveling surface.

Then, conditions changed. At Lake LaBarge on New Year's Eve it grew bitterly cold. On they went. Finally out of dog food, they fed the animals from their own stores, mainly from their rapidly diminishing supply of flour. On the smooth lake ice, for one brief day they managed to make better time even in their exhausted state.

Along came a band of Tagish Indians. The run-down duo tried to draft the Natives to accompany them. But the locals, knowing the deeply buried state of the pass and casting a calculating eye at the weather, forecast deteriorating conditions and strongly warned the men against proceeding.

Shortly after, a blizzard struck, blowing full in their faces. The driven men fought on another twenty miles before they were forced to stop. Awaking to a heavy snow, they made another ten miles, camping midway along the lake. One dog grew too exhausted to work, so they left him and abandoned their sled. The next two days they managed only five miles total.

The weather grew even worse. Forced to dig in and wait it out, Williams and Bob spent five days in a snow shelter. Their only nourishment was a small amount of dry flour eaten out of hand. Inside their lair, Williams deterioration accelerated. He grew feverish with pneumonia. Weakened to near delirium, he lost awareness, allowing his fingers and toes to freeze. On the sixth day, though the blizzard still raged, they realized they must abandon their shelter or die there.

Everything but the clothes on their backs they left behind. In just a short distance, Williams collapsed. Bob helped him to stand. Supported by the young Indian boy, Williams struggled to walk. Finally, he gave out altogether. The emaciated Bob heroically put Williams on his back. Plowing through deep snow he carried him a few yards at a time. For five days, as the blizzard still raged around the summit of the Chilkoot Pass, Bob continued, picking Williams up, staggering weakly through the deep pack and drifts, putting him down, then placing him on his back again to yet once more lurch as far as he could. Over and over, a few yards a time, it took Bob five days to gain 12 miles with his still living, but dying burden.

In the final stages of starvation, just when all strength was drained and hope had ebbed, they were seen by a party of Chilkat hunters. Quickly loading the two on their sleds, the Tlingits towed them the rest of the way out of the mountains and to the Healy and Wilson trading post at Dyea at the head of Lynn Canal.

To Wilson's questioning about why the two had undertaken such a seemingly foolhardy undertaking, Williams could manage only almost unintelligible mumblings, something about an important mission. Then breathing his last, the ravaged man died. Between the dying utterances of Tom Williams and the few English words of Bob, Trader Wilson gathered that something of importance had been left behind in the mountains. He mustered a party to follow the backtrail, but a blizzard stopped them before they reached the pass.

J. J. Healy, who had been on a trip to Juneau, returned. Taking in the situation he concluded that no one would make such an apparently ill-conceived trip of their own volition. He suspected they must be scoundrels forced to leave the country. Healy knew of such occurrences taking place from time to time following a miners' meeting. Therefore he suspected the dead Williams and his young sidekick were ne'er-do-wells found guilty of some serious infraction. Bob couldn't tell him, but Healy imagined commission of a crime such as thievery, cheating, or a breaking of the peace—crimes short of deserving hanging, but deserving harsh summary punishment—had resulted in banishment from the country . . . regardless of season.

Nevertheless, Healy hurriedly turned around, taking Bob to Juneau for treatment of exhaustion, starvation, and frostbite.

Loyal to his mission, Bob kept trying to convey the message. Using chunks of coal in one illustration, a handful of beans in another, he finally broke through the barrier enough that Healy now became convinced the two men from the Interior were bringing out news of a big strike, a concentration where nuggets at the discovery site lay around like those beans. Upon their return from Juneau, Healy sent a second party back into the mountains. This time they were able to make it all the way over the pass to the snow cave. There they found the bundle. Frozen in his final repose, one of the sled dogs lay curled up next to it, in death appearing to still faithfully guard the invaluable packet.

Reading the communiqué in the packet, Healy and Wilson learned the important reason for which Bob had performed his heroics and Williams had given his life. They got word to McQuesten in time and mailed the various other letters. At great cost, the *Code of the Prospector* had been kept.

The following summer many came over the pass in response to the news borne by Williams and Bob. Two men in particular who arrived in 1887 would become prominent, stamping their names on Alaska gold strikes and place names, Gordon Bettles and Jack Wade.

Breakup of the upper Yukon River usually took place between early and mid-May. However, upon occasion, Bering Sea ice could keep ocean-going vessels from gaining St. Michael until early July. Therefore, riverboats could sometimes make it all the way from the upper river down to the Yukon mouth before shipping from outside could reach the port of St. Michael which was upcoast of the Yukon mouth. Also, apart from supplies arriving from west coast ports, stores warehoused at St. Michael often were closed off by ice. Therefore, sometimes riverboats that had followed Yukon ice-out down, had to anchor up and wait departure of sea ice before they could connect with cargo and start back upriver.

Frederick Harte: "When Franklin and Madison struck gold downstream at the Fortymile the prior fall, Art Harper moved a lot of the Fort Nelson stock 120 miles down. But Al Mayo stayed at Nelson with the leftovers. By spring, faith, but everyone was desperate for food. None of us had a glimmer whether the message packet sent with Wilson and Bob the winter before even made it out to the coast. Or if it did, if it had connected with Jack out in 'Frisco. So we were all wonderin' if he'd sail north with any more stock than usual. But whether or not, we expected he'd be into St. Michael with at least the regular order of supplies. So Mayo took the *New Racket* downriver in a dash for food, trailin' hard behind the breakin' ice. As he arrived at the delta, ice cleared enough to allow him through to St. Michael.

Captain Al Mayo
James McQuiston Collection

"McQuesten was there, and yes, he'd gotten Art's note. He gave Al Mayo the news about Tom Williams' death. As Al digested the sad tidin's, they hurriedly threw a cargo on the *Racket*. The main supply would be comin' in his wake; this was just a relief run. So he kept it light, only ten tons and towin' no barges, to make fast time against spring flood.

"When Al steamed into Forty Mile, remember the settlement was brand-new that winter. There was no ACC post built yet. So the boat was the store. Al Mayo and I dispensed the food straight from the deck. As the starvin' miners came aboard and we assembled their orders, Arthur Harper kept records as clerk. Used a packing crate for a desk. When the bigger supply arrived ten days later, 100 tons, we three repeated as storekeepers from that deck."

Forty Mile sprang up as the first settlement worthy of the designation "town" on the upper Yukon. McQuesten and Harper shifted their main focus from their just-established Stewart River post down to the new mining center. There they soon built a station with a large warehouse and provisioned it with increased supplies Jack had just brought in from San Francisco.

Heretofore, the small steamers servicing the upper river had been able to supply only enough to allow about 100 men to winter over. The rest were forced to leave either up-or downriver each fall. The small stern-wheelers of the ACC fleet, consisting of the *Yukon, New Racket,* and *St. Michael* had little space for freight either above or below deck. Almost every square foot was taken up by engine, boiler, and fuel. To handle movement of the growing amount of cargo, each

Steamers St. Michael, New Racket, Yukon

Alaska State Library Historical Collections, Wickersham State Historic Site,
Schieffelin Brothers Yukon River Prospecting Trip, Charles O. Farciot, P277-017-032

time they went to St. Michael for supplies they shoved or towed a line of four or five small barges carrying about 10 tons each. According to William Ogilvie, it took about one month to complete a trip between St Michael and the vicinity of the Alaska-Canada border.

———————

Alfred Hulse Brooks: "William Ogilvie was a Canadian government surveyor who would later be appointed commissioner of Yukon Territory. In 1887, he performed much of the official surveying and mapping of the 141st parallel, the boundary between Alaska and Canada's Yukon. He and I later became friends. George Carmack, Skookum Jim, and Tagish Charlie packed Ogilvie's supplies over the Chilkoot, and traveled with his survey party to Forty Mile that summer. I mention the three packers because they would eventually play such an important part in the most defining moment in the history of the region.

"That same year, as part of the Ogilvie survey, Skookum Jim showed Captain William Moore the pass that paralleled the Chilkoot. Ogilvie named it the White Pass. The Natives had managed to keep its existence secret for 40 years after Robert Campbell of the Hudson's Bay Company had found out about the Chilkoot Pass. Captain Moore correctly analyzed possibilities for the White Pass as an important transportation corridor. Sizing things up, he later staked out strategically situated land, claiming the ground upon which would later grow Skagway, Alaska."

———————

While the men were occupied in the survey, a prospector worked his way 40 miles up Yukon District's Thron-diuck (Klondike) River. He reportedly found little.

The unique state of the Yukon Basin that had allowed it to be so well self-ruled by the free and the brave began to change with the founding of Forty Mile. Certainly, into the region's first town many as competent as the original entrants still came. But the distance, isolation, topography, and harsh climate were not such effective filters when men could nestle in a town setting. With a resource base far exceeding anything previously available and so much assistance at hand insulating the incompetent from results of their mistakes, it simply did not take the skill level and the resolute character to succeed in Forty Mile that it had when supplies were short and people dispersed. And so, the gathering at Forty Mile drew many of a different ilk than the vanguards: human leaches that invariably hang around gold camps sucking off the investment in risk and energy of the industrious. Their type neither would have been attracted to, nor could have made it in a less protected environment. As men of lesser character joined the process, the miners' meeting began to deteriorate in quality and effectiveness. All the old timers would look back on the year 1888 as the turning point. When they later more formally drew up papers for their fraternity, *Yukon Order of Pioneers*—YOOP—they established 1888 as the cutoff for qualification into the brotherhood.

In 1889, after discussing things with his longtime partner Jack McQuesten, Arthur Harper decided to leave Alaska Commercial Company in favor of private opportunity he saw upriver. The company

Yukon Order of Pioneers at Forty Mile
Alaska State Library Portrait File, ASL-Groups-PioneersOfAlaska-01

steamboat *Yukon* took him with materials and supplies about 225 miles above Forty Mile, where he reestablished Fort Selkirk near the Pelly mouth. Joe Ladue, who had earlier joined in partnership with Harper and McQuesten in their alliance with Alaska Commercial, broke away as well. He and Harper formed the firm of Harper and Ladue.

Harper and Ladue continued the practice of outfitting miners on a "pay-when-you-can" policy. A notable example of the trust and honor prevalent between the traders and the rough breed they catered to would occur a few years later. The partners had a several-ton shipment delivered at a time neither could be present to disburse it. They let it be known that any arriving miner could load up, leave a written account of what he took, and settle up when he got the chance. Eventually, of the whole cargo as listed on the delivery manifest, Harper and Ladue found a discrepancy of only six cans of condensed milk. Harper commented that he'd rather think that was due to a mistake by the shipping clerk than even the smallest dishonesty on the part of a prospector. The practice built a tremendous feeling of seller-buyer camaraderie and loyalty, but made for cash-flow problems and slow returns on investment. So the old practice necessitated charging higher prices.

The year 1889 saw the addition of a new stern-wheeler to the ACC fleet. The *Arctic* boasted a 140-ton capacity. With its addition, ACC looked capable of wintering over about 300 miners. However, too late in the season to be able to adjust to the loss, the *Arctic* wrecked on its maiden voyage. It had aboard provisions without which Forty Mile could not survive the winter. Jack McQuesten sounded the alarm. For all who would leave the country, he offered free passage on the *New Racket*. But they must move quickly. Ice was beginning to run as about 100 men swarmed aboard.

The steamer pointed its prow downriver carrying little food to feed the deckload of miners. Through the gathering ice flow, the *Racket* experienced mishaps that slowed them, and time-consuming stops at Rampart, Nuklukayet, and Kokrines to unload groups that decided to overwinter at those locations. Almost unable to maneuver in the thickening ice, just as they struggled into Nulato and worked the boat into a sheltered winter resting place the river locked down tight.

With limited resources, certainly a supply that did not anticipate such an influx, the Nulato post would not be able to feed the large number very long. So the men lined out on a forced march for St. Michael, 180 miles distant. Those wearing the few available sets of snowshoes took turns breaking trail through two feet of snow. Men following in their wake rotated their order in line. Nulato Natives aided with dog teams carried starvation rations for the men. All managed to make St. Michael, but in weakened condition.

The *Arctic* was refloated in 1890. Its addition to the fleet began to greatly increase supply to the growing population.

A major competitor to the Alaska Commercial Company arrived on the Yukon in 1892. Trader J. J. Healy (of Healy and Wilson of Dyea) created the Chicago-based North American Trade and Transportation Company (NAT&T) and began to establish stores along the Yukon. Differing from the business model of McQuesten and Harper-Ladue, the new company kept to a strict cash-and-carry policy. Quicker returns on investment for inventory allowed them to undercut the original traders' prices. That made for stiff competition, especially since so many new prospectors were arriving who had no prior grubstake relationships and trading loyalties with the original traders.

Those who did harbor old loyalties loved Jack McQuesten for his open-handedness, but disliked the tight-fisted Healy. That he would not grubstake them was taken as a lack of faith and trust. This caused the combative, vindictive Healy, a man who prided himself on loving contention and never forgetting, never forgiving, to develop a hatred for Jack and his loyals. Once, when Jack could not supply an item for one of his faithfuls, he sent him across the river to the rival store. Healy not only refused to sell to the man, he threw him off NAT&T property.

The big benefit of NAT&T's entrance was that of reintroducing the element of trading competition along the river. Having the two vying for the region's dollar served to bring down Alaska Commercial's prices and forced them to deliver better-quality goods. In just the few years since competition between ACC and Western Fur and Trading had cut profits to the point of buyout or business failure, the country had grown enough that two trading businesses could keep a keen, competetive edge, yet remain in the black.

When Forty Mile had been new back in early 1888, William Ogilvie had first reported to Canadian government officials about the town. He had stated that it was largely populated with Americans. With no Canadian government officials in the country, he told the Dominion that the men lived as if there were no international boundary. In what amounted to an American town on Canadian soil, they were dwelling in the settlement under their miners' code. However, he reported everything to be running smoothly enough. In that early day in Forty Mile's existence, he opined, any Canadian intrusion would surely be detrimental. He contended that the independent-spirited Americans would simply be driven to move west across the nearby boundary line onto American soil. And that, Ogilvie informed Ottawa, would only slow development of the Canadian Yukon.

Across the Fortymile mouth from the original town and McQuesten's ACC store, the new company, NAT&T established their own town, Fort Cudahy.

———————

Rod Perry: *In that day, one would have to travel three quarters of a thousand miles upriver and across the Coast Mountains to reach Juneau, the next "civilized" village of at least the size of Forty Mile–Fort Cudahy. And searching downriver for the next island of comparable civilization one would have to bypass Nulato and St. Michael as not big enough, cross the Bering Sea and either continue east across Siberia or turn down the Russian Far Eastern coast all the way to Vladivostok. Taking all of that into consideration, for someone to think of this isolated island of bustling habitation as two towns when it was separated by the mere narrow width of the Fortymile River over which dwellers crossed back and forth by a short footbridge, is quite a humorous, imaginative stretch.*

———————

Several years after Ogilvie had advocated that the government leave the Americans free to run this American town on Canadian soil, the town had grown. Now in the early 1890s, "Greater Forty Mile," (the combined town) had increased to include all of the two companies' stores and warehouses, a sawmill, eighty-odd cabins, two bakeries, a barber shop, a couple of blacksmith shops, an opera house, a few distilleries, a church, several saloons, billiard halls, and dance halls, a tinsmithy, a hardware store, two doctors, a watch repair shop, and a dressmaker serving the town of about 600 souls. Additionally, about thirty-five illegal stills thrived. Forty Mile was known as the town "where bread is often lacking, but whiskey's never scarce." Also, for the first time in the Far Northwest, enough of the wandering prospectors had gathered in one place that it became profitable for various lowlifes—those that invariably find their way into gold rush towns to mine the miners—to set up business in Forty Mile.

McQuesten loyalists still disliked J. J. Healy. When Healy—who before coming north had reportedly thumbed his nose at several constabularies and agencies over various and sundry whiskey-making and trading violations—committed a minor infraction of the Miners Code, old Yukoners hauled him before their tribunal. Used to running things their own way, they tagged Healy with a stiff fine. Smugly feeling they had the whip hand of the country, they demanded he pay.

Healy being Healy, was anything but the type to roll over. Deciding it was time to put the Yukoners in their place, he called on the faraway North West Mounted Police (NWMP). The appeal gained strength when William Ogilvie vouched that not only was it time for Canada to establish authority over the American-ruled town, but high time for Ottawa to begin collecting the thousands of dollars in customs due on American goods that were coming in and the large amount of duty the Canadians were losing on Dominion gold going out. And then, there was that little issue of the estimated three thousand gallons of whiskey yearly coming over the border or being distilled in the locality.

By 1895 twenty NWMP constables were building Fort Constantine, newly established on the Fortymile mouth. To the far Northwest had come Canadian sovereignty and law.

About 180 river miles downstream from the Alaska-Canada border, small findings in 1891 and 1892 had been followed by the most sizeable discovery of gold along the Yukon up to that time, the 1893 Birch Creek strike. Since that was the general area Jack McQuesten had originally been attracted to prospect upon his 1873 arrival at Fort

Yukon after hearing reports of Rev. Robert McDonald's 1860s find somewhere around Birch Creek, Jack had likely been expecting that sooner or later strikes would be made in that country. In fact, he had grubstaked the two Russian-Koyukon Creole discoverers who often worked for him, Sergei Cherosky and Pitka Pavaloff. On Preacher Creek, and along several other creeks near Birch Creek, prospectors made several other sizeable 1893 discoveries.

As Jack McQuesten steamed upriver in 1893, he came upon about seventy-five miners flagging him down. They had been waiting along the bank for his arrival. At a new location they had begun establishing a service center for this new Birch Creek strike area. They had plotted the townsite and about thirty cabins were going up. They needed supplies.

A spring flood in 1894 wiped out that new town. However, the miners, ever able to roll with a punch, quickly reestablished it on more suitable ground 12 miles downstream. Thinking it was on the Arctic Circle, they named their new town, Circle City. On July 29 the steamer *Arctic* arrived in Forty Mile carrying a letter from George Cary appealing to one and all to come down. Forthwith, Jack McQuesten offered to grubstake any who would move the 220 miles downstream to prospect that area. More than eighty men—mostly Forty Milers— took him up on his offer. They went down, fanned out, and made more strikes. Thereby, Jack McQuesten became one of the principal founders of Circle City, Alaska. By mid-1894, Miller, Mastodon and Independence creeks were discovered and became the core of the newly designated Circle Mining District. Over 300 men wintered in Circle City in 1894.

By 1895 the white population of the Yukon Basin was growing at an increased pace. With miners still mining in the Fortymile and Sixtymile and a few other streams back on the Canadian side, and with Circle having grown to 700, about one thousand whites inhabited the Basin. By the summer of 1896, drawn by reports of substantial finds on both sides of the border, the white population along the Upper Yukon reached about 1,500 to 2,000.

During this time period, particularly slowing the exodus to the Alaska side were finds on the Sixtymile. Miller Creek (different from

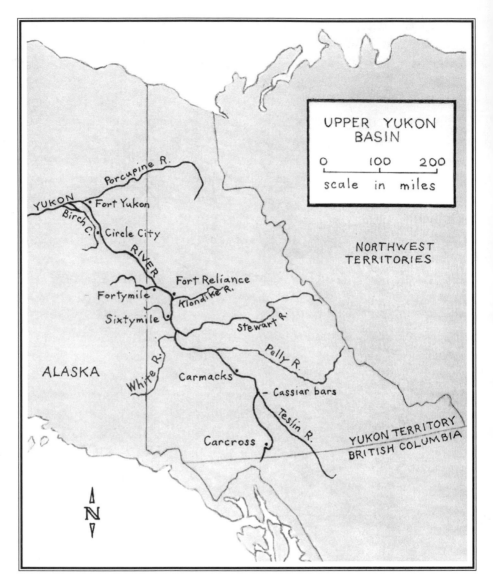

UPPER YUKON
BASIN

0   100   200

scale   in   miles

the Miller Creek of the Circle District), a tributary only 6 miles long, proved to be the richest ground found in the Yukon Basin to that date. Miners took over $300,000 out of there in 1894 and by 1896, $500,000 was mined there.

The confluences of the Sixtymile with the Yukon River and that of the Fortymile were ninety-seven miles apart. But because of the way the drainages lay, mines far up the Sixtymile could be readily accessed from the supply center of Forty Mile. Someone needing to haul light freight could, with minimal effort, make a moderately easy round trip. By canoeing a distance up the Fortymile River and carrying everything over a short portage south into the Sixtymile drainage, the traveler or freighter could go with Sixtymile current down to the Yukon mouth and float the Yukon downstream to Fortymile. All water except for the short distance up the Fortymile was downstream going.

———◆——◆———

Alma Preston: "Rod, maybe you've heard of The Goin' Kid. Talk about live energy! He could hardly sit still and was always happiest while on the move. Back in the old days he and his team were known from Skagway to Kotzebue and Seward to Coldfoot, one of the greatest names on the northern trails. He had an interesting way of talking; it was very fast and full of action. He told me about how it was just before the big strike."

———◆——◆———

The Goin' Kid: "Miss Alma, most miners workin' so-so Fortymile claims abandon their diggin's 'n stampede down t' the richer strikes . 'round Circle City. Most all the miners work in partnerships. Sworn on a solemn handshake. Nothin's fine's a true, loyal, hardworkin' pard. On better Fortymile locations, many partnerships diversify. One stays workin' Fortymile. Keeps their proven diggin's bringin' income. Smart; bird 'n the hand. His pard drops way down t' the Circle District tryin' t' find a bird 'n the bush t' expand joint holdin's. Those stayin' up'n the Fortymile keep producin'. In 1895, they take $400,000 out o' there. In 1896 on just two cricks alone in the Fortymile District, miners take out 'bout $300,000 in gold.

"But Miss Alma, as it's 'bout t' play out, most payin' thing some o' those Fortymilers ever do's stay put. In their wildest dreams they don't know it, but they're keepin' positioned close to a giant strike 'bout t' happen. That is, at least the ones around that're close t' town, not minin' way back up the Fortymile's farthest reaches. The close ones're ready t' be the first t' reach the most incredible placer gold diggins this world's ever seen. Get first stab at the claims. 'Fore a year's passed, many Fortymilers're goin' t' be hog-nasty rich. Course, that'll make their pard down 'n the Circle District right filthy, too."

Down in the Circle Mining District, the richest mines lay many miles back from the main river. However, because it was well situated on the stretch of the Yukon closest to the finds, and offered high ground for a townsite with water deep enough for riverboats to pull in, Circle City quickly grew as a service center for the district. So while Forty Mile, Yukon District was the first town on the Upper Yukon, Circle City was the first *Alaska town* on the Upper Yukon.

Jack McQuesten again moved in response to the miners' needs. In 1894 he established an Alaska Commercial Company store at Circle City. The following year the NAT&T built a rival store there. Circle City

McQuesten and Co. Trading and Supply Center at Circle.
Jack (Behind Dog) and Pal Fred Harte Stand Near Far Left.
James McQuiston Collection

became known as the largest log town in the world. At its peak it boasted a library, a school, a post office, a hospital, a newspaper: *The Yukon Press*, two theaters, and an opera house. The single Episcopal Church preached the evils of the eight dance halls, more than 25 saloons, and ever-present ladies of "The Row."

Bedrock along Birch Creek and its tributaries lay relatively close to the surface. Since most of the mining was shallow diggings, miners were saved a lot of work. But the nature of the mining made it so it could go on only during summers. Because it was so unproductive to accomplish anything but freighting after

Yukon Pioneers Jack McQuesten and Fred Harte.

Detail from previous photo

freeze-up, almost the whole nearby population came in from their outlying claims to winter in town. Those were idyllic days in Circle City, to which old-timers later nostalgically referred. The acknowledged leader of the community, by virtue of his sharp intelligence, open generosity, impeccable integrity, and trust in the eyes of his fellow pioneers was Jack McQuesten.

Years before, during his numerous trips to St. Michael he had become close friends with the famous biologist and ethnographer Edward W. Nelson. (For a few years, Nelson lived among and recorded life of Yupik Eskimos near the redoubt.) Nelson would go on to become one of the most famous naturalists in U.S. history, a prominent collector for the Smithsonian Institution, Chief of the Bureau of Biological Survey, and one of the fathers of the U.S. Fish and Wildlife Service. Out of their friendship Jack grew interested in helping Nelson collect specimens. Some reside to this day at the Smithsonian, most notably, the first Alaska-Yukon sheepskin ever made available for scientific examination. After McQuesten secured it from an Indian and shipped it to him, Nelson began the description of the species. He named it *Ovis dalli* for his cohort, William Healey Dall.

In one correspondence Jack announced to Nelson that he had collected for the Smithsonian a bear of a species surely new to science. Jack described the specimen as a mountain animal adapted to sidehill travel, having evolved long legs on one side, short legs on the other. Jack had previously sent hundreds of well-prepared bird and mammal skins and had recorded daily weather observations for Nelson. Familiar with Jack's history of serious scientific contributions, but unfamiliar with the extent of his sense of humor, Nelson and his biologist cohorts were momentarily puzzled over Jack's report, then laughed with their Yukoner friend at the bizarre notion of an animal genetically sentenced to spend life going in one direction.

Jack became famous for his huge vegetable gardens, especially his great crops of turnips. He raised and trained Susan and Kate, a pair of moose, to plow. He plowed with sled dogs as well.

In the year 1892, violence back in the States had revealed a symptom of economic tension a-brewing: eighteen had been killed in a steel-mill battle between union workers and Pinkerton guards. The year 1893 had seen the United States fall into a major depression. By the end of 1895 many of the continent's most powerful businesses had gone belly-up. Numerous huge trusts and conglomerates along with innumerable lesser corporations went down. Great railroads, banks, mortgage companies, and manufacturers crashed. Wave after wave of misfortune dashed on the rocks thousands of medium and small businesses. In Chicago, 100,000 workers and in New York, 70,000 found themselves on the street, unemployed. Immigrants who reached our shores milled about jobless and homeless. The nation's gold reserves were drained and what remained was hoarded by a population in fear. In desperation the country looked this way and that, searching for an escape—something, anything that would give them even a glimmer of hope. Within the population millions were at a loss to know where to find their next dollar, many even their next meal.

Forced into a search mode, more men turned their eyes north. As the United States and Canada were primed by the economic

Jack and Helper Plow His Garden.
James McQuiston Collection

depression, word of the gold finds along the Yukon circulated among opportunistic types who kept their ear to the ground. From mid-March through April of 1896, a notable increase in the number of gold-seekers left Seattle bound for Forty Mile, Circle City, or other Upper Yukon locations. William Ogilvie estimated that at its peak as many as 3,000 may have supplied themselves out of Circle City.

In the Circle District as at Forty Mile, hundreds of tons of supplies could be boated up the Yukon and off-loaded into warehouses where it awaited either consumption in town or winter transport by sled far back to the mines. Also during the ice-free summers, because many Circle District discoveries lay relatively close to Birch Creek water at least reachable by tracking and poling, as much as possible was boated in closer to some of the mines by smaller craft.

After freeze-up, however, nothing could be boated closer than upper Lynn Canal. From Circle City that was some 850 tortuous, peril-fraught winter trail miles away up the Yukon and over Chilkoot Pass. Distance, difficulty, and danger combined to make the trip out of the question for anything but mail, and almost prohibitive for even that. The situation cried out for a faster, easier overland winter transport connection to ocean shipping waters. Since McQuesten, Harper, and their groups had arrived two decades earlier they had faced the same state of affairs: seven to eight months a year was a long time to go without contact or supply from the outside world. Now with population along the Yukon growing at an increasing rate, demand for better winter travel, transport, and communication climbed apace.

Of course, through the years while there were yet too few people in the North, the early strikes had been too small to raise more than passing interest among the general populations of the United States and Canada. The Far Northwest had remained out-of-sight, out-of-mind to distant governments. There was no chance that the powers-that-be would consider going to the expense and effort of constructing year-round surface transportation lines. But all of that was about to see dramatic change.

The single greatest watershed occurrence, the very seminal moment in the history of the North was in the offing. It was destined to blow the lid off everything that held back development of travel and supply systems serving the Yukon Basin.

Chapter 11

The Fabulous Klondike Strike

TWO YEARS AFTER PACKING AS FAR AS FORTY MILE for William Ogilvie during Ogilvie's survey of the Alaska Yukon boundary in 1887, George Carmack with his wife Kate moved from Carcross, where they had been living with Skookum Jim and the rest of their Tagish relatives. The couple began to headquarter hundreds of miles downstream.

Seven years later, on July 1, 1896 at Forty Mile, Jack McQuesten grubstaked the most important foray in the history of the Northland. Carmack requested to be staked so that he might make a trip to the Thron-diuck River. There he intended to combine prospecting (for building logs and gold) and fishing. He promised Jack that if his prospecting failed to turn up anything he would repay in dried salmon, always a valuable commodity to Jack for his dogs. Upon securing $130 worth of supplies, that day George and Kate began boating up the Yukon toward the Thron-diuck.

By whatever method information along the river traveled, 500 miles upstream word reached Skookum Jim that George and Kate would be fishing on the Thron-diuck River. He and his relative, Tagish Charlie, and Charlie's nephew, Patsy Henderson, ventured downriver to join the Carmacks. Such a trip must have been carefully considered. Though the three vigorous men could have easily made the trip down in half a week by doing little more than merely drifting passively around the clock with the speed of the current, their return trip requiring laborious poling and tracking against the flow would have required several weeks.

Rod Perry: *However, as circumstances would soon play out, were the Tagish men to wish to buy outright the finest steamboat on the river to*

179

take them back to the head of navigation, they would be able to afford the queen of the fleet itself by the next shipping season!

———◆—◆———

The three found the pair fishing for salmon at a long-established Native fish camp at the mouth of the Thron-diuck. That river of beautifully clear water flows into the Yukon from the northeast. Its confluence is located about ninety-two miles above the United States-Canada boundary, fifty-two above Forty Mile, and just six miles—barely more than shouting distance—above the old site of Jack McQuesten's Fort Reliance.

Shortly, the group met Robert Henderson, a miner from Nova Scotia. In their wildest imaginations, never could Carmack and Henderson have dreamed that the chance encounter would not only dramatically impact the lives of everyone present but that the happenstance was destined to explode upon and change the history of all of northwestern North America.

Henderson had turned to professional prospecting some years before in Colorado. He had come over the Chilkoot Pass in 1894. Headed for either Forty Mile or Birch Creek, he happened to meet Joe Ladue. The firm of Harper and Ladue had recently established a trading post at the mouth of the Sixtymile River, naming the site Ogilvie. Like Harper, McQuesten, and Mayo, Ladue possessed an unbridled enthusiasm for the future of the Yukon Basin. He had particular faith in the potential of the area draining into the Yukon near his new post. Joe Ladue and Robert Henderson hit it off immediately. The trading post owner convinced the newcomer to remain in the area. Like the rest of the Canadian Yukon, the area outside the main mining center of Miller Creek on the Sixtymile and the producing areas along the Fortymile had been nearly deserted following the rush to the Circle District. However, many who had initially rushed down, but failed to find anything substantial in those downriver diggings had returned upstream to reexamine the Stewart, Sixtymile, and other upper Yukon areas. To such, Harper and Ladue served as their supply source.

The Nova Scotian secured a grubstake from his new friend. He then launched a dedicated search for gold up the Indian River, which drains into the Yukon just south of the Thron-diuck. With a companion he prospected his way along until they ascended a northern tributary, Quartz Creek, to the divide where they could look over into Thron-diuck drainage. Impressed enough to try the creek, the men went back to get more supplies from Ladue. They devoted the next year to mining Quartz Creek and prospecting Indian River.

From the Quartz Creek bars, Henderson had mined about $600 in the spring of 1896. That amounted to almost a year's wages for a laborer back in civilized Canada. Buoyed by that success and optimistic that the region held something even better, with four others he had again ascended Quartz Creek. Then they crossed over the divide into the Thron-diuck drainage into which he had previously gazed. Prospecting down that tributary creek Henderson named Gold Bottom, the men found good prospects and began mining. Taking the first gold from the basin, Robert Henderson became the true discoverer of the Thron-diuck—about to be renamed the Klondike.

Rod Perry: *Interestingly, of the four big gold strikes of northern Alaska, the discoverer of the first (the Klondike) and codiscoverer of the last (Iditarod)—Henderson and John Beaton, respectively—issued from the small maritime province of Nova Scotia.*

By the time the men had $700 to show for their efforts they had run out of food. Henderson made a resupply run to Ogilvie. (Using Ogilvie as his resupply point instead of Forty Mile, the only place in the nearby region where miners could officially file a claim, would later cost Henderson dearly.)

His return route from Ogilvie would take him forty-five miles down the Yukon to the Thron-diuck, thence up to Gold Bottom. (By that time everyone knew it was fifty-one miles down to Reliance—six miles below the Thron-diuck—not sixty as per the early estimates.) Robert Henderson's appearance with a boatload of supplies turning into the Thron-diuck outflow surprised George Carmack at his fish camp.

Honor-bound to follow the traditional *Code of the Prospector*, Henderson openly informed Carmack of his discoveries and his general belief that the nearby country held great promise. Henderson encouraged him to prospect in the vicinity. He even invited him to stake a claim near his own. He requested that he be quickly informed if Carmack found anything profitable.

So far the interchange had gone swimmingly. Then, tragically for Henderson, he abruptly turned it sour. Holding Carmack's Tagish relatives in scathing disdain, Henderson emphatically stated that he did not want any "d—d Siwashes" (meaning Indians) mining near him! When the offended Carmack shot back that he would be loyal to his wife and relatives in any venture, the two men parted somewhat disagreeably.

Over the years, Carmack had been, at most, a casual gold prospector. At the time he was thinking more about prospects for cutting a raft of building logs for which he had an offer and floating them down to Forty Mile. His family group looked for suitable timber up the *Thron-diuck*, hunting moose as they went. Finally, being out of food and tobacco, and deciding to look over Henderson's prospects, Carmack and the men took a route up a tributary known to the Natives as Rabbit Creek. Dabbling at prospecting, they found a few colors as they went, and once even a ten-cent pan. At the time that was considered a very good prospect, but they were hungry and went on. They proceeded over a divide, laboriously bushwhacking twenty-five miles from their camp to Henderson's.

———————

George Carmack: "Twenty-five miles beating the thick brush and mosquitoes cross-country is tedious and fatiguing. It takes a lot out of you anytime, but especially when you're hungry. When we got there, Henderson sure gave us the cold shoulder. He did sell us a little food, a meal or two just to get us back to our camp. But he flatly refused my relatives tobacco. Henderson strongly stated again, 'I told you once and I'll tell you again, I do not want them mining anywhere close to me!' As I was later quoted, 'His childish, unreasoning prejudice would not even allow him to stake on the same creek with the despised Siwashes so his obstinacy cost him a fortune.'"

Rod Perry: *By most accounts, because of the rebuff, Carmack withheld telling Henderson of the ten-cent pan. However, Carmack later insisted that he had informed him, but that Henderson declined because he wanted to reach bedrock to see what Gold Bottom held.*

Carmack and his company straggled back. Famished, they diligently hunted moose. As they hunted, they kept looking for stands of suitable house logs and continued evaluating Rabbit Creek to see if it were possible to float them down its course. Additionally, from the head of the drainage down, they checked for gold. But as their hunger took them to the point of weakness, desire to hunt anything but food waned.

By all accounts, no one had ever prospected the stream. During his years at Fort Reliance, Jack McQuesten had tramped over it while hunting. Joe Ladue had camped one night on a tributary, which would be named El Dorado Creek and later become the site of mines worth not just millions, but billions. But he, too, had been trying to fill the cooking pot, not gold pan. The few gold seekers who had previously searched up the main Thron-diuck had missed Rabbit Creek entirely. Its confluence was doubly hidden from anyone passing up or down the river; not only did an island block view of its mouth, the juncture was obscured because just before its confluence, the lesser stream spread out into a low area of shallow slackwater.

Near where they had grown too famished to continue prospecting, Jim killed a moose. They camped to butcher and eat. Jim went down to the stream to dip a pot of water, by chance at a point where bedrock rose to the surface. There Skookum Jim made a startling discovery, rich almost beyond belief. Carmack later said that as they lifted slabs of rock, gold appeared "like cheese on a sandwich!" With the moose to sustain them, the men prospected hard for two days, searching for what they thought would be the richest ground. On August 17, George

Carmack four-sided a small spruce in the middle of the valley and wrote on it with pencil words that would turn the history of the Canadian Yukon and Alaska: "To Whom It May Concern: I do, this day, locate and claim, by right of discovery, five hundred feet, running up stream from this notice. Located this 17th day of August, 1896. G.W. Carmack."

For Jim they staked One Above. Carmack took, beside Discovery, One Below. (In Canada's Yukon the person who was recorded as the discoverer of a new strike was due a second claim.) And Two Below went to Charlie.

The group renamed the stream, Bonanza Creek. The area held such rich deposits that over $30 million—about $4.5 billion adjusting for more than 100 years of inflation and the vast increase in the price of gold—eventually would be taken from the gravel of El Dorado Creek, just one, five-mile-long tributary to Bonanza Creek!

There arose some disagreement about who would get the discovery claim. Yes, Jim made the find. But it was George who headed up their party and had been directing movements and activities. It was George whom Henderson had encouraged and it was George who had the market for logs that was a big reason for them checking the Rabbit Creek drainage. The group finally agreed that it made good sense for Carmack to record as the discoverer. They reasoned that, given the prevalent racist attitudes, other miners would not recognize the claim of a native. Therefore, George Carmack is widely credited with the discovery. In a way he was indeed due credit. He and Jim agreed that they would partner on the extra discovery claim.

On their way to Forty Mile to record, at the mouth of Rabbit Creek they met four prospectors heading up the Thron-diuck River. Carmack redirected them up Rabbit Creek. He did the same with two Frenchmen they ran into at the Thron-duick mouth. All of that human presence concerned Carmack enough that he sent Jim back to look after their interests and begin setting up a sawpit to whipsaw lumber for sluice boxes. Carmack tipped off other miners they passed on their way down to Forty Mile, holding to the *Code of the Prospector*.

To his everlasting discredit, Carmack, in his offended pride, refused to honor the Code to the one he owed the most. He could have taken the moral high road and risen above Henderson's racial insults. He could have sent one of his party to Gold Bottom to inform the man who was greatly responsible for Carmack even looking for gold on Rabbit Creek, prejudiced though the man was. Instead, George Carmack headed to Forty Mile to record the claim without sending word, leaving Robert Henderson to unknowingly mine lesser ground just a long day's walk over the divide.

———————

George Carmack: "When we went over to his camp on Gold Bottom, and he didn't want my relatives around, what's it to him who's working a claim that's not his? Especially if we had staked claims well separated up or down the creek from his. He was so narrow-minded and hateful. When he insulted my relatives he was denigrating me for marrying into their people. I suppose I could have sent Charlie over to his camp again to give Henderson the heads-up. But I'll tell you, with no trail, a fifty-mile round trip beating the brush isn't something to be taken lightly; even a woodsman good as a Tagish doesn't do it with a wave of the hand. And after Henderson's hateful rejection just a few days before? If it was still grating on me, just imagine how Charlie must have felt to be so despised. Think how it would have been between Charlie and me if I had twisted his arm to go against his will.

"I don't know, maybe I should have seen to it that he get the early tip. Maybe returning good for evil and letting him feel small and cheap would have made for adequate payback.

"We had found that gold by the moose, but who knew whether there were much better prospects up or down the valley? We couldn't lollygag because we couldn't tell if we might be all alone or maybe someone else is poking around the drainage. Time was of the essence. So we all set to driving ourselves hard, and we needed the benefit of every one of us helping look to see if there's richer ground, not just stake the first place we struck. How could we spare one of us to be a runner over to Henderson? We've got to come to a decision on a stretch of creek, stake, and race for Forty Mile to secure the discovery claim. If someone swooped in, staked, and beat me to town to record, he'd pick off discovery rights. As the ground turned out, we'd have

George Carmack

lost a king's ransom. I think anyone in my shoes would have been in a hurry to do exactly what we did.

"Join that reasoning with the combination of our excitement and our feelings about Henderson and you can see why I did what I did. And to say it again, everyone should forever remember this: he told us he didn't want to mine anywhere near any Siwashes, didn't he? Well, if he didn't even want my relatives on the same creek with him over on his Gold Bottom show, how would he have been satisfied working Bonanza with Kate, Jim and Charlie anywhere on the same drainage? You could say we were just honoring his own stated boundaries."

Chapter 12

———◆———

Miners Positioned in the Yukon
Lead the Stampede

The Goin' Kid: "In Forty Mile, most o' the hands 'n town're new t' the country, just cheechakos. Lotta old-timers're way back on the cricks workin' their distant claims. Many o' the greenhorns're just millin' 'round idle. Aren't lazy, most've given the country all they got. Tuckered themselves getting' into the Yukon 'n prospectin' hard all summer. All with no luck. Now summer's endin'. Most're hangin' 'round, faces long as a horse. Down 'n dejected 'n plannin' t' quit the country. Quite a few've tied on a long drunk. More sober o' the drunks c'n only stand by holdin' onto somethin'.

"Then Carmack blows in.

"Before recordin', Carmack stands before a group 'n Bill McPhee's saloon 'n announces 'is find. Ol-timers think o' George as lackin' motivation. Not much of a prospector. Always braggin' t' make 'imself look good. They never thought 'is word t' be altogether trusted. So the few sourdoughs 'n town sway the newcomers t' think down on 'im. First off, nobody believes 'im. But you know, seein's believin'.

"Kinda theatrical like, George Carmack unpockets this cartridge case and holds it up. Twists out a willow plug. Then 'e dribbles the contents out 'n the table. It's not the amount, it's the look of it. The ol'-timers know every crick's gold carries its own signature. This looks like nothin' from anywhere they know. Got t' be new ground. One minute everyone's lookin' at the gold, list'nin' as the ol' sourdoughs mutter their comments. Next minute, the bar door's not big enough. Starts right there at that moment, Miss Alma, most marvelous gold stampede o' the age. A rush that's the beat o' any this world's ever known blows sky high.

"One's almost a cheechako, a bartender standin' by. McPhee agrees t' grubstake 'im as he's tearin' off 'is apron 'n turnin' t' run. Don't know much 'bout gold huntin', 'e don't, even though once previous 'e worked a claim. But 'n a year Clarence Berry'll be a 'Klondike King' known all over this green earth.

"By the followin mornin', the bustlin' town o' Forty Mile's bustlin' no longer. Coulda heard a spider tip-toein' across McPhee's saloon floor. Every man Jack just pours outta Forty Mile like that gold outta George's cartridge case. Day after, you c'n almost hear the dust settle on Bill's bar. 'Bout no one left but the traders 'n North West Mounted Police. Actually, the Mounties even get gold fever. A bunch're granted leave t' go stake.

"Remember I told you how lucky 'twas goin' t' turn out fer men t' stay around instead o' rushin' down t' Circle City? Circle's about 270 miles down the Yukon from the strike. But Forty Mile's only fifty-two miles downriver from the Klondike. Forty Milers'll be the first big group t' reach Bonanza and Eldorado cricks. News spreads fast as men c'n run, pole 'n paddle."

———◆—◆———

AFTER ALERTING THE CROWD, Carmack strode to the North West Mounted Police post to record the four claims. Imagine the irony and his dismay when he was told that the gold he had brought was insufficient to pay the filing fees! However, consistent with the character admired by all along the upper river, Inspector Charles Constantine settled Carmack's fears by gracing him with time to go back and pan out enough to pay.

———◆—◆———

Old Ben Atwater: : "Al, even a few of the Forty Milers who'd been wasted in a drunken stupor for weeks weren't left behind. Loyal friends and partners dumped them in the bottom of their boats. Just shipped them upriver like so much deadweight ballast. Most of 'em scarcely realized they were passengers. It's a two-day pole up to the Klondike, but in this case just one going day and night in such a fever. One souse I knew of didn't sober up enough to know he'd even left Forty Mile until his partners had him within fifteen miles of the strike. Same's if he had good sense, hanged if that drunk didn't stumble into one of the richest claims in the country!

"The first few there raced up the creeks and down. Al, you know how it would be. You get there and you don't want to stake the first place you come to on the creek. You want to test enough to find the thickest concentrations. But with the hordes following close on your heels, you know you haven't got much time. Let's say you take time to test ten separated spots to make up your mind. By the time you decide maybe it's heaviest back on the fourth location you tested, you race back and chances are some other guy's already staked it. So in a stampede like that you have to keep contemplations to a minimum. You take a stab and trust a lot to Dame Fortune.

"Well, within a few days of the first frenzy some of the early dust started to settle. Word swept up and down the creeks about what others were finding. Some claims didn't have much showing at the surface at all. But on enough claims there was plenty near the top. The general impression prevailed the ground held deposits the like of which none had ever seen or heard. Or even dreamed. Fortymile miners'd been averaging about $800 a year. Now on the Klondike, some claims showing strongest at the surface, a man could work out that much in part of a day. (Later, as they went deeper into the heaviest concentrations, a story of at least one $800 pan was reported.)

"Soon as people had their stakes set, those with friends and partners working elsewhere hurried to send word to those they could reach. The cry went up the Yukon, the cry went down. The Bonanza and El Dorado claim holders themselves couldn't leave. So a lot hired Indians as messengers. Told them to pull out all stops—just burn up their moccasins and paddles—to go fetch their friends. Letters carried on the moccasin and birch-bark express urged miners in other districts to drop everything. Here's a sample note:

August 26 Joe, you got to pay close attention to this here. I don't care how good you think the deposit is your working. DROP IT! It ain't worth the deposit behind the log compared to what I got on Rabbit Creek. This here's the stampede for the ages. Get yourself down to the Tron-duck. Find me at 6 above. I tell you leave most everything but the shirt on your back and high-tail it. Some stretches still not staked. Lots of fractions. Set the trail on fire cause hombres pouring in more by the hour. Minutes count. Don't sleep or sit to rest and if you fall down don't even stop to get up just keep right on coming.   Zeke

"Oh, I tell you Al, the great stampede was on, alright, was it ever on! Klondike fever spreading faster than a smallpox epidemic. Miners up on Sixtymile River just forty-five miles above the Klondike showed Ladue's Ogilvie station a fast-disappearing stern. Whah! Even Joe Ladue himself showed Ogilvie a fast-disappearing stern! A short distance farther above Ogilvie the boys still mining the Stewart River bounded for their boats. Quick as messengers reached other upriver diggings, miners threw down what they were doing when they were handed the letters. Most never slowed enough to snatch up anything much beyond the essential pick, shovel, pan, and gum boots.

"Except for one big encampment. They thought it'd be worth just a few minutes to go better prepared. Pell-mell, tearing wild around the camp, on the dead run they scooped things up they thought they needed most. They threw armloads in the boats, wheeled without stopping, and churned back for another grab. Racing back and forth between the tents and the boats, the scene was all crazed arms and legs—looked like a handful o' durned spiders tossed on a hot stove. They sprang in their boats and turned the Yukon to a froth, off to the Klondike in full howl."

———•——•———

Rod Perry: *As it is written, "The rain falls on both the just and unjust." It must have been maddening and discouraging to the worthy old-timers that a disproportionate amount of the good fortune fell on others. Circumstances dealt such a cruel blow to many of the most knowledgeable, dedicated miners, those who had been in the country the longest and were the most industrious. The persistence and diligent labor that had previously rewarded many of them with paying mines now worked against them.*

When news of Carmack's strike reached Forty Mile and the other supply hubs for the various mining districts, many of the real sourdoughs were hard at work on their distant claims far back on the creeks (where an average of 25 cents a pan was considered top paydirt). So they were the last to get the report. Shopkeepers, newcomers, drunks, gamblers, and others who happened to be around the supply centers were therefore the most available to stampede to the Klondike (where, as Ben Atwater said, fables of a single pan of $800 would eventually be told). They staked their choice of the most promising-looking ground long before news reached most of the top miners.

Old Ben Atwater: "Knew a guy named Bill Liggett. A real first-class prospector. And smart as anything. When Bill first heard the rumors he just shrugged them off. Seasoned sourdoughs like us, we all remembered many a stampede that'd led excited men, usually tenderfoot cheechakos, to rush off to a nothing more'n a whole lot of nuthin'. That just wasted what little time, energy, and money they had. Like I said, Bill was an excellent prospector. And he was a careful businessman. During his years in the region he'd already developed some successful finds. Always took his money Outside and invested it. At the time Lyin' George and his party made the Klondike strike, Liggett was working a very profitable claim. He had no intention to leave it for some goose chase.

"So at first he pooh-poohed the fabulous rumors. He kept thinking the tales ridin' the winds from claim to claim up and down the creeks seemed so far-fetched. Just way too tall to be true. Nobody'd ever heard of such concentrations. But Bill told me finally reports just stacked up too fast one on top of the other. He couldn't keep discounting them. The moment he believed, he made a lightning-quick decision.

"Remember, I mentioned how financially wise Bill Liggett was? Never gambled, never wasted. Just tighter than bark on a birch when it came to him holding onto his hard-earned. But you know what? Bill told me he just dropped his pick right where he stood. He hot-footed to his cabin, snatched up only a very few essentials and dashed down to the Yukon. He left behind his lucrative claim. And his snug little cabin and cache. Most valuable, he left behind a year's stock of provisions. Bill did what not many would do. But it turned out he knew what he was doing. Even a minute's difference in that great stampede could let a competitor beat you out for a claim you'd have staked. In such a race for riches that could mean the difference in setting you up for life or missing out. So for Liggett, keeping things light and fast was most important. He even left his tools, camp gear, and rifle. Never saw hide nor hair of a bit of it ever again.

"Liggett bounded into his skiff. The man poled and paddled like the devil himself was sitting on the stern glaring, prodding with his pitchfork and threatening hell as a consequence if Bill let up one bit. He pushed to his limits day and night 'til he reached the Klondike. But when he got up there, all he found was a sea of fresh-skinned spruce stakes gleaming white as porcupine quills. Every piece of decent ground along the two main creeks was already staked.

"A number of other sourdoughs like me had finally come to see. Was it just another snipe hunt or a real find? Most of us old experienced hands thought the surface indications were all wrong. 'Willows lean the wrong way,' some said, an we nodded. 'Valley's too broad. Soil's wrong. Water doesn't taste right.' And we turned our back on it. Left the discovery mostly to the know-nothings. They went out and staked the whole blame country.

"Liggett was smarter. He could see the landscape didn't look right. Yet he looked into it more carefully. He saw the early test pans'd showed it held gold, maybe lots of gold. He walked around and rubbed his chin. Ligget picked out what he thought looked like the most promising part of the new show. He just goes right up to one of the claimholders. Not Swiftwater Bill but one of the others on No. 13 above. The guy was a newcomer. And he didn't really know what the ground held yet. Ol' Liggett offers the guy more money than he'd seen in all his born days. Just too tempting to turn down. A three-eights share in Thirteen Above, El Dorado is what changed hands. That little part of one claim made Bill Liggett one of the richest of the Klondike kings.

"Everybody that's heard about the rush read about how Ol' Swiftwater cast gold from his part of Thirteen Above around like it was dirt. Whiskey, dance hall floozies an' strumpets and thousands bet on the turn of a card, Wagh! comparing wouldda made the very prodigal son himself look like an alter boy. Well, Liggett didn't broadcast the wealth he took from his part of that same claim, but from what we all know about that gnat-brained fool Swiftwater, it's an easy guess. And Bill Liggett kept every ounce of his."

"George, Jim, and Charlie staked Discovery where they did 'cause they saw bedrock was so close to the surface. It didn't take them long to work out enough to file. The three took $1,400 down to Forty Mile and on September 24, 1896 they recorded."

———◆—◆———

Rod Perry: *And what became of Robert Henderson, who gained credit as being the discoverer of gold on the Klondike? In perhaps a case of poetic justice, Henderson indeed got to maintain his prejudiced parameters: He did not have to mine near any "d—d Siwashes." Though he was working just over the hill, he did not learn about the great strike until three weeks after Carmack and his Native relatives struck it rich.*

By then it was too late. Within just two weeks, by the end of August 1896, the whole length of Bonanza and El Dorado creeks had been staked. When he belatedly heard the news, he just sat down and buried his face in his hands. In the depths of his utter disappointment he was unable to so much as speak. Later, the Canadian government would recognize him for his part in the discovery and reward him with a small pension.

Actually, though Henderson and his fellows were first to work at mining gold from the Klondike drainage, they were far from the original discoverers. *Joe Ladue, John and Pete Nelson, and Dan Sprague beat Henderson by a decade when they found a little gold while prospecting the river's upper reaches in 1886. They just didn't find enough to be worth mining.*

———◆—◆———

Old Ben Atwater: "I forgot to tell the important part about Joe Ladue racing away from his and Harper's Ogilvie post when he found the strike was a big one. When he pulled in down at the Klondike, Joe, real quick, scanned not for gold, but the mining support situation. From the Yukon, the only natural place to start back into the country to the diggings was from the Klondike mouth. Any fool could see plain as the hand in front of your face that a supply point to the mines would have to be built where Yukon steamers could tie up at the confluence. It happened a flat piece of land was located smack there. It was the only ground fit for a townsite. He real fast claimed most of the flat.

"He knew he was in a race. Miners and suppliers would start demanding ground. And winter was right around the corner, coming fast. So he had a messenger take his claim down to Forty Mile. While it was getting recorded. Joe pushed the forty-five miles back up to his Ogilvie post. Quick as he could, he floated supplies and his sawmill back down. Along with his monopoly on town lots, he also sold most of the logs and lumber that built the town. He named his town Dawson for a man he admired. George M. Dawson was a geologist who Joe met when the Canadian government sent the man in to explore and map the upper Yukon back in '87. But Joe could have just as well named his town, 'Ladue.'"

Watching the rush, Joe Ladue saw that to travel light and get there quickly, several hundred early entrants into the district had left their food and gear behind. He lost no time moving contents of the Ogilvie trading post at Sixtymile downriver to his new town location. Ladue and Harper had only originally provisioned the beautifully constructed Ogilvie post for the much smaller number of miners that had been working that immediate area. So when their Ogilvie supply reached Dawson it was not nearly sufficient to sustain through the winter what amounted to a gathering of almost the entire white population of the upper Yukon Basin.

The Goin' Kid: "Back 'n the Fortymile, news spreads upstream. Claim t' claim, it gets there quick t' miners 'n the lower reaches nearer town. But the main center o' minin' activity lies eighty-five miles up the Fortymile River. On the most distant forks some're workin' ground over a hundred up. The way some on the middle 'n upper reaches get in on it, they start noticin' a funny thing. Somethin' mighty queer's goin on, a definite pattern. No miner who goes down fer supplies ever comes back. So some of 'em upriver sniff that somethin' mighty important must be holdin' 'em. But fer others who don't respond t' such flimsy suspicions, they have t' wait'l the river freezes. Then we dog-team freighters c'n first mush their supply orders upstream. Not'll we pull in does word o' the Klondike penetrate t' the most distant camps. By then the stampede's old as Adam and Eve.

"You know what? When they do hear, some run. But many o' the ol sourdoughs with the most years under 'em choose t' stay put. They're least likely t' leave profitable diggin's t' go flyin' off chasin' after wild tales. Sounds downright outlandish to 'em. Whoever heard o' gold that thick? An' the delay stretches even worse fer 'em. While some rumors tell o' unbelievable indications, others're discouragin'. So, again, 'nother bunch o' the savvy ol' sourdoughs leave the Klondike t' the cheechakos.

"Out'n Bonanza 'n El Dorado themselves, it's hard 'nough fer the new Klondikers t' get a good idea what their own claims might hold. An' they're standin' right there. They c'n only tell what's up top. Test holes'd only flood if they started diggin' very deep in early fall. So they only do what they can, dabblin' 'round on the surface. An' they get their cabins up, firewood cut, 'n windlasses built, lumber ready fer sluice boxes, 'n haul what supplies they can. Have t' wait'll the ground freezes 'fore they start down t' bedrock. Heaviest deposits'll eventually be found twelve t' twenty feet down, a few somewhat deeper. So if the Klondike miners themselves find it hard t' get a handle on it, the old Fortymilers, some of 'em 150 miles travel from Klondike action, got no prayer t' know from the thin 'n conflictin' information reachin' 'em."

Old Ben Atwater: "That fall, the steamer, *Arctic* got herself temporarily ice-bound at Forty Mile. Then river broke loose enough to let her make the mouth of the Klondike. They dumped off some supplies and another hundred prospectors. They also took out the last letters of the season.

"Most of the best ground on the Bonanza and El Dorado bottoms was long before staked by the time those of the old headwaters Fortymilers who answered the cry got there. If that wasn't bad enough, they faced an additional problem: they had to somehow get by on starvation rations. We dog punchers had already freighted half their yearly supplies to their former diggings far up the Fortymile. When the men abandoned their claims and rushed off for the Klondike, just like Bill Liggett they turned their backs on all their supplies and left 'em behind.

"Right after freeze-up's a busy time for freighters anyways. But now, plus the usual hauling we had to turn around, go up, and haul from a lot of the claims back down to Forty Mile. The round trip from a lot of the heaviest upstream mining action averaged maybe 170 miles. Next, from Forty Mile the supplies had to be sledded up the Yukon to the Klondike and out to the miner's new claims. Depending on the location, that could be another eighty miles.

"Every dog puncher in the Upper Country was employed full-time. The Malemute Kid, The Goin' Kid, Art Walden, me, and a few others. Maybe the Seventymile Kid, too—I don't remember. We all just drove ourselves and our teams with little rest. The dogs, they got so sour, even when you went out to feed they'd try to hide. And that's no exaggeration. We tried to pace them, but we knew men might starve if we didn't keep ahead of it.

"The cost of shipping supplies from 'Frisco or Seattle to St. Michael and up the Yukon was steep. Then tack on cost of our original freighting from the trading company warehouses on the Yukon out to the mines. Now add costs of our rehauls to that already-sky-high food and equipment. By then, couldn't have been much more expensive if every item was platinum coated. That made it extremely tough on them. I don't doubt a starving man would pay a fancy price for our service, much more than the going rate. But none of us gouged them. We didn't want to take advantage of their straits. On the other hand, as the Good Word says, *A workman's worthy of his hire* and we and our dogs were well worth our pay. We worked so constantly, all of us dog punchers came out of that fall with a nice tidy income. Oh, what would the North be, Al, without dogs?"

———◆———

As experienced as McQuesten, Harper and Ladue, and NAT&T were, supplying their trading posts had always been speculative, involving a lot of educated guesswork. If they overestimated business, they ended up sitting on stock that did not move quickly and experienced cash-flow problems. On the other hand, if they underestimated and ran out before those depending upon them filled their needs, severe privation could discourage prospecting and mining activity and either cause their customers to leave the area or open the way for competitors to move in. Only if they supplied their stores with close to the exact amount needed did they experience a fast turnaround on their investment, keep their market thriving, and their business profitable.

The great, continuing problem remained the lack of winter communication and transport. Being limited to the four-month river shipping season forced suppliers into sending out orders at the end of summer for an inventory that wouldn't arrive until the beginning of the following summer. It was an inventory that would have to last until the summer after that. For instance, the last boats to make it out of the river before ice-up in September and October of 1896 not only carried last-minute notes to friends and relatives about the new strike on the Klondike, but they also carried orders for supplies that would not begin arriving until early June 1897 and keep coming in through the '97 summer. Miners would desperately depend upon those supplies to keep them fed and equipped until June 1898 when the '98 shipping season would begin. September 1896 to June 1898 was closing in on two years. Obviously, having to prognosticate the number of prospectors that would be in the country and trying to forecast where, along hundreds of miles of the Yukon their shifting activity might place them made it a great guessing game and held back development of the country.

For McQuesten, Mayo, Harper, and Ladue, and the other trading and supply ventures, by the 1890s, almost all the supplies were shipped out of San Francisco and Seattle. Because Seattle was also the port of embarkation and return for most of the gold seekers, the traders were able to keep fairly close tabs. For the two decades leading up to the Klondike strike yearly tallies had always showed small numbers very gradually climbing. That had allowed the suppliers to generally come close to keeping up with the increasing demand.

But there was no way in the fall of 1895—when they had been ordering their supplies for June 1896 through June 1897, they could have guessed what was coming. How could they have known how to adequately provision the Klondike?

Picture the supply-order situation in the fall of 1896. Traders and boat captains know that prospectors located nearby are rushing to the Klondike. But by the time traders hightail it out on the last steamers to beat the early freeze-up that year no one yet knows the full scope of the strike. In Seattle or San Francisco, engaged in their winter buying they have no way of guessing that the population will far more than double in the 1897 season.

If it was that hard to guess correctly for the first year of the rush, how in their wildest dreams could they imagine that in two years the population of Dawson alone—not counting the numbers mining out on the claims and scattered around the remainder of the Yukon Basin—would be some twenty times what it had been before the Klondike strike!

———————

Old Ben Atwater: "I told you about miners who'd stampeded off to the Klondike and left their outfit behind. And about us freighters going up the Fortymile to fetch back their supplies. Up the Stewart and Sixtymile, too. Well, there were a lot of men that couldn't afford to relocate their food from their old claims like that.

"And it was frustrating for the suppliers, too. Following all their careful expediting and shipping down in 'Frisco and Seattle, in that fall of 1896, traders were just flat stuck there in the North frozen in with no way to respond and nothing to respond with. For all of their preplanning, the end result was a good supply of food scattered about the country abandoned. Might as well have dumped it in the Yukon in the first place and saved everyone going to the trouble and expense of distributing it. Only ones who ended up benefitting were the mice, squirrels, and bears."

———————

The North West Mounted Police report for 1896 noted that an unusually early cold snap hit the upper Yukon that fall. Ice began to run heavily September 2, almost stopping navigation. After opening up for a few days it froze tight, bringing navigation to an untimely halt.

Chapter 13

---◈---

Early Stampeders from "Outside"
Beat the Big Rush

IN THE FALL OF 1896, William Ogilvie, stationed at Forty Mile, had sent word of the discovery out to his superiors in Ottawa by one of the last outbound steamboats of the season. He sensed that the strike was big. However, when the last boats fled ahead of the freezeup, the strike was only days old and no one yet had any more than indications of the actual richness. His early report received but minimal government attention.

When surface waters out on the claims froze deeply enough, the miners were finally able to sink test holes without flooding out. Eagerly, they headed for bedrock. As sample pans were tested up and down Bonanza and El Dorado, more concrete indications of the worth of the new strike began to be revealed. By late December they thought it to be stupendous.

Feeling that getting word out to Canadian officials was crucial, Ogilvie decided the urgency outweighed the great risk; he would, as Harper had done a decade before, send a messenger snowshoeing out to civilization. This time, the trip would be even farther: 627 miles (by Ogilvie's own survey) from Forty Mile up the Yukon and over the perilous mountains to Dyea.

In the years since the trip had killed Tom Williams, others had come to the brink of sharing his fate. On that long, cruel trek, trying to cross the treacherous Coast Mountains buried under literally hundreds of inches of snow, two men stopped by a vicious blizzard turned their dogs loose so that each animal could find its own best shelter. Then the two hunkered down to exist on dried dog salmon and raw cornmeal. The dogs sought out their best shelter, alright. When the men emerged to harness up and resume their passage they were greatly surprised. To their amazement they discovered that, even given the voracious appetites of the hungry dogs which usually welded them tightly to their food source, the beckoning of more merciful elevations had yet been stronger. The men never saw any of those dogs again.

Another trekker fashioned a crude shelter and sat wretchedly, wrapped in his furs. For nine days he subsisted on dry oatmeal and tallow candles. Still another, Whiskey Thompson, to come out alive on the far end of his tribulation, survived the sufferings by eating raw dog flesh.

Knowing all these stories and more, Ogilvie put his important message and the fate of the journey in the hands of a lone, seventy-four-year-old man!

But the man who accepted the challenge and pointed his webs up the Yukon was no ordinary seventy-four-year-old, no ordinary trailsman. Ogilvie turned to none other than his trusted old stalwart from boundary survey days, Captain William Moore.

———————◆—◆—◆———————

Rod Perry: *How did a lone traveler in 1896 make it out 627 miles to Dyea? How did a seventy-four-year-old make it through in the dead of winter when back in 1886 the trip of 508 miles starting from Fort Nelson had killed Tom Williams traveling with a companion?*

First—unlike Williams who was only a riverboat man, Moore was not only a well-known riverboat captain, but a seasoned man of the trail. The old Yukoner had many a winter under his belt living and traveling in the country.

Second—it is unlikely Moore had to battle anything like the freakishly horrible trail conditions which oppressed Williams and Bob.

Third—by 1896 there was a little more human presence along the way, most notably Ladue's Ogilvie post, about 100 miles along, which still held some supplies and, especially, Arthur Harper's post at Fort Selkirk, 225 miles into the journey. Such oases would have given Moore a chance to go relatively light between points, then rest and reprovision. The toughest stretch would be the 400 miles beyond the

Pelly mouth. The kindly Harper, with memories surely still haunting him of sending Williams and Bob to Dyea on an almost exact same mission, would have given Moore every aid at his disposal. Harper's aid could well have included sending some of the post Indians along, well provisioned, breaking trail and transporting Moore's supplies until he was far on his way.

It could well be that Moore would have been first to fill Arthur in on the Klondike strike. Harper would have to have been at Selkirk before the river locked up, and that was only a couple of weeks after the strike became known. That, as we have seen, was before anything concrete was known, with only frenzied speculation about what might lie underground. So even if Harper knew there was a rush underway—maybe his partner Joe Ladue sent early tidings by Indian messenger the 125 miles up from Ogilvie or 170 up from the Klondike—it would have been too early to tell Art much.

Because opinion that the strike was probably a blockbuster only came into general agreement as test holes went down in November and December, Moore's up-to-the-minute information would have probably been that which provided prospecting fanatic Arthur Harper the news that vindicated the belief he'd held for a quarter century— that the Yukon Basin held fabulous wealth.

Back to why Moore was able to make the 627-mile-long trip in good shape—

Fourth—Moore would have been familiar with the relatives of his former trailmate, Skookum Jim. Back in 1887 the two had no doubt stopped in Jim's village, Carcross, when Jim guided Moore to make him the first white man through White Pass. It's almost inconceivable that the old captain would not have planned from the start to rest and even reprovision a bit at the Tagish village, poor though they were. He would have known they would be overjoyed to learn that Skookum Jim, Tagish Charlie, Kate and Carmacks had made the great strike and found incredible riches. Also, back in 1886–87, Wilson and Bob had been admonished by Tagish hunters not to try the pass. The Tagish would have no doubt taken the two in and shared their meager fare had Tom and Bob asked. Imagining Moore leaving there on the last stage of his long tramp, some of those villagers might have even snowshoed along, carrying his load and breaking his trail part of the way.

Fifth—because Moore had been the white "discoverer" of White Pass, he probably took that route. It offered a way much lower in elevation and without the steep climb and descent of Williams and Bob's route over the Chilkoot Pass.

Yet, all in all, a 627-mile-long tramp on snowshoes in the depths of a Yukon winter was heroic for a man of any age, much more so for the venerable old sourdough of seventy-four.

A few other early reports besides Ogilvie's—those letters that had just made it out on the last boats that fall—did have an effect. Probably mainly limited to Yukoner's private communiqués to relatives and personal friends, the news did not attract very widespread media notice. Even if it had, the unknowing would not have thought it sounded different enough from other announcements of periodic discoveries that had come down from the North over the preceding two decades to create more than casual interest.

However, to people who had been personal recipients of the inside information, those early tidings of the Klondike strike were convincing enough to cause great excitement. From those insiders, word must have radiated out to numerous others, inside tips that the strike gave indications that it could well surpass all others in the annals of the North. Amid visions of instant wealth simply waiting to be claimed, many began assembling prospecting outfits and preparing to head to the Yukon early in the spring of 1897.

As glowing as the reports sounded to those northbound possessors of early information, they could not have guessed the full extent of the discovery, for even most of the miners themselves who were mucking away that winter in the Klondike would not know for sure until May of 1897. That was when they would begin to wash out their winter dumps, those huge mounds of frozen accumulations of gold-bearing muck and gravel brought up from underground during their winter's labor.

Old Ben Atwater: "Because many men on the Klondike were former Fortymile miners, lots had partners in Circle City. You can imagine, Al, they sure wanted to get news of the great strike down to 'em. But, o'course, if you're a Klondiker maybe determining how soon you'll be rich by how much of a dump you pile up, are you going to put down pick and shovel and take a couple months off to play messenger boy? 'Course not. Their claims appeared so fabulous they just bowed their backs to the mining.

"Remember, the last steamers out downriver couldn't have took much news the 275 miles from Dawson down to Circle City. Long before the extent of the strike got known, the early freeze-up had drove riverboats into winter moorage.

"Dog teams hadn't been at first available to run the news down either. Like I said, Al, all us upriver drivers were in harness. We were busy under contract to relocate supplies from the Fortymile, Sixtymile, Stewart, and other outlying locations to the new diggings. However, in December a freight team driven by Walden—that's my sometimes partner Art Walden—finally broke away and headed to Circle City. He carried a packet of letters from the new strike. On his way he was caught up by the first official U.S. Mail team to make a regular run from Lynn Canal hauling Circle City mail. The two teams pulled into the village not far apart in January.

"I heard what happened from Walden. Word circulated in a flash that the first dog teams of the season'd come in with mail. Every man in Circle City quickly gathered at Harry Ash's tavern. Art threw his packet down on the bar and ordered a mug of beef tea. Harry grabbed the bundle, paid Walden's order no never-mind, and told him to just make his own. Thumbed through fast as he could 'til he found a letter from his partner. As he read, his pulse must've been going like a trip hammer. Suddenly, Ash vaulted right over the bar, Walden told me. Ash shouted out to the crowd, 'I'm bound for the Klondike, boys. Have at my whiskey, the whole works—it's on me!' Letter after letter told those Circle boys they were partners in claims that might make them rich beyond their wildest dreams. They didn't even wait to uncork the bottles. Simply knocked the necks off to get at the whiskey and started dancing and whooping like wild men.

"You know, Al, that packet of mail snuffed out Circle City as a boom town. Just rang the death knell. It'd live on as an inhabited village, alright. But it'd never again have the population. And it wouldn't be the center of commerce and society it used to be.

"Up to then, going price for a town lot and cabin was $500. Sled dogs'd been selling for $25 to $50 each. Now Walden was immediately offered three of the best cabins for any one dog in his team. He later laughingly told me that must mean that the price of a dog just shot up to $1,500! Either that or it meant the price of a cabin'd cratered out at $8 to $17. Actually, he figured the real values for both settled somewhere in between. The animals were in such demand, during the rare times they went up for sale they started being sold by their weight. They were going for $1.50 at first. Finally they worked up to $2.50 a pound.

"The news had Circle City by its ears, alright. It was going to be a real ordeal. About a 275-mile trudge up to Dawson. On the upper Yukon just like around Nome, no one worth his salt'd be caught without a hand sled, and every man jack flew to loading his. The town all but emptied. A long line started to stretch out with the miners necking their sleds up the river.

"Every man understood perfectly he couldn't hope to buy so much as a morsel of food or any supplies in such a new camp when they got to Dawson. They knew the first steamboat wouldn't make it in 'til the middle of the next July. Half a year. Clear to then they'd have to scrape by on what they themselves could drag upriver from Circle City.

"The miners figured a sledload of 200 pounds to be about the absolute limit one good man could tow. At least if he was going to still knock down his fifteen miles a day. That was their common expectation when the going was so exhausting. Men traveled in pairs. Each one necked a sled, but they only took one camp outfit to save weight. Any way you figure it, it seems impossible for a man to haul on a hand sled enough food to get him by for six months. Especially when part of the load's taken up with trail gear and tools. And even more especially with the terrific labor of pulling a steel-shod sled 275 miles in temperatures far below zero. And over trails that continually blew in. The cold and tough trail ate up energy. That demanded eating lots of the load during the march itself.

"Somehow those rawhide-tough miners'd all make it through to Dawson. But you can bet by then each one had worn every last washer off his scrawny tail end! It took a mighty tight belt and a feather-light tooth, but somehow they'd winter over on what they brought. By spring ice-out, it wasn't surprising many would be down to diets of almost nothing but flour. But doggone it, every one of them would eake by 'til the first supply boat.

"At the going rate of $1.20 a pound, I joined Walden and the Malemute Kid and a couple other freighters hauling up from Circle City all winter long. Some of us made three round trips, 1,700 miles. And that was after our earlier work between the Fortymile and the Klondike."

———————

Out on the Klondike creeks, beyond the sinking of test holes, few could progress into extensive mining development of their claims through the winter of 1896-97 because the labor it required was hard to hire. Most of the people in the country were too busy working on their own claims to work for someone else. The majority worked on speculation. They were driven on by reports coming from the few claims that could hire labor to thaw underground drifts following pay streaks. First, reports spread of wonderful test pans before bedrock was even reached. Then tales of staggering wealth at the bottom electrified the country. The miners bent to the task in a feverish effort to sink shafts through the frozen overburden to bedrock. Driving themselves to their utter limit, they hardly stopped to eat, sleep, bathe, or change clothes. Someone described them as "millionaires too lacking in food to eat, too busy to bathe."

The typical prospect hole was two-and-one-half feet wide by six feet long. The men built a fire of six-foot dry logs then completely covered the fire with green logs. To seal off the cracks between the green logs the men banked the fire with dirt. With the limited flow of oxygen the fire would burn all night and the covering of barely burnable green wood and dirt kept much of the heat available to thaw downward. The next morning they first removed the unburned logs, banking dirt, and what ground they had thawed. Next they worked all day removing what they could manage to pick and shovel from the frozen ground below. Ten inches by thawing and six inches by pick and shovel was considered good progress. They repeated the process each day.

After digging down ten or eleven feet, it grew impossible to efficiently throw dirt out of the hole with a shovel, so the men constructed over the hole a log frame and a crude windlass with a seven-inch log for a drum. One man turned the windlass, another worked at the bottom. As soon as they hit gravel they checked their prospect by running a test pan every foot until they hit bedrock. If they found gold in paying quantity (paydirt), they melted and picked (drifted) their way sideways, tunneling to follow the paystreak. The frozen ground generally needed no shoring to prevent cave-ins.

Paydirt along Bonanza and El Dorado Creeks generally lay on the ancient streambed twelve to twenty feet below the surface.

It was difficult to see what the frozen ground held. However, as they periodically washed out a test pan with melted snow they commonly tested out at between $5 and $100 to the pan. Miners used to previously finding eight or ten cents to the pan on the best claims almost refused to believe what they were seeing, even as they held the riches right in their hands. Excitement over the results drove the men on.

On March 25, 1897—spring in the south but still winter in the Yukon—the *City of Mexico* left Seattle with over 600 stampeders, doubtlessly mostly responders to the last letters that made it out of the Yukon before fall freeze-up. For the rest of the spring, eager gold-seekers jammed every northbound ship, the forerunners of the great rush that would follow.

Little did these in the vanguard realize that by early September the previous fall, most of Bonanza and El Dorado were claimed. By November 20, 338 claims had been staked. The number had hit 500 on January 6. Then the Circle miners who had trekked up during January and February had staked more after that. These newcomers coming up from Outside would find that every worthwhile foot of Bonanza and El Dorado Creek bottom had been claimed months before they even embarked from Seattle. And they were a year ahead of the multitudes who would make famous the great rush of 1898.

Up north, back in the Klondike, many miners began to look emaciated by springtime. There they were, starving—some showing obvious symptoms of scurvy—while sitting atop piles of muck and gravel worth fortunes. Every waking moment the men dreamed of extravagant meals their hoped-for money could buy in far-off cities. However, though many would soon be unimaginably wealthy, there in the Klondike they could not buy so much as a loaf of bread. And there they were, "wearing their skins like iron," coated with months-long accumulations of perspiration mixed with the grime of their excavating, miners too engrossed in the uncovering of their future riches to worry over hygiene. Filthy rich.

After such a long, hard winter, the Klondikers could hardly wait to find out what had been the fruits of their labors. As soon as the first available water began to run in the creeks, the miners built sluice boxes and proceeded to "clean up." As through the long sluice boxes they washed the dumps, what those who had staked the most productive claims found settled behind the riffles made their eyes bulge out like doorknobs. It was reported that pans were found that spring as rich as $500. By comparison, the best pans in California had run thirty-five to forty cents and had been thought of as unbelievably rich.

When spring cleanup revealed that their winter labors had made many Klondike miners fabulously rich, the strike became news of truly stupendous proportions. However, what is news but private information if it cannot be broadcast and there is no one to hear or read of it? This information of the great strike would have to wait to become news until someone could reach the outside world to break it. The first to take the word out were some of the miners themselves.

Immediately on the heels of breakup, in mid-June, 1897 the Alaska Commercial steamer, *Alice* came into Dawson with much-needed supplies. Two days later the NAT&T's *Portius B. Weare* tied up there at the Klondike mouth. More than eighty miners booked passage. Some had sold their claims, thinking their pay streak would play out. Others just needed a break from the privation. They had only begun to tap the wealth, but their claims would be there when they got back.

It was later reported that the weight of the miners' gold—carried aboard in whiskey bottles and other crude containers—kept close to their persons in the *Weare's* second-tier staterooms, began to make the deck supports creak and groan, forcing the crew to shore up the structure.

Rod Perry: *As the* Alice *began downriver June 16, two bound south for a brief respite were former California fruit farmer and Forty Mile bartender, Clarence Berry and his wife, Ethel (who the previous year as a new bride, had been the first woman to cross the Chilkoot Pass.)*

Quickly believing Carmack's story in Bill McPhee's bar, he and his brother Fred had poled up to the Klondike and staked Forty-two Above Discovery. Initial work convinced the two they should acquire better property. They were able to trade half interest for Six Above on El Dorado. With Ethel there to keep the cabin heated and the men fed, the two excavated faster than most. At thirty feet they hit a deep paystreak of unbelievable richness, each shovelfull worth hundreds of dollars. Before worth of the ground leaked out they were able to purchase adjacent claims, Four and Five Above.

Upon return from their quick trip out to the States, they would bring north a dozen of their loyal former fruit orchard workers. In a day when laborers in the United States were commonly making fifty dollars monthly, and farm workers far less, the Berrys would pay their men an ounce of gold daily (at $16.00 an ounce.) The couple could afford to be liberal. At the close of each day, in but a few minutes Berry would wash out enough to pay off his entire workforce. The generous Berrys would treat women and children visiting their claim to a veritable Easter egg hunt, allowing them to pick up a few nuggets. They would also leave a bucket of nuggets and a bottle of whiskey outside their front door on El Dorado with a sign inviting passers-by to "Help Yourself."

Later, Berry would make rich strikes in the Fairbanks District. Today's Ester, Alaska was first Berry, Alaska. Following their mining days, the astute Berrys were destined to make a fortune in oil. In 1985 the company would go public on the New York Stock Exchange and in 1996 Berry Petroleum would produce its one hundred millionth barrel.

A decade after the Berrys left Alaska, word reached them that Bill McPhee's bar in Fairbanks had burned down. The man who years before in Forty Mile had grubstaked his bartender soon received instructions to begin rebuilding. A Fairbanks bank had received money to cover the entire cost of construction.

But back to the telling of how news of fabulous Klondike riches first broke upon the world . . ."

———————————

Down the Yukon, the *Alice* pulled into St. Michael June 23, the *Weare* two days later. However, with Bering Sea pack ice still blocking shipping, no ocean steamer had been able to get through. Finally, on June 30, the steamship *Excelsior*, which had pushed through the ice the last forty miles, docked at St. Michael. Four hours later the *Portland* made it in through the pack.

On the *Portland*, sixty-eight left for Seattle, a 2,700-mile voyage. The *Excelsior*, headed for Alaska Commercial Company headquarters in San Francisco, being the faster vessel, gained three days on the *Portland*. On July 14, 1897, the *Excelsior* tied up at the San Francisco dock. A number of Klondike miners disembarked with one-half million dollars in gold. Converted to year 2000 dollars, their gold would have been worth about $12 million. Wondrous stories hit the news wires and swept the nation like wildfire.

———————————

Al Preston: : "The story was told of one of those miners. He'd lived a solitary existence for several years on his remote mine on the Fortymile. Then he'd rushed to the Klondike and overwintered on his claim. Upon reaching San Francisco and registering at his hotel, the first thing he does is start running a bath. As the tub fills and he begins peeling off clothes, he comes unexpectedly upon a pair of woolen long johns and two pairs of socks he'd totally forgotten he owned.

"Once bathed and dressed, he sits down in the restaurant and orders a lavish dinner fit for a king—or three kings. Before the waiter leaves with the order, the old sourdough has a plateful of beans set in front of him.

"As the waiter approaches with the first course, he notices the bush rat muttering intently into his plate. The old-timer's apparently engaged in an earnest and animated discourse with the beans.

"At the waiter's arrival, the man from the Klondike looks up briefly, then resumes his conversation. Shaking a finger at the beans as he pushes the plate aside, he sternly orders, 'OK, boys, now you just stand back and watch a man eat a real meal!'"

———————

Three days after the *Excelsior* reached San Francisco, the rusted hulk of the Pacific Whaling Company steamship *Portland* eased into Seattle harbor. An excited crowd of over 5,000 waited at the dock. Standing ready was an armed force of Wells Fargo Express Company guards. Throngs used to thinking in terms of a common laborer earning $500 to $700 a year watched as sixty-eight gaunt, weather-beaten men in patched and mended garments brought almost three-quarters of a million dollars in gold (about $18 million in year 2000 dollars) down the gangplank in whiskey bottles, old satchels, wooden boxes, tin cans and bags of canvas and moosehide tied up with rope.

One of the most famous headlines in U.S. newspaper history dominated the top of the front page of the *The Seattle Post-Intelligencer*.

LATEST NEWS FROM THE KLONDIKE

Saturday, June 17, 1897

9 O-CLOCK EDITION

GOLD! GOLD! GOLD! GOLD!

Sixty-Eight Rich Men on the Steamer Portland

STACKS OF YELLOW METAL!

Some Have $5,000, Many Have More, and a Few Bring Out $100,000 Each.

THE STEAMER CARRIES $700,000.

Docking of the *Portland* and the famous headline that described the event would be one of the most enduring images in Seattle history, handing the young city a large part of its identity. A century later, one writer would observe, "In a sense, Seattle itself arrived on the steamer *Portland.*"

The continent was primed to catch gold fever. Citizens had been mired in the despair of the severe depression of which they could see no end. In the United States, the luster was off the promise of a developing nation that had previously offered unlimited opportunity.

From colonial times, anyone who wished to create a new beginning had been able to heed the call, "Go West, Young Man!" But by the 1890s the country had been all but settled coast to coast. The economic aspect of the siren call that had attracted the world's downtrodden, huddled masses had ceased to deliver to immigrants in the same measure that it had for over 200 years. Millions lived in poverty, having no outlook offering hope that their situation would brighten.

The press played on the sensational discovery. Exaggerated reports blew an already giant strike into mythical proportions. They painted the picture of a land where anyone could dig almost anywhere and bring back riches. Once they had created hysteria, newspapers fanned the flames. Thousands swallowed the bait.

The excitement swung the mood of the nation. One informal investigation into the passenger makeup of railways heading west found some 210,000 who stated that their goal was the Klondike. Adding to those railway travelers were the many who stampeded to the Klondike from the far reaches of the earth. The great rush seemed to be on everyone's lips. Money that had been hoarded came out and began to circulate. The country's atmosphere became one of festive self-confidence.

The *Portland* turned right around, leaving for St. Michael six days after docking. One who was aboard was former Washington governor, John McGraw. Another who caught the fever was William D. Wood. Immediately he had resigned as mayor of Seattle to become a gold hunter. Ten thousand others scrambled to head north immediately.

The last days of summer and the autumn of 1897 saw the first ships full of the media-driven masses head north to beat the onset of winter across the Chilkoot Pass and White Pass.

Craft of every description and state of seaworthiness—anything available from Tierra del Fuego to Barrow, retired or active, joined the fleet. Even derelicts that had lain in "bone yards" for years were resurrected and pressed into service.

One collier, having been emptied of its usual cargo, had its filthy black hold hastily furbished with what passed for "berths" for 600 passengers. Another ship, terribly overloaded, weighed anchor for the North Country with a deckload piled so high that the helmsman could not see directly ahead. A small launch embarked stuffed with men so consumed with visions of gold they seemed not to care that the closest qualification its captain had for piloting an ocean-going vessel had been driving a horse-drawn milk wagon on the streets of San Francisco!

The voyage of the ship *Eliza Anderson* seemed doomed to failure at the beginning, but by its finish, its passengers must have hoped the blind luck that accompanied their voyage would transfer unchecked once they reached the goldfields. First, the ship cast off from Seattle headed north—at least the captain hoped they were headed north—without a compass. They soon rammed another ship. Next, crossing the dangerous Gulf of Alaska, they barely survived a driving storm. Then, only halfway to the mouth of the Yukon, their destination, they ran out of fuel.

Incredibly, their luck swung around. Somehow, they managed to safely make their way into a sheltered cove on Kodiak Island. Then, while walking the nearby shoreline, someone discovered a rich vein of coal. Farther along on the voyage, just when it seemed that all would be lost as the ship was close to being dashed on the rocks, a remarkably gifted stowaway emerged from hiding and saved the ship!

Though the season saw an increase in the incidence of shipwrecks, many made it through. As soon as the gold-crazed hordes disembarked at the head of Lynn Canal, Skagway and Dyea sprang up as instant towns to service them.

The earliest arrivals of the onrushing horde began to pull into Dawson and rush out to the Klondike creeks to stake their fortunes.

———————

Rod Perry: *Far north, up on the Klondike the misconceptions of various new arrivals may be grouped under several headings: two are cynical and the third harbors false hopes. In the first group, many experienced miners among the earliest arrivals turn negative without so much as brushing the surface. "It just doesn't look right," they say. In the second group are a number like Robert Henderson. He arrives three weeks after the strike but turns away in disgust when he finds virtually all of Bonanza and El Dorado creeks staked. This second group assumes there is no worthwhile ground left. The third group, a* *naïve wave of newcomers, comes roaring in thinking they will find the whole discovery open to their staking and they're as good as rich just because they are many months ahead of the hordes who follow. Of course, the reality is that the main creeks had been staked end to end months before word of the strike even reached them. Many immediately leave, shocked when their false hopes are dashed.*

All the groups were wrong. Rich deposits still lay hidden nearby.

———◆———

Old Ben Atwater: "Al, you remember me saying t a bunch of us old sourdoughs looked at the surface indications, the way the willows leaned wrong, the water didn't taste right and so forth and talked ourselves right out of staking? Well, the gold seemed to play another cruel trick on many of us most experienced miners. It caused our very experience we'd gained through seasons of back-breaking labor and privation to play against us. Wherever we'd prospected through the American West, British Columbia and elsewhere along the Yukon we had always found gold settled at the lowest point. It's the heaviest material in the formation. The lowest point is in the valley bottoms. For sure it's never on the hillsides above. So when us old hands arrived just a few days or weeks late or even months, and saw all the rich Bonanza and El Dorado creek bottoms staked, our so-called "knowledge" led us to turn away to look elsewhere without another thought. We just left it to raw, inexperienced Johnny-come-latelies who'd come in the next summer and didn't know any better, to prospect above on the hillsides. It was the greenest cheechakos you ever saw that located the fabulous bench claims in places like the famous White Channel.

"Those turned out to be ancient stream courses. Bonanza and El Dorado flowed up there in past ages and left deposits worth millions of dollars."

———◆———

During the first winter of the strike, 1896-97, most of the miners from all the other mining districts in the Yukon Basin relocated in the Klondike. By April 1897 the population of Dawson had hit 1,500. But by fall, with the coming of the first seekers from the outside world, those who had heeded the initial word of the strike and headed north before the first Klondike gold had arrived at San Francisco and Seattle, the town had swelled to 3,500.

Old Ben Atwater: "Like I told you before, most of these new gold seekers were of a different cut than the experienced prospectors before the Klondike Strike. Yeah, Al, no doubt the new ones included a fair number of hardened outdoorsmen. But a big share had little, if any experience to prepare them for such a trip and life. Shopkeepers, bankers, tradesmen, doctors, attorneys, farmers, factory workers, menial laborers and the like. Many were town and city dwellers. Not many knew anything firsthand of scaling mountains, building boats and running wild rivers, traveling the wilderness, enduring mosquitoes and black flies or, especially, living and working year-round near the Arctic Circle. Few but the farmers knew a thing of working draft animals. Result was thousands of horses dying on the trail. They didn't know how to dress, how to outfit for the trip to the Klondike or what they'd need once they got here. Many traveled light to get here quick. The fools thought they'd be able to buy needed supplies and gear at Dawson. They'd be in for a very rude awakening. Sure, there were plenty of exceptions, but I'd lump most of the Ninety-eighters under the heading of 'hopeful innocents.' And quite a few 'misguided fools and bumblers.'

"What use did these cheechakos make of the long experience and expertise of us old-timers? Precious little to none at all. For one, in the great rush we got minimized, minimalized or whatever you call it. Just sort of counted unimportant and lost in the shuffle. Second, they had no time to learn from us. What we saw them doing was just, en masse, throw their thin experience, and civilized, warmer-climate habits, and their ignorance against the distances, the climate, the mountains and rivers, against the whole savage country. In the Yukon, ignorance and incompetence had always before been so deadly. But when they hurled themselves at the obstacles in such a mighty wave, most managed who couldn't have made it by themselves."

Alfred Hulse Brooks: "Regarding supplying the region, there were no more knowledgeable people in the North than the established trading companies. It can hardly be imagined how frustrated and frantic they must have felt. With all their experience in the feeding and equipping of Yukon miners over the past seasons, they fell far short in their estimates regarding the numbers. And being used to experienced outdoorsmen coming into the country, they could not have guessed at the general lack of preparedness of the crowds that would descend upon them by the fall of 1897. With no precedent to refer to, how could they or anyone else accurately guess the country's supply needs? Lacking swift communications to the outside to place a quick order and without all-season transportation to get a timely shipment back, there was no way to adjust."

Chapter 14

———◆———

The 1897–1898 Food Shortage

WHILE THE FIRST WHO STAKED THE KLONDIKE had mucked and moiled and starved on their claims through the winter of 1896–97, those last letters of the season they had managed to send out of the Yukon to friends and relatives via the final downriver boats before freeze-up were effecting foundations of a repeat food shortage the following winter of 1897–98. The earliest respondents to the previous fall's letters had shipped north beginning in March and on through the summer in time to enter the upper Yukon during the short northern access window. They trickled into Dawson through the summer. By fall new entrees from over the passes were arriving at the rate of about seventy-five a day.

Not one in ten brought provisions enough to feed himself until the opening of shipping the following summer. Word of fifteen dollars-a-day wages and gold being carelessly cast about had begun to seep out. Incoming pilgrims deduced that the Yukon must be a land of abundance. Most had traveled light to beat the rush and naively depended upon being able to gain equipment and supplies once they got to Dawson. Once they arrived it took awhile for the reality to set in that while steamers from downriver had supplied Dawson with plenty of whiskey to last the winter, they had not brought nearly enough food. While that might have satisfied some, those who did not relish the idea of starvation began to worry.

By the time reality set in, it was too late for many to escape. In the fall of 1897 the big river dropped to an unusually low level, preventing the last few steamers that had been expected from getting up over the shallow Yukon Flats ahead of the initial freeze-up. An evident disaster loomed.

Then the river, though running ice, reopened barely enough to allow navigation. The Alaska Commercial Company, having a steamboat docked in Dawson, hurriedly sent a picked crew under Captain Hanson down to Fort Yukon, some 355 miles away, hoping they could beat the final freeze-up and bring up a load of food the company had stored there. On the way down it was noticed that the water level was dropping at an alarming rate.

They churned into Fort Yukon, loaded 300 to 400 tons of food in record time and pulled out on the high boil. But only twenty miles upriver the steamer grounded on a sandbar. Dropping down a few miles, they off-loaded half of the goods on an island. Then turning back upstream, they tried to make it over the shallows with the lightened load. But the river had fallen still farther and again prevented their passage. They dropped down to the island again and off-loaded the rest of the cargo.

They had failed to relieve Dawson's impending food crisis. Now it was doubly vital that the gold town be alerted that hoped-for provisions would not be coming. As many as possible needed to flee the country before the final freeze-up stopped navigation. Captain Hanson and the men returned to try to get over the shallows, this time with an empty boat. But the river had continued to fall. Once more they could not get across.

The steamer dropped back down to Fort Yukon whereupon Captain Hanson began one of the noblest missions in the annals of the North. He hired some Fort Yukon Indians and their birch-bark canoe to take him to warn the citizens of Dawson, warn them to boat down to Fort Yukon—where there was food—while they still had the chance, that no more steamers could be expected. Immediately they pointed their bow toward the Klondike, 355 miles away against the swift current.

Most of the crew steamed downriver, the captain having promised free transportation to San Francisco if they could beat ice-up and get the boat to St. Michael. Three others, desperate to get back upriver to their Klondike gold claims, food or no, flew at the task of building a poling boat and heading upriver to beat the ice.

Two of the crew, dog drivers, decided to spend the winter freelancing, buying dogs at Fort Yukon and hauling goods from the island cache up to Dawson.

———————

Alma Preston: "Rod, our friend, The Goin' Kid was right in the middle of that whole debacle and here's the way he told the incredible story to me . . ."

———————

The Goin' Kid: "Miss Alma, Art Walden—he's kind of a quirky sort, but sometimes we work t'gether—he 'n I take one o' the steamer's lifeboats. A few days later we start polin' up t' the food cache on the island. Gotta secure it fer the winter. Now that round-bottom 'n fore'n aft rocker no doubt let the lifeboat pivot 'n ride stormy sea waves like a gull. But the shape makes it almost impossible t' pole upstream. The consarned beast'll just not keel. Wants t' spin like a dang bowl. But's all we have so we bend t' the task. 'Exasperatin!' says Walden, 'long with a lotta stronger language I wouldn't repeat to a lady.

"When we come up 'n the island a few days later, what do we behold? There's a crazy runnin' up 'n down the bank wildly wavin' us in t' land. Who should it turn out, but Capt'n Hanson. The birch-bark he'd hired had leaked so bad the Indians dropped 'im off at the food cache. Promised t' get another canoe at Fort Yukon. Said they'd come back for 'im t' keep their mission goin'. So he'd built 'im a shelter o' packin boxes. Just sittin' there most a week readin' labels. An worryin' 'imself sick 'bout the folk up'n Dawson. An' frettin' 'bout losin' time 'cause freeze-up's not gonna wait. The new canoe and Fort Yukon men haven't showed up.

"Art n' I change plans instantly. Now we're in with Hanson in 'is rescue mission. An extra man t' line the boat helps. But then, the first snow, a half a foot, makes the footin hellacious. Takes four days o' the most terrible labor trackin' the sixty miles 'long the bank from the island t' Circle City. Capt'n Hanson hires 'nother birch-bark n' new crew o' Natives. Tells Walden n' me t' follow any way we can 'n off 'e goes on 'is desperate dash. Dawson's now 'bout 275 miles away against the current.

"All that Walden and I c'n find's a leaky birch-bark. We take two days t' cover it with canvas. No one's ever seen the likes, but 'n those two days the Yukon begins t' rise. Now all the ol' Circle City sourdoughs predict another steamboat'll make it up over the flats."

———◆—◆———

Rod Perry: *Not only Dawson, but Circle City itself is in dire straits. After the town exodus to the Klondike the winter before, only eighty miners remained working the district. Not a crumb of food had been dropped at Circle since the year before. Though each passing steamer promised that the one coming behind would offload provisions, riverboat after riverboat bypassed Circle City, running their cargos on up to Dawson where the desperate demand had driven up prices.*

The Circle City men were in no danger of actual starvation because they could make their way eighty miles down to Fort Yukon where warehouses held plenty. However, because their mines were located so many miles back in the country behind Circle City, most operations had to be supplied by sled hauling from Circle City warehouses over winter trails to their diggings. That task required a whole winter of repetitive trips. If, instead of spending the season freighting from Circle City to their claims, the miners were forced to take up the whole winter sledding their supplies from Fort Yukon to Circle City, they faced losing the entire following year of mining, just consuming what they had brought up from Fort Yukon, and many would be financially ruined.

———◆—◆———

The Goin' Kid: "At a miners' meetin' the men decide t' stage a nice, orderly, civilized holdup o' the next Dawson-bound boat. If indeed one even makes it up over the flats. The boys'll make it polite, but it'll be forceful. They mean business, they're desperate. If the boat goes on by Circle City, a group o' the boys camped out above'll get a signal. They'll stop the boat at a swift narrows above the town with a shot 'r two through the pilothouse. The meetin' agrees they'll help unload Circle City's own cargo 'n pay fer it at Dawson prices.

"We don't have long t' wait. The N.A.T.&T. flagship *Portius B. Weare* rounds the bend. Not suspectin' a thing, they nose in, tie up, 'n drop the plank. The company superintendent comes ashore. The miners, just calm 'n polite's c'n be, confront the supe' with their case. But the man has 'is own company orders. He turns 'n barks out fer a deckhand t' the cast off the hawser from its tie-up t' a stump. Next thing the deckhand sees is a dozen leveled Winchesters. He freezes. A pilot then steps t' the bow all brave. He's 'bout t' take 'n axe t' the line. Then 'e looks again. Now the same dozen muzzles're swung 'round 'n him. He sees the grim glares down their barrels 'n thinks better of it.

"The supe' refuses the miners' demands. He tells these boys in their Alaska town that 'is whole load's bonded t' the British side o' the border. Bond 'r no bond, the miners say, they're not doin' without. They refuse t' allow the boat t' leave. Three whole days while the supe' folds 'is arms 'n the Winchesters threaten, it's a standoff. Time wastes. Signs of oncomin' winter're everywhere. More ice starts runnin'. The capt'n knows once it begins heavy, he's stuck right where 'e is fer the winter. For all 'e knows, the boat might well be destroyed in the crush o' runnin' ice next spring.

"The Circle City boys all have friends 'n partners up'n the Klondike 'n don't want t' see 'em starve. They still insist on getting' their supplies, but're antsy t' see the Weare get movin' on up t' Dawson. A few leaders reason if they force things they c'n relieve the capt'n o' responsibility t' 'is company because 'e didn't give permission. They think 'e might even be hopin' that's what they'll do so 'e can get goin'. Sellin' some supplies at Circle City 'stead o' Dawson isn't anywhere close t's bad's losin' the NAT&T's flagship, their fanciest boat 'cause it gets frozen in where it's not protected. So they end the stalemate by forcefully off-loadin' eighty outfits from the hold themselves. Mannerly's ya please, they carry the goods in t' the company store. Pay full Dawson prices t' the NAT&T agent. Then they empty the shelves 'n take the goods t' their own cabins.

"Walden 'n I're refused passage upriver. Not only's the capt'n in a hostile mood toward Circle City in general, everybody knows Walden 'n I contract a lot for the rival Alaska Commercial Company. But we 'n four others march aboard. Just dare the man t' throw us off. Not wantin' more trouble and wasted time, he gives in, casts off 'n steams upriver.

"Everything goes well 'nough at first. Then we come up'n those Dawson miners polin' their newbuilt boat up from Fort Yukon. When the capt'n finds they'd come downriver hired on Hanson's A.C.C. boat 'n especially friends o' us six who'd forced passage, 'e refuses t' pick 'em up. But the pilot prob'ly figures he'd rather lose 'is job th'n face the wrath o' the whole river. He defies orders, swings over 'n takes 'em aboard. While they're tyin' their boat 'n tow, I wink at Walden 'n nod my head toward the capt'n: later, he's still gonna look good t' company bosses when they find out 'e ordered the pilot not t' pick up those rivals.

"Meanwhile, good Capt'n Hanson's been drivin' 'imself 'n 'is hired canoemen night 'n day. He's bucked the swift current 355 miles since Fort Yukon 'n flowin' ice the last part. *'Just valiant! An epic feat of heroism'* is what Walden calls it. Hanson's birch-bark'd only just pulled in t' the big eddy in front o' Dawson 'n hour before. He's right'n the middle o' pleadin' t' the big crowd. 'Get out o' the town,' he's beggin' 'em. 'Go while ya still got the chance. That'r risk starvation. No paddlewheeler c'n possibly make it up over the flats,' he's just explainin' t' the crowd, when 'e practic'ly stops'n midword 'n signals fer silence. Everyone listens.

"A long, drawn-out whistle echoes up the river. It's the approachin' *Portius B. Weare.*"

———————

Rod Perry: *However, the good Captain's convincing warning does bear fruit. It primes many to leave when they discover that the Weare, the same as the trusty old Bella which comes in close behind, is only carrying a light load of consumables, not much of which could be considered nutritionally sustaining.*

———————

The Goin' Kid: "A good part o' the cargo's whiskey. Enough folk leave, there might be sufficient stock to keep the remainin' residents in such a stupor all winter they won't know they're starvin'.

"Many Dawsonites do ship out immediately, some 'n the steamboats, others 'n small boats o' their own. A number drop down t' winter in Fort Yukon. Rest o' the evacuees grab the chance t' get completely out o' the starvin' country by way o' St. Michael. They'e hopin' t' catch the last ships o' the season outbound t' Seattle, Portland 'n Frisco. Capt'n Hanson's effective reduction o' Dawson's pop'lation ends up helpin' save the town. Relieves demands 'n the thin food supply just 'nough fer everyone t' narrowly scrape by'n starvation rations."

Chapter 15

◆

The Great Klondike Rush of 1898

SAN FRANCISCO, PORTLAND, SEATTLE, AND VICTORIA vied to establish themselves as the main supply point for Alaska and the Yukon. In October 1897, a Seattle newspaper had printed an eight-page Klondike edition and sent it to every postmaster and public library in the country as well as to thousands of businessmen and politicians.

Rod Perry: *As we have seen, many, if not most among the first wave who had rushed from the outside into the Klondike had gone in without adequate supplies. The two companies that dominated trade and transportation on the river had pulled out all the stops in a race against falling temperatures and water levels to bolster supplies 1,600 miles upriver. Leslie's Weekly, a publication with strong interest in the North, had reported that if even one of the steamers that left Saint Michael were to fail to make it to Dawson before freeze-up, one-third of the Klondike population could starve.*

As we know, barely enough supplies did reach Dawson before ice-up the fall of 1897 to just fend off starvation of the number already there. And the rush had barely started.

With a teeming horde on the way, the North West Mounted Police could see a looming disaster. In February 1898 they announced a policy that no one else would be allowed into Yukon Territory unless they brought in one ton of supplies and gear, considered enough to make them self-sufficient for one year. The Mounties set up scales near the summit of the Chilkoot and White passes to weigh the miners' outfits.

About seven of the first twelve miles of the Chilkoot Trail lay either over level ground or climbed slowly enough to make it possible to pull sleds and transport heavy loads. Once the incline became steeper, however, it became necessary to divide each man's "ton" into lighter increments. Carried in 100-pound parcels, the ton took twenty trips. Many men broke their loads down to fifty pounds for the hardest going. It was said that for every mile of the steep parts of the trail, the average stampeder walked ahead forty miles packed, then returned forty empty. The famous final pitch of 1,500 steps carved in the ice up which men trudged in a crowded, slow-moving line to the summit took an average of five hours each trip.

Until the way grew too steep, horses were used by many. When their final load was packed that far, they were abandoned for others to use or were shot.

Canyon City was set up as a permanent settlement seven miles from the top. Entrepreneurs built a steam-powered tram that included the longest cable span in the world, 2,200 feet. When running at capacity, it could haul nine tons per hour for those who could pay. Professional packers offered their services to carry loads the final pitch to the summit for $1 per pound.

Once they had their ton at the top, getting it down to Yukon headwaters was much faster and easier. Without taking a light load down first to scout the route ahead, one group of four lashed 500 pounds to each of their two eight-foot-long handsleds and jumped aboard, a pair to each sled. Before they knew it they were flying down the grade at the horrific speed of a runaway express. As their speed and momentum grew more terrifying and they at times cleared the snow in thirty-foot leaps, they wondered how they'd stop. Abruptly they found out. As the sleds hit a tilted rough spot and crashed, the load burst its lashings and for a couple of moments the canyon air was reported to have been "flush with camp gear, sides of bacon, bags of rice, mining tools, and energetic, ardent profanity."

Tent cities sprang up along the trail featuring supply dumps, saloons, bunkhouses, brothels, casinos and, as one stampeder put it, "humanity pressed so close you can hardly breathe."

Unusually heavy snows fell on the Chilkoot during February and March 1898, followed by several warm days and fresh snow. Experienced mountaineers warned of impending danger and cautioned the throngs to wait. The Chilkat chief literally drove his packers out of the danger zone at a run. The lure of gold was too strong, however, and thousands pressed on.

The Goin' Kid: "At 2 a.m. on April 2, 1898, Palm Sunday, a small avalanche buries 'bout twenty men. Another slide at 9:30 a.m. covers three. All 'r rescued. 'Bout 200 decide to heed warnin's 'n evacuate. Just before noon, a massive avalanche bears down on some o' the evacuees 'n a number o' men diggin' supplies out from the prior slides. About sixty men're buried under thirty feet o' snow. So tragic, Miss Alma, so pitifully tragic. So many families'll never see their loved ones again. Oh, an' I know ya' love dogs. Only Shorty Fisher's freight dog Jack, survives. By the time they get to 'im he's been buried eight days. Someone claims 'im, gives 'im a couple o' days to catch up, 'n Jack's put right back to work. Might seem kinda heartless, but then again, that's what Jack's tuned t' do."

Promoters billed the White Pass as an easy wagon road the entire way. After a relatively broad, but terribly muddy first few miles, the way narrowed. Then it traversed steep sections where one misstep could mean a tumble of hundreds of feet. Some places were too narrow for two laden horses to pass. All of the repetitive ferrying of loads tempted stampeders, many of whom had no experience using beasts of burden, to greatly overload their pack animals. Horses broke legs negotiating boulder fields, strained themselves in the deep quagmires and tumbled down precipices. They perished by the thousands.

By September 1897, conditions deteriorated to where the White Pass trail was virtually impassible. Strong men, it was reported, were seen returning, tears streaming down their cheeks, completely physically and emotionally broken. The stream of gold-crazed humanity passed on, indifferent to their sufferings.

Through the mountains, stampeders following both trails risked disease, malnutrition, hypothermia and even, it was reported, death from suicide and murder. Of the estimated 5,000 who missed getting to Skagway earlier and did not set out until the fall of 1897, some estimated that no more than 500 made it through that winter.

———◆—◆——◆———

Alma Preston: "Rod, here is what I clipped from an article quoting Canada's Minister of the Interior, Clifford Sifton. Remember, he's commenting on that winter between the winter of Carmack's discovery in 1896–97 and the main rush to come later, in the summer of 1898. The minister is writing at the end of the 1897–98 winter. 'The inhumanity this trail had been witness to, the heartbreak and suffering which so many have undergone, cannot be imagined.

———◆—◆——◆———

Compiled records of various railway companies indicated that some quarter million citizens started west intending to join the rush. Of the approximately 100,000 men and women who actually started in 1897 and 1898, no more than 40,000—probably far fewer— eventually reached the Yukon. Everywhere along the trail were piles of left-behind supplies, many marked with signs welcoming others to "help yourself."

After the Mounties' "ton-or-turn-back" requirement went into effect, the average time it took to cover the thirty-two-mile-long Chilkoot Pass or the forty-mile-long White Pass totaled three months. Those who made it over the passes gathered where the trails converged at Lake Bennett. There, they stopped to fell trees, whipsaw lumber and build boats, quickly denuding the slopes of timber. On May 29, 1898, the ice went out and an armada of several thousand craft began their float of almost 600 danger-fraught miles to Dawson.

Several perilous rapids between the headwaters and Dawson took their toll in lives and lost outfits. Most of the gold seekers were inexperienced boat builders and lacked river-running skills. The crafts were almost universally built too small, and headed downriver courting disaster, laden almost to the gunwales, leaving little freeboard. Most careful travelers unloaded and portaged all or most of their cargo around Whitehorse Rapids and Five Finger Rapids. But the portages were so long and the work took so many days that the lure of arriving at the foot of the torrent in a brief few minutes influenced many to cast their fate to the tumult and "shoot the chutes." Some chose to just shove their unmanned, empty craft into the current above, hope for the best and catch them below from another boat. Reportedly, the first man to successfully brave the rapids with a full cargo shot through with his boat laden to the gunwales with whiskey.

───◆────────◆───

Old Ben Atwater: "Grand sweepstakes for the all-time most bizarre load had to go to the enterprising opportunist who brought in a whole dad-gum scowload of cats. Just how on earth did the man cage, feed, care for, and relay that many panthers from salt water over the mountains to Yukon headwaters? Nobody knows. But think about it; his logistics must have been something to behold!

"Now at the summit of the pass, when he checked in to clear customs, he really set those Canadian officials to commence scratching their craniums. Never in all their born days had they laid eyes on such an import. They had no written guidelines on what to assess the cat man. What they finally hit on was their usual charge to trappers: a buck each, for duty on the fur. I remember when I told Walden of it he 'bout laughed himself blue.

"When the scow reached Dawson, I'll tell you Al, that cargo sold as fast as the townspeople could slap down an ounce of gold per kitty. You shoulda seen those new arrivals dive into the town's booming mouse population. Just going through the vermin like a dose of salts through the hired hand! Their pace of mouse extermination was only exceeded by the speed the felines themselves were cleaned out by Dawson's loose huskies!"

───◆────────◆───

Following the disappointment of finding that they were almost two years too late, and that gold did not, indeed lie under every rock, most of the late hopefuls did not even go prospecting. Only some 4,000 who reached the Klondike found so much as a trace of gold. Even so, it was a few of the most driven of the 98'ers who, finding everything staked closer to Dawson, did make some of most remote discoveries far back on the fringes of the district. Thousands of the newcomers left the country at first opportunity. Many others, however, either went to work laboring in the various support service industries or toiling at the standard $15 a day wage for the few hundred whose claims held substantial deposits.

Chapter 16

Travel Options to the Klondike in '98

SOME WHO TRAVELED TO THE GOLDFIELDS took the "poor man's route" and trekked by way of the Chilkoot Pass or its close neighbor, the White Pass, into the upper Yukon. Others, who had the resources to pay and could find space on the overcrowded boats, took the "rich man's route," traveling by water all the way to the diggings. There were several other ways to reach the northern goldfields but only a small minority took them.

The Dalton Trail, which began at the present location of Haines, Alaska, was perceived by many, at least those with pack animals, to be the best route of all. It was the third of the three "grease trails" of the Chilkat Tlingits. It went overland about 245 long, but relatively easy, miles, following the route of today's Haines Cutoff. It hit the Yukon at Fort Selkirk.

One reason it was not more popular during the Klondike rush was that since Jack Dalton had learned the way by following Chilkat packers in 1890, he had established a lucrative trading business along the trail and regarded the route, save for Native use, as his private cattle drive trail for supplying inland miners. Therefore, until about 1896, when he began operating it as a for-profit toll road, he did not advertise it as a way to reach the gold fields. By that time, the Chilkoot and White passes were so widely known that few goldseekers took other pathways to reach the Klondike.

Rod Perry: *Jack Dalton led a long, fabulously adventurous, sometimes violent life. He served a pivotal role in many business explorations and commercial ventures central to a significant part of early-day Alaskan development. Dalton's second son, James W. Dalton, an engineer,*

231

served in Dutch Harbor alongside Al Preston in the Naval Construction Battalion, the "Sea Bees." (Like many of Alaska's miners, Al patriotically put down his pick and shovel to serve his nation at war. Al was working at Dutch Harbor when the Japanese bombed the base on Alaska's Aleutian Islands on June 3, 1942.)

Later, James Dalton served as a supervisor of the Distant Early Warning System (DEW Line) Cold War defense system in Alaska. Early on, oil companies exploring Alaska's North Slope consulted with him for his expertise in arctic engineering. The 414-mile-long supply road to Alaska's oil fields on the Arctic Ocean was named the James W. Dalton Highway in his honor.

James Dalton's young wife, Kathleen "Mike" Dalton, widowed when he died of a sudden heart attack in 1957, continued to be prominent in the civic life of Fairbanks. In the early winter of 1983–84, I was privileged to work shoulder-to-shoulder with Mike as she dived into helping Yukon Quest International Sled Dog Race founder Leroy Shank and our core group, get the thousand-mile event that leads between Fairbanks, Alaska, and Whitehorse, Yukon Territory, off and running.

———◆———

For transportation of passengers, both the poor man's and rich man's routes had their advantages and disadvantages. The Chilkoot and White Pass routes were shorter, only 1,600 miles or so north from Seattle to the Klondike River. They began with a relatively short, easy ocean voyage. From Seattle, for most of the almost 1,000 miles up the coast of British Columbia and Southeastern Alaska, shipping cruised within the protected waters of the Inside Passage. From the head of Lynn Canal, it was "only thirty-two miles" over the Chilkoot Trail and "slightly more than forty miles" over the White Pass to the headwaters of the Yukon. (But, oh, what miles they were!) From there they could float downstream with the current, albeit, a current that included two sets of perilous rapids.

Goldseekers taking either of the poor man's routes could also start earlier in the season. By crossing the passes well before ice-out and building boats or rafts, they could be poised to float to the diggings the moment the Yukon broke up.

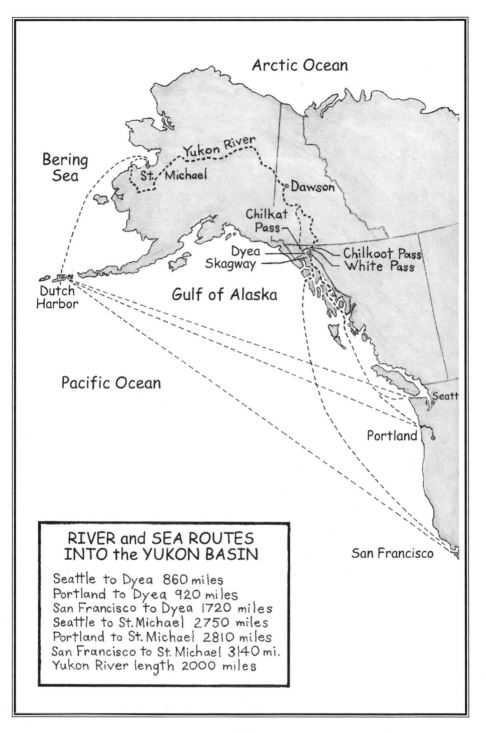

Arctic Ocean

Bering
Sea

Yukon River

St. Michael

Dawson

Chilkat
Pass

Dyea
Skagway

Chilkoot Pass
White Pass

Dutch
Harbor

Gulf of Alaska

Pacific Ocean

Seatt

Portland

**RIVER and SEA ROUTES
INTO the YUKON BASIN**

Seattle to Dyea 860 miles
Portland to Dyea 920 miles
San Francisco to Dyea 1720 miles
Seattle to St. Michael 2750 miles
Portland to St. Michael 2810 miles
San Francisco to St. Michael 3140 mi.
Yukon River length 2000 miles

San Francisco

The offsetting disadvantages were several. The final pitch to the summit of the Chilkoot Pass was so steep that the trekker could reach out and touch the ground ahead. In winter, avalanches thundered down from the slopes above. The White Pass was not much better, evidenced by the fact that several thousand horses died as stampeders attempted to use pack animals in the crossing.

Once they packed across either pass and descended to the chain of lakes connected to the upper river, it was necessary for travelers to stop and construct rafts or painstakingly whipsaw lumber and build boats from native materials. Beyond the lakes, they floated anywhere from 300 to 800 miles of river, depending upon where they stopped to prospect. Once they reached their destination, they had but a bare minimum of supplies and gear to support their prospecting efforts.

The advantage for goldseekers taking the all-water passage from Seattle to the upper Yukon was that they could outfit themselves as heavily as they wished and get it there with little or no physical effort of their own. As sail and steam did the work, passengers could sit back and view the scenery all the way.

Passage on stern-wheelers plying the Yukon was hard to come by. There were only a few such specialized craft working the river, just enough to take care of the pre-rush needs. It would take shipbuilders awhile to catch up with the exploding demand. Therefore, boat owners charged premium prices.

The all-water route held several other disadvantages. First, to go from Seattle by ship all the way up the coast, across the Gulf of Alaska, around the Alaska Peninsula and across the Bering Sea to the Yukon mouth was a trip of over 2,750 miles in length, more or less, and the voyage was often ravaged by tremendous storms. It was a far greater undertaking than the short, easy sail up the inside passage to Skagway or Dyea. Naturally, it was much more expensive.

Second, the Yukon River quite often cleared of ice before the sea ice cleared enough to let oceangoing ships through to St. Michael. And hazardous navigational conditions from ice-out ended on the upper river before they did far downstream. That combination allowed river travel to begin from the headwaters significantly before steamers could head upstream from the mouth. Therefore, in a race to a new strike, especially a strike located on the far upper river, those waiting at the Yukon mouth would lose to those who went over either the Chilkoot Pass or White Pass early enough in spring to have their boats built and waiting to push off at headwaters ice-out.

Now when it came to the commercial movement of freight and mail, as stated, not only was the Chilkoot Trail many times too steep to negotiate readily by draft or pack animals, the climb was so demanding that loads had to be broken down into parcels and packed over the summit in repetitious trips. And we have seen that the White Pass offered different challenges but was just about as difficult. Therefore, while the Chilkoot and White Pass Trails served adequately for the mere passage of early miners hauling just enough to get them into the country to start prospecting, the effort required was far too labor-intensive to be practical for commercial enterprises such as trading posts and stores to use in the large-scale transport of the heavy supply upon which the miners who stayed in the North depended.

To move large amounts of equipment and supplies into the gold country, shipment by water was the only practical way. Not only was it economically efficient, but beyond loading and offloading, delivering the tonnage required minimal physical effort. Very little that equipped and supplied any of the diggings along the Yukon River and its tributaries prior to 1900 came into the country any other way.

Alfred Hulse Brooks: "Before the Klondike rush, the major holdup to the region's development had been that the gold country was isolated from the industrialized world for two-thirds of the year. Cut off from freeze-up in mid-September to breakup in late May, the lack of travel, communication, and supply simply strangled the region.

"I say eight months because, in addition to deep winter, hazardous river ice conditions during spring and fall stopped traffic completely. In spring there was a period as the ice weakened that it was unsafe for dog team travel. Then until the river cleared of ice water travel was impossible. In fall it was reversed between when flowing ice stopped steamboat traffic and the ice became strong enough to safely run on. It varied with the character of the breakup and freeze-up each year, but together, those spring and fall transition periods could add up to two or even three months without any kind of freight, mail or personal movement between salt water and the Yukon Basin.

"Before 1898–99, there were so few prospectors and miners working the country, with just a limited amount of gold being produced that there were relatively small requirements for supply of food and equipment. So this had never come close to mounting official pressure to make worthy the slightest consideration for a road project of the size and scope needed to breach the mountain barrier. That changed with the great rush to the Klondike."

Chapter 17

---◆---

The White Pass Railroad
and Overland Wagon Road

IT TOOK SOMETHING CATACLYSMIC, an explosion the size of the booming Klondike strike, to blow things wide open for development of winter transportation into the northern interior. Until 1896, the population of Yukon Territory stood at about 5,000, First Nations people plus the very hardiest, most intrepid explorers, fur traders, prospectors, missionaries, and a handful of merchant companies and river transportation interests. The Yukon River on the Alaska side was likewise sparsely populated with the same mix. But by 1899, the great rush of humanity into the Klondike caused a previously almost unpeopled area in an almost unmapped region of the North to explode into an instant wilderness metropolis of as many as for 40,000 inhabitants, and perhaps even 50,000 if the count took in the nearby region. It comprised the largest Canadian population center west of Winnipeg, Manitoba.

Before, in both Canada and the United States, the few stories coming out of the Yukon River had been colorful, but of minor importance on the overall scale of national news. The great rush, however, commonly created sensational, front-page national coverage and became an everyday conversational topic across the continent. Among the people of Canada and the United States, the Yukon District and Alaska grew greatly within the public perception as valued possessions.

---■---

Old Ben Atwater: "Interesting to note, Al, at Dawson's peak, I figured U.S. citizens outnumbered Canadians at least ten to one, maybe fifteen to one. Americans held most of the claims. No wonder United

States citizens felt such a strong connection to the Klondike. We felt like our stake east of Ogilvie's survey line was as important as the Canadians' part."

————◆—————◆————

Alfred Hulse Brooks: "With the exploding population and emerging economic importance, the Far North was desperate for a better transportation system. Not only could such a booming area not *thrive* with a mere four-month transportation system, such a large population and that much industry could hardly *survive*. How could the region grow, having to cope as it did with virtually all movement of travelers, mail and freight to and from the outside world shut down eight months a year? And how about having to guess ahead up to twenty months in advance the number of inhabitants and where they'd be? One can see how nearly impossible it was without year-round, high-volume, ready transportation to and from the outside world to adequately serve the travel, communication, and supply needs of Far North people and industry."

————◆—————◆————

Rod Perry: *According to some reports, population of the Klondike area at its peak reached about two-thirds the population of Seattle. Imagine how Seattle would have fared had it been closed off from all ground and sea shipping eight months yearly!*

The Yukon and Alaska, according to the prevailing mind of the day, probably held untold hidden mineral wealth. Popular opinion held that the Klondike discovery was likely only the tip of the iceberg. With the boom and its excitement driving thousands of prospectors to search out every nook and cranny, other rich locations, it was felt, were sure to be found. Even the most casual observation showed that lack of adequate year-round transportation constricted development of the Dawson area. How much more, analysts were saying, would it choke a country when a number of such finds were made?

————◆—————◆————

Capturing the attention and romantic emotions of the continent, the roaring Klondike strike brought tremendous pressure upon the Canadian government to provide an efficient, high-capacity transportation system over which people, mail, and supplies could readily flow regardless of season. In addition, it opened up lucrative opportunity for industry to throw its might into its building.

Men of action sped to build a railroad from salt water into the gold country. At the last of the nineteenth century, developers did not become bogged down in today's endless permit processes, congressional hearings, partisan politics, environmental concerns, and the like. North America was in an empire-building mode and developers were encouraged to open up the country.

At the very peak of the Klondike Gold Rush, on May 28, 1898—the day before the ice went out on the Yukon, allowing the great armada of the Chilkoot and White Pass stampeders to begin their float toward Dawson—construction of the White Pass and Yukon Railway began at Skagway.

In just one year, in a remarkable feat enabled by British financing, American engineering, and Canadian contracting, and powered with almost superhuman effort, the narrow-gauge roadbed was cut, filled, and blasted, tunneled, and trestled through the rugged Coast Mountains barrier into the Interior. Rails reached Lake Bennett in the summer of 1899. A year later, on July 29, 1900, only twenty-five months after the start of construction, the 110 miles of track connected Whitehorse to salt water.

No longer was the Yukon Basin so completely walled off.

———◆—◆———

Al Preston: "I remember an old-timer of the country describing the absolute night-and-day changes he found in the new railroad: 'A journey that used to be an odyssey that took us old prospectors weeks, even months of incredible, severe exertion has now become a relaxing ride. Now, while carrying as much luggage or freight as I decide to ship in, tons at a time if I want, I can lean back in my cushioned seat while I take in glorious vistas. In a short few hours, I now pull into Whitehorse, relaxed and uplifted.' "

239

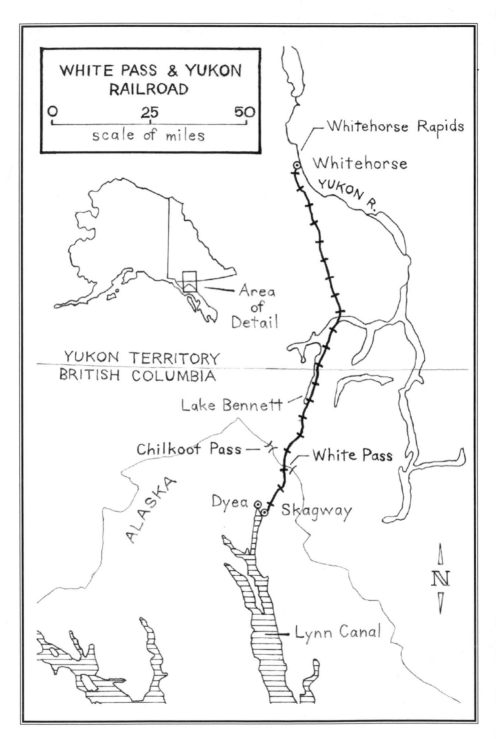

WHITE PASS & YUKON RAILROAD

0   25   50
scale of miles

Whitehorse Rapids

Whitehorse

YUKON R.

Area of Detail

YUKON TERRITORY
BRITISH COLUMBIA

Lake Bennett

Chilkoot Pass —

White Pass

Dyea   Skagway

ALASKA

Lynn Canal

N

Not only was it shorter, now 330 miles long, the improved route, because it was located off the river, eliminated holdups and dangers inherent in traveling Yukon River ice with its vagaries. The Overland Road thereby substantially enhanced conditions for freighting and gained several weeks annually for shipping and travel.

Even with the coming of the road, during the four months of open water, heavy use of the waterway between Whitehorse and Dawson by steamboats still provided by far the most efficient and economical shipping. Therefore, by careful preplanning, businesses and individuals had most of the region's freight brought in during shipping season. However, with the advent of the Overland Road, during the eight months that the river was non-navigable, at least teamsters were able to regularly move mail and materials by the *ton* into the brawling Canadian supply hub. They not only carried much more, they did it faster than dog teams ever had over the old, longer river route.

The Arctic Limited stage line, which regularly changed to fresh teams at waypoints along the way, covered the 330-mile distance between Whitehorse and Dawson once each week carrying passengers, baggage and light freight. At slower speeds than the Limited's fliers, private contractors moved heavy freight.

Alfred Hulse Brooks: "The White Pass and Yukon Route (WP&YR)— the combined railroad and Overland Road—was the most valuable addition to the developing infrastructure of the Yukon Territory and Alaska since the advent of the steamboat and trading post system on the Yukon River. Before the WP&YR, there had been no viable way to swiftly travel, communicate, or transport anything or in and out of the North once freeze-up shut down the great waterway. Prior to the railroad, supplying the Yukon Basin depended totally upon accurately guessing the numbers and whereabouts of the population and its needs sometimes approaching two years in advance. That was not always possible, as evidenced during the great shortages of the Klondike Rush.

"Finally, though, with the coming of the railroad, summer or winter, supplies and equipment could be brought into the Interior not just by the ton, but by the hundreds of tons. Mail service became regular and travelers could move readily in and out of the North. If freight were needed badly enough, even in winter an order could be sent from Dawson to Seattle and it was possible to receive it within the month, sometimes faster.

"Before, no matter how badly mail, freight, or people had needed to be moved between the States and the North during winter, it had been a virtual impossibility. However, once the railroad established year-round transport from the North Pacific through to the Yukon drainage it relaxed winter's stranglehold. Now anywhere in the entire Yukon Drainage and beyond, if a person wanted something from the States badly enough it was entirely accessible. That is, if he was willing to pay the high cost of dog team freighting."

Once mountains of supplies began to reach the Klondike year around, and mail and travelers could readily flow both ways, other strikes that had not been big enough to demand construction of such a winter supply system began to greatly benefit. Immediately, Alaskan dog drivers, such as Ben Atwater, beat in winter trails along several hundred miles of the upper Yukon River. Accessing the supply wealth of Dawson, they took goods to hubs serving older gold discovery sites of the late 1880s and early 1890s such as Fortymile, Belle Isle, Circle City, and even to an extent, Fort Yukon, Rampart and Beaver. The biggest benefit was regular mail.

Rod Perry: *One young Upper Yukon dog driver of the day, Harry Karstens, a.k.a. The Seventy-Mile Kid was already well known in the North when Charles Sheldon, avid hunter, naturalist, and wealthy friend of Theodore Roosevelt ventured into the Alaska Range north and east of Mount McKinley to explore, study the flora and fauna, observe the change of seasons, and collect museum specimens. Sheldon hired Karstens to assist him. When Sheldon's work resulted in the creation of Mount McKinley—now Denali—National Park, Sheldon pushed to make Karstens its first superintendent.*

When Hudson Stuck, archdeacon of the Episcopal Church in Alaska, organized the first successful climb of Mount McKinley, he chose Karstens to lead the climb. The route he chose, later named Karstens Ridge proved the most practical way to the summit until the Alaska Earthquake of Good Friday, 1964 destroyed it as an easy route. (Author's recommendation: Read The Wilderness of Denali *by Charles Sheldon,* Ten Thousand Miles on a Dog Sled *and* The Ascent of Denali *by Hudson Stuck, and* My Life of High Adventure *by Grant Pearson.)*

Chapter 18

———◆———

Early Dog Team Freighting on the Upper Yukon

ALL THE GOLD STRIKES WERE LOCATED well back from the Yukon along the Klondike, Sixtymile and Fortymile rivers, Birch Creek, Preacher Creek, and other tributaries. Distances as far as 100 trail miles separated some of the diggings from the main river. Therefore, freighting by dog team was crucial to moving supplies and equipment back to the mines.

———◆———

Rod Perry: *Hardly any of the miners during the gold rush era owned dogs; they were too busy prospecting and mining to afford the money, time, and trouble to keep a team. About the only dog teams in the country besides small teams kept by the Natives were owned by hard-working professional freighters, mail carriers, and white trappers. These great dog men, upon whom everyone else so depended were known and looked up to throughout the whole North.*

When reporters converged upon the North to feed a nation hungry for romantic tales of gold-rush adventure, writers glorified feats of some the foremost dog punchers, grew them larger than life, and they became luminaries known 'round the globe. Some of their names: Frank Tondreau, aka The Malamute Kid; Harry Karstens, The Seventy-Mile Kid; Captain Ulysses Grant Norton, the Tireless Trojan of the Trails; The Wandering Japanese, Jujira Wada; and the great Eskimo driver, Split-the-Wind. Less known to readers Outside but just as highly esteemed by men throughout the North were others such as The Goin' Kid and Ben Atwater, among others. These men contracted with either the Alaska Commercial Company, the North American Trade and Transportation Company, a few lesser commercial suppliers, or with the miners themselves. Some, such as Ben Atwater, contracted to carry U.S. mail.

A picture of Ben and his team was the most popular picture sold at the 1909 World's Fair held in Seattle, the Alaska-Yukon-Pacific Exposition.

The price of goods sitting in company warehouses was already high, and understandably so. Trading companies had to cover the expense of the procurement and expediting in the States, the sea voyage to St. Michael, the 1,100-to 1,700-mile stern-wheeler trip against the current from the mouth up to the various supply centers and all the attendant costs such as labor, fuel, storage, capital construction and maintenance, coverage of risk from loss at sea and fires, and, of course, profit to investors. Freighting supplies and equipment from company warehouses out to the miners added greatly to the cost. At the height of the Klondike rush the going rate rose to $1.25 a pound from Dawson to the most distant claims. But there were no other options. Without the dog teams, much of the mining would have ground to a halt.

Alma Preston: "Rod,those dog drivers worked, literally, hundreds of thousands of cumulative winter trail miles. As they did, they invented and perfected methods and means. None I know of describes these better than our old friend, The Goin' Kid. . . ."

The Goin' Kid: "Most professional freighters in those early years 'long the upper Yukon used a system we perfected. 'Twas geared t' the conditions 'n kinda work we were doin'. Miss Alma, by the time you came up 'n started workin' for the Colonel out o' Seward, it'd disappeared. Now I hardly ever see dog freightin' done like it anymore. Here's the way it works: Yukon sleds, not basket sleds're used. They have flat beds usually seven feet long, twenty inches wide. Supportin' cross bents clear the trail four inches under the load. Runners're just sixteen inches, outside t' outside, t' follow narrow trails. We hitch three sleds t' track close one behind 'nother by cross chainin' 'em in t' a train. Right crossin' t' left 'n left crossin' t' right, short lengths o' chain fixed t' the front corners o' the trailin' sled attach t' the opposite rear corners o' the sled ahead. This forces the trailers t' follow just about perfectly 'n the tracks o' the sled 'n front.

"Freightin' back then's very heavy. Trails're rough as a cob. That triple Yukon sled method works better'n any other. Makes possible fer one lone man t' work heavier loads 'n other ways used anywhere else 'n the North. Three seven-foot sleds spread the load over a much longer bearin' surface 'n if you use just one, standard, twelve-foot basket sled. Keeps the center o' gravity lower. The jointed sled train flexes over obstacles. Think of a chain draggin' over a log. Snakes through forest trails so twistin' ya could never get a longer sled through. When one 'r more sleds tip over, one lone driver c'n usually right one at a time without havin' t' unload. An' when ya come t' places too steep, ya just take 'em apart 'n go with one at a time up 'r down.

"The load everyone thinks of as a standard contract load, at least over flat 'r gently rollin' country's 1,200 pounds. We're careful t' figure "draft" 'n arrange the loads t' get the weight's close t' the power's we can. The cargo's ideally loaded 600 pounds on the lead, 400 on the mid, 'n 200 on the trailer sled. On each sled, we want the center o' gravity a third back from the front.

"Drivers figure six 'r seven big dogs make a full team. An' these're big dogs. We dog punchers used a lotta malamutes. They're coastal Eskimo dogs 'bout 100 pounds weight. In fall they're brought up from the coast on the steamboats. But for heavy freightin' you can't beat Mackenzie River Huskies. Also crosses to the old Native breeds of the Mackenzie prob'ly put together decades before by the Hudson's Bay Company. They're larger, stronger 'n better draft animals 'n the coastal dogs. Finest team I've seen has a couple that weigh 160 pounds. All go not far shy o' that. And that's dogs 'n the lean, hard, workin' weight o' late winter.

"Team's harnessed single file. Dogs pull from leather collars akin t' horse collars. The tubular leather structures're stuffed tight. Usually with caribou hair. Traces from the lead dog run from 'is collar t' 'bout four inches in back o' the hips o' dog behind. There, they snap into a ring on that second dog's traces. This hookup's repeated all the way back 'til it reaches the last two dogs. Both of 'em're attached t' a spreader bar called a whiffle-tree. The whiffle-tree's far enough

One Version of Single File Hookup.
Note Freight Collars and Modified Yukon Sled.

Alaska Museum at Rasmuson Center, John Urban Collection,
Loman and Hanford Stationery and Printing Co., AMRC-b64-1-89

behind the rear dog—called the 'sled dog' on the upper Yukon back then—'e can readily jump out from between the traces. That's t' help the driver maneuver the sled 'roun tight corners. The whiffle-tree's attached t' the sled bridle with a five-foot-long tow line. The driver straddles the tow line, walkin' 'tween the sled dog 'n the sled.

"He steers with a gee pole attached t' the side o' the front o' the lead sled. Grasps it in 'is right hand. Les he's left-handed o'course, then uses a haw pole. Over smoother trails, the gee pole's angled t' waist height 'n used as a powerful steerin' lever. But over tussock-ridden trails roughed in from the Yukon t' the mines, most drivers angle it up t' shoulder height. Higher-angled gee pole's a vertical lever, too. Keeps the lead sled from tippin' over the same time it's a side-to-side lever for steerin'. Keep the heaviest sled in front from tippin' 'n that sled stayin' upright helps hold the second o' the trailers from tippin' 'cause they're cross chained so close.

"Yukon sleds got no brake like on a basket sled. Goin' down hills, the driver unsnaps the towline from the sled bridle. Just turns the dogs loose as a harnessed team. Then 'e takes the sleds down by 'imself. If the hill's gentle, 'e just eans back on the gee pole 'n digs in 'is heels t' brake. But 1,200 pounds're too much on steep downhills.

Several freighters have been killed 'n crashes. One's gee pole broke 'n the stub ran 'im through. Down steepest slopes, safe way's sleds're levered over 'n turned on their sides 'n dragged down one atta time.

"Goin' out loaded, dogs make only 'bout three miles'n hour. Diggin' inta their work, they don't need much room 'tween 'em. They're harnessed up separated, nose t' tail, less'n a dog length 'tween. Keeps total team length short. Power stays close t' the load. But empty, you come back atta smart trot. Sometimes even break in t' a lope. Then the team does better havin' the traces lengthened. More freedom o' motion. 'Stead o' snappin' the traces o' the dog in front in t' rings four inches behind the next dog back, they're snapped in t' another set o' rings midway along the ribs o' the followin' dog. Gives each dog a couple extra feet. Comin' back empty at five, six miles'n hour, the driver still trots most o' the time. No place t' stand on a Yukon sled. If the goin's flat 'n smooth 'n the driver wants t' ride, 'e has t' sit'r kneel perched on the load. Load goin' home carries camp 'n trail gear. Mid 'n trailer sleds'r lashed on top. He positioned dog food caches fer the return trip on the way out.

"Shelter cabins (not tended roadhouses) 'r built'n average day's travel—'bout twenty miles—apart 'long the main trails t' the mines. They're simple—log walls, sod roofs, dirt floors, window 'r two, a door, a woodstove. Pole bunks'r piled with wild hay. Freighters haul 'n cook their own food 'n cut their own stove wood.

"Drivers work their teams 'bout eight hours a day durin' short winter light. Leaves 'em lots o' time stopped. On faint trails t' more off-beaten-track diggin's, there's no shelter cabins. Dog punchers camp 'n the open like this:

"A camp location's picked where two trees stand 'bout four t' six feet apart. Against 'em we pile a half cord o' six-foot green logs. Makes a high wall t' reflect heat. Front o' the pile a big fire's kindled o' dead, dry wood. Then it's fed green logs from the pile. Side o' the fire opposite the pile, the puncher puts down a thick bed o' spruce feathers. Next a canvas, then a caribou hide, hair side up, then 'is fur sleepin' robe. Last the canvas wraps over the top fer warmth 'n t' guard the robe from sparks. T' keep the side o' the bed away from the fire from losin' heat ya pile up a high wall o' snow. That 'r hang a canvas fer a reflector. Such a camp setup's comfortable at forty below. Keeps it bearable way lower.

"People who don't know a lick 'bout life in cold country think you better not ever go t' sleep, you'll never wake up. Miss Alma, you'n I know that's plain corral dust. If they'd think 'bout it, when they're home a'bed 'n get a bit chilly, what happens? Makes 'em uncomfortable 'n wakes 'em up. Add a quilt 'n go back t' sleep. Same thing 'n the trail. Wakes ya up long 'fore you're cold 'nough t' matter. Just stay right 'n bed. Reach out with a long pole with a stub of a branch for a hook. Pull a few logs down. Roll 'em from the top o' the stack in t' the fire. This ol' camp method's largely replaced. Now most everybody uses light wall tents 'n Yukon stoves.

"Sled dogs 'n the days 'fore the big rush 'r extremely valued. But they used t' have a hard life. Usually short. 'Fore the multitudes came in, a workin' husky can usually be had for three t' five dollars. But the great Klondike Rush skyrockets demand way beyond the number o' local native dogs. Goldfields and the country couldn'ta been developed without dogs. As demand rises, steamboats begin shippin' malamutes in from the coast. Men from the States comin' up bring every large dog they c'n lay hands on that looks able t' tighten 'is traces. Even with the added supply few're extra fer purchase. Boom years o' the rush, goin' price fer a proven sled dog rises t' $300.

"Miss Alma, like you, I'm attached t' my dogs 'n glad they have it a lot better these days. But back then, sought-after as the animals are while they're workin' through the long winters, they drop'n value t' nex t' nothin at end o' the freightin' season. Before the White Pass 'n Yukon Route 'n Overland Wagon Road created regular supply lines, facin' near starvation used t' be expected every winter fer the miners themselves. Summers're spent workin' 'n scrapin' up 'nough t' make it through the next winter. With humans so threatened, even in summer the old-timers didn't have anything t' feed nonworkin' dogs. Common practice was t' save only the very best. They'd shoot the rest each spring. Spared the poor animals misery of a summer o' starvation. Nobody liked it. But 'twas reality of a harsh life. Dog punchers depended on findin' replacements 'fore next freeze-up."

Rod Perry: *Surviving dogs were turned loose to fend for themselves over the summer. Most on-the-spot chronicles of the gold rush devote some space to the tremendous cunning and skill the voracious animals developed as thieves. All who would succeed along the Yukon had to learn to "think like a dog" in this aspect of dog behavior. The animals would rarely let an opportunity escape them, whether it was biting through tin cans, making catlike climbs newcomers would swear no canine could accomplish, or curling up innocently near a tent, feigning sleep, patiently waiting for hours for the inhabitants to leave so that they might move in and ransack it.*

Old Ben Atwater: "Two prospectors boated down to Circle City on business. They fixed their loaded boat to a running line and pulled it a ways offshore to keep it safe. Then they commenced to walk into town. When they got back, they were amazed and roaring angry over what they found: a pack of loose dogs'd obviously sized things up, swum out, bit through the rope holding the boat, and dragged the craft ashore. Starving critters hadn't left one single bag of provisions unripped. They were gorged on the contents. Even ate the dry flour and the dishrag.

"Another time in Circle City a desperate, starving sled dog saw his chance when a Native woman turned her back for a moment. He dashed into a cabin and made off with the body of the baby his grieving mother'd been preparing for burial. As the dog dashed through town with his prize, miners gave chase. A passel of them ran him 'til the animal dropped the little corpse. Then all the men helped the poor woman bury her baby."

Rod Perry: *In most situations it was not the wild animals so much as the tenacity and depredations of the loose dogs that provided the chief motivation behind innovation of one of the most useful structures and picturesque symbols of the North, the elevated food cache.*

Old Ben Atwater: "Even with all the damage they could cause, in winter dogs were too precious to destroy. So sometimes we had to tether them. Before chain got common up here, we used an age-old Native trick. We drilled a hole an inch in from each end of a two-inch diameter, four-or five-foot-long pole. A rawhide thong passed through one hole and around a tree or other solid station with a loop that let the pole swing or circle. The other end was snubbed so close to a loop snugly circling the dog's neck, any try to turn to gnaw the pole only pushed it out of reach or tightened the loop on his neck so tight he gave up trying.

"On the trail, I never do, but after the evening feeding, some drivers practiced turning their huskies loose to choose their own place to bed down. They didn't wander far; didn't want to leave the source of food. When the driver was ready to move out, well-trained dogs would come mill around in position near their own collar, ready to be harnessed."

The Goin' Kid: "Me, I never turn workin' dogs loose fer the night. Surefire way t' lose your lash-up. Hunger of a husky fer leather's got no limit. Leave their moose-hair-stuffed, leather work collars where a loose dog can get at 'em, they'll be eat up by mornin'. Most o' us teamsters built our traces o' webbin' rather'n leather. Makes 'em unappealin'. But if you're not careful 'n ever get a little splash o' grease 'r feed soaked in t' 'em, dogs'll eat those, too. Even when workin', the puncher's got t' watch 'is harnesses 'n lines like a hawk. While stopped, better keep the animals strung out. Bunch together 'n they eat each other's collars. Sooner 'r later, even if ya try t' stay watchful, ya can't spend every second on the alert, 'n they'll eat up their own gear. Out'n the cold, a man works up a powerful hunger. But it's left far behind by the appetite of a dog.

"Campin' on the trail, one dog puncher friend o' mine has a dog slip 'is tether. In the mornin' the animal's fast asleep. Shows no sign— other'n bein' untied—he's been up to any deviltry durin' the night.

But then my friend gets busy loadin' 'is sled and harnessin' up. Item by item 'e discovers the husky's night's work. The dog's completely eat up the driver's valued pair o' large gauntlet gloves. Chewed down every inch o' babiche from the laborious lacin' of a snowshoe. Munched a whole, long, braided whip—includin' part o' the wooden handle. Gobbled a long leather gun case strap, nibbled away the leather bindin' on a canvas container 'n devoured part o' 'is own harness."

———————————

Rod Perry: *Better supply lines from salt water into the Yukon Basin vastly improved the lot of not only the human, but the canine population. A growing number of enterprising individuals began catching, drying, and selling salmon to the dog drivers. That allowed the animals to be summered over. Equipment improved. Gold strikes on the west coast exposed upriver drivers to Russian and Eskimo sled designs and their ways of harnessing, arranging, and driving a dog team.*

Dog driving on the upper Yukon evolved and many of the freighting methods of the early days faded out.

One thing that did not seem to fade out is the language that old-time dog drivers thought necessary for the successful plying of their craft. The early French and Metis drivers of the Hudson's Bay Company were legendary at keeping the air blue with the vilest of cursings. But even refined gentlemen thought rough language basic. As a frontier Moravian missionary doctor, founder of hospitals in Seward and Nenana, esteemed pioneer doctor practicing in Anchorage, mayor of Alaska's biggest city, and author of the book, Dog Team Doctor, *Dr. J. Herman Romig claimed he needed to be trilingual, requiring one language for the practice of medicine, one for the pulpit, and an altogether separate tongue for the driving of dogs.*

William Healy Dall, one of the greatest biologists the United States has ever produced, and the son of a kindly, mild-mannered pastor, had this to say about his experiences driving dogs during his years in Alaska during the 1860s: "It is said that no man can drive dogs without swearing. I think it is in a manner true. At all events, he must have a ready store of energetic expletives to keep them on the qui vive. *In Russian America we always used the indigenous epithets, which, as we did not understand them, were hardly sinful . . . it was lucky for Job that he was not set to dog driving: if he had been, I fear his posthumous reputation would have suffered."*

Chapter 19

---◆---

Winter Mail in the Early Days

PRIOR TO THE GREAT RUSH to the Klondike, almost no winter travel at all took place between the Yukon Basin and salt water. One winter when Circle City was at its peak by William Ogilvie's estimate as many as 3,000 headquartered out of the town; only one dog team ventured to make the perilous trip of 850 miles out to Lynn Canal and just two made it in. This passage required starting with the mountainous load of gear and food required to survive the trip. There was simply little or no capacity on the sled for anything else such as mail.

There were no official mail carriers. Mail *to* the miners stacked up down in Juneau and mail *from* the miners accumulated in the trading posts. Anyone traveling in or out who was willing to add to his sledload carried the mail at a dollar a letter. Those sending letters accepted that there was a good chance that the mail would never reach its destination. The trip was so long and almost impossibly difficult that everyone regarded it as a gamble whether or not even the traveler himself could make it through at all. And that was without carrying anything extra. With neither a broken trail, a source of resupply, nor any chance of assistance in that desolate, uninhabited country, the journey often broke down into a driver's desperate battle for his very own survival. When things became that grim, the first thing to go was the mail. Letters were usually burned to protect their private nature.

In the normal course of things, a miner might write a letter and, if he received a reply within a year or eighteen months, he felt fortunate that the mail had made it both ways. Of course, answers to questions he had asked a year and a half before often puzzled him. Chances were good that not only could he not remember just what it was that he had asked, by that time he probably could not remember that he had asked anything at all.

During the great Klondike rush, multitudes pushing through at all seasons kept the trail broken and there were more resources for resupply and aid along the way. That opened opportunity for cargo to be included in the sledload beyond what was required for bare survival.

At first, people like famed "Klondike Mike" Mahoney filled part of the winter demand. In 1897 he carried mail at one dollar a letter between Dawson and Skagway. His 1,200-mile round trips took one month. As he started, his sled carried 250 pounds of mail and 500 pounds of gear and food for himself and his dogs. He brought outdated newspapers which were read (by others—he hadn't yet learned to read) to gathered miners for a fee as he distributed the mail in the far-flung camps. By late winter, after having been cut off from the civilized world since ice-up closed navigation the prior fall, the miners were so starved for news they devoured each sentence with ravenous voracity.

By 1898 the population in the Klondike overwhelmed Mahoney's efforts to fill the postal need. The North West Mounted Police took over the mail run. Relays of men and teams going day and night could complete the trip one way in a week.

———————

Rod Perry: *It was one thing for the Mounties to haul 250 pounds of mail at a time on those Pony Express–like relays. But if it had been 250 pounds of freight it would have provided but a mere drop in the bucket compared to the vast supply needs of 40,000–50,000 inhabitants of the Upper Yukon. Clearly, during the two-thirds of the year the Klondike was ice-locked, the region cried out for something with infinitely greater carrying capacity than piecemeal dog team transport.*

Actually, as the population skyrocketed, 250 pounds of mail per trip became a mere drop in the bucket compared to the total postal demand. It may be that, overwhelmed, the Mounties had to limit their service to Canadian mail. Whether or not that was the cause, between freeze-up of the Yukon in September 1898 and January 1899 there was no American delivery into Dawson. U.S. mail mounded up, warehoused in Skagway. Desperate Americans in Dawson as well as citizens back home in the States pressured the Postal Service until they began to award contracts for dog-team mail delivery. Ben Atwater was awarded one of the first—if not the very first—Skagway-to-Dawson contracts. Soon, following the Nome discovery, his contract extended to that great Seward Peninsula strike, making his round trip a 4,600-mile-long run.

(And "run" is exactly what it was for Old Ben. In his famous picture below he is hauling the mail on two Yukon sleds—hand sleds—cross-lashed to form a train. Notice there are neither runner tails extending behind the sleds upon which Atwater could stand, nor structure extending above the bed to which he could hold for balance. Ben Atwater did what all drivers of the day did, trotted along under his own power between sled and dogs, steering, as he is pictured here, with right hand on the gee-pole.

When the White Pass and Yukon Route breeched the mountain stronghold in 1899 to connect ice-free salt water to the Upper Yukon interior of course it changed mail delivery dramatically. Prior to the railroad, the great bottleneck for all passage—freight, communication,

Ben Atwater and His Dogsled Team Arriving at Bennett Lake from Circle City, Alaska with U.S. Mail

University of Washington Libraries, Special Collections, Hegg 064

Train of Three Yukon Sleds Freighting to Nome
From Ships Standing Offshore

Anchorage Museum at Rasmuson Center, O.D. Goetze Collection,
O.D. Goetze (Otto Daniel), AMRC-601-41-209

and personal travel—had been the extremely brutal and perilous crossing of the blizzard-ridden Coast Mountains. Once rails reached Lake Bennett in 1899 dog teams could use the end of steel as their trailhead and they no longer had to negotiate the treacherous mountain stretch.

Clouds moving in from the exceedingly high-rainfall area of the adjacent coast—where some locations receive more than 100 inches of annual precipitation—dump prodigious snowfalls as they encounter the crags rimming the Pacific. (Rule-of-thumb conversion ratio of rain to wet coastal snow is about 1—10.) The pileup of literally hundreds of inches of winter pack in the mountains leaves little moisture to be dropped on the interior side of the range, creating a rain shadow. The Whitehorse area receives but six inches of precipitation yearly. What snow does reach the upper Yukon Basin tends to be dry and powdery.

Not only was the snow easier to cope with once the Interior was gained, but the railroad eliminated the steep elevation pitch up or down that had so greatly limited what a dog team could carry into or out of the region. After railroad engines had done the heavy lifting, mail carriers had an essentially level run over the two thousand miles of the Yukon River Trail between Lake Bennett and St. Michael. Elevation difference at those opposite ends was but about 700 feet. Essentially level going allowed transport of heavy loads.

Chapter 20

---◆---

Thoroughfare of the North

THE GREAT YUKON RIVER HIGHWAY is an age-old trail, broken before the dawn of man's arrival there. Before the earliest inhabitants came, its two-thousand-mile-long course had been cleared and leveled into a grand thoroughfare by waters draining the interior of an entire subcontinent following the path of least resistance to the sea. When the ancients immigrated into this vast, 327,000-square-mile basin, they found it braided with a veritable superhighway system, a huge web of connected travel routes leading to and from the farthest reaches. The great drainage consists not only of the main trunk, but includes so many major and minor tributaries, and feeders to the tributaries that the routes they offered were almost uncountable. This system of wonderful waterways simply beckoned to be paddled and poled in summer. When winter morphed their flow into frozen ribbons, they waited to be broken and packed by the footfall of men and their dogs.

For millennia aboriginal peoples around the great system were the only users. That suddenly changed in the early mid-1800s with the coming of Russian American Company traders to the lower Yukon and Hudson's Bay Company traders to the upper river. Not only did these foreign users add traffic, Native groups began to travel it more frequently. To what had formerly been their almost purely subsistence lifestyle they added greatly stepped-up trapping and trading activity enhanced by their increased use of dogs for travel.

The 1867 purchase of Alaska by the United States almost instantly brought about a dynamic acceleration in the trapping and trading industry with the introduction of steamboats to support the trading posts. No longer were the remote posts so remote. No longer did they cling to edge of economic existence as they awaited piecemeal supply of trade goods canoeful by canoeful and sledload by sledload, propelled there by mere muscle of men and dogs. Now upstream against the powerful current, steam power could readily stock the stations, bringing the equivalent of hundreds of canoe-or sledloads at a time (and bringing them faster) from the distant supply depot at St. Michael near the Yukon mouth.

In the last quarter of the nineteenth century, mining came to the Yukon Basin. Fortunately, all the major finds could be approached closely by steamboats plying the great waterway or its larger tributaries. As the various early gold discoveries brought more and more prospectors, miners, and camp followers into the region, more trading stations, gold camps, and villages sprang into being, ratcheting up steamboat traffic. In 1869, one lone steamboat had begun servicing the river. Gradually over the years, one here, one there, was added until by 1896 a half dozen or so churned the waters of the Yukon.

Then the mother of all gold strikes precipitated the fabulous rush to the Klondike in 1897 and 1898. Where there had been a small but steady increase in river traffic since Alaska had come into U.S. hands thirty years before, the cataclysmic boom of the marvelous find increased the population of the region many-fold. At the peak of the Klondike activity between 1897 and 1900, 137 sternwheelers, tugs, barges, and launches were working the Yukon River transportation industry.

Towns along the Yukon grew larger and more energized. Church missions and mission schools thrived at several locations on its shores. With that many steamboat boilers holding an insatiable hunger for fuel, wood-cutting camps, beehives of activity employing many men year around, proliferated between villages.

Another active presence came into being when the military arrived to keep law and order. The great gold rush lured many seamy characters north. Tales of lawlessness and even murder reached Washington D.C. With the eyes of the world on the Yukon, the federal government could not very well continue to ignore their neglected northern possession. In 1897 the U.S. Army sent Captain P. H. Ray to investigate. He recommended that a system of military forts be established at strategic locations. Three of the most important would be positioned along the length of the Yukon River within Alaska. Fort Egbert would be built near where the river entered Alaska from Canada. Midway, Fort Gibbon would be erected at the confluence of the Tanana River. At the bustling shipping center of St. Michael on the Bering Sea north of the Yukon Delta, Fort St. Michael would be added.

As the army came to help enforce order, they began plans to install and operate a military-run communications system to serve both military and civil needs of Alaska. They would string a submarine cable and suspended land lines to join the contiguous states with Alaska by telegraph. From Fort Liscum in Valdez it would run over 400 miles along a new military trail to Fort Egbert, and from there downstream, connecting the forts of the upper, middle, and lower Alaskan Yukon River. Along the river, to fill in the hundreds of miles between the three forts, many telegraph maintenance stations would be manned. It would constitute the first successful long-distance radio operation in the world. The military-run telegraph system into Alaska and down the Yukon River would be the first major contribution provided by the federal government to the infrastructure, the beginning of the government's central role in developing Alaska.

At the time of the Russian sale, the vast Alaskan and Canadian Yukon drainage had been one great, silent, undivided wilderness disconnected from the outside world and all but unknown to it. But by the close of the nineteenth century the river had grown into a corridor of pulsing transportation and communication, a stream of energized, ascending habitations humming with industry and vigor. Running north–south through most of Yukon District, then east–west completely across Alaska's very heartland, the Great Inland Highway had become a swath of what might be called "frontier-modern" civilization dividing the wilderness.

What shortly before had been one unbroken wilderness of a size that had seemed veritably infinite, had now been effectively split into what might be thought of as roughly north and south halves. Of course, because of the enormity of the original whole, those halves were yet immense, each nearly the area of Texas. But to the prospector or trapper the vastness had been halved into manageable portions. Attaining their farthest reaches was far less than half as daunting as before.

Almost all northern trails ran south to it, almost all southern trails headed north to it, and most traffic feeding into it flowed along it, this Thoroughfare of the North, the great Yukon Trail.

———————

Rod Perry: *Looking ahead to where I intend for this book to take us on our educational journey, I want to pause right here before going on. Understanding this short chapter, Thoroughfare of the North will be indispensible. So please do not lose sight of the importance and prominence of this great river corridor, significant even before the coming of the white man, and now peaking in importance fully ten years before the Iditarod Gold Strike. As Alma Preston and her old friend, Anton Radovitch, have done their best to guide us, one will never be able to understand the ultimate end of this writing— explaining creation and use of the old Iditarod Trail—without first learning of the historical setting and progression of the prior gold rushes and gold rush trails.*

Watch for this later in the book: a famous highway engineer, surveyor, and builder of the Iditarod Trail is going to use the phrase, **the line of travel.** *Well, in that day there was only one major line of travel that mattered as far as that Alaska Road Commission official— or any other knowledgeable person in Alaska—was concerned, and that was along the Yukon River, the dominant Yukon trail of winter and highly trafficked waterway of summer.*

The Yukon Trail would be famous long before the Iditarod strike, continue in its prominence during the Iditarod Gold Rush, and would remain well beaten for decades after the Iditarod Trail faded into silent oblivion.

This orientation regarding the preeminence of the Yukon River Trail and its relationship to the later Iditarod Trail is so vitally important that we will, from time to time, revisit this subject to emphasize its importance. But now, lest we get too far ahead of ourselves, let's return to our chronology.

Chapter 21

---◆---

End of an Era

PRIOR TO THE KLONDIKE RUSH, especially in the years before the rush to the Fortymile River in 1888 began to bring a new breed in, the Yukon Basin scene could be capsuled this way: a sparse rabble of driven misfits in a fanatical quest for gold, battling nature amidst an almost uninhabited world of their own so isolated that advancements of the industrialized world and societal developments, including their nation's wars, had no effect upon them.

Then in 1897–98, the great rush to the Klondike vaulted the region, the event, and its new wave of characters—the 98ers—into the forefront of world attention. As the great tide of humanity flooded into the Upper Yukon, those stalwart forerunners, the "pioneer pioneers"—were marginalized—save Joe Ladue—by the sheer immensity of the whole event.

So what became of François Mercier, Jack McQuesten, Arthur Harper, and Al Mayo, the four pioneer-pioneers?

As business along the great river turned increasingly to supply of the miners, François Mercier found it less and less appealing. He was, in his heart of hearts, a fur trader among the Indians. In 1885, after having spent seventeen years setting up, administering, and anchoring the Yukon Basin fur trade, he retired to Montreal. Before the death of François Xavier Mercier of a heart attack at his Montreal home at 606 rue Saint-Denis, January 4, 1906, "l'éxplorateur bien connu" ("the well-known explorer") as one writer described him, traveled widely, at least once returning to Alaska.

When the first gold down from the Klondike aboard the steamship *Excelsior* broke the news of the fabulous strike to the nation, the eyes of those who gathered on the San Francisco waterfront to see the ship dock were riveted on the motley, disheveled men who staggered onto the wharf under the weight of fortunes. Let us now go back and look on.

Look over there: a crowd of reporters surround that swarthy man with the large moustache. Tabbing Joe LaDue "mayor of Dawson," they hound him relentlessly for copy.

And see that burly, mustachioed man striding down from the ship with the well-dressed, attractive Indian woman and their handsome, well-mannered children? That is none but the great Jack McQuesten leading his faithful Katherine and their family. Correctly predicting that the first surge of poorly provisioned miners into the Klondike will precipitate a veritable famine in the entire Yukon Basin, Jack is permanently moving his family out of the North Country.

Now notice that old sourdough over there; amid the excitement, are you and I the only ones aware of that lone, emaciated, gray-bearded passenger who, unnoticed, totters so weakly down the *Excelsior* gangplank? In this shipside bedlam, do they not recognize this well-loved pioneer? Do they not know this sickly man is one to whom not only the rich men cornering the charged attention on the dock owe so much, and the rest of those claim holders who stayed back north on the Yukon River owe so much, but also the citizenry of both Canada and the United States owe so much for his prominent part in vaulting their far-off possessions into value and prominence?

He is poor Arthur Harper. Broken physically from the many deprivations he has suffered and racked with tuberculosis, sadly, our old gold hunter has come Outside to die. Having willed his assets—said by some to amount to $200,000, a grand fortune at this time—to his beloved family, he is headed for Yuma, Arizona. There, he has been advised, the climate will be therapeutic. Now here he walks unsteadily over the San Francisco dock, coming toward where we stand.

Now look; there is Jack leaving the children with Kate and pushing his way through the crowd to reach Art. Near us, we see him take Art's hands in his own. The two are talking earnestly. We strain to eavesdrop, but the clamoring crowd makes it impossible. We can only imagine what final, parting words are passing between Jack McQuesten and Arthur Harper, the two greatest of those gold hunter-trader pioneer-pioneers, the two who endured and accomplished so much together.

As they separate, we leave the scene, a lump in our throat, making our way out of the throng and away from the historic docking.

Arthur Harper, Pioneer Discoverer of Gold in the Yukon Basin.

James McQuiston Collection

On November 11, 1897 Arthur Harper will die in Yuma at age sixty-two. He will not witness the gold rush he was so key in starting fully reach its zenith. He will never know how his vision and faith and tireless groundwork will help spawn all the major gold finds of the North that follow: Nome, Fairbanks, and Iditarod, as well as many lesser discoveries.

That Jack McQuesten will be remembered by history variously as "Golden Rule Jack," the "Father of Alaska," the "Father of the Yukon," "Father of the Country," or "The Guardian Angel of the Miners" indicates the honor and esteem in which he is held. There is no more universally beloved soul in the entire North. As one observer, William Haskell, stated, "He had come in contact with nearly all of the men who had risked their lives in search of gold in its frozen soil, and had ever been their friend. It has been said that he has outfitted, supported, and grubstaked more men, and kept them through the long winters when they were down on their luck, than any other person on the Yukon. Hundreds of men now on the river owe all of the success they have to his help, and they know it and appreciate it."

Comb diligently the annals of Alaska and Yukon Territory gold rush history; search as you might, you will not unearth a single unkind or critical word referring to Jack McQuesten. Unusual indeed it is to come upon an individual so highly revered in his own time.

Some accounts claimed that Jack McQuesten died in poverty. But, thankfully, they could not more greatly err. McQuesten not only survived to see the trio's faith vindicated that the country held vast wealth, he acquired an appreciable amount of it. A Boston newspaper article paying tribute to Jack (likely gaining the information from Jack's family still living in his birthplace of Litchfield, New Hampshire) reported that Jack and Katherine took south two million dollars gained from his mines on the Stewart River as well as from Dominion Creek, where they stated he was the third to stake following discovery. Other reports claim he invested in two of the richest Bonanza and El Dorado claims. As well, loved as he was for his open-handed generosity, and as many claim holders as there were who owed their very discoveries to Jack's faith demonstrated by his advance of supplies that allowed them to keep on looking, it is hard to believe he was not rewarded tangibly with at least minor shares in many paying mines throughout the various districts.

And so, by all well-reasoned evidence a multimillionaire, he moved his family to the San Francisco Bay area, where he had come so often over the years to buy supplies for the partners' river posts. There they lived in their Berkeley mansion until Leroy Napoleon McQuesten went to his eternal reward. In his seventy-second year, in 1909 the man lauded as "one who turned the heads of the civilized world," while readying to travel to Seattle to serve as "ambassador" at the Seattle World's Fair Alaska–Yukon–Pacific Exposition, came down with pneumonia and died at home.

———◆———

Rod Perry: *Those readers who cannot bear to have Jack McQuesten taken from them may bring him back for a further visit. Jack's "close distant" relative, my friend Jim McQuiston, author of* Celtic Guide *(www.celticguide.com) has also authored the most definitive, thorough work ever written about the great pioneer.* Captain Jack McQuesten, Father of the Yukon *may be purchased through Amazon.com."*

———◆———

In The faithful and talented Katherine, twenty-four years his junior and married to him thirty-one years, lived on there in Berkeley, comfortable in their Victorian home on thirteen beautiful acres of well-kept lawns and orchards. During her husband's years on the Yukon, he felt that if he expected the highest and best of his fellow man, they would honor his trust. According to river legend, Jack had never sent out a bill, yet was never shortchanged for his generosity. Though Jack's qualities made him esteemed by all, some close observers said that sterling debt payment record could be credited to Kate's diligence in looking after his collections. She skillfully managed the family estate until her passing in 1918 at age 61.

And Al Mayo? Of the three, he alone lived out his days in the North. Known far and wide as "Captain" or "Cap" Mayo, because it was he who usually captained the *New Racket,* he settled in the mining town of Rampart on the Yukon River. There he lived as de facto mayor surrounded by his family until, in 1924, he died at age 77.

*Frederick Harte,
Yukon Basin Pioneer*
James McQuiston Collection

The pioneer-pioneers had opened the North. Almost all subsequent development of the interior and west coast of the entire northwestern subcontinent can be traced at least in part to their founding efforts.

Frederick Harte did not achieve the wide fame of "The Big Three"—McQuesten, Harper, and Mayo—with whom he originally voyaged into the upper Yukon. He spent most of his time prospecting and mining and serving in his old friends' trading posts. That he was held in high esteem by his fellow miners is evidenced by his being elected by the Yukon Order of Pioneers as their second president—next to serve after Jack McQuesten. Harte was another of those early stalwarts who did not live to see the big rush fully develop. Worn down like his lifelong friend Arthur Harper, the two old pals, both born in 1835, died virtually simultaneously. Records show that Harte passed from this world November 7, 1897. Buried November 12, 1897 he was first to be placed by the Yukon Order of Pioneers in their Eighth Avenue, Dawson cemetery. That was the day following Harper's November 11, 1897 death in Yuma, Arizona.

At Dawson's peak, when possibly more than forty thousand inhabited the boomtown, with no land left, some of the lots changed hands for up to twenty thousand dollars. Joe Ladue would become a millionaire, retire to Plattsburg, New York and marry his childhood sweetheart. Sadly, however, he would die there almost immediately, passing away in 1901, like Art Harper, of tuberculosis.

The New Racket, sold by the partners to the Alaska Commercial Company in 1893, was wrecked on the Koyukuk River by the outgoing ice in 1897.

After Harper and McQuesten dismantled Fort Reliance for its logs and took them upstream to build Fort Nelson, the rest of the remains of Reliance were soon consumed as steamboat fuel. Today, few historians or others visit its former location, marked by mere shallow depressions in the soil.

Remaining Forty Mile and Selkirk structures are succumbing to time and the elements. Fort Yukon, Circle City (now Circle) and St. Michael remain active villages, and Dawson an active town, though the latter three retain but a fraction of their gold-rush-era vibrancy and population.

Numerically, far fewer took part in the Klondike gold rush than the rush to California, which in turn drew numbers second to those of the Australian rush. So it was not the magnitude, but the conditions that rocketed the Klondike into prominence as the most grandiose, picturesque, and sensational of all the world's gold rushes. The only reason it did not gain even more stardom was the sudden shifting of world eyes and journalists' pens when in Havana Harbor the battleship *Maine* was blown up, arousing Americans to outrage and launching the Spanish-American War.

From the Sled:
Progress Assessment and Perspective

Rod Perry: *Back at the beginning, you accepted my invitation to climb aboard my sled and travel with me on an adventure through history. You have proven yourself an able traveler and faithful companion. We are progressing. Our huskies have covered the miles and we are well along toward our destination: Iditarod. On long uphill pulls and through blizzards the pace has been slowed. Then at times it has quickened when the way is level and hard-packed. Sometimes the trail has been so winding we have looked high into the night sky ahead and noted the Dipper. We have looked again and it was high on our right, then again we saw it high on our left. Upon occasion we even had to turn on the sled to see it shining over our shoulders. But though the way turned briefly east, west, north, or even south to best get us through the country and our history, we've trusted the trail and the trail has been taking us northwest. Yes, we are well on our way toward Iditarod.*

We pause by trailside to take stock of our progress. Looking back, the lock has been forced on the great, silent, unknown Northwest. Indeed, it still largely remains a land of almost limitless wild expanses and great solitudes, only beginning to be explored. But the biggest obstacles have been surmounted. For over 2,000 miles through the center of its vast heartland, the mighty river that drains it pulses with energy, travel, and commerce. The Yukon now provides a solid base to venture out from or return to.

Ice-up of the great river has always turned it into a frozen highway, but now it is a well-traveled frozen highway. Winter activity along the broad thoroughfare has grown apace with summer steamboat commerce. Traffic now far exceeds that of the past as settlement grows along its banks. A modern railroad regularly and rapidly hauls in from the sea hundreds of tons at a time, passing through ragged crags that not long before posed such an effective barrier to all but a man with a backpack.

267

Freight and mail delivery and passenger traffic are mainly between salt water and Dawson. The modern transportation, communication, and supply hub of up to forty thousand that booms with vigor and industry bustles with traffic to and from smaller settlements of the upper Yukon Basin, particularly Forty Mile, Circle City, and Fort Yukon.

Some commercial and private traffic flows farther, some much farther. Now with the railroad delivering so readily into the Upper Yukon, it is the only source of supply during the long winter months while ice blocks shipping. Then, the whole 1,600 miles of river below Dawson is dependent upon flow to and from Dawson. Some freight, a fair number of travelers, and all winter mail now course back and forth up and down the great Yukon Trail. It might be a long way, but it is the only way yet developed to get to and from the outside world once ice locks down the North.

Just upcoast of the Yukon Delta, the old redoubt of St. Michael the Russians had originally built of logs and milled lumber shipped up from their base in Southeast Alaska, has become a booming port on the Bering Sea. Over thirty shipping companies are using it as a shipyard, wintering haven, cargo transfer and storage station, supply depot, and staging point. The Hotel Healy is able to house 500 guests. Over twenty thousand have stopped over in St. Michael during 1897 and 1898.

Three U.S. Army Signal Corps outposts are being established along the Alaskan Yukon River, Fort Egbert at Eagle near the Canadian border, Fort Gibbon at the confluence with the Tanana, and Fort St. Michael near the Yukon mouth. They will operate and maintain the telegraph line that will run from the western United States up the coast to Valdez, then overland to Eagle, thence down the Yukon to its mouth.

The key has been the creation of an effective transportation corridor. Because of its development the eastern side of the country is no longer limited to sporadic travel, communication and freight flow from the industrialized world in summer, nor is it choked off almost completely from that flow as it used to be in winter.

However, away to the west, far over a thousand trail miles distant lies a peninsula jutting into the Bering Sea that is yet largely unknown and unsettled, without any of the developed amenities we have just come from. And that is where our trail is heading . . . on its way to Iditarod.

Chapter 22

The Nome Strike

THE SEWARD PENINSULA FORMS the westernmost promontory of the Alaska mainland. From the mountain above the Eskimo village of Wales, located at the tip of the peninsula, Siberia may be seen on a clear day only about fifty-five miles distant across the Bering Straits. Though the Seward Peninsula coastline had been known since early Russian exploration, its interior lay dormant until 1866. Then as part of the grand plan to connect the United States to Europe, the Western Union Telegraph project established a route for its line across the peninsula and workers began there. Crews had strung but fifteen miles of cable when the whole idea was abruptly aborted. Once the construction gangs pulled out, the inland area of the peninsula remained almost deserted for the following thirty years. Because the caribou population was at low ebb during that time, not even Eskimo hunters commonly ventured there. Almost without exception, the few Americans who knew of the place considered the Seward Peninsula a worthless waste.

Although some prospecting took place resulting in small finds of galena and even gold, the region did not receive concerted attention until the worldwide excitement over the Klondike strike sent gold seekers searching every nook and cranny of the North. When news of Yukon gold swept San Francisco, Daniel B. Libby gathered a group that included Henry L. Blake, A. P. Mordaunt and L. F. Melsing and shipped north. They headed not for the Klondike, but for Niukluk River country on the Seward Peninsula. There Libby had found gold as a young man more than thirty years before while supervising work on the Western Union cable project.

The Libby party discovered gold on a tributary of the Niukluk in the spring of 1898. Somewhat later that year, they made a fairly rich strike at nearby Ophir Creek which yielded $75,000 in gold. Another group that prospected nearby included missionary Nels O. Hulteberg, mission teacher P.H. Anderson, mission doctor A.N. Kittilsen and Lapp reindeer herder Johan S. Thornesis. They staked claims nearby. The two groups established the Discovery and El Dorado Mining Districts. The town of Council came into being as the ensuing small rush brought miners to the area. However, the strike was relatively minor in the light of the blockbuster discovery that lay right around the corner, not far west.

Rod Perry: *As early as the New Year's Day edition of the Nome Nugget for1900, which would feature an article, "Who Discovered Nome's Gold?" there would be vastly varying versions regarding the whos and hows of the great Seward Peninsula strike. Too bad the paper did not have on staff a highly skilled investigative reporter to cross-examine the principals while all of them remained close by and the happenings were still fresh. Alas, apparently no newsman of such skill and inclination was present. Besides, as usually happens during the tumult of many of the world's great events, people are too immersed in the happening itself to place much value on establishing a correct history for the benefit of future generations. They are too physically busy to set aside time to write it. At the peak of Nome's gold frenzy, the sorting out of facts probably occupied a rock-bottom rank on everyone's list of priorities."*

Henry Blake of the Libby party and the missionary, Nels Hulteberg, then looked farther west. Blake had been shown ore from the Cape Nome area by Toorig Luck, an Eskimo who, in midwinter, took Blake to his source. The two decided to return after the land thawed the following summer to more adequately prospect the area. Apparently, on another reconnaissance tramp across the mountains and tundra from Council to the coast west of Cape Nome, Blake gained information regarding gold in the area from Charley Garden and his Eskimo wife, Sinuk Mary. The pair lived a simple subsistence lifestyle,

PIONEERING ALASKA'S IDITAROD

hunting, fishing, gathering, and panning enough gold from the Sinuk River to buy staples when they took their yearly boat trip down the coast to trade.

———◆——————◆———

Rod Perry: *Among a few others, the so-called Three Lucky Swedes enter into the story: Erik Lindblom [different reports spell his first name also as Eric and his last name also as Lindbloom] and John Brynteson, immigrants from Sweden, and Jafet Lindeberg, a half Lapp, half Norwegian. From there, the chronology and details of the movements of the principal discoverers of Nome's gold, as far as who went where, with whom, in what order, and what did and did not take place, are so laden with controversy and conflicting first-person testimony, remote hearsay, and general gold-rush legend that, if Nome's leading newspaper could not correctly sort it out within two years of the strike, it should raise eyebrows if today anyone claims to have settled it definitively, more than 100 years after the fact. I am confident in stating that it remains a confusion impervious to time and attempts at clarification."*

———◆——————◆———

Erik Lindblom, a tailor, had been plying his trade in San Francisco when the steamship Excelsior docked there with its cargo of Klondike gold. Smitten with the fever that swept the nation but lacking cash for passage, he signed as a seaman on a whaler headed north. It was not until the voyage was well underway that the Swede, understanding little English, found that his contract bound him to chase whales around the Arctic Ocean for two long years! Seeing his chance to break free when the craft anchored at Port Clarence (near today's village of Teller) to take on fresh water, the little tailor jumped ship and made a run for it. He had gained the North free of charge and by good fortune had avoided going to the Klondike, where most of the productive ground was already claimed. By sheer luck, the direction in which he ran would take him through the very area of his destiny, over ground where he would soon become a discoverer of one of the world's great gold deposits.

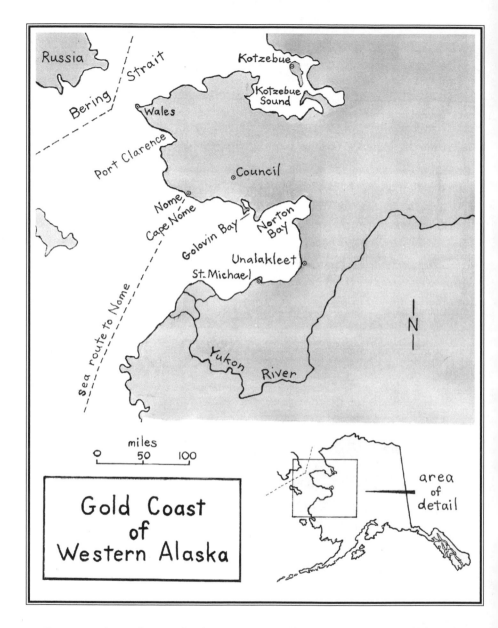

Gold Coast
of
Western Alaska

area
of
detail

miles
0   50   100

In a version of Nome's discovery attributed to him, Lindblom later stated that during the flight south from Port Clarence he ran into Blake as the latter visited the cabin of Charley Garden and Sinuk Mary. There he was said to have broken the news of the Klondike stampede to the others, among whom he claimed there had been no prior knowledge. In reality, the very reason the Libby party, of which Blake was a member, had come north seeking gold was that news of the Klondike strike had excited them.

Charley Garden and Blake gave the runaway directions toward Hultberg's Swedish mission on Golovin Bay. As Lindblom's way and Blake's return route to Council would take the same course for many miles before dividing, the two were said to have traveled together. The way the story goes, as they briefly paused to prospect around the area Charley Garden had described, Lindblom and Blake discovered gold together, Blake panning while Lindblom looked over his shoulder. Lindblom related that as soon as color began to show in the pan, Blake dumped the contents, dismissing it as insignificant, counting on Lindblom's lack of experience to throw him off track and keep the naïve Swede from staking a claim. Lindblom's story had them continuing together until their ways split, whereupon he legged with all speed the many remaining miles to the mission. There, he said that he broke the news to Hultberg and others who were present. The listening group included John Brynteson, who, according to this version, first heard of Nome's riches (as, purportedly, did Hultberg) as the exhausted man staggered in and semicoherently began raving about finding gold. Brynteson was said to have been the only one present to believe in and desire to respond to the tailor's tale.

John Brynteson, like Lindblom, was a Swedish-born naturalized American citizen. A giant of a man for his day at six feet, six inches, he had left the back-breaking physical labor and low rewards of Michigan's coal mines in hopes of unearthing something far more valuable in the North. According to yet another discovery story, following the aforementioned January trip taken by Blake and Hultberg with Toorig Luck to the site of the Eskimo's find, in July the two white men boated back to the area, as planned. Their party included four others, among whom were the Swedes John Hagelin and Brynteson, both recently arrived at Golovin.

Later, Hultberg was to claim that he invited Blake and all four of the others. Blake, though, recorded that, as he did not want the party to be dominated by Swedes, he included two of his friends, Henry Porter and Chris Kimber (which apparently greatly angered Hultberg).

273

If this did not confuse the record enough, Brynteson later stated that he and Hagelin were the ones who first organized the trip, and then invited Hultberg, who in turn included Blake and his friends.

As the party neared their Snake River destination at the end of their five-day voyage, a severe storm built. Striving to enter the river mouth, they swamped in the heavy surf. All of them made shore, but most of their supplies and gear were swept away.

Following the night around a bonfire, they made for the site Toorig Luck had shown Blake and Hultberg the previous winter. Reaching the watercourse later to be named Anvil Creek, four miles north of the future site of Nome, Blake and his friends stopped to work the lower streambed while Hultberg pressed on to look farther upstream. Later, when Blake hiked up to see how Hultberg was faring, the missionary, seeing Blake approaching some way off, hastily turned from his prospecting. Walking down to join Blake, Hultberg informed him that his investigation had drawn a blank, which eventually proved to be a blatant deception.

By his following performance, it seemed obvious that Hultberg was hatching a plan to get everyone away from the area before anyone could stake. He would return to Golovin Bay. Then, as soon as he could shake Blake and his cohorts, he would return on a better-equipped expedition including no one but the other Swedes and his mission friends.

The men, lacking everything required for a long stay, prepared to leave. Hultberg either actually became sick or feigned illness, lying in a tent. Once he had lulled everyone, he sneaked away in the night, gaining a head start for his Golovin mission. Blake later testified that upon Hultberg's arrival there, the missionary (who actually was sick and exhausted by then) enlisted Lindblom and another "Swede," the Lapp-Norwegian, Jafet Lindeberg, gave them a small sailboat and a detailed map of exactly where on Anvil Creek to go and sent them off with not only his own power of attorney, but also that of every Swedish missionary in the Golovin area, wherewith they claimed, as Blake put it, "the whole country."

Prior to these events, Jafet Lindeberg had come to the North as part of the Reverend Sheldon Jackson's project in which 500 reindeer

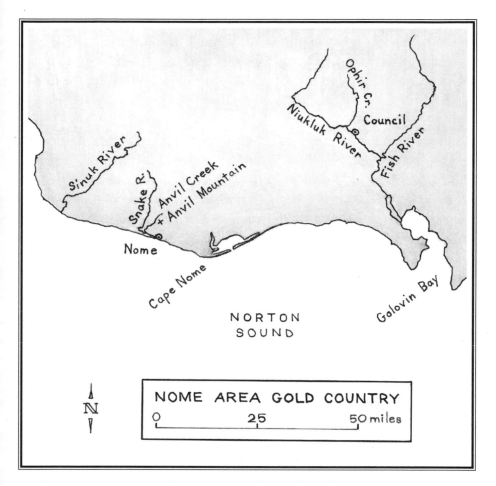

NOME AREA GOLD COUNTRY

0   25   50 miles

and twenty Lapp families were to be shipped in to teach Alaskan Eskimos how to tend and use the animals. Lindeberg had heard the siren call of Yukon gold and, chomping at the bit, had been looking for a way to get to Alaska. He had grown up in northern Norway where the Lapps brought their reindeer seasonally and knew just enough about the animals to gain a position in Jackson's enterprise. Just before he left Vardo, Norway, that winter, an old whaler was said to have found him and pressed the then considerable amount of $2,000 upon the young man after securing his promise to "buy him a gold mine" with the sum.

By the time Lindeberg's services were no longer needed by Reverend Jackson, the project barge had taken him as far as the mission on

Golovin Bay. By then he had learned that $2,000 was too little with which to purchase a paying mine. What it would buy, he correctly reasoned, was the necessary provisions and gear that it would take to look for one. He bought what the old prospectors called an "outfit."

———◆———

Rod Perry: *There are, of course, many other versions of the Nome gold discovery. Another prominent variation had the Swedes, sent by Hultberg to work his claims at Council, overhearing Blake talking at the Libby party's cabin about the whereabouts of Nome gold whereupon they reported the information to Hultberg. But introducing other versions only makes looking into the issue all the more like staring into a tub of spaghetti. Whoever actually went where and did what with whom and when, remains a question, but it is fact that Erik Lindblom and John Brynteson teamed up, brought in Jafet Lindeberg for his outfit—food, clothing, shelter, tools, a few building materials, medicines—the basic supplies and equipment to live and work for a year—and the three sailed from Golovin Bay on a borrowed mission barge, leaving September 11, 1898 for the Snake River and Anvil Creek."*

———◆———

Reaching the Snake, the trio of neophyte gold seekers did not even seek a secure anchorage, but just splashed the hook as soon as they entered the unprotected river mouth. They grabbed a few essentials and quickly made their way over the tundra to Hultberg's spot on Anvil Creek.

Brynteson filled a pan from the stream bottom. In but a few moments of the usual swirling, shaking, and tipping, the bottom of the pan gleamed. Looking at the others, he calmly stated, "We are millionaires."

A storm blew up that day. The Bering Sea off Nome is very shallow, allowing onshore winds to whip the waters into a seething fury. Exposed to the destructive breakers as they had left it, the barge with its contents was dashed to pieces and lost.

John Brynteson blew out of the site bound for Golovin to round up all the supplies he could quickly lay his hands on. As the huge miner quickly receded into the distance, his powerful, long strides must have given the impression he had donned the proverbial "seven-league boots."

Lindblom and Lindeberg threw themselves into building a rough cabin, staking a number of claims for the trio as well as their friends, relatives and backers. They quickly panned enough gold to buy winter supplies. In due time, presumably before Brynteson could return from Golovin, they, too, went back to the mission. The three quietly let Dr. Kittilsen and Gabriel Price know about their find.

Desiring to return to Nome in October, the men begged command of another of the seemingly endless supply of the Swedish mission's small craft, this time a schooner.

Rod Perry: *Though ice-up loomed, Hultberg would not allow them its use until they had built him a church! The finished product, complete with the steeple the missionary insisted upon, must have been some cathedral, slapped up as it was in but five days by the anxious-to-be-away miners, not one of whom possessed a lick of carpentry skills. With the structure finished, the men loaded the schooner with what remained of Lindeberg's original five-ton outfit, added to it some provisions purchased from a trader, piled on a small supply of lumber and weighed anchor for Nome.*

They beat the ice by just a few hours. The day after they arrived and laboriously wrestled the little schooner into the Snake, the river froze in solidly for the winter. Then the men bowed their backs to moving the cargo, as well as all the driftwood they could collect for firewood, up to Anvil Creek.

With Dr. Kittilsen serving as chairman and Gabriel Price as recording secretary, on October 15, 1898, the miners officially created the Cape Nome Mining District. They went back and more carefully measured and marked the boundaries of Lindblom's and Lindeberg's original stakings. Then they located numerous other claims up and down Anvil Creek and the Snake River and on other likely-looking ground in the vicinity.

Leaving the ice-bound schooner locked in its winter moorage, the miners returned to Golovin by sled. Back at the mission, Gabriel Price sent a letter up to Council City hoping to quietly alert just a few of his closest friends. He bade them slip away and stake claims at the new discovery but cautioned them to keep the information close to the vest to avoid a rush.

———◆———

Rod Perry: *Leaning into the very teeth of a blizzard, miner after miner who had been let in on the secret, slipped furtively away, showing the suddenly shrinking burg their snow shoe tails. However, one does not dare set off into an early winter storm on a round-trip trek of 160 miles across the desolate Seward Peninsula for the purpose of locating and staking claims without having first assembled at least a skeleton outfit and loading the pile into a pack or onto a sled. That process would have been hard to hide. And be it mukluks, snowshoes, or runners, they all leave tracks. Within one day of the letter's arrival, neither hide nor hair of even one Councilite could be found in the deserted town.*

———◆———

The next stampede took place when Lindeberg and Kittilsen arrived in St. Michael November 30 in quest of more supplies and mining equipment. There they found a mishmash of people heading in different directions on different quests in several states of mind: excited heights of hope, frustrated impatience, and deep depression.

The port town was booming. The Klondike rush had dropped a gold mine into the lap of the Alaska Commercial Company. North American Trade and Transportation, too, was thriving across the bay as a town of its own; their Hotel Healy could house 500 guests. And not only was business jumping for that pair of companies. Where there had been but two main trading and transportation enterprises on the Yukon River just two years before, now over thirty had dived into the lucrative shipping business. They had constructed machine shops, stores, warehouses, personal dwellings, a hotel, and shipyards.

Where there had been only a half dozen steamboats plying the Yukon two years before, now 137 craft of various descriptions had become involved in the river trade.

With so much capital invested, the various interests were bent on milking the rush as hard and long as possible. Even after it was understood by anyone who knew anything about the Klondike that the main body of stampeders arrived two years too late, the steamship companies shamelessly continued to promote the find and the newspapers which carried their advertisements, knowing Klondike fever stimulated circulation, worked hand in hand with the shippers. The port cities of San Francisco, Portland, Seattle, as well as Vancouver and Victoria, British Columbia, striving to capitalize, continued to pump the Klondike.

Most of the old Yukoners and experienced trading companies well knew there had been no way to prepare adequately for the hordes which descended upon the Upper Yukon. Army Captain Patrick Henry Ray, who had been sent to reconnoiter the Alaska situation, envisioned a looming spectre: a swarm of out-of-luck, out-of-food stampeders combing the country in starving, predatory packs. Ray predicted that armed, desperate and dangerous, they would take food wherever they found it, but would, he thought, ultimately die of scurvy, starvation, and cold.

With indications of an unseasonably early freeze-up and with famine so seemingly imminent in that country 1,600 miles upriver, ACC and NAT&T pulled out all stops to beat the congealing river with their final supply runs of the season. If they could make it in, they hoped to relieve the situation by bringing as many stampeders as possible back out.

While a possible life-and-death scenario was playing out far inland, ocean shipping companies kept bringing more passengers to the river mouth. Deboarding ship, these new arrivals competed to find steam-boat passage in to Dawson, hoping to get there in time to stake claims before winter set in. In their frenzied quest to squeeze the last dollar out of the season some of the riverboat companies pocketed the fares of these hopeful innocents, took them aboard, and began steaming up against the Yukon current, already perilously flowing ice.

———————

Old Ben Atwater: "Here we were way up in the Upper Yukon with legions of newcomers trying for all they're worth to leave. Some wanted to quit the country because of disappointment over finding they'd arrived in the upper Yukon too late; all the good ground'd been taken going on two years. Others were downhearted after finding this gold hunting wasn't nearly such an easy sure bet as they'd imagined; it didn't simply lie under every rock. Then there were plenty of smart ones that saw they'd better beat it out of the country to keep from starving. Add the dumb ones who don't have sense God gave a goose, but we're finally able to convince they gotta leave because of the shortage of food. It doesn't matter what their reason for going, we're just sending as many as we can out not only to save them, but to whittle the remaining population down to a level we can overwinter.

"Same time as this exodus, those shyster companies down at the mouth were sending more in. I've never seen the like, Al, it sure beats everything. So many trying so hard to reach a place so many others were trying so desperately to escape. If those incoming could've only heard the heartrending tales of woe moaned by the disappointed."

———————

In addition to the Arctic climate, the great differences in rushes farther south and those to the Yukon and Alaska had to do largely with the extreme difficulties of personal travel and transportation of one's supplies into the gold country due to cross-continental and oceanic distances, wilderness remoteness, topographical blockades, surface conditions and climate. Stacked one upon another, these factors ruled out any chance for most cheechakos to regroup and resupply for a fresh start. Additionally, many had sold the entirety of their worldly possessions and spent it all outfitting themselves and getting to the goldfields in the first place.

For many, most of the firelight once lit by hopes of riches won in an instant flickered out with the fading sun of autumn, slowing the major part of the human flood of 98ers coming into Dawson. Then, whatever positive notions lingered froze into gloom and despair as the polar cold intensified, and the flood into Dawson stopped. Finally, Dawson flood movement picked up again, but reversed direction; thoughts had turned toward escape. A great evacuation got underway.

The most demoralized of the 98er evacuees mixed with many of the downcast who had come in the previous year and even then found themselves a year too late. These formed a groundswell of dejected humanity outflushing down the Yukon. Some would get to St. Michael early enough to board a steamship bound for west coast ports; others would miss the last ships south.

———

Rod Perry: *Remember what Alma Preston and old Anton Radovitch told us about one gold rush spawning the next and gold rush trails being interconnected?*

Not everyone left at once and not everyone so soon gave up on their quest for gold. The great Klondike rush so populated the region that for several years, chiefly 1898–1903, the holdover would contribute outsurges feeding other rushes. Additionally, some of the down-and-outers, desperate to make enough to book steamship passage to the west coast and rail passage from there home, would find their way to Valdez, where they would work on a government trail-building project that would provide an all-American access corridor used by all major Alaska gold rushes to follow. But let's not get too far ahead of our story . . .

———

The unsuccessful Klondikers who had made it down the Yukon, but too late to gain passage on the season's last ships south, now found themselves icebound for the next seven months. Mingling with that would-be outgoing tide was a small flood of incoming late arrivals from the States who had intended to steam up to Dawson, but had reached the Yukon mouth too late to beat freeze-up. Heading out or heading in, no matter what either of these groups wanted to do next, they were caught in St. Michael with no choice but to winter over. Some others were there just biding time in the supply center, avoiding the starvation threatening the Upper Yukon. They intended to go back to prospecting first thing after iceout next May. Additionally, sixty-eight steamers were reportedly caught partway up the Yukon as as the river froze. That trapped many of those who had hoped to make it to the Klondike before winter. At least 550 of them walked back over the ice, some hundreds of miles, to reach St. Michael.

One more group was in St. Michael that early winter: a small return tide of prospectors whose enthusiasm, originally kindled by Klondike gold, had led them on an unsuccessful search around Kotzebue Sound and the Kobuk River some 500 sea miles up the coast from the Yukon River mouth. Failing to turn up anything worthwhile, most of these had made their way back to the port.

And so, wintering there in St. Michael, most were discouraged and broke. All they could focus on was boarding the next southbound ship. However, among even those retreating hordes were numerous souls within whom still burned a glimmer of hope.

Of the minority who had just arrived by ship too late to reach Dawson, those who were able to remain uncontaminated by the tales of despair of the Klondike woebegone still stood at various levels of enthusiasm for the hunt. The rest of the populace were chiefly employees of the trading and transportation companies, the regular townspeople. Perhaps the most interesting of those town dwellers that fall of 1898 was Tex Rickard, who would later become the most famed fight promoter of his day, builder of the third incarnation of Madison Square Garden, builder of Boston Garden and founder of the New York Rangers. Rickard was there in St. Michael as a twenty-eight-year-old budding entrepreneur, running his gambling casino.

Here into this trading and transportation headquarters of shippers and merchants competing for business, of people crowding into available housing or erecting tents or crude shelters, into this cauldron of bustling activity and flowing rumors came Jafet Lindeberg and Dr. Kittilsen for their supplies and equipment. They wended their way among the piles of freight for the stocking of St. Michael warehouses and freight destined for upstream trading posts, missions, villages, and Dawson City. They wound past stacks of prospectors' outfits in their respective piles, and came at last to the big stores where they filled their orders.

When the Swedes paid in Seward Peninsula gold the news swept the town.

St. Michael simply erupted. In frantic bedlam, men ran to load provisions and gear on sleds. The big dog teams of the trading companies pulled out first. Others, who owned no dogs, raced hither and yon, some to the neighboring Eskimo village, making exorbitant offers for as many malamutes as they could secure. Soon, with the almost emptied town of St. Michael fading behind them, these former inhabitants strung out in a lengthening line up the coast, with the big, fast-moving teams stretching away in the distance, the smaller teams following at a slower pace, men pulling hand sleds helped by a dog or two behind them. In the rear, stampeders in singles and pairs, necking their Yukon sleds piled with heavy loads, laboriously tramped toward the Seward Peninsula and Anvil Creek. Stampeders pushed their endurance to the utmost.

———◆—◆———

Rod Perry: *Shortly after the St. Michael stampeders had joined those from Golovin Bay and Council City, over 300 claims had been located inland from the Nome beach. With news of the apparently rich strike, almost everyone who heard of it quickly rushed to be among the first arrivals. Therefore, with the traffic flow almost entirely toward Nome, and with not many left with the wherewithal or inclination to head in the opposite direction, word did not quickly emanate upriver. Someone, though, must have resisted the pull to become rich as Midas and started the news moving up the Yukon River Trail. By late winter, word of the find reached even Dawson, some 1,600 miles from St. Michael.*

———◆—◆———

The population and demographics of the Klondike area duplicated those commonly following all gold discoveries, major and minor. In the age-old pattern, once the stampede frenzy settled into the laborious process of extracting what had been claimed, for every fortunate finder who struck it rich there were left multitudes who struck out. Of those who came up empty, many returned home, their grand dreams of riches dashed. Of those who stayed, some with an eye for business saw the opportunity to "mine the miners" by providing services in high demand. They established sawmills, hotels, restaurants, laundries, gambling halls, brothels, freight-hauling businesses, newspapers, and the rest of the infrastructure.

----◆----

Rod Perry: *By far the majority who stayed, however, like Al and Alma Preston's old rest-home friend Anton Radovitch, had done in his younger days, settled for hiring out to the successful miners and business owners as menial laborers. As the venerable Mr. Radovitch told us, he was an example of this group, which being already positioned in the North, made up a restless horde ready to stampede to the next find."*

----◆----

Not wanting to wait for more verified reports or for the opening of river navigation, some of the most optimistic, energetic, and prepared individuals in the Klondike began the 1,400-mile-long odyssey to Nome. Like the exodus from St. Michael, those few with dogs led the way. Gold seekers necking hand sleds, many equipped with sails to take advantage of prevailing downriver wind, followed.

A number of Dawsonites owned the first bicycles brought into the country. Several owners, dubbed "wheelmen," began furiously pedaling toward Nome on the hard-beaten Yukon Trail. Several hundred miles downriver, a Native noted a strange sight far out on the river. Not being able to see the thin lines of the bicycle so far away, all he could make out was the hard-to-explain posture and action of the cyclist. Shaking his head in amazement, he reported, "Crazy man go down river, sit down, walk like devil!"

Throughout the winter, gold seekers, a few at a time, continued to arrive in Nome. By breakup as many as 1,000 populated the site. Most of the latecomers who made up the majority, looked around and, finding that the nearby creeks and gulches had been staked end to end, assumed to their frustration that all worthwhile ground had

Klondike Miner Heeding the Call to Nome
University of Alaska Fairbanks, Frank Buteau Collection

been taken. Adding to the maddening situation, with so many claims registered by the earlier arrivals through power of attorney for friends, relatives, and backers who were absent, a high percentage of the locations was not even being worked. To the general anger was added a catalyst which greatly multiplied the confusion: more than a few claims were recorded for "phantoms," that did not even exist. The very last straw that broke the back of their sanity was that many of the claim holders were of foreign birth. Some, like the Lapp reindeer herders, were thought to be aliens. Others had so recently immigrated and gained U.S. citizenship that they spoke little or no English and were lumped with the supposed aliens as foreigners. Tempers flared.

———⬩—⬩———

Rod Perry: *The angry latecomers should have spent their energies combing the adjacent country in quest of new diggings. Though they trailed the very earliest stampeders, they had still arrived well ahead of the huge rush that would burst upon Nome as soon as shipping opened. As would be proven later, some of the very richest placers in the country were yet to be found, and many of them lay waiting virtually within sight of where the anger of the restless crowd boiled.*

———⬩—⬩———

Remember that in the earliest days of the Upper Yukon what law existed depended upon the inhabitants themselves in the form of miners' meetings. In the 1880s and early 1890s, when few inhabitants lived in the upper country, almost everyone knew one another and largely coexisted in a spirit of goodwill and cooperation. They were sifted by the very nature of the difficulties of entry into the country and, once there, by the vicissitudes of survival, so that almost to a man, they were of high ethical character. In such a setting, miners' meetings had worked superbly. However, with the great gold strikes and the arrival of more people, the quality of the institution had deteriorated terribly. In Canada's Yukon, the Mounted Police arrived just in time to be ready for the great rush to the Klondike and wonderfully upheld law and order.

However, on the U.S. side, America had so ignored its farthest north possession that only the sketchiest of enforcement was found. Entry to Nome featured no such sifting process as had entry into the Upper Yukon in earliest days. To Nome the weak came as easily as the strong and the riff-raff had no morale or resolve-testing distances and harsh vicissitous to strain out those lacking ethical character. Amidst Nome's well-supplied throngs life was much easier than life had been in the early-day Yukon. In Nome, anyone—including the most nefarious— could easily sail right up to the beach with as much as he could afford to bring, step right off, be in the thick of the discovery, and easily mix himself into the crowd.

———— • ———— • ————

Old Ben Atwater: "Compared to the Canadian Klondike the Nome strike was so lawless, it was said that God, upon hearing reports and coming down for a firsthand look, just rolled his eyes, threw up his hands, spun on his heel, and shaking his head, pulled out on the last boat."

———— • ———— • ————

As the angered Nome population seethed, a small core of connivers hatched a plan to use the general unrest to their personal advantage. They called a miners' meeting intended to revoke the ownership of existing claims. Unbeknownst to the assemblage, the ringleaders had stationed cohorts on the heights several miles from Nome to watch for a signal fire from the town. The smoke would tell them that the meeting had made all of the so-called "foreigner's" claims illegal. At that cue they were to swoop down and restake them.

However, they had not counted on the quick action and bravery of Lieutenant Spaulding, sent to Nome from the barracks in St. Michael with a detachment of ten troops. Smelling a rat, he attended the meeting. Yes, indeed under federal law it was certainly not lawful for aliens to own claims unless they could show they had officially filed their intent to become citizens. But no one had proof that the Swedes and Lapps had not at least filed that intent. Indeed, for all anyone knew, they may have already gained full-fledged citizenship. If so, they were due as many rights as those who fanned the flames of unrest. Therefore, the most illegal thing taking place was the way the miners disregarded due process and took the law into their own hands. So as soon as the motion was made to declare existing claims null and void and throw the country open to stake over from scratch, the lieutenant moved for adjournment. Not only that, upon his order his troops cleared the hall with fixed bayonets.

Chaos had been averted, but order might not have prevailed for long had it not been for an amazing occurrence. Some versions say that it was one of Spaulding's idle soldiers, others say that it was a man sitting on the beach convalescing from an ailment, but whoever it was, someone took up a pan of beach sand, swirled it and found gold. Excitement over gold distributed seemingly endlessly along miles of beach available to everyone equally diverted attention far from the Three Lucky Swedes, the Lapps, and the other "foreigners."

As fast as Nome's idle population could appropriate almost nonexistent boards with which to fashion rockers they forgot all about claim jumping and swarmed to the beaches.

————◆——◆————

Al Preston: "Rod, that discovery of the Golden Sands made Nome unique as a double gold strike. First you had the rich upland placers where only those owners of staked and recorded locations or their assignees had rights to mine them. Then, second, there was the open-to-entry beach access where anyone was free to just pick a spot, set up a rocker and begin mining. The two-in-one strike once more set the North on end. It grabbed worldwide headlines like the Klondike strike so recently before it."

————◆——◆————

In the early summer of 1899, as the pack ice opened and ocean-going ships filled with gold seekers from the United States bound for the Klondike arrived in St. Michael, word of the Nome find swept the fleet. Learning they would be latecomers if they continued their course toward the Klondike, instead of disembarking to take river steamers up the Yukon to Dawson, almost every gold seeker chose to remain aboard and go on up the coast to the new, ground-floor opportunity.

Upon reaching Nome, the deep-hulled ships had to stand offshore in the roads. Shallow-draft lighters then brought men and their outfits in to where the new arrivals waded through the surf right into the amazing beach mining pandemonium. Hurriedly off-loading their outfits and securing them above high-tide level, they, too, dove headlong into the frenzied activity.

Far away, over 1,800 miles by sea and river from the golden sands of Nome, thousands of disconsolate Klondike have-nots eked out a mere living, working odd jobs in town or wielding pick and shovel helping wealthy claim holders become richer. Their former visions of golden fortunes dashed, many were too destitute or too embarrassed to return home. As soon as the ice went out on the Yukon, verified reports steamed to the inland goldfields that the Nome find was much, much more than the unverified rumor that had reached Dawson by dog team earlier. Indeed, it portended to be the richest find, by far, yet made in Alaska. With confirmed news of the amazing new strike where, in truth, everyone could find gold, as soon as those riverboats could turn around, over 8,000 Klondikers crowded aboard and formed another huge outgoing tide, headed for the new El Dorado, Nome.

<hr />

Al Preston: "Rod, the Nome beach was everyman's strike. It was so easily reachable compared to the strikes of the far Interior. No long overland trips packing of a ton of gear over tortuous mountain terrain. No boat building or running deadly rapids. No need to be first or be left out. Just sail from Seattle, be lightered in with your gear, land on the Nome shore, and immediately begin mining the very beach sand under your feet.

"It was the richest tidewater diggings ever discovered. I'll tell you about the Nome beach show. The beach gold was extremely fine, mixed with ruby sand. Miners dug between high-and low-water lines. They shoveled the gold-sand mix into rockers. Rockers were portable, easy to move between locations. A man worked his hole as long as he could stay with it. Each incoming tide displaced everyone and smoothed over the beach. Soon as the tide began receding, mining followed it out. Claims couldn't be staked on the beach; men could only hold their spot by working it. The moment they quit, anyone was free to move in. For mile after mile the beach was a teeming swarm of 'hind ends and elbows' and swinging shovels. And often, swinging fists.

"Now, the owner of a rich gold claim inland could leverage himself and extract great wealth by setting up a more permanent operation including a crew of menial wage earners and elaborate systems for moving the overburden and separating the gold. But no one could get rich on the beach because miners were limited to one shovel length on either side of their rocker. That held every beach operation to a one-man show. And the tide made even those tiny "claims" temporary. But everyone who really worked at it could make excellent money on Nome's beach.

"Legally, beach diggers were supposed to stop at the high-water mark. That's because holders of legal inland claims had staked everything clear out to the beach edge of the tundra. However, that didn't stop beach miners from burrowing under the tundra whenever they could get away with it. They dug under by thawing the frozen ground with driftwood fires.

"Leave it to those crazy miners! Here and there, Eskimos lived in sod igloos along the tundra just above the beach. One time a miner burned and tunneled his way so close to an igloo that his smoke came up through the floor and suffocated a bedridden old man. Another time, occupants of another sod house and the miner both were startled when the igloo floor dropped into a tunnel!"

———◆—◆———

Naturally, it became almost impossible for the Three Lucky Swedes and other inland claim holders to keep hired laborers working their placers. After all, the going wage they paid was no more than $15 a day, while the beach miners could expect anywhere from $25 to $300 for a good day's effort. But lack of available labor soon became the least of the upland miners' concerns.

———◆—◆———

Rod Perry: *A new threat to displace them appeared on the scene, by far more dangerous than the disorganized rabble they had faced at the recent miners' meeting. What Nome's rightful claim-holders (particularly the newly naturalized Scandinavians) needed was security, relief from the threat of future mob actions. Now what they got was "relief" all right, relief in the form of a sinister new conspiracy to relieve them of their claims.*

———————

District Judge Arthur H. Noyes and a small contingent of lesser officials sent to their rescue by the U.S. government did indeed keep their claims from falling into the hands of the mob. However, that protection was not for the Scandinavians, but for the shyster Noyes himself and his corrupt government crooks.

During "resolution" of claim-jumping that had become rampant, while supposedly sorting out the phantoms, foreigners, and usurpers from the legitimate claim holders, these outlaws in officials' clothing took advantage of the chaos and deluge of litigation. They twisted the law into a scheme to gain control of Nome's rich inland placers not for the rightful owners but for themselves. They counted on the great distance from higher government oversight to allow them to get away with it.

The Swedes and other lawful claim holders found themselves up against the very might of the federal government. And the U.S. Army, which had so recently heroically saved their interests from the mob, now had to back the court in removing them from their claims.

If Noyes were not of despicable enough character, he had come north accompanied by a treacherous, powerful civilian friend in the person of Alexander McDonald who held considerable influence over the judge. McDonald had friends and connections in some of the highest offices in the nation, including the presidency.

The Nome government "lawfully" (per their twisted interpretation) set about hiring crews and mining the rich ground for themselves. Day in and day out, as gold disappeared from their placers on pack horses taking it to the safes of Noyes, McDonald and their cronies, the maddened miners could do nothing but stand by wringing their hands.

Since the shysters themselves were the highest authority in Alaska, and the Army was duty-bound to back up their actions, seemingly nothing could be done to stop them. Nothing locally, that is.

Charles Lane had, prior to the great strike, sent Gabriel Price to Alaska to look into prospects and promote Lane's interests. When Lane arrived to manage the claims Price had secured, he also bought out the interests of many of the original prospectors, making him perhaps the most powerful miner in the Nome Mining District. When the government deviants usurped his holdings, they fouled the wrong man. Lane, a man of wealth and political connection, was also a man of high moral character and action. Determined to stop the outrage not only for his own benefit but also for that of the rest of Nome's displaced miners, he slipped out of Nome in a small boat. The most accepted version of his getaway had him hiding in an empty barrel as the boat took him out to a southbound ship ready to weigh anchor.

Once he had made port on the West Coast he traveled by fast rail to the seat of his political connections in the East. There, Charles Lane's solid reputation and testimony soon got the process rolling that would clean up Nome, albeit only after the scofflaws first ignored the federal government's initial mandate to right their wrongs. Eventually, Washington had to forcefully send in replacements. The crooks were ousted and given their legal comeuppance. (However, considering the law they had thumbed their noses at and the financial harm they had caused, it was widely agreed their penalties were not nearly stiff enough.) The miners of Nome were returned to their claims. However, only a fraction of the treasure robbed from their placers ever found its way back into the rightful hands.

While the shyster Judge Noyes and his crooked pals were plying their skulduggery, every ship plying salt water the nearly 3,000 miles between Nome and Seattle carried more news to the waiting media proclaiming the availability of Nome's gold. By the time the sea ice froze in the fall of 1899, the population of Nome stood at 10,000 people. Numbers froze around that level through the usual near-stoppage imposed by winter conditions upon transportation. But soon after the opening of navigation in 1900, the population of the Nome area exploded. To the number arriving from points south was added

The "Three Lucky Swedes" John Brynteson,
Jafet Lindeberg, Erik Lindblom
Alaska State Library Historical Collections,
Alaska Purchase Centennial Collection, ASL-P20-088

another wave of Dawsonites abandoning the Klondike. The Nome District swelled to between twenty and thirty thousand gold seekers.

The tent city became a temporary metropolis, stretching for miles along the beach. The more permanent structures of Nome proper went up almost as fast. Because building materials were shipped in so easily, right up to the beach in front of town, and sometimes within a few yards of their destination—some entire buildings even came north in prefabricated sections—the city sprang up almost overnight.

Alfred Hulse Brooks: "Remember that I explained how overflow from the Klondike spurred other gold strikes and development in Alaska? The overflow of which I spoke was both in men which were drawn north and excitement which stimulated exploration and development. That very Klondike bubbling-over led directly to the Nome strike.

"The flow of Dawson-to-Nome stampeders really escalated winter use of the River Trail down the Yukon to Kaltag and heavy trail traffic between Kaltag and Unalakleet over the old Kaltag Portage and on up the Coastal Trail to Nome.

"Additionally, the timing of the first large wave of miners to the Nome strike, 1899, fortuitously coincided with the partial completion of the faraway White Pass and Yukon Railway. The swiftly developing transportation system from Skagway to Dawson was ready to fulfill Nome's winter transportation and communication needs."

———◆———◆———

Rod Perry: *Again, carefully note the heavy use of the Yukon River Corridor, Kaltag Portage, and Coastal Trail connecting Dawson and Nome during their peak populations. Additionally, observe that this busy traffic began a full decade before the Iditarod discovery and fully twelve years prior to the first heavy use of the Iditarod Trail. Consider why this route traveled by thousands between these two great gold-rush cities will be referred to later as the prevalent "line of travel."*

———◆———◆———

Old Ben Atwater: "That year of 1899 the railroad builders of the White Pass and Yukon Route got rails down fifty-six miles through the Coast Mountains as far as Carcross. What an huge advancement that was! It meant us dog-team carriers could pick up the mail in the Yukon interior. Relieved us so we didn't have to go all the way to the coast to get it like we used to. Before the railroad, it used to be sometimes getting through the mountain passage was just flat impossible. Even when we could do it, the mountain crossing was brutally punishing and dangerous. Steep, deep, heavy snows, awful lotta trail breaking, and constant avalanche danger. It really limited the loads we could carry and added immensely to the time mail took to reach the gold country."

———◆———◆———

Alfred Hulse Brooks: During the 1900 summer, construction crews completed the final 69 miles of the railroad from Carcross on into Whitehorse, the permanent end of steel. Coincidentally, in that summer of 1900, Nome's population hit its all-time peak. The timing was perfect. Because the Nome stampede did not become full-blown until two years after the main Klondike rush, the lag provided the Canadians with just enough time to finish their all-season railway connection."

At the turn of the new century, Nome's post office boasted the largest general delivery address in the United States. Letters addressed to stampeders named Johnson alone filled several boxes. For an area population of twenty to thirty thousand the need for year-round mail delivery was monumental. Once ice-up closed shipping, the newly completed railroad allowed Nome to look east for its mail.

That year of 1900, the United States Post Office deemed the difficulty of the trip had been enough reduced, and they were persuaded to let contracts to run weekly mail from Dawson to the golden city on the Seward Peninsula. That decision was based upon several factors. First, completion of the railway to Whitehorse had further decreased the distance over which everything had to hauled by beasts of burden. Second, the rest of the way ran virtually level almost the entire distance. Third, numerous gold-strike towns, Native villages, steamboat wood-supply pickup points and missions spread along the way could act as shelters and supply havens. The distance was long, but a city of that size could not very well go seven months a year cut off from communication with the rest of the world. And, besides the three Lynn Canal passes, there was no other route then known that allowed connection from the Interior through the mountain barrier to ice-free shipping waters of Southeastern and Southcentral Alaska, none whatsoever.

Rod Perry: *Of course, just because mail left Dawson bound for Nome on a weekly basis, it did not mean that a letter leaving Dawson would reach Nome in one week!*

Old Ben Atwater: "As you know, Al, I got awarded the mail route from Skagway into Dawson and Circle, then soon later, all the way to Nome. I can tell you, not much winter *freight* went all the way over that long mail route. Or passengers going with me. After all, from the wharf at Skagway, through the Klondike, down the Yukon River Trail, over the Kaltag Portage and up the Bering Sea coast to Nome is about a couple thousand miles. But if someone wanted to get in or out of Nome badly enough, he at least had some route where he could do it. Or maybe he just had to have some absolutely necessary item. Say

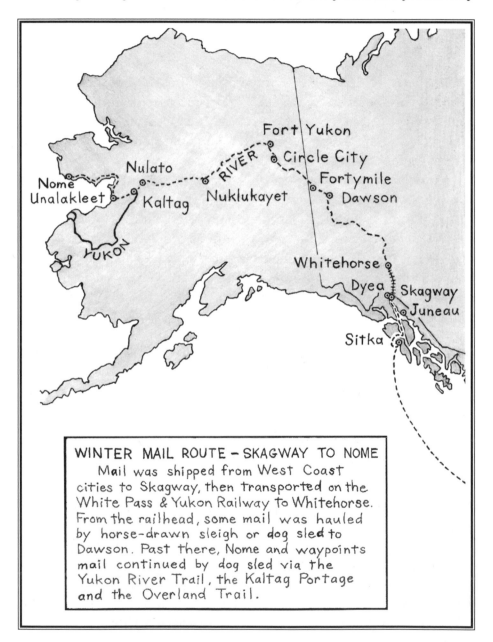

WINTER MAIL ROUTE – SKAGWAY TO NOME
Mail was shipped from West Coast cities to Skagway, then transported on the White Pass & Yukon Railway to Whitehorse. From the railhead, some mail was hauled by horse-drawn sleigh or dog sled to Dawson. Past there, Nome and waypoints mail continued by dog sled via the Yukon River Trail, the Kaltag Portage and the Overland Trail.

he couldn't wait for ocean shipping the following summer to bring it cheap and easy right to Nome's beach. If he had to get it that bad, and the high cost of taking it by dogsled was something he was willing to bear, at least penetration of the railroad through the mountain barrier into the Interior in the faraway Yukon Territory made it possible."

When the final upgrade came two years later with the building of the twelve-foot-wide Dawson Overland Trail from Whitehorse to Dawson, the use of horse-drawn sleds and wagons over the stretch allowed freight by the ton to be brought into Dawson from the head of steel during winter. This new transport further reduced the distance over which mail, travelers, and freight had to be transported in dogsled-sized loads.

In winter, everything heading the remaining distance to Nome left Dawson and traveled down the Yukon River Trail pulled by dogs. The great "Inland Highway" had boomed with the great Klondike rush. Now, winter traffic simply skyrocketed when the fabulous Nome strike dramatically turned 1,100 miles of the Yukon's frozen back between Dawson and Kaltag into a hard-beaten thoroughfare as several waves of Dawsonites left the Klondike headed for Nome. There were but two great cities in the North and the Yukon River Trail led most of the way between them. Not only dog teams carrying mail, freight, and passengers, but hikers and a few on bicycles coursed down the Yukon Trail to get to Kaltag where traffic branched off the river and followed linking trails 290 miles to Nome.

At the Athapaskan Indian village of Kaltag, the Yukon bends closer to the sea than anywhere else until nearing its mouth. There, fortuitously, lies a gentle pass through the mountains. For untold generations, the Yukon Indians and Bering Sea Eskimos from the Unalakleet area had used the ancient portage to meet with one another, sometimes for trade, others for war.

The instant population explosion at Nome created a heavy demand to move mail, freight, and travelers from the Yukon River over to the sea and up the coast to the Golden City by the shortest, easiest, safest route practicable. The Kaltag Portage became a heavily trafficked highway. The 290-mile distance from Kaltag to Nome was composed of the 85-mile-long portage and a little over 200 miles of following the sea coast north and west to Nome.

Nome still had no other viable winter mail and supply option. Anything coming into Nome over that terribly roundabout United States–Canada–United States course via Dawson had to come over 2,000 miles by rail and beast of burden after leaving Skagway on the Southeastern Alaska coast. It was a long, laborious, complicated way to haul a passenger, freight, or a letter. Nomites wished for something more expeditious. They wouldn't have long to wait.

From the Trail:
Trip Progress Assessment

———◆——◆———

Rod Perry: *Our long and winding trip through this Northland history has progressed to about the halfway point. When you climbed on the sled at my invitation, you didn't know your guide. By this time, however, we've become familiar, travel-hardened companions. Sharing a sled will do that.*

Now the trail toward our destination takes a turn that might surprise someone not familiar with the route: Geographically, the trail doubles back on itself! But not to worry, it is only geographical. Even though our sled will take us many hundreds of miles back over the same physical trail that brought us from the Klondike to Nome, historywise, storywise, it is as if we're not retracing our steps at all, but are heading into untraveled country. Trust the trail! It may twist and turn and even double back, my friend, but trust the trail. It takes us to Iditarod.

Before we turn the team, let's orient ourselves. The North has been unlocked. It booms in the east as Dawson in Canada's formerly remote Yukon Territory has exploded into being. At its recent peak, the city on the Klondike and its surrounds boasted a population of perhaps as many as 40,000 or even 50,000 using it as a supply base. It is served by an efficient, year-round transportation system. The world is gripped in the age-old magnetism of gold. The yellow metal's irresistible force has drawn men from almost every nation on earth, not only to the Klondike, but to other regions of the North where they hope to unearth their own bonanza.

Now the great find to the east has precipitated Alaska's own blockbuster discovery. The North Country's West has blown wide open with the great strike at Nome! The Golden City and outlying gold camps and small towns have reached a combined peak population not far behind that of Dawson at its recent height. Commerce, travel, and communication between the two centers and connection through the mountains to West Coast shipping and the industry of the United States and Canada have caused a great increase in traffic up and down the Yukon River Trail.

But Nome has no close winter-transportation link to ice-free shipping waters. That means, for seven months of the year, if it is to connect to the industrialized world, Nome must depend upon Canadian routes and transportation systems. Access requires traveling a distance so great that it approximates two-thirds the breadth of the United States. Because that so crimps Western Alaska's vitality and potential, it heads us surely toward Iditarod.

To get there, however, we must first turn the team back and travel the Yukon River Trail about halfway back to Dawson before turning up the Tanana River Trail to gain our destination point. It is yet undiscovered and unnamed, but soon it will be called Fairbanks.

Hold tight to the driving bow. Can you feel the energy of our spirited team transmitted through the tug lines, back along the towline and through the hickory of the sled to your mittened grip? Winding though the way might be, our faithful huskies yet run strongly and our runners track true to the trail . . . toward Iditarod.

Chapter 23

———◆———

The Fairbanks Strike

———

IN THE SUMMER OF 1898, while the throngs who had arrived too late in the Klondike filled menial jobs or established service industries around Dawson, and while the Three Lucky Swedes were staking their claims at Nome, a savvy Italian prospector named Felix Pedro came upon the richest gold-bearing stream he had ever found. Out of food, he and his partner could not stay and headed back to the supply sources along the Yukon, 200 miles away.

———

Rod Perry: *In Alaska, miners had widely prospected the country sloping north toward the Yukon River and had found gold in many drainages. Felix Pedro and some others no doubt knew that Arthur Harper, two decades earlier, had found traces along the Tanana River, which gathers waters draining south away from the Yukon. They concluded that, over the height of land separating the Yukon from the Tanana drainage, a good chance existed that streambeds running toward the Tanana probably held gold as well.*

———

Al Preston: "You know, Rod, it's like Nome, discovery stories are dime a dozen, though the Fairbanks details aren't nearly as crazy. There are several versions of how Fairbanks was discovered, but mostly it's just little twists on small details. Old Ben Atwater couldn't very well run his mail route during summer so he went down and helped construct some of the first buildings in the town. He knew Pedro, Gilmore, Barnette, Wickersham, all of them. Here's the way he told me it happened."

Felix Pedro, Discoverer of Fairbanks Gold

Old Ben Atwater: "Felix Pedro was born around Bologna, Italy. Felice Pedroni was his real name. He said his family was already dirt poor—subsistence farming and mining. Then his father died when he was young. That put his family in even harder straits. His uncles were coal miners. So as a kid, Felix started mining. I don't know whether he mined in Italy, but he did in France. When he emigrated to the United States he mined in Illinois, Oklahoma, Washington, some other places. I know he said he went to British Columbia's Caribou in 1893. Al, I remember him looking around Alaska's Fortymile country when the Klondike was struck. Like a lot of us who were nearby, he missed the first part of the rush.

"In 1898 Felix and a young mining engineer went on a long prospecting trip. From Fortymile country they went over the height of land into the upper Tanana. After going a couple hundred miles through tough country, they followed a Tanana tributary up to a pup. Up the valley of that pup, while the engineer was looking over a quartz vein, Felix prospected a bar and found encouraging colors. They'da stayed, but winter was around the corner. With too few supplies to stay they headed back to Forty Mile. Pedro tried to keep the landmarks in his head so he could come back. They were so driven by hunger, maybe that made his memory fuzzy. He tried to relocate the site in 1899 and 1900, but couldn't.

"In ought-one, a prospector we all respected named Tom Gilmore joined him in the search for "Lost Crick." In late June they headed out of Eagle Crick in the Circle District. Their plan was to take a compass course southwest all the way to the Tanana. Wouldn't you know it, after a very few days they lost the blamed compass. So they just followed the ridge separating the Chena and Chatanika rivers. Several days along they reached Fish Crick. Their pans showed colors, but not enough to hold their interest. They turned their back upon that thin showing and kept going. As they went, Felix climbed a nearby dome later named for him, Pedro Dome. They kept following the drainage and got to a point about a mile away from the future settlement of Fox. Again Felix and Tom got out their shovels and pans. This time they found better prospects. In fact, everywhere in the area they looked they found prospects. A clear tip, they figured, they were working a wide area of mineralization.

"After a month in the Bush, grub began running thin. Luckily, a number of days earlier, a group of four miners left Circle City on Pedro and Gilmore's track. I said *luckily* because each led a horse packing provisions. They hoped the trail might lead them to a find. Maybe Lost Crick. With the trail already cut, those followers made excellent time. They caught up, meeting on Fox Gulch. Usually Pedro and Gilmore would have been really bent over such a development. In their present case, though, they were glad to partner with the others. It meant a resupply of food. A tripling of trail-cutting help, too.

"On August 26 of ought-one the group climbed Ester Dome to overlook the country. Glassing, the men saw distant smoke. Through binoculars Pedro found the source. He watched the steamer, *LaVelle Young,* turning back from trying to buck a stretch of the Tanana. It'd been unusually dry weather. Nice for the prospectors' going overland, but falling levels'd made a point of swift water on the big river too shallow. He saw the *Young* turn and drop down into the mouth of the tributary Chena River. They ran a short distance upstream, and splashed anchor. Felix recognized the boat as a trading boat carrying supplies. He and the boys decided on the best course to reach it. Then the party camped for the night.

"Felix Pedro was a very competent prospector. However, little did even he guess what he was right above. Everything was so covered by wind-blown sediments and hid by thick vegetation it would have been tough to guess. But smack under where they camped on Ester Dome and under his very footsteps as he later hiked over the Ester Crick headwaters, lay unbelievable riches."

———————✦———✦———————

Rod Perry: *Reportedly, the Ester Mining District would eventually yield more gold than all other strikes in Alaska combined.*

The majority of gold seekers who came in following almost every major strike were newcomers, ignorant of how to effectively look for gold. They set out either under the impression that gold lay everywhere for the taking or assumed that finding a deposit was purely a matter of dumb luck.

Not so, however, the wandering breed that combed the country doing the basic searching and making most of the strikes. Experienced prospectors, these peripatetic men tended to be fair amateur geologists; they intuitively knew what areas and land forms held the most promise and possessed an uncanny ability to visualize what lay below the surface. Many in those days, when looking for placer deposits, based their analysis upon the model of a biblical, worldwide flood. Where would heavy, loose gold most likely settle, they asked themselves, first amid the racing floodwaters of the deluge and second, during rapid drainage as the tremendous volume ran off in torrents?

———————✦———✦———————

Old Ben Atwater: "Pedro and one of the others beat their way over the rough course to the boat. What should they find when they got there but a big squabble. The boat's owner and E. T. Barnette were jawing. Really getting into it about off-loading the cargo. The boat owner had contracted to haul a large supply of Barnette's goods from St. Michael up the Yukon, then fork up the Tanana. Barnette planned to set up a trading post way farther upriver at Tanacross. He was convinced a planned railroad would take the route of the Valdez trail to Eagle. He figured they'd cross the Tanana at the old Indian ford at Tanacross. But now low water and rapids had stopped the *Lavelle Young.* The good captain reminded Barnette of the terms of their contract. They'd agreed if they couldn't reach Tanacross, they were to off-load as far up as they could make it. And this was far's they could make it, as any fool could see. Period.

"Pedro wedged in and convinced Barnette that gold prospects in the locality looked promising. Felix told him that other Circle City prospectors were in the country round about. He allowed to Barnette that if he were to set up a supply center at that point on the Chena River, he could expect business. Pedro explained that prospectors already in the region would begin to base out of his place. Why wouldn't they? It beat wasting themselves on a several-hundred-mile round trip back to resupply at Circle City. Furthermore, Felix said, other prospectors who had stayed away because of the difficulty of the trip could be expected to come. Barnette's wife blubbered her eyes out at the thought of being stuck on such a worthless-looking, mosquito-infested backwater. But the man off-loaded there. And the City of Fairbanks had its beginning.

"Now the prospecting party was flush with supplies. Pedro and Gilmore and the other crew set off seventy miles to the southeast looking for "Lost Crick." They found what Pedro thought was it. Named it "'98 Crick," honoring the original date of the find.

"They prospected 'til late fall. Found good enough color all of them decided to work the place over. With winter coming, Felix and three others headed to Circle City for more chuck plus winter gear. Had themselves quite an ordeal, he told me. It'd been raining like a moose peein' on a flat rock. Rivers and cricks running brim-full. Crossings were time consuming and perilous. They ran out of food. Lost all their horses, save one. Even had their dog wander off and lose his pack. Well, they came a whisker from going under, but they finally straggled in to their Eagle Crick base.

"The word spread around the Circle miners. A number geared up and made the long trip back with Pedro's crew. They all went to work building quarters and sinking test holes, burning their way down. They did find indications, top to bottom. But all their work never turned up anything that would really pay.

"Everybody grew mighty disgusted. For three years, all the big hoopla over that 'Lost Crick' of Pedro's and this is all it turned out? So when Felix and Tom tried to get them to go to Barnette's Cache with them and comb country they knew was gold bearing, those Circle City boys said no thank you, if you quit there to come here, how good could your Barnette's area be?

"That spring of ought-two, Pedro and Gilmore were back down near Barnette's Cache. They spent about everything they had reoutfitting. About then, a little kid from a nearby Indian village ran a sharp willow stick way into his leg. The villagers came for help. Ol' Felix, he was a pretty good bush doctor. He treated the young'un and the kid healed right up. Now they thought he was a pretty skookum medicine man. The elders whispered to Felix if he went up Bear Crick, he'd find all kinds of gold. Gilmore told me Fairbanks Crick looked better to them, but the two figured they'd better heed the locals, so prospected Bear. (Al, let me say, and you prob'ly already understand, I'm calling these cricks by today's names on the white man's maps.)

"Well, Bear Crick hadn't put enough in the poke for them to buy more grub. They talked and agreed to keep one man there while the other got away to ease up on their remaining stash. Tom went back to Circle City alone. I hope you remember, every time I say this, the trip the way they went was maybe 150 to 200 miles each way.

"Felix prospected the area north of Barnette's all summer. On or near July 22 of ought-two he was on Pedro Crick. That was about twelve miles north of the Cache, close to the confluence of Gilmore and Goldstream Cricks. After days of sinking a fourteen-foot test he was at bedrock. Don't need to tell you, Al, how much work that would be without a partner to crank the buckets up with a windlass! Not you, Al. The pay he found, though, was all worth it. And then some.

"You've heard the famous phrase, 'There's gold in them there hills!' Bet you don't know it was Felix Pedro himself who coined it.

"Now ol' Felix, he was one of the kindest, most unselfish men I ever knew. He pulled out on that several-hundred-mile round trip hike to Circle country to bring back Gilmore. He had some gold to show so rounded up some others. Ground around Pedro's strike got staked pretty quick.

"As more came in, business for Barnette was hopping. But he wasn't satisfied. He sent the so-called Wandering Japanese, Jujiro

Wada, to Dawson to stir things up. Almost 450 miles in the dead of winter, but he was a traveling little machine. The tough little man came swirling into that town three days after Christmas. The *Dawson Daily News* and the *Yukon Sun* both ran headlines about the rich new strike over on the Tanana. Maybe as many as a thousand men stampeded. It was looking up at fifty below most of the trip.

"Now when they got there they found most ground staked. What did the fools expect? Happens with most strikes. And the other thing, deposits lay so deep compared to most Klondike area finds. It just took a lot longer to make a showing. On most of the claims they hadn't reached bedrock or drifted very far yet. These Dawson boys maybe expected gold to be bulging the miners' pokes. So when at first gander they saw slim pickin's they accused the news Barnette sent to Dawson was overblown. So they get all bent and start threatening Barnette. Rumors and stories get told they were about to hold a necktie party, a hemp dance with a little Japanese dangling. But I can tell you, Al, that was just a concoction. They were mad at Barnette for what they considered false promotions. And to boot, they threatened him for his high price for flour. But it's hogwash the crowd threatened to hang little Wada.

"Most turned tail back to Dawson. But those that stuck mostly found a paying claim and ended up in the money.

"Felix went back to Italy and tried to get hitched to some miss in the old country. Turned him down. So he came back and married an Irish floozie of the town, name of Mary Doran. Wretched wench. Poor Felix deserved better. Heart attack? Whaaah! Nothing wrong with his heart! He was hard-working. Never drank. Honest. And he was loyal and unselfish. We all admired our Felix Pedro. I'll tell you, Al, it was really sad to lose him."

——— ♦ ———

Rod Perry: *Felix Pedro died in St. Joseph's Hospital in Fairbanks July 22, 1910, eight years to the day after making his strike. Although the reported cause of his death at age fifty-two was heart attack, foul play at the hands of his wife was suspected. One of his old friends and partners, Vincenzo Gambiani, being questioned on his own*

*deathbed, was asked for a final testimony about the cause of Pedro's
death. Too weak to even speak, he scribbled two words,* moglie-veleno
("wife poison.")

*Pedro's body had been embalmed, sent to San Francisco and buried
in nearby Colma. On October 12, 1972 Cortelloni Ameto located his
grave. The remains were exhumed and moved to his birthplace in
Fanano, Italy for permanent burial. In the process, an autopsy was
performed. Analysis of hair samples proved he had, indeed, died
of poisoning.*

*Fairbanks celebrates Felix Pedro yearly during Discovery Days
festivities. Fairbanks and Fanano, Italy are joined as sister cities.*

Soon after Felix Pedro struck gold on Pedro Creek prospectors
discovered Ester and a number of other locations close by. The main
town of Fairbanks exploded in population, several outlying
communities sprang up, and the new city became the territory's
economic center. When Judge James Wickersham established his
court in Fairbanks, it became the governmental center of Alaska as
well. As with Dawson and Nome, the boom necessitated both summer
and winter movement of vast quantities of supplies as well as in- and
outbound mail and travelers.

Steamboat traffic flowed into Fairbanks from both ends of the river.
Some freight came in from Lynn Canal over the railroad to the end of
steel in Whitehorse. From there, steamboats plying the Whitehorse–
Fairbanks run took it with the Yukon flow 850 miles down to the
Tanana mouth, then 300 up against the Tanana current to Fairbanks.
Because these Upper Yukon steamboats returned straightway to
Dawson and Whitehorse after their Fairbanks delivery, passengers
coming in from Lynn Canal through Canada who were bound for
destinations downstream from the Tanana confluence had to debark
there and await a St. Michael-based steamer heading down following
a Fairbanks run.

Steamboats coming up from St. Michael had a haul of almost
identical length, approximately 1,200 miles. But theirs was upstream,
breasting the current the entire way to Fairbanks.

During the four months yearly that water transportation was functional, nothing yet available to Fairbanks could beat bringing in most of their supplies via steamboats and barges that could haul hundreds of tons at a time. But when winter locked up the Yukon and Tanana, any additional freight had to move a few hundred pounds at a time by dogsled.

Al Preston: "A lot of writers who wrote about dog-team transport over the old trails were far more interested in romanticizing the telling than telling the truth. They blew some of it up into something more than it actually was. Rod, to hear some tell it, whole northern cities depended upon dog teams bringing in all the supplies they needed during the months waterways were frozen.

"First of all, running hundreds of miles over mountain ranges and through blizzards and deep snow, say the musher never stops, just keeps making round trips all winter. How many people do you think one, lone driver and team could keep supplied? Not very many. So physically, it wasn't possible.

"Second, for four months a year—five in Nome because it's salt water which doesn't freeze up or stay frozen as easy—steam power can bring hundreds of tons—I said, *hundreds of tons!*—right to the docks of the biggest towns cheap and simple. Don't you think every store keeper and business man, and even some of the more stable citizens, if they have even one brain cell working, don't you think they're going to plan ahead down to the smallest detail and have it shipped in during summer?

"You can't do that with mail, and you can't always do that with travelers, but you can with most freight needed to supply a town or mining district."

Old Ben Atwater: "You know, being a mail carrier and freighter, I carried tons of mail in my day with my dog team and once in a while a paying passenger. But when I hauled freight all the way in from the Skagway to Dawson, or from Dawson all the way to Fairbanks, or later from Valdez in to Fairbanks or all the way to

Nome, it was always something special that couldn't be planned for way ahead and brought in by water. And with the price I charged being sometimes a hundred times as much per pound as what a steamboat could land it for, whatever they had me haul had blamed well better be something they couldn't live without or didn't have time to wait for.

"Back at old Forty Mile, Jack's ACC warehouse stocks'd come almost 5,000 miles by combined sea and river shipping from Frisco. He'd get a steamboat delivery from St. Michael of maybe 140 tons. Total shipping charge to that point was maybe a few pennies a pound. Then as soon as the river would freeze up for good traveling, I'd start hauling it up the Fortymile as far as a hundred miles to the mines. My charge to take it that far was a dollar or more a pound. You can see water is so much more efficient and affordable; you want to take full advantage of summer shipping and haul everything possible as close to the miner as you can get it by boat.

"One time a big mining company near Fox broke a piece of their hydraulic machinery. Had their whole operation stopped cold. It was late September. They couldn't very well sit there on their hands waiting for shipping to open the following summer. So they got a letter out to a foundry in Seattle to cast a replacement. When they calculated enough time had elapsed for the mail out to Seattle, the foundry work, the saltwater shipping back up to Skagway, the train to bring it to Whitehorse, and the horse-drawn wagon to haul it to Dawson, when they thought it was time the Fox mining company sent me to pick it up. Paid my stay in a Dawson hotel 'til it arrived. Al, that was one expensive chunk of equipment. But it got them back mining by December. That was a case of money for dog-team freighting being no object.

"Then sometimes it was some small, lightweight, but important item. One rich miner wanted some special perfume for his favorite dance hall queen. Another guy I remember was a Hungarian cook who made goulash so addictive made you foam at the mouth and bay at the moon and just quiver all over thinking about it. Twice a day folks'd back up in long lines waiting at his little kitchen. Never sold anything else, didn't need to. He'd scoop you extra if you brought your own bowl and spoon to save him washing dishes. Well, one day his hired dishwasher bumped the whole open container of the man's secret spice mix into the dishwater. Turned the air blue the Hungarian did, and knocked that clumsy helper near into the middle of next week. He was just dead in business until he got more spice in.

"I carried his letter to Dawson. Took almost two months for his order to go out and his new supply to come back. Next mail run I made to Dawson, I hauled it back to Fairbanks along with the mail. Freight like that's so light I didn't even notice the extra three or four pounds. But I'll tell you, I charged him plenty. You think I'd accept money? No siree! Al, I aint the fool that I look. I let him work off the charge in goulash. Froze it in blocks and took it with me to heat at night on the trail. By comparison with how valuable that spice was to the man, my high freight price didn't amount to much.

"One more example: Ol' Yablonski, the blacksmith, had his whole year's horseshoe and nail supply lost when the *Lady Caprina* went down with all hands. It was too late for a reorder to come by water before freeze-up. It was either have his winter supply brought by dog team from Valdez or lose business to his competition. So he contracted with me. My charge was maybe a hundred times more than his competition had to pay to have shoes and nails shipped in by water in summer. Yablonski had to stay competitive. So he couldn't charge more for his labor or his shoes to make up for higher shipping. Well, he kept his customers, but he must not've made a dime shoeing horses. Yablonski was lucky there's more to his trade and he wasn't just a farrier.

"So even after a couple more trails were developed from salt water to the Interior, as far as winter freight coming all the way from the coast by dog team went, it was very important for special shipments. But it sure wasn't the major way the main body of goods in general reached the Interior goldfields. The main traffic on the winter trails was freight that had already been brought into the Interior up the Yukon and Tanana by steam power. Then us freighters got hired to shake it out to end destinations, out from the main river trading center warehouses.

So what use did the trails get the entire distance between the Interior and the coast? Not much freighting but a whole lot of foot traffic and dog team passage of travelers in and out. And, of course, the all-important hauling of the mail.

"But back to what you said about those writers, Al. All the way hundreds of miles from salt water in winter by dog team? With a sled able to haul in only a few hundred pounds at a time? And maybe only capable of making two round trips a month? Bringing supplies like groceries and all other staples that way and thinking you're going to keep a big interior mining town or city going? Huhh! Makes you wonder about some writers' basic intelligence."

————◆—◆————

Since it was miners headquartered out of Circle City on the Yukon River that had made the Fairbanks discovery, the way between the two communities became well-beaten. The early prospectors' trail was quickly improved. That gave them access to the great Yukon River Trail and the well developed transportation line into Yukon Territory. So during winter, like Nome, they were able to take advantage of the dependable Canadian rails into Whitehorse and wagon transportation system from Whitehorse on down to Dawson.

But that was roughly a thousand miles by combined transportation methods, Fairbanks to Skagway. Fairbanks interests wanted a much shorter winter trail of their own.

————◆—◆————

Alfred Hulse Brooks: "Back in 1898, well before the Fairbanks discovery, the United States government had seen the potential benefits if a share of traffic to and from the gold fields could be attracted to course over more U.S. soil than just the few miles to the Coast Mountains summit in from Skagway and Dyea. Also, they reckoned that if they were to stimulate development during a time when the imagination of the continent had been captured by exiting headline news flowing out of north almost daily, they could turn around the entrenched national mindset that the purchase of 'Seward's Icebox' thirty years before had been money thrown away on a worthless, frozen northern wasteland. Congress directed the U.S.

Army to send exploration teams to Alaska to locate a practical way to the Yukon goldfields over U.S. lands.

"In command of the party exploring the Copper River was Lt. William Abercrombie. He concluded that a trail to the Yukon River should be built not up the Copper, but beginning at the port of Valdez on Prince William Sound. Valdez was already beginning to grow as a port of entry and supply base for prospectors bound for the Klondike over a route discovered in January 1898 that led up the Valdez Glacier. Passage over the ice was extremely exhausting and treacherous, and many had lost their lives in the crossing. Abercrombie advocated an alternative route."

━━━━━━━●━━●━━━━━━━

In the spring of 1899, construction of a pack trail had been started. Government work crews were supplemented by hundreds of destitute stampeders who had failed in their attempt to strike it rich in the Klondike. Now desperate for a way to earn passage to escape the North, they had hired on for $50 a month plus board. Progress on the five-foot-wide pack trail had been so rapid that by fall, the first forty miles including the most difficult section up the Keystone Canyon and over Thompson's Pass, had been completed. Ahead of the finished trail, ninety-three additional miles had been surveyed and cleared.

━━━━━━━●━━●━━━━━━━

Alfred Hulse Brooks: "Coinciding with Abercrombie's 1899 work, the U.S. Army had also been progressing north in its laying of the Washington–Alaska Military Communication Army Telegraph System, termed WAMCATS. The next year, the last section of line was laid over Abercrombie's route and extended to Fort Egbert, at today's Eagle, Alaska, located on the Yukon River close to the Canadian boundary. In the process, WAMCATS workers improved Abercrombie's pack trail."

━━━━━━━●━━●━━━━━━━

Rod Perry: *An energetic young lieutenant worked on the project. In the process, he fell in love with Alaska and with driving sled dogs. Lt. Billy*

Mitchell went on to gain fame as one of the pioneers of military aviation and would eventually go down in history as one of the country's great military thinkers and innovators. His portrait as a young dog driver hangs in the Dog Mushers Hall of Fame in Knik, Alaska.

It was over this telegraph route that Fairbanks founder E. T. Barnette had been led to believe a railroad would be built, crossing the Tanana at Tanacross. That crossing point was his destination when he chartered the Lovelle Young to transport supplies for establishment of his trading post.

Alfred Hulse Brooks: "Fairbanks quickly grew in size and importance as a governmental and commercial center for the Alaska Interior. As that took place, the town needed a shorter, more efficient winter supply line than going over a thousand miles through Yukon Territory to Skagway. Simultaneously, the prevalent spirit of nationalism drove the city to push for an "all-American" transportation line of its own through United States territory. To accomplish those ends, Fairbanks interests put in a trail heading south to link with the recently completed Valdez–Eagle telegraph and military pack trail. Their connecting trail of approximately 250 miles ran up the Tanana and Delta rivers, over the Alaska Range through Isabelle Pass, and down the Gulkana River to Gakona Junction. There it joined Abercrombie's trail and the WAMCATS line. The port of Valdez boomed to serve Fairbanks."

Rod Perry: *For over two decades, until the completion of the Alaska Railroad, the majority of what entered Fairbanks during winter would come in over the almost 400-mile-long route.*

Once Fairbanks established its Valdez connection, much of Nome's winter transport shifted from running over the Canadian system to the new route. To reach Nome, it first moved from Valdez north over the Chugach and Alaska ranges to Fairbanks. It then traveled west

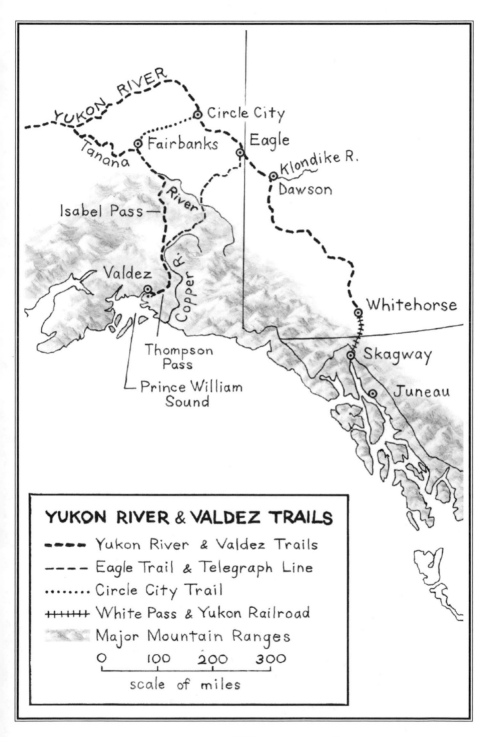

YUKON RIVER

YUKON RIVER

Tanana

Circle City

Fairbanks

Eagle

Klondike R.

Dawson

Isabel Pass—

River

Valdez

Copper R.

Whitehorse

Thompson
Pass

Skagway

Prince William
Sound

Juneau

YUKON RIVER & VALDEZ TRAILS

- - - - Yukon River & Valdez Trails

- - - - Eagle Trail & Telegraph Line

.... Circle City Trail

++++++ White Pass & Yukon Railroad

Major Mountain Ranges

0   100   200   300

scale of miles

down the Tanana River to the Yukon and down the heavily traveled Yukon River Trail–Kaltag Portage–Coastal Trail route to Nome.

◆——◆——◆

Rod Perry: *To continue preparing the reader to understand the Iditarod Trail, note that Fairbanks, located between Dawson and Nome has been added as the third major city along the dominant "line of travel" generally connected by the Yukon River."*

◆——◆——◆

Though Nome valued the Valdez–Fairbanks–Tanana Trail connected to the Yukon as an all-American route that was indeed shorter than going through the Dawson, Yukon Territory (Canada had elevated the former North-West Territories "district" to full territorial status), advantage of the reduction in distance was somewhat offset. The Valdez–Fairbanks Trail had to cross two mountain ranges, whereas from Dawson the trail ran essentially level. At best, both trails were thought to be too time-, energy-and money-sapping. Nomites still yearned, like Fairbanks had yearned before them, for a shorter, more economical winter route of their own to ice-free shipping waters.

◆——◆——◆

Rod Perry: *The problem keeping Nome from doing what Fairbanks had done in constructing a winter transportation route of its own to ice-free salt water was two-pronged. First, the distance and physical obstacles separating Nome from the nearest ice-free port were far greater than what Fairbanks had faced. Second, whereas Fairbanks (like Dawson before it) had constructed its saltwater link while its boom was at its peak, Nome's cry for a trail did not become full-blown until its great boom was well past and its population had diminished to one-tenth of its gold-rush size. Therefore, the length and degree of construction difficulty combined with a decreased demand forced Nome to continue to depend upon the winter transportation systems of Dawson and Fairbanks.*

From the Sled:
Progress Assessment and Overview

———◆———

Rod Perry: *My friend, our journey has taken us to the northwestern subcontinent, paused on its east side, rushed across its wide span to its west coast, then reversed direction to travel halfway back to our beginning. You and I have traveled so many miles together through this northland history that trail and camp procedures now come second nature to you. By now we're quite a team.*

We've witnessed development of the transportation corridor to the east that so effectively served to develop the Dawson region. That Canadian system was vital, difficult as the great distance made it, to Nome's early life and growth. From Nome, our odyssey has taken us back eastward to Fairbanks. Even though the heartland city grew up hundreds of miles closer to Dawson and could thereby take advantage of transportation through the Canadian town far more economically than could Nome, Fairbanks saw the advantages of an even shorter winter transportation system connecting it to its own year-round port. It moved quickly to establish a trail link to Valdez.

Fairbanks' switch to using its new route to the sea for its winter needs also gave Nome a significantly shorter route. Even so, Valdez to Nome is still a long, long trip.

Not much time elapsed before visionaries in Nome could see the possibility for an even shorter way of their own to winter shipping. However, as things stood, the great volume of transportation between the three major population centers of the North had so developed the winter trail system connecting them that it would only be by some tremendous, overriding developments that a new trail system could be created with enough logistical and economic advantages to induce professional dog drivers to abandon the established system and adopt a new one. That would be especially true when it came to allowing carriers submitting bids to haul U.S. mail over a new route a chance to

317

win contracts in competition with bidders using the well-established Yukon River route.

And so now, my friend, our journey must proceed back toward Nome. Our goal? To look into one of the most remote and little explored regions left in Alaska, the distant country between the Upper Iditarod River and Susitna Station through the mighty Alaska Range. We'll see if such a trail is possible.

While I manage the sled, go on up and help our trusty leader turn the team. Once again, we're reversing direction and heading back over the Yukon River Trail toward Nome. Don't grow disoriented at this repeat turning about; instead, keep your eyes on the horizon. As before, this back and forth repetition is only geographic. As far as the trail through our history is concerned, we're once more headed into new country. Rely on your guide; he knows where he's taking you. Trust the trail. The way now tends downhill. We feel new energy coming back through the sled and by the set of the dogs' heads and ears we know that our surging huskies sense something ahead. Hang on! They pick up the pace, taking us surely, now swiftly . . . toward Iditarod.

Chapter 24

---◆---

The Railroad Makes a Good Start

IT HAS BEEN SAID AMONG MARINERS that, along with New York and Sydney, Australia, Alaska's Resurrection Bay is one of the three most perfect natural harbors in the world. Seward, formally founded in 1903 at its head, also happens to be the closest ice-free port to Nome. A trail out of Seward started working its way in the direction of Nome through a seemingly unrelated development.

With the early emergence of gold mining on the Kenai Peninsula and elsewhere around Cook Inlet, the quality and strategic location of its harbor quickly vaulted Seward to prominence as the main year-round deepwater port for the Cook Inlet region.

Coincidentally, a route running from Seward offered the best combination of an excellent ice-free harbor, a gentle gradient, and a buildable roadbed for a railway through the Alaska Range to Alaska's commercial and governmental center, Fairbanks.

Not only the burgeoning city of Fairbanks, but also mining activity around places like Kantishna and other significant gold discovery sites located north of the Alaska Range depended upon transport along the Yukon River. On the south side of the range, prospecting and mining were not only thriving on the Kenai Peninsula, but making starts in the Susitna Valley. But they had only primitive means of winter supply. Though these locations were far-flung and mostly well away from the rail route, a railroad from Seward north to Fairbanks would pass close enough to serve all of them. Even those strikes in locations along the Yukon and its tributaries quite distant from the route would benefit, for such a railroad would at least bring shipments much closer and greatly shorten their winter supply lines.

Those obvious advantages stimulated an investment group to begin construction of the Alaska Central Railroad.

319

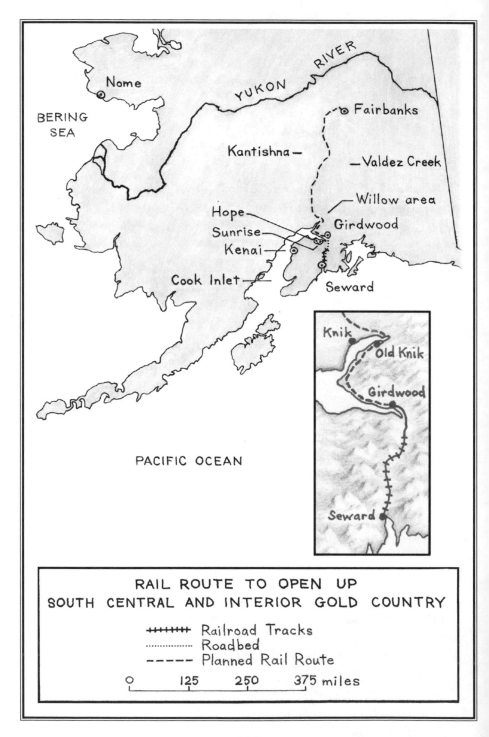

RAIL ROUTE TO OPEN UP
SOUTH CENTRAL AND INTERIOR GOLD COUNTRY

++++++ Railroad Tracks
.... Roadbed
- - - - - Planned Rail Route

o   125   250   375 miles

The railroad was not completed until the 1920s, two decades after the Fairbanks Rush, but construction had begun from the Seward end in 1903. Although the effort went broke in the financial panic of 1907, crews had constructed seventy-two miles of roadbed and laid fifty-two miles of track before the venture ceased operations. Therefore, for some years before trains began winter service, its roadbed blessed foot travelers and dog teams by providing them a serviceable winter trail for seventy-two miles out of Resurrection Bay toward various diggings around Cook Inlet. It particularly aided travelers where the railroad had blasted tunnels and built trestles to gain passage through an otherwise impassable stretch of cliffs and canyons in the Kenai Mountains. Past the tunnels the roadbed extended nearly to the mining activity at Girdwood on Turnagain Arm. Between Seward and Girdwood, foot travel became common and dog teams often made the trip.

The foot and dog team travel simply kept a well-packed thoroughfare beaten in between the rails, and beyond, where crews preparing the roadbed worked well ahead of those installing ties and rail. So, as construction progressed northward, travelers were able to take increasing advantage of the easy grade.

From Girdwood, the Crow Pass cutoff trail left the railroad route, took a shortcut north over the mountains and reconnected with the rail route farther on. It received less frequent winter use, but mail carriers, miners, and trappers entering or leaving the Matanuska and Susitna drainages during winter went that way. By dog team the climb over the pass was almost too steep to be negotiated. Over the other side it dropped sharply into the Eagle River valley. Near the present townsite of Eagle River, the trail rejoined the Alaska Central Railroad pack trail, which followed the future right-of-way that surveyors slashed out far ahead of crews preparing the roadbed.

The path continued past the Native village of Old Knik (present day Eklutna), crossed the Knik and Matanuska rivers and led across what is now called the Palmer Hay Flats. There, the beginnings of a trail toward Nome turned away west, leaving the rail route's north heading.

The developing railbed and pack trail gave northbound travelers a great advantage. Prior to that construction, gaining the Matanuska-

U.S. Mail Team Blessed with a
Nearly Perfect Trail out of Seward

Peterson Postcard Album, UAF-1998-53-7, Archives and Manuscripts,
Alaska and Polar Regions, University of Alaska Fairbanks

Susitna Valley country in winter by foot or dog team had been terribly imposing. But the work of the Alaska Central crews presented those who had a compelling enough reason to go that way a doable, if difficult trail.

And so, though railroad builders were thinking only of Fairbanks as a destination and their objective was limited to the opening up of the country along the rail belt and the central Tanana-Yukon Interior, their construction was unintentionally presenting a great side benefit: they were building Nome a 160-mile-long start on a trail issuing from Resurrection Bay.

Chapter 25

———◆———

Nome Winter Trail Desires Get a Boost
Midway Gold Strikes Add Demand

WIDESPREAD, GOLD-RUSH-DRIVEN ATTENTION on Alaska prompted the federal government to order a number of expeditions north to look for useful transportation corridors. Several were directed to inspect routes issuing from Cook Inlet. One such route was explored by Josia Spurr in 1898 and soon afterward by others. It led up the Susitna River and its main tributary system flowing in from the west, through a pass in the Alaska Range over a most beautiful scenic pass he named Rainy Pass, and on down into headwaters of the Kuskokwim River.

———————

Rod Perry: *I was fortunate to be among the first five dog drivers of the modern era to crest Rainy Pass, the more circuitous side route through Ptarmigan Pass having been taken instead on the first four Iditarod Trail Sled Dog Races. Pausing at the summit after a long jog uphill behind the sled, I stood awed by the transcendent view. If you, too, are by some design or chance fortunate enough to find yourself on that crest at brightest midday and drinking in the vistas as I did, you will lean back to gaze high at shimmering mountainsides slanting steeply over you— too brilliant to permit a long stare. Looking down, the deep, shadowed canyon of the fabled Dalzell lies ahead. Perhaps you will, as I did amidst that surpassing grandeur, lapse into an inner grandiloquence as you inadequately attempt to express your impressions, as well as reflect on how it would take a jaded and callous person indeed not to be struck by the magnificence of the creation and humbled before its omnipotent, magnanimous Creator.*

———————

For years following the Nome Rush there glimmered hope among Nomites who were aware of the explorers' reports of the remote pass. They were intrigued by possibilities that the little-known way might offer a suitable shortcut from ice-free salt water to Nome.

Even with the railroad's help providing the great start of a better trail out of Seward, the approach to Rainy Pass is long, very long. From Seward, dog team and foot traffic in the earliest days of the route's use had to travel about 250 miles of rough trail—a laborious trip of ten to twenty days depending upon whether the way was broken or not—before reaching even the beginning climb of the lowest Alaska Range foothills.

About 160 miles into the journey, near the present site of Wasilla, the trail left the rail route and split off to the northwest toward the pass. It led across the rolling lowlands and gradually ascended the successive valleys of the Susitna, Yentna, and Skwentna rivers. A steeper climb beginning at the Happy River finally gained the summit of Rainy Pass.

Though cresting the pass put several hundred very hard-won miles behind, several hundred more lay ahead before the intended route could break out of almost unexplored wilderness to emerge at Kaltag, at that hard-beaten junction of the Yukon River Trail and Kaltag Portage.

Because of its length through desolate, uninhabited country and fears of insufficient use there was a great question about whether building such a trail could be justified. Need, which as the years went by declined as Nome's population dwindled to one-tenth of its gold-rush numbers, appeared to be offset by the probable difficulty and expense of trail building, upkeep, and operation.

Al Preston: "As you know, I mined near Nome. So I can tell you quite a lot about the state of affairs as we thought about our trail situation up there in the early years. Rod, about the time of the Nome Rush, the government explored Rainy Pass country. A few years later congress created the Alaska Road Commission (ARC) as a branch of the U.S. Army. The ARC was set up to take charge of building and maintaining

Gulkana Roadhouse on the Well-Developed Valdez Trail

Albert Johnson Collection, Albert Johnson, UAF-1989-166-110,
Archives and Manuscripts, Alaska and Polar Regions Collections,
University of Alaska Fairbanks

trails and roads. Alaska was so primitive the federal government deemed transportation corridors to be a national security interest.

"Of course the ARC office in Nome had copies of the explorers' report and maps. When we Nomites found out about the pass someone came up with the idea of a trail through there to shorten up our way to winter shipping somewhere down on the Gulf. The idea caught on and circulated around town. From then on almost all of us held a glimmer of hope that some day, some way such a trail could be put in. The cabin I rented in Nome was next door to an ARC employee who was a pretty close friend. If the trail were to go in, he'd probably be in on the work. So the idea of a Rainy Pass trail was something I got to talk about in depth more than most.

"It's great to have dreams because they lead you to creativity. But a lot of those Nome dreamers weren't being very realistic. It wasn't all rosy. There were some big obstacles apparently in the way. At least raising serious doubts. For one, if we were right in guessing where it might go, it looked like the trail would lead through maybe 400 or more miles of the most desolate wilderness.

"That remote part of the country—it had hardly been visited since Russian times. If even then. The Commission knew that in the whole length it was only inhabited with a couple or three Native villages.

"Next, the timing was wrong. The big demand for such a trail had passed Nome by. Instead of that booming gold-rush city, we had dwindled to a small town. With decreased population and activity, there was a great question about whether that route would ever get a small fraction of the traffic it would need to make it worth putting in and keeping up. If the Road Commission had existed while the Seward Peninsula was still crawling with thirty thousand, and Turnagain Arm on Cook Inlet still had maybe two or three thousand mining down there, the government would have ordered that trail put in without a second's hesitation. But by the time the ARC came into being and the explorers' reports became known, nine out of ten stampeders had pulled up stakes.

"Because it was such a long, long haul over the established way from Nome to Valdez, and it appeared the distance between Nome and some place like Seward must be hundreds of miles shorter, that comparison of miles, alone, took over almost everyone's thinking. As if there were no other factors to consider than a distance differential.

"But face it; Nome's winter travel and mail delivery going through Fairbanks were already working just fine the way they were. Summer and winter that route to salt water worked so smooth. The trail up the Yukon and Tanana and on to Valdez was so loaded with settlement and resources. It was plain to the Road Commission and everyone who could draw a rational comparison that a new route through raw wilderness would have to reduce the distance tremendously to counterbalance all the advantages the trail up the Yukon through Fairbanks and on to Valdez offered.

"Look especially at the Yukon River Trail with all the roadhouses, trading posts, villages, missions, wood-cutting stations, settlers' cabins, and fish camps studding the way, there were shelters aplenty.

Well Dressed Passengers Ride in Comfort.
Stage Travel on the Valdez Trail.
Alaska State Library Historical Collections, ASL-P01-2301

Steamboats were running by the dozens back and forth all summer. They could stock every place along the Yukon, and Fairbanks on the tributary Tanana, so easily and comparatively inexpensively. And by then the Fairbanks–Valdez trail had already been improved to accommodate horse-drawn wagons, sleighs, and sledges and there were plenty of upscale roadhouses operating.

"A lot of people didn't stop to think about comparing those advantages with having to laboriously and expensively stock distant roadhouses along a new route through raw wilderness piecemeal, a few pounds hauled one sled load at a time long distances by dog team.

"Then along the Yukon River route, there were the factors that made it easy on the drivers. To hand them ready feed, the highest-quality, fattest salmon in Alaska swam by the millions right up to the cutting tables and drying racks. And to make the going good, there was such constant traffic the trail was always being rebroken. In case a really big snow fell or an extra strong wind drifted the trail in deep, everyone just waited for the mail team to come through. The carriers *had* to go: they were bound by their contract schedule. If the mail driver thought it was really tough, to conserve his own team he could hire a big, fresh team from a nearby riverside village to plow through with an empty sled and break it out.

"You compare all of that with the emptiness and remoteness of the Rainy Pass route. It was pretty plain the newly proposed way couldn't come close to duplicating the Valdez-to-Fairbanks and Yukon Trail's advantages. The only way for Rainy Pass to overcome its disadvantages enough to make that route feasible would be if the distance were to be found to shorten the trip enough, and the trail quality proved to be fast enough. Would the new way cut five days off the trip? Ten days? At a certain point the business advantage would have to swing from the old trail over to the new one. But until the route could be looked over, no one knew either distance or difficulty of the terrain.

"As much as the idea of a shorter way intrigued you, trail-savvy folk visualized trail conditions and pondered some questions: Unless the distance was so shortened it could take a big share of the business away from the existing Yukon River Trail route, who in tarnation was going to travel it? Would anyone build, supply, and staff so much as the simplest roadhouse if all that comes through once in a while is some poor, crazy mail carrier—some misguided fool who's hungry enough to take a contract when it means wallowing through deep, unbroken snow all the way because he's the only traffic? A roadhouse business can't run on thin air, now, can it? And how's a shorter trail going to benefit Nome if it takes longer to cover the distance slogging over the mountains on snowshoes breaking trail alone, than over the old, smoothly functioning way where you cover the well-broken, level river miles at a nice brisk trot?"

<hr/>

Rod Perry: *For a great illustration comparing dog team travel over trackless country where men and teams struggle to wallow ahead perhaps five to ten miles in a hard-fought day vs. travel over well broken trails where teams can move at a mile eating trot, look ahead to pages 439 and 440.*

<hr/>

Al Preston: "You had to look at it this way: the long-distance way through Fairbanks was indeed time-consuming and expensive, no argument. But the way the officials seemed to view it, the cost was being spread out, shouldered by individuals and businesses, use by use, if that makes sense. In a nutshell, it was expensive to transport freight, mail, and travelers the old, long way, but didn't take a huge, new capital investment.

"That meant, to those making the trail-building decisions and controlling the purse strings, that allocating a sizeable lump of government funding to cut through what trail builders would likely find out there—the expansive standing forests, downed timber and dense brush—plus construction work to bridge numerous small streams, erect thousands of trail markers, and build shelter cabins, then afterwards maintain the hundreds of miles of an entirely new (in some ways duplicative) trail system, Rod, all of that apparently looked like funding an unnecessary upgrade, if not a luxury."

———————

But then the situation began to change. Several minor gold rushes took place in the little-traveled wilderness located midway along this proposed trail route. The small boom towns that sprang up and the many outlying mines populated the area with perhaps one thousand souls. The occurrence tipped the scales enough in the minds of government road builders to initiate an investigative expedition in the winter of 1908. Alas, the reconnaissance only bore out their former trepidations. Though the way did indeed appear to provide a good route, they deemed it too expensive to build and keep up.

As Al Preston pointed out, road builders saw that building and maintaining the trail would not be the only expense. Most of the route between Seward and the Yukon led through off-the-beaten-path country virtually devoid of habitation. It offered almost no support to travelers. Therefore, a roadhouse and supply system would have to be built, staffed, supplied, and run at government expense or at least subsidized. The thin population bases of Seward and Cook Inlet on the southern end, the minor importance of the midway gold strikes, and the dwindling population of Nome predicted few travelers. With traffic so sparse, a roadhouse venture would hardly attract entrepreneurs. And no mail carrier was going to win a bid—or even want to bid in the first place—when there was little or no traffic and he had to constantly break all the trail by himself. Authorities decided to keep to the status quo and continue using the established routes.

The northwesternmost break through the mountains over Rainy Pass would never have seen much more than an occasional trickle of use had it not been for a blockbuster occurrence: From one of Alaska's most remote, little-prospected regions, the almost unknown upper Iditarod River, the cry once more rang out, "GOLD!"

The location of the final great strike of the gold rush era happened to be not far to the west and about midway along the proposed Seward-to-Nome mail route!

The last, old-fashioned, hell-bent-for-leather gold rush in North America was on. When that final, glorious stampede burst upon the scene and Iditarod quickly grew to become, briefly, Alaska's largest city, the thousands of the gold town's dwellers desperately needed winter transportation routes. Suddenly road builders had rationale aplenty dropped in their laps to go to the effort and expense of putting in the trail over Rainy Pass. Would-be entrepreneurs, dollar signs dancing in their eyes at the thought of heavy traffic, chomped at the bit to establish waypoint roadhouse businesses.

Of the five hard-beaten cracks through the almost impregnable armor of the great, thousand-mile mountain fortress north and west of Wrangell, only this last trail to the Northwest—the Iditarod Trail—would never be replaced with a railroad or highway. Traversing swampy quagmires and sodden, tussock-ridden muskegs and crossing so many waterways, it was suitable for travel only in winter's frozen state. Even with all of the traffic it received at its zenith, the Iditarod afforded Nome only a long, rugged path allowing foot travel and difficult passenger, mail, and freight delivery by dog team.

Rod Perry: *As a trail it began, as a trail it lived gloriously, and when the gold petered out and the rush was over, as a trail it died. That no* road was ever built over the route and that the country it traverses remained largely raw wilderness would preserve its primitive character and its colorful, romantic gold-rush luster through the decades of abandonment as if the trail had an appointment with destiny.

The trail's romantic allure may be attributed one of the main reasons the Iditarod would one day live again. A half century after heavy trail use died out, in a man-and-team-against-the-wilderness setting, the old path would experience a glorious rebirth. From its long slumber it would awake once more to hear the barely audible hiss of runners and the creaking of sled joints; it would feel the staccato footfall and listen to the panting of trotting huskies. The world's longest, most grueling sled-dog race, termed "The Last Great Race on Earth" would be held over its spectacular course, capturing international imagination.

But I forget at times and get ahead of myself in the telling, as this is all so alive to me. Let's go back and examine more completely the interesting details of the Iditarod Trail's founding . . .

Following Nome's boom, once the easily discovered and mined upland placer and beach gold had played out, Nome had followed the predictable pattern all of the great discoveries of the North: Mining had gone from being labor intensive at the first stages, during which gold was available with simple hand tools and manual labor, to capital intensive. It required capital to buy, set up, and operate expensive hydraulic systems featuring huge hoses and nozzles to wash out and sluice less concentrated deposits that were harder to access, buried as they were under deep overburdens. Floating dredges, behemoths that cost even more to install than hydraulic systems, could economically operate where gold was even deeper and even less concentrated. Equipment replaced men.

As the tens of thousands of boomers folded their tents and left, Nome settled into an economically sustainable extraction mode based upon systematic development of the gold findings. The resident population had then dropped to a mere tenth of its gold-rush swarms. Therefore, though Nomites that stayed continued to yearn for a shorter, more economical winter route of their own to ice-clear salt water, the demand of the few thousand remaining could not counterbalance the cost of building and maintaining a trail of such length and difficulty.

As already seen, all the gold strikes in the Far North were linked by winter trails. Obviously, they were linked as well by the flow of humanity (often the same people) that ran from one discovery to the other.

To reiterate, during the Nome rush, the entire length of the Yukon River, the great Highway of the North became a hard-packed thoroughfare in winter as streams of the leftover "have-nots" of the Klondike Rush surged downriver from Dawson, using more than 1,100 miles of the river's frozen back on their way to the Seward Peninsula diggings. Then, with the Fairbanks strike, many "strikeouts" from Nome rushed back up the Yukon Trail into the Interior. Also, some still up in the Klondike stampeded down the Yukon River Trail to the Fairbanks discovery.

Alfred Hulse Brooks: "During the next few years immediately following the three great gold rushes, the north's primary population was situated either in Dawson, Nome, or Fairbanks or in villages along the trail system of the Great Inland Highway. The three big towns were the only centers north of the Alaska Panhandle that could boast of almost every component of modern cities down in the States. Almost all winter travel, mail, and freight moved along the connecting trails between the three bustling centers as well as along the branch trails which ran to minor strikes and habitations away from the main trunk line. The point is that the major population and activity of the North was confined to an area connected by the Yukon River Trail system."

Rod Perry: *Thinking about Nome's hoped-for trail of its own, and looking at such a trail from both ends, it was plain that much of the route was already in place. From Nome, the first 300 miles as far as Kaltag had long been a heavily beaten thoroughfare from years of being part of the "main line of travel," fielding the back and forth traffic between Nome and Fairbanks and Dawson.*

Alma Preston: "Now Rod, from the Seward end here's the way things stacked up. The Alaska Central Railroad railbed and survey trail gave occasional hikers and dog drivers a great start. Following that beginning, just after crossing the Matanuska River the most-traveled trail left the railroad right-of-way to head off on its own. It went west across the Hay Flats until it gained the north shoreline of Knik Arm (of Cook Inlet.) The first objective of this branch trail was the tiny settlement of New Knik (now Knik.) In those days it consisted of George Palmer's store, an Alaska Commercial post and a few log buildings. Knik was visited by sporadic summer shipping. It served as a supply point for the nearby area.

"The second destination of the branch was Susitna Station, where there was another Alaska Commercial post and a few other businesses. It was a steamboat stop about thirty-five trail miles beyond New Knik, a snug little community nestled on the Susitna River. The population had grown to maybe as many as a couple of hundred people, enough to call for a school. There were perhaps 100-plus men prospecting and trapping in the region. It was really hard to keep track of such a shifting population. Su Station had gained its importance as a supply center serving that thriving little group of people plus the round-about Indian population. Our mail contract route from Seward had its terminus there. There was a fairly well-beaten trail out to a minor strike near the Yentna River. Other than that, beyond Su Station were found only the thin threads of snowshoe and hand-sled tracks. They were left by individuals fanning out here and there to lonely prospects, traplines and Native habitations and hunting grounds."

Rod Perry: *Obviously, from Seward north to Susitna Station, a distance of roughly 200 miles, the trail was established. It was rough and lacking amenities and not heavily traveled compared to a trail such as the Yukon River Trail, but it was established. By the years right after the turn of the century, the dog teams of Seward pioneer and mail contractor Alfred Lowell and his brother-in-law "Colonel" Harry Revell*

(Alma's employers) were carrying winter mail over the distance a few times each winter. Though seeing but a small fraction of the traffic that coursed back and forth over the great winter thoroughfares of the Interior, and though the way featured little in the way of roadhouses or resupply points except at Glacier Creek on Turnagain Arm and at the Knik and Susitna Station posts at the far north end, the way was at least defined and used enough to feature a trail base of sorts that was intermittently rebroken.

With both ends in place, 300 miles from Nome down to Kaltag and 200 miles from Seward up to Su Station, the obvious, logical question that some kept asking was, why not just finish the middle portion to connect the ends?

Chapter 26

———◆———

Native Routes vs Useful Mail Trails

Rod Perry: *One hundred years after Nomites were no doubt wondering why the hard-beaten first 300 miles south from Nome were not joined to the established (albeit rough) 200 miles north out of Seward, it is common to read copy penned by unknowledgeable writers of Iditarod Trail Sled Dog Race background history and embellishers of gold-rush trail romance that an ancient, Native trade trail or system of such trails led from Cook Inlet over Rainy Pass into the upper Kuskokwim and on to Kaltag and Nome. They claim that early gold rush travelers coursed over them and trail builders essentially followed and used them as a foundation.*

Did the Natives along the trail route at one time or another travel every foot of the country over which the trail passes? Of course they did. Did they move about the country trading with one another? Absolutely. But were any of their trails of a character to constitute a ready-made, serviceable, continuous, direct trail between Susitna Station and Kaltag? Any close look into the situation strongly indicates that that is a most fanciful stretch.

———◆———

Al Preston: "You know, there was a guy came into Nome fresh up from America. He puttered around a few months and all of a sudden he becomes a self-proclaimed authority on the country. He took up demand for the trail as his pet cause. Kept sounding off to everyone who'd give him half an ear. Said the Indians had easy-to-follow paths they used to trade with each other, trails we could use to go all the way through.

"Did he take us for fools? Did he think we were blind and stupid? If the Natives had such perfect trails in place through the middle country before we got here, that would have meant the existing north and south ends of our longed-for Seward-to-Nome Trail were already joined! If so, all you'd have had to do was put the sled on their trail and whistle up your team to get going. Convenient!

"Does it make sense that a few thousand of us would have been wishing so longingly for something that was already there? Did he take himself for knowing so much more about what's out there than all of us prospectors who'd been poking around the country for years before he got here, a lot of us with Indian friends and some marrying their women and living in their villages? Fact is, the guy was daft; there wasn't any such trail system that was useable to us.

"I had a friend, Mishka, who lived at his village of Dishkaket. I'm no anthropologist, but I spent quite a lot of time with him in the Bush. Within their own area his people knew the country like the back of their hand. They were tremendous woodsmen. Perfect sense of direction. Photographic memory for every physical feature. When on his ancestral grounds Mishka new exactly where he was day or night, summer or winter. When I traveled with him you could see his people didn't need much more of a cleared path than a lynx. If they could readily make it through, the barest trace served. They went around a lot of obstacles we'd cut out. They had subsistence priorities that far outweighed using their time to clear boulevards. The result was, their trails were usually too narrow and twisting for our winter use. Our sleds were bigger. Freighters and mail carriers carried heavy loads. And we usually used bigger teams than the Natives. We needed a wide swath cleared of obstacles. And long, sweeping turns.

"But if being too narrow and twisting had been all that was wrong, we would have just widened and straightened them. The main thing was they seldom went very far in the direction we wanted to go. Exceptions were places like the Kaltag Portage and the passes where the mountains on both sides kept only one choice for where a trail could lead. A lot of their trails out in broader, flatter country took them here and there in quest for food. Trails criss-crossing their country from a caribou fence to a fish trap to a system of beaver ponds. If those trails were mapped it would look like you threw a handful of worms on a paper coated with wet paint. That's not likely to make for a Seward-to-Nome beeline.

"Even their trade routes didn't give us what we needed. To hear that blowhard in Nome talk, you'd have thought the Indians of Upper Cook Inlet had a lively trade going directly with the Eskimos of the Bering Sea and had a direct line marching right across the lands of all the tribes in between. Well, obviously, they usually weren't that polite and accommodating with each other. But man, if that kind of trail had actually existed, that is indeed the kind we needed, one that took us in a straight shot right across the lands of Native groups regardless of jealously held borders.

"Here's the way their trade trails really worked: the groups pretty much just traded with those adjacent to them. The Upper Cook Inlet villages would cross the mountains and trade with bands living closest to the other side of the range. Then they'd turn around and go back to the Inlet.

"Those bands just over the range would go this direction and that to trade with groups scattered on their borders. Those would in turn fan out to all points of the compass to trade with still others on the edge of their lands. I don't say none at all, but not many of their trade trails were of use when you needed a beeline to take you to a particular destination maybe hundreds of miles away.

"Rod, remember I said when I'd come in from my mining claim I had a little cabin in Nome? Recall I said it was next door to a friend with the Alaska Road Commission that built and maintained roads and trails? The man was Ross Kinney. One day at the post office Ross and I heard that windbag newcomer spouting off his Indian-trail-through-to-Cook-Inlet bunkum. Those in the crowd picking up mail who really knew the facts took no heed of him. Ross just rolled his eyes. He and I talked about the guy's numbskull ideas as we walked home."

———————

Ross Kinney: "Preston, one thing, that guy must have never traveled the country in winter beyond the beaten track. If he had, he'd know it doesn't matter how many summer Indian trails crisscross the area—once it snows they get hidden. To stay on their trail in winter you have to be like one of them who's lived his entire life on his own home turf. An Indian knows every tree and rock in his own neck of the woods so perfectly he can come through on snowshoes right over top of his summer trail. He doesn't need it to be cut and marked like we do. The best outdoorsmen among us can't match a Native's intimacy with his own stomping grounds. That takes a lifetime in one area and old ones to teach the young.

"The Alaska Road Commission builds trails visible enough they may be easily followed in a blinding blizzard even by folk who've never been there before. So we need a plain trail cut through the woods and brush and tripods across open country. For commercial purposes we need quite a thoroughfare compared with those of the Natives.

"You're right, Preston, when you predict that no Indian trail in its present state between Susitna Station and Kaltag would be of the least use for our purposes. If the ARC does a reconnaissance I'll be on the crew. I can lay you dollars to donuts that when we get out there in winter with snow covering everything we won't find a trace. In forested country only tangles of trees, brush, and blowdowns. In open country just blank expanses. If we end up having to build a trail over the route, we won't be just enhancing something that's already there. It'll have to be from scratch.

"Now if that know-it-all would use the term *route* he'd make more sense. Some of the Native routes were useful. When the first white explorers like Spurr and Herron came over, they needed to know which drainages led them where they desired to go, and where the passes were and so forth. The Indians knew that perfectly and showed the way. On Herron's exploration his men worked themselves to the bone struggling to move his pack train ahead only about three miles a day over a good share of the route. Although they were showed the way by local Indians, there was no suitable trail through the woods and brush so they had to laboriously cut one.

"If folks who've never battled through untraveled wilderness could only understand, *route* is a more general term than *trail*. Description of a route might tell you that to get to a pass through the mountains you take a certain river valley, then branch off up a particular side valley. If mountains wall in the valleys, you can't lose the route. But shoot! Those valleys might be ten miles wide. The whole width and length could be thick forest, a tangle of brush and blowdowns, a morass of beaver swamps, a big, winding river you have to cross and recross maybe by raft, and large, roaring tributaries you have to spend a lot of time finding a way to ford. I've put in weeks of warfare against such an untracked route. I remember some days fighting it dawn to dark being lucky to make two or three miles along a mere route with no trail.

"Now what if there was a cut and marked *trail* up that valley? What if you found a swath had been cleared through the tangle? What if it circumvented the swamps and followed a way that avoided the need to raft across the main river, picked the side of the valley where tributaries were fewer and smaller and the path took you straight to nice fords? I've made twenty, thirty miles a day taking a string of horses over trails like that.

"That's the difference between traveling a mere route and a defined trail. They take you to the same destination, but there's world's of difference.

"I've told you that with all the pressure the people of Nome are putting on the Commission, the inside thinking is we expect that the big brass are going to have to eventually respond. We'll be sent out to look the country over. Colonel Goodwin and I have investigated it about as thoroughly as the limited information allows. We have a fair idea of the route that proposed mail trail needs to take. It's the logical way for us. Some of it has been the logical way for the Indians. So after our recon, if we end up going back and building a passage through to Seward, yea, sure Preston, we'll naturally go by some of the general routes Natives have used maybe thousands of years. But where we do, we'll usually find it looking the same as if it had never felt the footfall of man; we'll have to find the best way and cut and mark our own trail just the same as if no Indian had ever seen it."

Chapter 27

---◆---

Providence Hands Nome Another 200 Miles

JUST AFTER THE TURN OF THE CENTURY, at a time when the citizens of Nome first began calling for their own trail, there existed no white habitation over the entire distance between Kaltag and Susitna Station. Both the vastness and the remoteness of that great wilderness made spanning the distance a formidable construction project. Trail builders doubted it would be worth it. They knew that even if they went through all it would take to build such a trail, if they presented it to travelers as an option, travel over those (roughly) 450 miles with no source of resupply would present such a daunting test of survival that few, if any, would so much as consider traveling it. With few passing over it, the way would not stay broken. Then it would only be a nicely defined pathway lying feet deep under untrodden snow. Struggling, wallowing through the loose depths, travelers would be forced to transport mountainous loads of dog and human food to last the duration of a laborious, snail's-pace, dangerous traverse.

---◆---

Rod Perry: *Indeed, in those pretrail days, it truly would have been far, far easier for a Nome-bound musher sitting in Seward to catch a ship to Valdez and go all the way around over the Valdez and Yukon trails. Even though he would be adding many hundreds of miles, he would find a heavily traveled, usually concrete-hard trail with roadhouses conveniently spaced along the way for rest stops and abundant provisioning.*

If, instead, he dared gamble going by way of Susitna Station to reach Kaltag, he would find the first 200 miles between Seward and Su Station difficult enough. Though established, it was not yet constantly traveled. Thus, the packed trail often lay beneath a depth of soft snow.

340

*Drivers and Dog Teams Wallowing Through Untracked Snow
Struggle to Make Five or Ten Miles a Day*
Alaska State Library Historical Collections, Wickersham State Historic Site,
Schieffelin Brothers Yukon River Prospecting Trip, Charles O. Farciot,
ASL-P277-017-042

*But difficult as Seward to Susitna was, it was a sissy's picnic held up
against the ordeal of the second stretch, the approximately 400 to 450
miles from Su Station to Kaltag. Other travelers going that way being
rare to nonexistent, the musher could count on wading impeding depths
almost all the way. His team, wallowing belly- deep with little traction,
would strain to haul a barely movable load. That load would not only
include a full complement of winter camp and trail gear. It would also
include something like one and one-half months of food. Counting on
supplementing with game would place one's very life dependent on a
source that tended to be iffy. The struggle of inching ahead a few miles
daily would stress a musher and team to their limits. Such a risky,
close-to-impossible trip would verge on the unthinkable to many
experienced travelers when there was an easier, risk-free choice.*

*A trailsman taking the much longer Valdez–Fairbanks–Yukon Trail
would be able to trot his team briskly from roadhouse to roadhouse
pulling a light load because provisions for man and dogs awaited and
he could do his "camping" eating at a table and sleeping in a warm bunk.*

Record-Setting Team Made One Hundred Miles a Day
over Developed Valdez Trail

Ocha Potter Papers, UAF-2003-163-6m, Archives and Manuscripts, Alaska and
Polar Regions Collections, University of Alaska Fairbanks

Therefore, no matter how much Nome wanted a Seward Trail put in,
the way things stood just after the turn of the new century, rational
minds had to dismiss such a project.

But as if fate had ordained Nome's Seward Trail, a progression of
seemingly unrelated developments began that, as they stacked one
upon the other, made the project look increasingly worthy of consideration. The first was that aforementioned 1903 commencement of
construction of the Alaska Central Railroad heading from Seward
toward the Interior and the advantages that gave dogteam and foot
travel. Although there had already been a dogteam and foot trail out of
Seward to the sizeable mining operation of Girdwood on Cook Inlet's
Turnagain Arm, it had been a long, tough one in its roundabout course
and its hard climbs and descents through the Kenai Mountains.
Pushing steel farther north out of Seward with each year's work, and
preparing the roadbed well ahead of the advancing rail construction

342

gave travelers an almost level roadway leading straight to the head of the Arm. Additionally, ranging far in front of the roadbed, the surveyors pack trail greatly reduced the traveler's difficulty.

The very next year, in 1904, hundreds of miles to the northwest a steamboat churned far up the great Kuskokwim, second-largest river in Alaska. At a point where the Takotna River flows in, related villagers from Nikolomas, Big River, Telida, and distant Lake Minchumina had a traditional gathering place. There Abraham Appel nosed his boat up to the bank and established a trading operation. Not only was Appel's location well situated at the Native gathering place, it stood at the head of practical steamboat navigation on the river. No one would be likely to move in above him to shortcut upstream trade.

Although he must have considered those advantages, he had no way to predict that his chosen location would be made far more strategic and profitable by upcoming developments. And he could never have guessed those developments were right around the corner.

Appel's establishment happened to be close to the best natural course for a Seward-to-Nome trail. Not only that, but he had landed perfectly positioned about midway along the proposed route. To trail visionaries Appel's post offered wonderful prospects for a strategically placed shelter and supply waypoint. Comparing the wilderness between Kaltag on the Yukon River and Susitna Station near Cook Inlet to a desert so wide that no camel can drink and carry enough water to make it to the far side, Appel's would provide the necessary midway oasis between Kaltag and Susitna Station.

For lucky Abraham, a main trail running through would dump in his lap far more commerce than his trade with the far-flung Athapaskan villages he had founded his business upon.

Still, without other developments, establishment of Appel's midway oasis alone was not enough, not nearly enough, to spur trail builders to seriously consider starting construction. His was yet only a tiny pinpoint in the midst of a great, desolate wilderness the size of Washington State. Yes, north out of Appel's toward Kaltag, the rich riverine habitats were dotted with numerous canoe camp sites used in summer by villagers of Old Shageluk, Holikatchuk, Dimenti, and Dishkaket. But since the Russian Lieutenant L. A. Zagoskin had momentarily visited on his way through sixty years before, that country of the Upper Innoko that lay between the Kuskokwim and Yukon had been almost untraveled and all but ignored by white men. Would-be trail builders knew almost nothing about it.

Now turning to look the other way from Appel's post, toward the great Alaska Range and faraway Susitna Station, the distance and difficulty posed a barrier so chilling to the imagination that Abraham probably shuddered to think about it—if indeed the slightest consideration of connecting with civilization in that direction so much as crossed his mind.

———————

Rod Perry: *Unconnected to civilization by anything but his summer supply by steamboat, Abraham Appel probably harbored no thought of anything but maintaining his remote outpost for Native trade. Nevertheless, his lucky streak not only continued, but accelerated.*

———————

Only two years after Appel founded his trading post, in September of 1906, four prospectors—Thomas Ganes, Mike Roke, John Maki, and F. C. H. Spencer—boated up the Kuskokwim and hiked over a Native portage to look around the remote Upper Innoko. Stopping for a lunch break on a small Innoko tributary, Thomas Ganes tried a test pan and found gold.

Upon ascertaining that the find was substantial, the men ventured to Appel's. Finding him too short on supplies, they went back to the Innoko and took its tortuous course hundreds of miles down to the Yukon. Sledding back with supplies in the winter of 1906–1907, they met a few others and told them of their find. Word first spread about Ganes Creek to a few Kuskokwim prospectors. That brought a small rush from that side. By spring, news of the discovery worked its way out the other way and reached the Yukon village of Nulato. From there it was telegraphed to Nome and Nome spread the tidings.

Over 1,000 stampeders rushed to the area, coming mainly from Nome and Fairbanks and the villages along the northern Yukon River trunkline. Prospectors struck gold at Ophir in February 1908. Other nearby discoveries quickly followed. The boom created a loose cluster of instant settlements: Ganesville, Moore City, Ophir, and Takotna.

Rod Perry: *By continuing great good fortune, Appel found himself close to the new strikes; none were farther than about fifty miles distant as the raven flies. In a land as big as Alaska, especially in the midst of one of the most desolate stretches of almost uninhabited wilderness in that part of the territory, fifty miles was considered practically next door. Appel was right there, set to serve as a supply and transportation hub. His post began to grow its own little population.*

The new gold strikes escalated Nome's hopes that the trail connecting Susitna Station and Kaltag would be built. Appel's outpost had originated as the lone pinpoint of white activity for hundreds of miles, at first seeming rather lost out in the midst of the great wild. His trade with the Indians had initially created but an almost unnoticeable stirring amid the silence. But these instant, small boom towns suddenly interrupted the quiet with a growing little beehive of human presence and energy. There between the Kuskokwim and Yukon rivers, the general area of the mining activity—some fifty miles across and expanding—became popularly known as the "Inland Empire."

The area's settlements needed easier winter trails for personal travel and transportation of mail and freight. A Seward Trail would not only serve to link Nome to its nearest ice-free harbor, but in passing through these new midway gold settlements it would link them to both towns. Just as importantly—perhaps even more importantly—it would give the new boom area a fast link to the main thoroughfare, the Yukon River Trail.

During the boom Peter McGrath was sent into the area by the Nome court to serve as sheriff and U.S. Commissioner. He recorded claims for the mining district. Not long after his arrival he noted Appel's perfect location and built a trading post of his own at the site. The place came to be called "McGrath's."

Al Preston: "Rod, I knew Pete McGrath in Nome. He later told me how things progressed out there in the early years regarding development of trails through the Inland Empire.

Pete McGrath: "Coming from Nome, like most, I'd been highly interested in a mail trail through to Seward. Mr. Preston, when I got to my commission location on the Kuskokwim and got my feet under me as far as a feel for the lay of the land, something became pretty

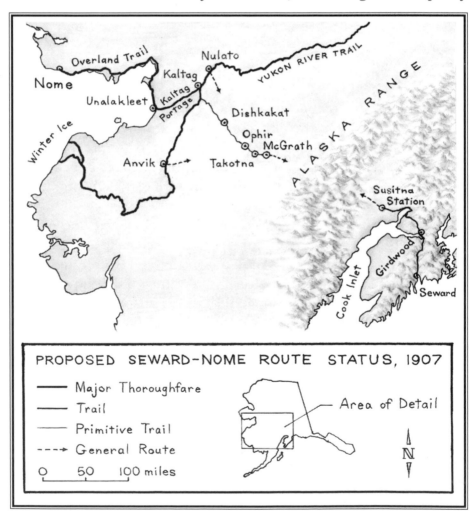

PROPOSED SEWARD–NOME ROUTE STATUS, 1907

— Major Thoroughfare
— Trail
— Primitive Trail
---→ General Route
0   50   100 miles

Area of Detail

N

plain. This gave me all the more reason to construct my store at Appel's site. I figured, generally, it was very roughly maybe 200 miles between my place and Kaltag on the Yukon River. That might be overestimating, but the miners' original trail was so rough and crooked it was hard to figure.

"Look at the map and you'll see what I mean by "connect the dots" and how logical it was. Providence must've been behind our trail. Four Inland Empire towns—Takotna, Ganesville, Moore City, and Ophir sprang up somewhat close to one another. Not only were they generally north, the direction they needed to be, but look—draw a line through them and it runs smack over a pretty good course for a direct trail out to Kaltag. Nobody even had to step in and get a special trail project going. Just taking its natural course, the mining activity had perfectly spread the first fifty miles or so with small settlements. They gave us shelter and supply points with rough paths between.

"If there'd been nothing else out there, I was guessing that would've left maybe 150 of the miles out beyond those villages without a break all the way to Kaltag. But look again at the map. Again, Providence must have been on the trail's side. It was hard to judge distances, but out there in that 150-or-so miles, and in just the right direction, lies Dishkaket. You've been there Mr. Preston, your old friend Mishka's village. I'm guessing Dishkaket's possibly sixty-five north from Ophir and let's call it eighty-five from there on to Kaltag. Even before the rush it held a good Native population. Now with the boom it's got about 100 of Mishka's people, a dozen or so whites, a couple stores, a saloon, and I'm told even a roadhouse for travelers. Another advantage for our Inland Empire trail is there's already a long-used Native trail from Dishkaket to Kaltag.

"You'd think it'd end there as far as Providence blessing our trail. But it doesn't end there. Traffic on the Dishkaket–Kaltag trail had grown heavy enough, someone with an eye for business slapped up a roadhouse near the mouth of Kaiyuh Slough. Now that long distance between Dishkaket and Kaltag was broken in two. All said and done, the whole way from my place to Kaltag was dotted with shelter and supply points and strung together with rough trails beaten in. How's that, Mr. Preston?"

"At least to the north that great wilderness stretch was being filled in a fair part of the way with at least the rudimentary trail featuring minimal shelter and supply. I could see the way things were progressing it seemed like a foregone conclusion the ARC would come in and connect the dots professionally with their surveyed lines and we'd get us a straightened mail trail from Appel's out there to the Yukon Trail.

Ross Kinney: "For a professional roadbuilder, it was truly amazing to see that whole stretch from McGrath's to Kaltag just incrementally fall into place by chance. And all in less than two years. It was as if the trail had a mind of its own. In a destiny it contrived, it just went out and built itself. Think about the chances of all of those burgs springing up in a line. And when you think of all the possible points of the compass, what are the chances such a line of settlements would point in the exact direction you need?

"Of course, with that many miners out there calling for mail and freight, it takes quality trails to cut the cost of delivery. Unless these booms subside, we fully expect that our Nome Road Commission office will get ordered out there sometime soon to unkink it. Maybe completely replace their crude trails. But for now, they seem to be getting them by as is."

Pete McGrath: "With these Inland Empire strikes, this area of the Upper Innoko that had been so ignored and almost unknown began to see exploration, travel, and development aplenty. In summer, the only way to travel the country is by water, so stampeders used the Innoko. It was hundreds of winding miles up that snake of a river from the Yukon. But quite a few came that way to reach the diggings by steamboat or by poling boats or canoes. The briefest glance at the area reveals that with so many streams, sloughs, lakes, ponds, muskegs and swampy lowland, you'd find it infeasible to travel overland in summer. But for seven months a year the reverse is true. When everything freezes solid, boats don't work so well. Trails do.

"The crude trails were beat in by the gold seekers themselves. Planning, as far as building the best trail for future use, was not part of the thinking. Most of the first arrivals came in from various points along the Yukon. Since they were madly scrambling during the stampedes, trying to get to the new strikes the fastest way they could, they just kind of beat the trails in as they went. Winding around obstacles following paths of least resistance instead of cutting a straight path, they serpentined almost as much as the Innoko. One went in from near Anvik and another was said to roughly follow the old Indian route from the trading center of Nulato, and yet another came in from Kaltag to connect to the old portage route to Nome.

"As I mentioned, in their dash to get there, no one took the time to carefully survey and cut the way. Creating the best possible permanent trail for the next traveler or with an eye toward their own future travel was not part of their thinking. You've been out there, Mr. Preston. You know how such overland travel proceeds if no one has gone ahead to make a trail and you're trying to get someplace fast. You just expediently follow meandering ways of least resistance. If the yards ahead show a relatively clear path, even if it takes you left of the desired direct line of travel, then that is the way to go. Then the next time you see a clear way that deviates right, maybe you take it to make up for the previous left. You watch your compass, and a good navigator finds it pretty easy to keep close to the desired line. But man oh man, does it ever make for a snake of a trail.

"The next person, he wants only to get to the new diggings himself. He finds someone's broken trail and just follows his tracks. He might do something, cut out a log or lop off a branch, but he doesn't take much time to make the trail better. And no one in his right mind is going to be breaking a brand-new, straighter route when he has a hard trail base laid down for him. Therefore, the trails in from the Yukon were very rough and terribly tortuous. Even after the stampedes settled down into the extraction mode, travelers, mail carriers, and freighters just kept using the crooked trails to connect the strike with the Yukon River Trail and the Kaltag Portage. But it was far from the kind of trail professional contractors needed."

—◆———◆—

Ross Kinney: "So by the end of 1907 and very first of 1908 that whole approximately 200-mile-long wilderness segment south from Kaltag to McGrath's had been relatively tamed as it just incrementally kind of fell into place on its own. Of course, Preston, that just makes it all the more likely the Road Commission will get ordered to go out sometime to straighten and shorten it."

—◆———◆—

Rod Perry: *Yes, the McGrath's–Kaltag leg had been established all right, although not in a form someone with any other choice would have taken. One traveler reported that it was so crooked, one day as he mushed along, thinking he was the only one on the trail, winding around a tight corner he was startled to run smack into a musher coming toward him. What really surprised him, though, was the quick recognition that the other guy was him!*

—◆———◆—

Back to consideration of the original need to connect the 450-mile-long Su Station–Kaltag gap in order to have a Seward-to-Nome trail—it was no longer 450; now the McGrath's–Kaltag 200 was roughed in. That left only the stretch in the opposite direction—what they thought to be roughly 250 miles between McGrath's and Susitna Station—as the last remaining trailless gap along the proposed Seward-to-Nome route. But oh, what a gap it was!

So standing at Peter McGrath's front door in late 1907 and earliest 1908, it was one thing to think about traveling—or think about doing trail upgrade work—northwest over the new, primitive settlement-to-settlement trail to Kaltag. But turn and look southeast. Before you looms the great expanse toward Susitna Station that includes the imposing Alaska Range: some 250 miles of desolate and potentially deadly wilderness.

Chapter 28

Braving the Primitive Passage
Misconceptions and Realities

Pete McGrath: "Until Ganes struck gold, as far as I can figure no more than maybe a dozen or fewer white men had ever been known to have made the trek between my post and Su Station. It wasn't merely almost untraveled; no, to white men that route was barely known at all.

"After our Inland Empire gold strikes that way of access out to Cook Inlet country became somewhat more understood. But even then it stayed merely a broad, vague description of wilderness landmarks. Once past the village of Nickolomas, nowhere along the way was there so much as one hint of human presence. That meant, of course, no chance whatsoever of reprovisioning. So you had to take on such a huge load at the start you could hardly pack or pull it and it really slowed you down. Then you just prayed it would be enough to see you all the way through.

"Looking from the door of my post east, all that lies before you is a vast, untrodden waste. Primeval forests. Winding courses of frozen rivers featuring every peril inherent in traveling river ice. Blizzards. Horrible temperatures. Hundreds of miles of deep snow. And that towering, ominous mountain range. If you were touched enough to even give the slightest consideration to going out that way . . . well, I'd say the kindest thing I could do for you would be to put you out of your misery, then and there. A quick stroke with a pole axe to save you from the trip. It's a trek seriously considered only by fools!"

A musher (from the French word meaning march) bound for Cook Inlet from the supply center of McGrath's would, by inquiring around, understand that he must head up the Kuskokwim to where it flowed out of the mountains. By descriptions of landmarks and estimations of distances he had been given he could accurately guide himself away from the main stream and up the correct side drainages that led either to Rainy Pass or Ptarmigan Pass. The trekker would have learned that, after crossing the height of land, his descent would take him to a succession of Susitna River tributaries. He'd finally reach the main Susitna and then, Susitna Station.

Within those broad parameters, the path one took to get there was whatever way he snowshoed in himself. Immediate directional decisions along a wide, braided river or broad valley were a matter of individual choice. The way judged clearest, safest, and least obstructed that could be seen just ahead was taken as long as it conformed closely enough to the line of the general route. Such is the character of following a "route" with no defined trail.

Starting from the McGrath end, for an example, it was not always that simple to even find the way. The Kuskokwim is so wide, with so many braided channels, islands and side sloughs that two miners heading for Seward in the winter of 1908 became lost for 12 days before relocating the main channel. One superbly competent explorer opined, as he surveyed the Dalzell River below Rainy Pass, "I saw how one could easily get lost (at least temporarily) if coming upstream, as the canyons are so deceptive and the country so big." A major U.S. government expedition sent out to explore and map the country failed to even see several prominent rivers a later official reconnaissance party did record. The later party, on the other hand, entirely missed the mouths of the Dillinger and Tonzona rivers, two major tributaries that the first government expedition had found and mapped.

If he were heading in from the Susitna side bound for the midway diggings, a traveler knew the way led up the valleys of successive Susitna River tributaries (the Yentna, Skwentna, and Happy rivers and Pass Creek). Then it crossed the Alaska Range and followed down the Dalzell, Rohn, and Kuskokwim into the Interior.

Rod Perry: *Some modern writers claim that with the Nome Gold Rush beginning in 1898, and even more so with the 1906–1907 coming of mining to the Inland Empire, mushers immediately commenced whizzing back and forth over the way through Rainy Pass.*

That could not be farther from the truth. Such writing demonstrates an absence of understanding of long-distance wilderness dogteam travel and a lack of research into trail history as well. Unknowing writers just repeat what they read—that being written by some other unknowing writer—and so it goes back and back and back.

It may be truly stated that as a writer or teacher ventures toward realms in which he has no experience, the accuracy and veracity of his writing or teaching grows less and less reliable as he approaches the limits of his knowledge. And when he goes beyond, and his writing or teaching stands on no solid foundation, it is not worth much at all.

To one who knows, the constant errors and misinformation in newspapers, magazines, books, brochures, tourist information, television coverage, and the Internet stand out and mark the writers' ignorance of the subject.

Few today have experience traveling great wilderness distances over deep, soft, virgin snow in subzero temperatures. There is a vast gulf between the ease of following a defined path, and the multiplied difficulties of having but a general idea of the lay of the land and needing to make choices every step of the way about which stretch of landscape immediately ahead to take.

Through wooded areas, there is a sea of difference between traveling through a cleared swath, and having to hack and saw the course through trees, brush, and blowdowns.

And there is an absolute ocean of contrast between moving at a brisk pace over a hard-packed trail and plowing through hundreds of miles of bottomless, tractionless fluff.

Carrying enough food and essential gear to support progress and survival for the duration of a McGrath's–Susitna Station journey stretched man and team to the limits. Snowshoeing ahead and helping his dog team haul a mountainous load, or carrying a pack or necking

Hard Mushing Without Dogs.

Repeated for seventy days, these men necked half of their load ahead ten miles and made camp, then next day went back to their previous camp and brought up the remaining half load. Average advancement—five miles daily.

Ocha Potter Papers, Ocha Potter, UAF-2003-163-7m, Archives and Manuscripts,
Alaska and Polar Regions Collections, University of Alaska Fairbanks

and gee-poling a mountainous load on a hand sled ground a man and dogs or a teamless traveler down almost beyond the ends of endurance.

For enlightenment's sake, make up a detailed equipment, clothing, and food list that you would put together for a thirty-day wilderness trek of 300 miles. Remember that much of the way will pass through bottomless deep snow. It will cross the greatest mountain range in North America. You'll be battling temperatures that will surely range down to thirty degrees below zero and could well plummet to sixty below. The short, subarctic daylight will limit your daily travel time. Carefully total up the weight of the gear and supplies. Though your list will include today's high-tech, lightweight gear and freeze-dried food, if you can shoulder it at all, your load will be staggering.

Pack a sled bearing a like weight. Take it to the nearest area of deep snow. Strap on the fifty- to sixty-inch-long, eight-to-ten-inch-wide snowshoes required to hold you up in the dry, fluffy snow of Interior Alaska. Now sample the work of hauling the load behind you. Consider, however, that if your test is performed where the snow is less than waist-deep, where the snow has greater moisture content than the dry snows of northern Alaska and where temperatures are above zero, you won't be able to duplicate actual northern Alaska conditions. You will not be able to gain a valid idea of the difficulty of dealing with bottomless fluff nor a sled that resists sliding through subzero, dry snow like you had mixed sand with it. Oh, yes, I almost forgot; instead of today's slick plastic, you must shoe your runners with steel. If your snow is light, dry, and subzero feel the steel drag and almost screech in protest! How long can you last at the task?

Think you could do it more easily with dogs? Not so fast—maybe, maybe not. Ask a seasoned Iditarod racer about the weight of one dog's daily ration. Multiply that by the number of dogs you would take on such a 300-mile-long ordeal. Multiply again by the expected thirty days. Absolutely staggering.

Do you think today's light, fast dogs racing the Iditarod burn more calories? Maybe, maybe not. Racing dogs don't have to pull much. The sled is lightly loaded. Over a level, packed, fast trail, a team of eight or more flies along and the sled doesn't greatly affect their speed. Like marathon racers, they primarily burn calories through the distance they cover.

So ask any Iditarod competitor to tell you what he thinks it would be like, even over the modern, fast race trail, to start from Susitna Station with the entire, just-calculated load of dog and human food plus the rest of your equipment—and haul it all the way to McGrath. One thing is probable: To bring it off he would have to go with a sled far larger than any he has ever driven, or probably, ever seen!

He is likely to tell you that even hauling that weight, he could make the trip in far fewer than thirty days. And he would be correct. Therefore, to make it more comparable with the old days we must perform the freight haul differently. Ask him to explain what he thinks it would be like to travel this way: never touching the trail, parallel it the whole way 100 feet off to the side. Travel through deep snow with no cut path through areas of trees and brush. While he is thinking about that, ask the racer how it would be, while on snowshoes, to manage his huge load in the bottomless soft snow he and his dogs will be wading through out there. And see what he has to say about the dogs' struggle to move such a load while they are virtually swimming, able to gain almost no traction.

———◦———

Rod Perry: *Again, turn back and look at the picture of the wallowing team on page 341.*

———◦———

What is his opinion about how many calories dogs working like that might burn compared to a racing team? It might close to the same; they're both big-time calorie burners.

Those who know the Su Station-to-McGrath trail know that on some parts of the trip like the South Fork ice, dogs would speed you up, even hauling a big load. On other parts, though, they might hold you back and you'd possibly be far better off to be towing a sled on your own without dogs and the weight of their food. You can see that making the trip using sled dogs might or might not be to your advantage.

Gear and food of a century ago were terribly heavy. Clothing and bedding were of wool and sometimes fur. Tents were of cotton canvas. Cooking gear was made of steel. Axes, saws, and other commonly carried tools weighed a lot. Dehydrated food, of course, was not nearly as light as the freeze-dried food of today.

The winter traveler always faced a conflicting choice: Should he risk going light, gambling his very life on a swift passage? The hindrance of carrying or pulling a heavy load through hundreds of miles of virgin snow and obstacle-ridden wilderness caused some risk takers to head out with a minimal pack or sled load, chancing their very lives that they would not be held up by route-finding difficulties, blizzards, snow and ice conditions, accidents, equipment breakage, injuries, sickness, or exhaustion due to starvation.

The other choice was to prepare carefully to deal with contingencies. The more cautious traveler was inclined to consider the many possible difficulties and include more and heavier supplies and gear even if that meant going more slowly.

Difficulties stacked one upon the other. First, the energy expended in the Herculean effort and the calories required to combat temperatures that might fall nearly 100 degrees Fahrenheit below the frost point increased daily food intake far beyond requirements for summer travel. Dogs burn more calories under those conditions, too.

Not only was each winter day's ration heavier to carry, but the problem was further compounded: the plodding nature of choosing the course immediately ahead, breaking trail on snowshoes, sometimes cutting brush and trees to clear the way, then, if traveling by dog team, going back to widen the trail and help the dogs wrestle the sled through the difficult stretches, all combined to slow the forward progress to a crawl.

Also greatly slowing the pace was that, in those times preceding modern flashlights, the short, subarctic winter daylight severely limited daily trail time.

All of those elements diabolically combined to add days to the trip and force a trekker to take a more mountainous load.

Only the most daring travelers—Native or non-Native—gambled on the passage, the nature of which was "make it all the way through on your own or die."

So you see, today's "historians" who write that travel was common over the route during the era of those conditions reveal their lack of understanding of the nature of the primitive passage.

Back in those pretrail days, the crossing was obviously worlds apart from travel over a well-established trail such as the Yukon River Trail, which was hard-packed and studded with villages, roadhouses, and shelters. If, back 100 years ago, the nature of the passage over an undeveloped, hardly traveled, mere "route" was so different from that over a developed "trail," it should go without saying that the nature of the passage a century ago between Cook Inlet and McGrath country was so utterly disparate to today's dog-team racing as to have almost nothing in common other than that today it still involves dogs and mushers. And of course, today's sprint and distance racing is all that modern writers know.

To illustrate a comparison, say that early dog team travel over the trailless route could be thought of as akin to a solitary, heavily-burdened freight wagon being pulled by plodding, hardy oxen through country without any trace of a trail, along a route that will later become the Oregon Trail. In stark contrast, today's long-distance sled-dog races—staged over well-marked, packed trails featuring many resupply points and help in case of trouble—are like a dash from St. Joseph, Missouri to Portland, Oregon zooming over modern superhighways in an almost unburdened automobile. The comparison may be a stretch. But not by much.

Such travel as was undertaken over the route before any trail was put in is all but unknown, even within today's dog-racing community. Beyond a mere handful of the early Native competitors and a few others such as my brother Alan Perry, few others that have ever finished the Iditarod Race have taken winter trips by dog team, unsupported by a structured race organization, covering long distances in the Arctic or subarctic far from human habitation or other sources of resupply and lasting as many as two or three weeks or longer.

If one has to search far and wide among even today's dog drivers to find the rare musher who has experienced such travel, it stands to reason that among non-dog-driving writers and historians it is unlikely any may be found with the experiential frame of reference to write with understanding and insight about primitive movement over the route before the way became a trail.

———————————

Rod Perry: *In early 1977 I needed to get my team from our bush training location at Lake Minchumina out to the road system so that I could run the Iditarod. Accompanied by three others, and with my dogs split into two teams, we hauled long, freight sleds loaded to the extreme max. By the indirect route I chose, we traveled approximately 175 miles in much the way the early trailbreakers did. The arduous trip was one on snowshoes laboriously breaking trail ahead of the team, picking and cutting the way through dense brush and forest, essentially a map* *and compass in one hand, an ax in the other. We traveled with no other means of support than the supplies carried on the sleds and we camped wherever night overtook us. It required sixteen full days and parts of two others to reach the highway.*

To emphasize how different that sort of mushing is from modern racing, today it's possible for a middle-distance competitor skimming along on a lightly laden sled over a broken, well-marked race trail to cover such a distance within one day. And that includes several rest breaks.

To further emphasize how different travel over the primitive route was from the way it is now over an established Iditarod Trail over that old route we can go to the historical record.

Al Preston: "For all those jokers who think going between McGrath's and Susitna was a fast, slick trip before 1911 this ought to tell you how painfully laborious and risky it really was. One explorer I knew from the Alaska Road Commission's Nome office documented that in late 1907 about twenty prospectors, disappointed with their luck in the Innoko District, traveled in early-winter conditions (I'm guessing in pairs and small groups) over the mountains on their way out of the Interior. Walter said their trips were plagued with extreme hardships, including running out of food. To make about 250 miles the men took, variously, twenty-four to thirty-five days—*that's three and one-half to five weeks!* That figures out to making only seven to ten miles a day! It's probable that some of them "siwashed it." That means to keep their load bare-bones light they probably just took a piece of canvas and a couple of blankets for shelter and sleeping. Walter and my friend Ross Kinney said that all of those men did manage to straggle in to Susitna Station. But upon arrival their condition was described as "pitiful." Several barely made it.

"Another account tells of what may have been the only carefully planned, commercial freight haul over the route before it was developed by the Alaska Road Commission into a real trail. It was a gold shipment. Rod, I knew the man who conducted it; Bob had the U.S. Mail contract at Nome. The time that trip took sheds light on how difficult it was to make it through before the ARC work. Even though Bob was one of Alaska's most respected professional freighters and mail carriers, it took him a little more than five weeks to bring his "gold train" from the Inland Empire all the way out to Seward. I think I would be safe in saying that at least four of those five weeks must have gone into the section of the haul with no trail. Once they got to the trail at Susitna Station the rest of the trip would have gone way faster.

"Still another trip report is noteworthy because it came from none other than William Amos Dikeman. Remember, he's one of the two who made the Iditarod strike. It took him forty-seven days to mush from Seward to Iditarod. That's almost seven weeks. Does that sound like trail travel? Not if you know anything about the subject. What seven weeks to Iditarod should indicate is that no trail existed back in those days. No Indian trail, no white-man trail, no any kind of trail! Just a sea of virgin, untracked snow with no bottom. Slogging day after day at maybe a mile an hour, if that. Rod, think of the monstrous load of food he had to start with from Susitna Station. Either that, or be lucky taking game."

———— ◆——◆——◆ ————

Rod Perry: *Today, sled-dog racers feed at the checkpoints, seldom carry much food in their sleds, and, over the well-broken race trail, cover the stretch from near Su Station to McGrath in a little more than two days' travel, Willow to Iditarod in around four.*

———— ◆——◆——◆ ————

Formidable difficulties notwithstanding, as evidenced by the 1907 report from Susitna Station, occasionally there were individuals among the iron men of the day who felt a pressing need to travel during winter between the Innoko diggings and Cook Inlet. Such men were willing to take up the deadly gamble that one could make it through. So there was some traffic. However, it is plain that until the trail was cut, marked, and studded with roadhouses, the passage was so fraught with danger and difficulty that it took the strongest of travelers to the farthest fringes of endurance. So few made the trip that travelers of record seldom, if ever, found a broken trail.

—————◆—●—◆—————

Rod Perry: *Traveling the deep bush in winter, then as now, of the three amenities required for fast progress by foot and dog team travel alike, a cut, marked and broken trail is by far the most valuable. If you have hard footing you can go faster, your trip takes less time, and that reduces the food you must carry. Ranking second is resupply points. Again, that allows the traveler to reduce the weight of his load and he can move faster. In most conditions, a very distant third is "found shelter," such as arriving nightly at a warm cabin or roadhouse so that no camp has to be made in the deep snow or food cooked at far below zero. Especially when traveling by dog team, camp gear for a long journey doesn't weigh nearly as much as food. And it's not that difficult for a veteran trailsman to make comfortable camps. The tough thing is traveling trailless, untrafficked wilderness. To have to saw and hack through trees, brush, and downed timber, and stamp out a path through soft, deep snow, slows progress to a snail's pace. That forces the traveler and carry the mountain of food—which slows progress even more, which demands packing even more food, which slows—ad infinitum.*

—————◆—●—◆—————

There is a succinct, well-known quote regarding the difference in travel with or without a firm trail that has come down to us from a famous Alaskan explorer and dog driver. Into his words may be read a great comparison between the difficulty of travel in pretrail days when traffic was sparse, against the relative ease after 1911 when the Iditarod was cut and marked, studded with roadhouses, and heavily traveled.

From the pen of famous pioneer churchman and adventurer Archdeacon Hudson Stuck, who organized the first successful climb of Mount McKinley, traveled widely overseeing his diocese covering of much of Alaska, and authored *Ten Thousand Miles on a Dog Sled*: "The greatest gift that one man can bestow upon another in Alaska is a broken trail."

Chapter 29

———◆———

Seward-to-Nome Trail Status and Potential, 1906–1908

The winter freight, travel, and communication demands of the resident thousand souls of the Inland Empire continued to keep their rough, crooked trails to and from the Yukon Trail hard beaten. Also, those demands, plus the punctuation of settlements lined up from McGrath's to Kaltag added rationale for those who continued to push for a main trail all the way through.

———◆———

Al Preston: "With all the desire of the people of Nome coupled with the demands and strategic position of those new midway booms, it still seemed worlds away from adding up to enough cause to outweigh all the negatives that tipped the scales against starting trail work.

One night while having dinner at the Kinneys, Ross introduced some of his viewpoints that explained a lot about why the Seward-Nome project was held back."

———◆———

Ross Kinney: "Preston, what we have here are two populations, Nome and the Innoko miners, pressing the ARC with their wants and needs.

"Nome is already the most easily supplied big town in the Far North. Look at us; during shipping season oceangoing ships anchor offshore and lighters deliver right to the beach at our front door. That fills our warehouses bulging full. This town's got about everything we need to live as well-rounded a life as you'll live this near the Arctic Circle. If anyone wants to travel in winter, we have the best trails in the North heading out of here to Fairbanks and Dawson up the Yukon. And if need be, we can catch a winter ship out of Alaska by going that way. Sure, we'd like a *faster* mail trail, but that's really just an enhancement.

"Now you look at the situation of the Innoko miners. You have about a thousand people roundabout in the Upper Innoko country depending on their primitive, rough trails. Those settlements out there demand to be better connected for the flow of their travelers, mail, and freight. 'Inland Empire' sounds fancy, but they're really out there in the middle of primitive nowhere. What they really need is to be linked with a commercial-grade trail that gets them out to somewhere that qualifies as *somewhere*. Someplace they can access resources. Out to a main trail so if they need to go somewhere important, they can. So I'm expecting our ARC office will get orders to at least straighten the present trail from McGrath's out to Kaltag and the busy Yukon thoroughfare."

Al Preston: "Well, Ross, if you limit your project to putting in a trail through the Empire just connecting the Yukon Trail to McGrath's, you can bet all of the Seward–Nome Mail Trail advocates will jump right on it. Just picture yourself if they got you up to explain things in front of a big town meeting. I can see it now. They'd ask, 'Hey, Kinney, with the trail in as far as McGrath's, now you only have maybe 300 miles—could be as few as 250—separating you from Susitna Station. Why don't you guys get after it and just knock it out? That would not only serve the base needs of the Inland Empire, it would dress it up with handing them the option of either heading north to the Yukon or southeast toward Seward. And of course, just a trail from the Yukon to McGrath's doesn't do one thing for us Nomites. But adding those 250 to 300 connecting miles gives us our complete Seward Mail Trail.'

"Ross, I'd say that you'd be pretty hard pressed to deny their logic. Your back would be to the wall trying and you'd better have something pretty convincing prepared. So what do you have ready for a pro vs con argument that would get Nome off your back?

Ross Kinney: "That's where I was heading. Preston, as we go over this, remember I keep going over and over stressing that for Nome, because we're already so well supplied and our mail system already works so well from Valdez through Fairbanks and down the Yukon, a shorter trail's not a necessity; it's just an upgrade that might border on luxury. And for the inland settlements, they'll be well served as long as we just upgrade the way to get them out to the Yukon and the main line of travel.

"That said, if we *were* to put a connecting trail all the way through from Kaltag to Su Station, yes indeed, it could very well kill two birds with one stone, take care of the demands of both Nome and the Inland Empire miners. So now for the purposes of this discussion I'm leaving out arguments having to do with the Empire, just knowing that if we put in a Seward Trail they'll automatically get a serendipity. I'm switching entirely over to isolating pros and cons of either leaving Nome's mail run as it is connecting to Valdez, or shortening it mileswise by connecting to Seward.

"The way I see it, four big arguments rear their heads so high against putting in that trail toward Seward I doubt it will happen. These four major negatives, I told Colonel Goodwin I've named them the *Four D's*. It helps me lay it out in an organized form to make it plain to folks why we wouldn't go toward Seward. At least, not the way circumstances sit right now. It's not that you and I haven't discussed every one of these points every which way, Preston, but I want you to listen to this smooth way I figured out to organize it all. Let's just you and me imagine that Colonel Goodwin asks me to attend a big town meeting such as you visualize and speak on the subject of a Seward trail. Well, I've rehearsed it and here's about what my talk would sound like:

"'Good evening, folks. I know this crowd would love to hear me report that tomorrow our ARC crews are gathering at Kaltag to start building a Seward trail. Now sorry to throw cold water, but I want Nome to understand that it doesn't look at all promising. I know what I'm going to tell you might sound like some devil's advocate exercise. But you deserve to understand the realities. I've arranged the obstacles in an organized form that make everything easy to understand. Call it the Nome–Seward *Four D's.*

"'OK. *Four D's.* The first *D* stands for *Distance.* You can take this argument several directions. I know the first one most of you are thinking of is distance to salt water. By our map calculations, the way from Kaltag to Seward might be only half as far as the way we've used for years, Kaltag to Valdez. That's what always makes all of us Seward Trail fanatics up here rub our hands and salivate, doesn't it?

"'Now I don't want to talk down to you, but for anyone with much trail time on his mukluks there's a far more important *Distance* consideration: distance between supply and stopover points for the musher. You trailsmen in this crowd know that's such a huge, simply monumental consideration. Up the Yukon River Trail there are so many locations that're easily and cheaply stocked they're almost piled on top of each other. But in the whole distance from McGrath's to Susitna Station you have nothing, nothing at all. Just a huge, desolate waste that keeps your sledload limited to carrying almost nothing but the stuff of survival: camp gear and food for the trip.

"'The second *D* is *Difficulty.* Folks, there's not a lot of information at hand because just a handful of whites have ever made the crossing. But don't forget, we do know it does go over the greatest mountain range on the continent. Up to now, even without a trail, from what we hear, the small number of men making the trek between McGrath's and Su Station do manage to make it through. But it takes them up to five weeks. Reports say a lot of them straggle in almost more dead than alive.

"'Even if we pour all the expense and labor into building such a trail, we still predict few will use it. You ask, why? Well, look around you and pick out some of the experienced men of the trail standing here. After this meeting, corner them and ask if cutting and marking alone would make it that much easier. Yes, they'll tell you, a cleared, defined path would make it better because even if there are only a few that use it at least those few would go over the last guy's tracks. That builds at least a semblance of a trail base, giving the trail a bottom. But they'll also tell you that doesn't eliminate the sled-crushing loads of dog food and camp gear. Without roadhouses for resupply points along the way, the loads are too backbreaking and going's too slow. Your trailsman will tell you he'd rather keep using the slick, old Valdez-Fairbanks and Yukon River Trail system where he can clip along at a nice trot.

"'Think of how it goes round and round. Without the traffic to produce paying customers, would any one of you businessmen build a roadhouse out there? And you professional dog team freighters and mail carriers like you, Griffis—and yeah, I see you there, Radovitch, let's not leave out you foot travelers—without roadhouses for resupply and rest will you, or anyone else with any other option, give the trail your traffic? Unless you have constant traffic, the trail doesn't stay broken, does it? And without a broken trail few will travel it. So almost no traffic adds up to no roadhouses, and no roadhouses add up to no traffic. I hope that presents a clear understanding of my *D* for *Difficulty*.

"'Third *D* stands for *Direction*. Going toward Susitna Station and Seward means turning your back on the natural flow of winter traffic. You're going way outside the line of travel. Everyone standing here knows the major line out of Nome—almost the only line of travel that counts for us here in the North—is out to the Yukon Trail and along the big river with all of its connections and resources.

"'So when we're talking direction, folks, and line of travel, we all agree it's between Nome, Fairbanks, and Dawson, all connected by the Yukon River Trail and its branches. To us, they aren't just the largest population and commercial centers up in this country. North of Juneau they're our only islands of civilization and culture. They supply about everything basic we'd ever need, don't they? And even a few luxuries.

"'Out around Cook Inlet and Seward is a destination few of us want to end up. What's there? Really, nothing to speak of compared to the big cities up north. That is unless we want to just keep hustling right on through and catch a ship out to the States.

"'Fourth, the last *D* is *Demand*. People, we Nomites have to be realistic and face the facts. It's not like Nome's still booming with thirty thousand in the general area like a few years ago. Look at us— we're down to maybe four thousand aren't we. When you add the thousand or so mining out there in Innoko country, that's still only five thousand that're pushing for a trail through. And most of us so involved with our mining or business or families we don't travel by trail often, if ever. So we just can't see enough human pressure, people wanting to go by the route over the mountains between Nome and Seward or between the Inland Empire and Seward. We can't see economic pressure either.

"'Unless your objective's a shorter trip to catch a ship out of Alaska, nothing in the direction of Seward can measure up to what the Yukon River Trail offers.

"'About my fourth *D*, *Demand*, we think it would take a lot more travel than we can foresee to make it worth building. A lot more travelers than we can imagine, for it to entice anyone to build a roadhouse way out in that desolation where it's so expensive to freight in provisions it makes a businessman's overhead astronomical.

"'All things considered, at least the way things stand now, it's simply not cost-effective to go to the considerable labor and expense of constructing a trail between Cook Inlet and McGrath's.

"'This whole push for a Seward trail has gathered most of its steam from thoughts of faster mail. Well, you can ask our Bob Griffis standing here, if he or any other experienced mail contractor could ever win a bid for that route without roadhouses and traffic enough to keep the trail broken and fast. I see him over there chuckling and shaking his head. He'll tell you, if the trail didn't turn out a really big improvement—and I do mean a *huge* improvement cutting off a lot of time—it would never wrest the mail contract away from the boys running it down the present, slick, Valdez-through-Fairbanks route.

"'So there you have it, folks, the *Four D's*. I hope that makes the realities logical and understandable.'

"Well, Preston, what do you think about my layout?"

———————

Al Preston: "Russ, you've done a really good job with your logic and organization, and I think that would keep Nome's Seward Trail fanatics in off your back. But what about looking at it from the Seward end?"

———————

Ross Kinney: "I know that Seward would love a trail to Nome and it would no doubt be good for their town. But today the way things stand we sure can't see much traffic coming from the few people living south of the Range around Cook Inlet."

———————

Alma Preston: ""Rod, our Cook Inlet–Kenai Peninsula region as a whole had dwindled in population from its earliest gold-rush days. The number of miners and their families remaining at Girdwood, Hope, and Sunrise totaled no more than a few hundred. A couple of hundred prospectors were poking around the Susitna drainage, especially concentrated around the Yentna, where a small rush got going in about 1905. Susitna Station had a little population that was growing. But all of that didn't add up to anything to speak of. Railroad construction that once brought the Seward population back up was short-lived. When the Alaska Central went bust in 1907, population dropped again like a rock down a well.

"So, at the time of the small strikes up at Ganes Creek, Ophir, Moore City and Takotna, nothing existed in Southcentral Alaska remotely comparable to the big towns and trail and supply systems up north of the Alaska Range. That meant our Cook Inlet country and we at Seward had little of our own to contribute to the flow over the trail. The way things stood by 1908, the only reason we could think of for a trail through to Kaltag would have been mail to Nome. And Nome and way points mail would never have been enough to make such a trail work, economically and physically, not even close."

———————

Toward the close of the first decade of the new century, prospecting and mining activity and human populations throughout Alaska had already changed substantially since the great gold rushes. By 1907–1908 the climate of wild, crazed stampedes of a few years before had moderated. Though the relatively small McGrath's area strikes caused a minor blip in the trend, Alaska had mostly settled into a prolonged slowed-down pace of controlled extraction of the wealth.

Al Preston: "In a more staid, developmental mode, it made sense for most people to wait and take advantage of the easiest transportation. That usually meant waiting for summer to go by water. Almost always, if you intended to winter over you planned ahead and positioned yourself before freeze-up where you wanted to be until the rivers started to run the following summer. Most who intended to leave the Interior got out by boat before mid-September. Remember, as I've said before, very few besides professionals owned dog teams. Outside of commercial hauling and periodic mail runs by dog team, there was just not much winter dog team travel. If others decided they just had to travel during winter, it probably meant by shank's mare.

"Those few Nomites and residents of the Inland Empire who wanted to not only leave the new diggings, but also leave Alaska without waiting for spring, generally had two ways to choose from: Option one was take the Yukon River Trail to Fairbanks, then the Richardson Trail to Valdez. Man, from Nome that was a trip of something like 1,200 miles more or less. The way was long all right—over two months for a hiker who could keep up an average twenty miles a day. But that trail was almost constantly hard-packed, and that means the world. Combine that with its well-established roadhouse and supply system, and a man could hoof down the trail with close to nothing on his back or in his sled. If he took just one good dog, to pull a light sled or carry a pack he could really pick 'em up and put 'em down, maybe making thirty miles a lot of days. And once he reached Valdez, with all of the ships coming and going, he could count on passage south.

"Choice two? Take on the tremendous rigors and risk the dangers of going the little-traveled way over Rainy Pass. In that day of reduced population and winter movement, and with most who did travel to salt water choosing the more established route, foot and dogteam travel over Rainy Pass would have been not much more than nonexistent."

Chapter 30

———◆———

Goodwin's Pioneering
Reconnaissance of 1908

DESPITE THE NEGATIVES, planning for a Seward to Nome winter trail finally took on substance. Major Wilds Preston Richardson ordered the Army's Alaska Road Commission (ARC) Nome office to reconnoiter the country between Seward and the long-established Yukon River Trail at Kaltag. Their mission? To see if it offered a more practical alternative for hauling mail than the Valdez–Fairbanks–Nome route. Colonel Walter Goodwin, an engineer and the supervisor of the ARC's Nome District would lead the reconnaissance.

———◆———

Rod Perry: *If it turned out to look like a better route, how much better? Would it be surpassing enough in Goodwin's eyes to qualify as "more practical?" This much was certain: it would have to show mighty big advantages over the trail between Kaltag and Valdez to pull significant traffic away from the old and onto the new. If Goodwin did not see the advantage gap as wide enough he would not deem it worth going to the considerable expense and effort to build a trail over it.*

The Kaltag–Seward route Goodwin was scouting was up against a formidable opponent. As we have stated, the river trail from Kaltag to Fairbanks was superbly appointed. And in 1907 the Fairbanks–Valdez Trail had been upgraded to a summer wagon road and winter horse-drawn sleigh and sledge road. (By 1913 it would be passable by automobiles!) The route between Kaltag and Susitna Station would never be more than a narrow trail strictly limited to winter travel by dog team and foot.

———◆———

Walter Goodwin and his stalwarts would evaluate the trail between Seward and Susitna Station—crude and lightly trafficked—and the trails between Kaltag and Nome—formerly heavily trafficked, now less so, but still well traveled—for current usefulness and options for improvement. Over the great wilderness stretch between Susitna Station and Kaltag they would determine possibilities for building new, high-quality trails and the degree of difficulty and expense to construct them would be assessed. Mileage, elevations and grades would be measured. Latitude observations were to be taken and adjusted for magnetic declination.

—————◆—————

Rod Perry: *No doubt, as was common to all builders of quality ARC trails, Goodwin also considered of great priority the assessment of what percentage of the trail could be established in the timber or, at least, be kept off the rivers.*

A woods trail offered increased safety, freedom from overflow, better footing, usefulness earlier in the fall and later in the spring, a windbreak resisting blown snow from filling the trail and a clearly defined course.

—————◆—————

The trek would consist of five parts. First, the party would travel the seventy-two miles of railroad grade out of Seward. Next, Goodwin would analyze, with a road-builder's eye, the existing trail between Turnagain Arm and Susitna Station to determine if all of it was suitable for heavy, regular usage and if so, how it might be improved. The third and fourth parts would be through unmarked wilderness and would form the heart of the trip. They would explore the little-used passage between Susitna Station and the midway Innoko gold settlements. Then they planned to take a beeline through the rolling country from Ophir to Kaltag to see if a high-quality trail was possible. The fifth part would be over the heavily used old trails between Kaltag and Nome. The usefulness of that final 290-mile stretch was not in question, but they would determine if and how the age-old Kaltag Portage might be straightened and otherwise improved.

Having had most of their outfit, including two fourteen-foot sleds and eighteen dog harnesses assembled in Seattle, Colonel Goodwin sailed for Seward January 16, 1908 aboard the S. S. *Northwestern.* Accompanying him was expedition member Ross J. Kinney. Upon reaching Seward on January 25, they were joined by George E. Pulham and Frank Jackson. They spent five days finalizing their packing and testing dogs.

————◆————◆————

Rod Perry: *It seems very likely that the dogs used on the trip came from the dog lot of the Alfred Lowe–Harry Revell operation, which since 1905 had held the U.S. Mail contract for the region. There seems good probability Lowell and Revell were the only professional haulers around Seward with big enough operations to have rounded up eighteen extra sled dogs their business could get by without. Of course, that is only conjecture; Colonel Goodwin could well have prearranged some other gathering of animals to be ready when he arrived in Seward.*

————◆————◆————

On January 31, 1908, the four-man crew with (presumably) eighteen dogs pulled out of Seward traveling the railbed. On their way to Turnagain Arm they encountered considerable difficulty crossing the many narrow bridges. Previous foot traffic had beaten in a canyonlike trench up to seven feet deep that had become so mushroomed over at the top as to almost form a roof. It was too narrow for their big sleds. They were forced to make their way above and to the side of the trench.

Goodwin wrote that sometimes above dangerous heights, that meant traveling upon cornices that precariously extended up to three feet out beyond the ends of the ties!

The men had to shovel their way in and out of the half dozen tunnels where snow slides had heavily blockaded the mouths. Once inside, as obstacle-ridden as the tunnels were with darkness, loose rocks, lack of snow, slick glaciering and large stalactites of ice hanging from the roofs, the men were thankful that railroad construction had given them those through-the-mountain paths because the canyon of the raging river below was absolutely impassable, even in its frozen state.

Between two of the tunnels the party encountered glaciering that would have been suicide to attempt to cross without considerable improvement of the passage. Where the railroad had blasted a path along the sheer cliff face barely wide enough for the roadbed, seepage from the rock wall above had built up a deep layer of ice over the tracks. The flat road of summer had frozen into a long, slick sidehill sloping perilously toward the lip of the drop-off. The men took to their axes to level a three-foot-wide, 500-foot-long trail in the ice along the cliff.

Rod Perry: *Although Goodwin did not chronicle the details, anyone who has freighted heavy loads with spirited sled dogs pictures what the men must have done once they finished chopping their trail across the deadly stretch. They no doubt disassembled the loads and carried parcels across piece by piece. Probably, the lightened sleds were skidded along by one man in front and another in the rear. Finally, the dogs must have been "hopped" over one at a time. For close control of the powerful, surging animals, a man held the dog's head high by its collar, which kept its front feet off the ground, and the dog hopped along the ice trail on his hind legs. At the far end the huskies were staked out so they would not just run back and forth. That passage must have taken the better part of a day.*

From Girdwood, the party ascended Crow Pass then descended to Eagle River. That was the only part of the entire course to Nome that they deemed impractical for heavy use. The ARC desired to hold to their standard of a maximum four percent grade. Goodwin noted how ". . . over Crow Creek Pass it would be out of the question to handle Nome mail with an ascent of forty-five degrees for the last 1,500 feet and to an altitude of 3,550 feet and then down nearly as steep some places to Raven Creek and on down to Eagle River nine miles below."

Rod Perry: *Apparently, as far as Goodwin was concerned, if regular Nome-bound traffic were forced to include Crow Pass, the whole idea of a Seward-to-Nome rail route might as well be scrapped.*

———•—•—•———

However, from anecdotal information he gathered, Goodwin reported that Indian Pass a few miles to the west was said to be shorter and gentler. It sounded like it offered good possibilities for a trail feasible for travel by heavily laden sleds and big teams. Although he thought it should be examined; apparently he did not have the supplies or time to do it during the 1908 reconnaissance.

The reason the party did not continue west along Turnagain Arm from Girdwood and travel over Indian Pass instead of Crow Pass was that the railroad bed stopped at Girdwood. From there to Indian, the steep mountainside with its many canyons, cliffs, and rocky headlands falling into the swift waters and mudflats of the Arm formed an impassible barrier to dog-team travel.

———•—•—•———

Rod Perry: *Being an engineer and understanding Alaska's transportation needs, Walter Goodwin would have known that although the Alaska Central Railroad had folded, the idea of a railroad to the territory's political and economic center in the Interior made overwhelming good sense. Somebody would eventually lay tracks to Fairbanks. When that day arrived and construction began anew, the first fifteen miles of blasting and filling around Turnagain Arm in the resumed work would extend the roadbed to the entry of Indian Pass, with its gentler, more negotiable route.*

An interpretive sign once located on Eagle River end of the Crow Pass Trail spoke of the Crow Pass stretch being used by dog teams until the railroad was completed to Fairbanks in 1923. There appears to have been more priority placed on promotion of this stretch of trail by agencies, organizations, and communities that value a share of the famous trail's romantic past than on accurate scholarship.

Certainly, those who would make such claims demonstrate a lack of understanding of freighting by dog team. To climb 3,550 feet in a few short miles was stressful enough. But the final pitch to the top would have been an impossible gradient to pull going straight up. No dog team can haul heavy loads up a long, forty-five-degree slope, even on a hard trail. In deep, soft snow where the animals are virtually swimming it is absolutely impossible.

That means such a gradient must be traversed. A skier that allows his skis to lay flat on the slope will instantly find himself sliding sideways down the fall line. To hold the slope on a traverse, he must angle his skis into the hill to carve on the top edges of his skis. Unlike skis, heavy sleds cannot be held tipped up to carve on the top edge of the uphill runner, so they cannot traverse more than a very slight sidehill. Therefore, negotiation of the final steep pitch up Crow Pass probably required either shoveling out switchbacks or unloading and taking small amounts of the cargo up in multiple trips.

Neither could the drop down the other side have been negotiated safely except with small loads. Even with dog tie-out chains wrapped around the runners to "roughlock" them, a sled under heavy load could not have been kept from careening down out of control and overrunning the team, with the all too likely result of injured dogs and a damaged sled.

Going over Crow Pass was the better option for foot travelers because it was significantly shorter, they were not taking heavy loads across, and a man's boots or even snowshoes can handle slopes no sled can. But no thinking dog driver would have hauled up the terrible ascent and risked disaster down the dangerously steep descent once there was a gentler choice. As witness to that wish to escape the grueling and perilous Crow Pass for something better, in the spring right after Goodwin passed through, crews began laboriously building a trail along the Arm from Girdwood to Bird Creek.

The big breakthrough came in 1909. The railroad (under receiver-ship) started work again out of Girdwood. By the time construction crews had roughed out a pioneer trail along Turnagain Arm as far as Indian Creek, the much lower and more gradual Indian Pass could be accessed.

After a very few years, even the route over Indian Pass was left behind. When railroad construction crews took their work just fifteen additional miles along the Arm from Indian to Potter, mushers no longer had to go through the Chugach Mountains at all. The dog men were no

Construction Trail Extending Ahead of Railroad Bed

Anchorage Museum at Rasmuson Center, Alaska Engineering Commission
Collection, P.S. Hunt, AMRC-aec-g316

doubt glad to wash their hands of them; after all, they were not in the business for exercise and scenery! Though there were some short, steep climbs here and there through the rolling lowlands, from Potter until the beginning of the climb over the Alaska Range 175 miles farther on, they had no more serious long ascents and descents.

Once the railroad became operational in winter as far as Anchorage and then Wasilla, years before it was completed to Fairbanks, dog drivers made use of every mile of rail transport possible. As railroad construction pushed tracks north, the advancing end of the rails served as their extending trailhead. By 1922 most Iditarod Trail traffic did not even go through Knik and over the Alaska Range. Why climb the great range by dog team when you could relax aboard a train and let steam power carry your load beyond the mountains? On the north side of the range a new trail ran over flat or gently rolling country all the way to join the old Iditarod Trail near McGrath.

Referring to that sign, by 1923 when the railroad was completed, it had been thirteen to fourteen winters since almost all the dog team traffic had abandoned use of Crow Pass for easier routes.

———————

Goodwin and company continued around Cook Inlet country to Knik. There they left one of their basket sleds and added four Yukon sleds (the same conveyance referred to as "hand sleds" earlier on the Upper Yukon). The ubiquitous Yukon sleds were commercially manufactured Outside and sold by the untold thousands throughout Alaska. The stanchion bases were set into unique cast-iron sockets affixed to the runners and bolted to the cross bents or bridges by ingenious steel fixtures that allowed the sled to flex. Because the joinery was simple and they could be bolted together they were fast and cheap to mass-produce. Every trading post stocked stacks of them.

———————

Store Keeper and Wares
Seward City Library, SCL-1-525

Goodwin's basket sled, like most sleds of the day, had no runner tails extending behind the rear stanchions long enough for prolonged standing. The men walked or trotted along.

Goodwin thought it a big mistake to leave behind the basket sled and switch to Yukon sleds. However, Pulham had been placed in charge of transportation and the Colonel evidently chose not to argue. While at Knik, at Pulham's insistence they re-rigged their towlines so the dogs could pull single file. The party also bought more provisions.

———✦———

Rod Perry: *To those knowledgeable about prolonged bush travel by dog team through untracked wilderness, Pulham's decision speaks volumes. First, it gives the distinct impression that he was a man having more experience than Goodwin with this type of travel. Second, it points to an expectation that the trip would be characterized as one of giant loads being wallowed through deep, obstacle-ridden snows with no trace of a trail.*

Dividing the cargo into smaller parts would make it easier to wrestle through difficult passages. (Note: refer back to Chapter 18 for the Goin' Kid's description of this method.) And the dogs, now pulling straight ahead single file, would be able to pull more efficiently than when harnessed side by side, each pulling at an angle. As well, in single file, a dog team more effectively tracks behind snowshoes tramping out a new trail just ahead.

Following the Knik reconfiguration, the procession could have taken many arrangements—and most likely did as the men adjusted to meet the conditions—but it could have looked something like this: Two men leading the way breaking trail, snowshoe prints alternating. (The second man progresses planting his snowshoes "left-right" where the man in front had just planted his "right-left." In this way the unpacked gaps between the first man's steps are filled in, creating a more continuous packing.)

Next after the trailbreakers comes two lash-ups identical to that in which Old Ben Atwater is pictured back in Chapter 19 (two sets, each made up of two cross-chained sleds pulled by five dogs, and each sled tandem managed by one driver on the gee-pole.) Additionally, these drivers, themselves pulling with a necking line, would have been helping the dogs. A difference is that Goodwin's Yukon sled cargos would have made for far higher piles than that of Old Ben's mail.

Last in line comes an eight-dog team towing the big basket sled laden with the bulky items plus plenty of weight. Its driver would have been necking and gee-poling as well.

Through areas of extremely deep snow, all of the men would have stayed in their snowshoes morning 'til night. However, once in the Interior where snow was not so deep, some who followed behind could have perhaps done without. And of course, no one needed snowshoes where river winds of the Upper Kuskokwim kept the ice blown clear.

On February 15, the men arrived at Susitna Station. Goodwin wrote, "Here a three-quarter-blood Cree Indian was hired to go through as far as McGrath's and then return, and we took on flour, sugar, bacon, and other supplies as had been arranged for previously, and the real trip began, as this was our last base of supplies."

Rod Perry: *Goodwin had obviously either shipped his own supplies to the trading post prior to freeze-up or communicated with the operator to make sure that when the post ordered its own stock it would include specified items that would be reserved, awaiting the group's arrival.*

One of the unnamed "other supplies" they must have taken on no doubt formed the major bulk of their cargo. That would have been a large number of bales of dried salmon for the dogs.

For additional dog food they probably added several fifty-pound bags of rice and a plenteous supply of either lard or bacon (cheap in those days) in five-gallon buckets.

The load on every sled must have been absolutely mountainous. The powerful dogs used for freighting averaged about twice the weight of today's streamlined racing sled dogs and, of course, ate a lot. In the old days, mushers figured four pounds dry weight of salmon and rice

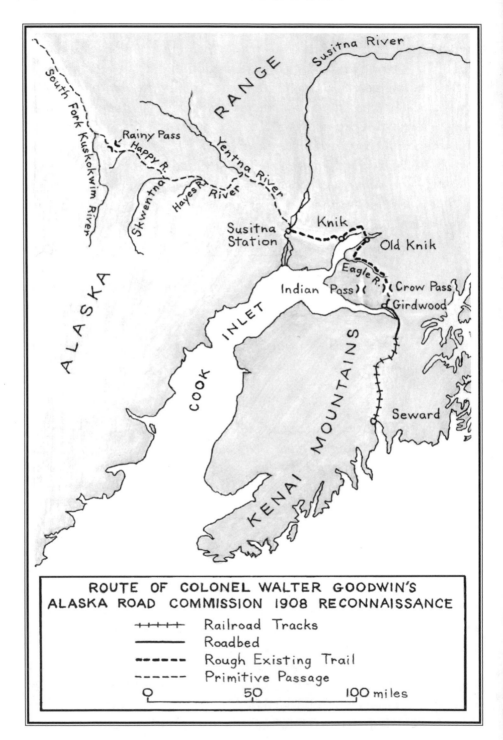

ROUTE OF COLONEL WALTER GOODWIN'S
ALASKA ROAD COMMISSION 1908 RECONNAISSANCE

┼┼┼┼┼	Railroad Tracks
─────	Roadbed
▬ ▬ ▬ ▬	Rough Existing Trail
─ ─ ─ ─	Primitive Passage

0   50   100 miles

plus fat was the standard daily ration per dog. Men and animals together must have eaten at least eighty pounds per day, even though most of the food stores—beans, rice, flour, sugar, dog salmon and the like—were dry. Fortunately, the sleds did not have to be carried, only slid.

Goodwin did not record whether the basket-sled runners were shod with steel or "ironbark," an extremely dense wood commonly used for runner shoes. Ironbark would be waxed or iced to run more smoothly than steel, especially in extremely cold weather. However, Yukon sleds came shod with steel and Goodwin did not mention reshoeing them during their equipment adjustment at Knik.

Good fortune smiled upon them when it came to moving their cargo. At the beginning, when their sleds were most ponderously top-heavy and oppressively weighted leaving Susitna Station, Goodwin and his men traveled a gradient that climbed so gradually it was effectively level. Their first hundred miles or so followed the twists of the Susitna and its successive tributaries, the Yentna, Skwentna, and Happy rivers all the way to the base of the Alaska Range. During that travel, the dogs were consuming as fuel from the sleds, 100 miles' worth of their load.

Still, it was not easy. Offsetting much of the advantage of level going were the deep snows that covered the river ice. Unless someone had not long before preceeded them, their way had to be laboriously snowshoed out.

———◆———◆———

Rod Perry: *Again and again, I read various writers (who have obviously never traveled raw country pioneering trails in the way of Goodwin) stating that during Goodwin's 1908 passage he "blazed" the trail.*

———◆———◆———

Colonel Goodwin did not blaze a trail. By tight definition, blazing indicates at least a rough marking of the way by cutting patches of bark from tree trunks, leaving "blaze marks." That process usually includes at least a rough slashing out of obstructions to allow passage, especially necessary to get a team and sled through.

In 1908, Goodwin was not sent out to "blaze" anything in this way. Not only were they not commissioned to build a permanent trail, they were not directed to as much as decide upon precise positioning. At that time, the Road Commission did not even know whether or not they would eventually decide to build such a trail at all. Even marking the way would have required far more time and manpower—and dog food!—than they had. From his own account, Goodwin's trip was one of reconnaissance. Orders for the expedition limited the men to looking over the country in a very general way. (When they built the trail three years later they did not even place the two greatest stretches very close to the same ground the 1908 trip covered.)

Goodwin knew that should their cursory assessment reveal that a mail trail should indeed be built, no permanent trail should ever run on the rivers unless it could not be helped. However, all that made sense for a one-time passage such as theirs was to travel out on the clear path the rivers gave them. They could make many miles on snow-covered river ice, winding though the course might be, for every mile they might have laboriously cut and slashed through the woods, brush and downed timber.

Traveling out on the broad river they were sometimes several hundred yards from the bank. The men would not have continuously snowshoed over to and up steep banks to blaze trees. Why mark a route up a river when the path is obvious? Why go to the effort where river ice probably would not end up being the trail location later?

Blaze can be also used in a loose sense to describe the passage of the first pioneers through. Writers of Goodwin's part in Iditarod Trail history who use the word loosely in that way, use it wrongly as well. Many—not multitudes, but many—travelers had passed over the route before he and his crew journeyed through.

Properly, Goodwin's 1908 Reconnaissance *looked over* or *scouted* the route in a general way.

Alaska Road Commission (ARC) personnel reported in 1908 that they had heard of an Indian trail beginning within a few miles of Susitna Station that cut cross-country in the direction of the Alaska Range. It was said to end somewhere near where the Talachulitna River empties into the Skwentna River. However, the ARC men chose

Walter Goodwin (left) with Companion and Sled

not to try to take it even though it paralleled their route and would have cut many miles of winding river travel from their trip. It may have been too hard to locate, too difficult to follow, or too narrow and twisting to accommodate dog team passage.

Rod Perry: *Again, as they headed toward the Alaska Range they mainly traveled the rivers, Susitna to the Yentna, Yentna to the Skwentna, Skwentna to the Happy, just following the twists and turns, rather than taking shorter, but uncut portages through the forest.*

However, here and there during the trip they may have gone through stretches of woods and willow. Through such forested areas and brush they would have intently searched immediately ahead for paths of least resistance through trees, brush, downed timber and across or around terrain features. "Paths" may be misleading—what they would usually have found were just ways to get through the woods and thickets that were somewhat thinner than the tangle on each side.

Going ahead of the teams, some of Goodwin's men would have cleared the way just enough to get the sleds through. During such going, the men in the lead would have had to return to the sleds time after time to help the dogs get past especially difficult places.

———⚬——

Heading out of Susitna Station, the party began to enter the zone of progressively deeper snows as they made their way toward the mountains. Typical of mountain ranges near the sea, clouds moving inland drop most of their precipitation on the seaward side of the Alaska Range. Snows in the Finger Lake area can accumulate to well over ten feet in depth.

———⚬——

Al Preston: "Rod, as we expected, my next-door neighbor, Ross Kinney was Colonel Goodwin's right hand man on the trip. Ross told me about getting the dog teams through that heavy snow belt as well as through other areas of fairly deep going."

———⚬——

Ross Kinney: "The uninitiated tend to think that a dog team is somehow able to magically skim lightly over the snow like Santa's reindeer. Not so. Preston, as you know, a lot of people ask me about our expeditions, so this is how I explain it to them:

"'A team pulling a load over a well-traveled, packed winter trail is like a person easily pulling a loaded wagon while walking on concrete-hard beach sand just above the water line.

"'A team pulling that load over the same packed trail, but after a new snow has covered it, say, to the depth of the dogs' bellies, would be tantamount to a person towing his loaded wagon while wading hip deep.

"'A team hauling its load behind a man on snowshoes breaking trail through deep virgin snow, where underneath there is nothing packed all the way to the ground, may be loosely compared to the man drawing his burden while swimming in deep water.'

"Preston, the latter is the condition we had to deal with on most of the reconnaissance from Su Station to McGrath's and a lot of it from there to Kaltag.

"And some 'Indian trail' to follow? You look out on a river and all you see is a wide ribbon of unmarked snow lying deep atop the ice. Or in exposed, windy stretches of the river, it's glare ice, gravel bars, and driftwood piles. You look at the woods and see no way through unless you cut it yourself. And where you come to wide-open spaces all you see is expanses of unbroken snow. For all traveling purposes, we found it to be the same as the Natives had always found it and left it; the whole way was as trailless as if those wastes had never once been pressed by the foot of man."

———— ◆ ————

It is impossible for anyone reading the account of Goodwin's trip to fully understand the task or appreciate the difficulty of the party's accomplishment unless they, too, have pioneered long wilderness trails by snowshoe and dog team.

———— ◆ ————

Rod Perry: *The almost eighteen-day, cross-country expedition I previously spoke of, the one I took with three others to bring my team from Lake Minchumina to the Parks Highway to run the 1977 Iditarod, that trek of some 175 circuitous miles on snowshoes breaking and cutting trail ahead of the teams, certainly equipped me with the background to appreciate Goodwin's feat. Others who have made similar treks by dog team, with no outside support, over such long, trailless stretches of the North, can picture with me what the passage was like for Goodwin and his men.*

———— ◆ ————

February at those latitudes began with but about eight hours of useable daylight. March began with about eleven hours. Every evening they would look for a good stand of spruce in which to camp.

The timber provided not only shelter from the wind, but also firewood, supports from which to string a ridge line for the wall tent and boughs for bedding. As every seasoned woodsman knows, it is appreciably warmer within a thick stand of trees. The forest canopy provides a barrier that reduces radiation as the north sky in winter draws heat, the tilted planet losing it from it's darker side into space. The crew would have used the day for traveling almost down to the last light, but pulled off of the river into the woods and worked at building a suitable camp just before it grew too dark to see.

Camp routine was set; each man had his tasks and the work progressed with speed and efficiency. The person experienced in subarctic winter travel by dog team can visualize that Goodwin's daily camping routine looked something like this: Two of the men set to stamping down a tent site, or, where the snow was shallow enough in the Interior, digging it out to ground level, using a snowshoe (with the toe slipped inside a flour sack) for a scoop. Quickly, they threw up a floorless wall tent, fired up the Yukon stove and began melting snow for cooking.

The cooks multitasked. While they readied the evening meal they probably worked ahead, presimmering beans or rice and reconstituting other dehydrated food for the following night. They would have made bannock (bread either fried in bacon drippings or baked atop the stove in a skillet with the lid on) enough to eat with the evening meal as well as for trail fare the next day.

Simultaneously, they cooked for the dogs, probably outside over an open fire. Dog drivers then, as now, took a lot of pride in keeping their dogs in good shape and working eagerly. That meant feeding them well. To a large cauldron of boiling snow water, the men likely added something such as rice and lard or bacon to go with one salmon per dog.

A third man cut dry timber and split enough firewood to last the night and next morning. A fourth cut green boughs for beds for both men and dogs. The fifth unharnessed the dogs, chained them out individually, put down some boughs for their beds and spread out the feed pans. As men finished their tasks they helped those who had not. The items from the sleds that needed to be brought into the tent were unpacked and carried in.

Over some stretches, such as up the Susitna and its tributaries as far as the mouth of the Happy River, the way ahead following the river was plain. It neither required Goodwin's presence to make route choices, nor daylight to see the way ahead. When the rest of the crew stopped to perform camp chores, one of the men may well have continued ahead to break trail for the first part of the next day's march. Snowshoeing out a few miles, turning around, alternating left-right with outgoing right-left prints, and widening the trail on the way back to camp, then having it set up hard while they slept would have given the men and teams a wonderfully advantageous start the following day. However, just as Goodwin did not include in his report many of the details of how they traveled and camped, he did not report whether he used such a strategy.

While the meals cooked and the stove heated the tent, by kerosene lantern or candlelight the men made efficient use of their time, hanging clothing and harnesses to dry, repairing clothing and equipment, sharpening axes and saws, and tending to whatever else demanded attention to keep them trail-ready. Goodwin would have worked on his journal, perhaps seated upon a salmon bale. Finally, with their meals eaten, the dishes cleaned and the dogs fed, they spread a canvas over the thick bough bed, lay down a caribou hide apiece (hair up) over which each man spread his sleeping robe, blew out the light and turned in.

Up in the predawn darkness, they built a quick fire in the stove, dressed, ate, repacked the sleds and harnessed the team. The tent, stovepipe and stove (filled with birch bark, kindling, and small-dimension firewood) were packed last so they could be unpacked first the next night. Each morning they were back on the trail as daylight first grayed the eastern sky.

The men would have piled even more food on the sleds at Susitna Station had they not hoped to supplement with game. "It is a veritable paradise for moose," Goodwin wrote as they ascended the steeper gradient of the Happy River, "and on the 28th of February, while some distance ahead of the party I killed a big bull moose. For the success of the trip we figured on a moose or plenty of ptarmigan . . . the moose dressed probably 650 pounds, and but for it we must have been on short rations toward the end of the trip . . . We saw, however, but about eighty ptarmigan on the entire trip and only had four of them, these were all near timber line."

Along the way they had just come they passed three parties totaling nine men, bound for the pass over the Alaska Range leading to the headwaters of the Kuskokwim. All of them were camping, killing moose, and awaiting more favorable traveling conditions.

———————

Rod Perry: *Talk about something to create "favorable traveling conditions." The five-man government party breaking trail on snowshoes with 18 dogs and five heavy sleds packing down a superhighway ahead of them must have seemed heaven sent!*

———————

As the colonel snowshoed ahead, he referred to the few rudimentary maps available in that day. Those made by the Spurr-Post expedition of 1898 and the Herron exploration of 1899 as well as the U.S. Geological Survey reconnaissance map of the Mount McKinley region made in 1904 were such maps. Some parts Goodwin found accurate, others in extreme error.

On March 2, the men and teams crested Rainy Pass south of Mount McKinley. It was beautifully clear and calm at the summit. Goodwin noted with pleasure that he found Rainy Pass easy of ascent and descent and near a direct line of the desired route.

The following day, after having descended from the pass down the Dalzell River, they reached the Rohn River. There, the party met two men on foot. Bound for Seward to get medical treatment for one man's thumb, they had been virtually lost for a number of days, even though one of them had been out to Seward once before. The ailing man happily received antiseptic tablets from Goodwin.

———————

Rod Perry: *But the greater gift given them, the one that the two no doubt accepted with joy and relief, was the party's backtrail to Susitna*

Station! Nothing packs a trail like dog feet. The stamped-out campsites they inherited—and bough beds if they yet remained free of snow— would have been the frosting on the cake.

———————

Down the Rohn River and the upper Kuskokwim, the group rejoiced in some easy sailing of their own. Just across the summit, on the interior side of the range, is a region of light snows. There, almost incessant mountain winds usually keep the ice of the upper river blown free. Except for patches of open water and overflow the way is clear. On some stretches over polished ice with the wind at their backs, the men were able to ride the sleds for the first and only part of the trip.

Continuing down from the upper Kuskokwim, as the reconnaissance party entered into the Interior, they left the mountains behind. Near the mouth of the Tonzona River they ran into Chief Nikolai with two women. Though the two groups had trouble communicating, the Natives guided the expedition twenty miles cross-country to Nicholomas, a Native village on the Kuskokwim opposite the mouth of Big River.

At the village, they met a white man who had just snowshoed from McGrath's. After gaining useful information about the nearby country from him, they followed the man's backtrail to the post. They had finished the most remote, physically demanding, and adventurous section of their reconnaissance.

The men halted for a day. There, as per their arrangement, they left "Johnson," the part Cree Indian. If he could have hurried back, he could have taken advantage of the hard trail-base, but he was fighting a bad case of pleurisy.

Presumably, the party reprovisioned to whatever extent they could, but the recent gold rush in the nearby country had all but exhausted supplies at McGrath's trading post. They found damaged flour selling for twelve dollars per hundred pounds and sugar at forty cents per pound. No other commodity was to be had.

At Moore City, a day's travel out from McGrath's, they found prices much higher because everything had to be laboriously brought there from the main river. Flour was thirty-five dollars per hundred, sugar and beans both fifty cents per pound and dried fruits sold for fifty-five cents per pound. As has been stated, the going daily wage in that era back in the States was about two dollars.

They found as well that Moore City had been almost totally abandoned. Two weeks before, the miners had stampeded to a new strike at Ophir, twelve trail miles away. The group stayed the night with the U.S. Commissioner still stationed at Moore City.

Goodwin gained a great deal of useful information about the country from him, including a hand-sketched map.

The next day the party traveled on to Ophir. Colonel Goodwin, as he had done every fifty miles, plotted the global position by taking observations on Polaris.

From Ophir, he would have preferred to take a direct line of travel cross-country to Kaltag, which he calculated to be some 100 miles away. However, from the body of information he had collected he knew that a beeline would require a great deal of cutting through trees and brush. He concluded that the season was growing late and they were almost out of food. Also, his orders were limited to looking over the country and reporting route feasibility to his superiors, not investing time and effort in building—or even marking—a trail the Road Commission still might decide against constructing.

The men and teams followed the beaten path, which progressed in the most crooked, roundabout way imaginable, snaking through muskegs, around thickets and over low, rolling hills until they reached Dishkaket. There, about 100 Natives and a dozen white people dwelled at what was then considered to be the head of low water navigation for supplies coming up the Innoko River from the Yukon. It featured two stores, a saloon, and a roadhouse.

Keeping to the twisting trail, they traveled on to a roadhouse near the mouth of Kaiyuh Slough amid plunging temperatures. The party reached Kaltag on March 19, 1908 as the thermometer showed forty-three degrees below zero, the coldest weather of the entire trip. Forty-nine days—seven weeks—had elapsed since they started from Seward, forty-three days actually spent traveling. They had snowshoed ahead of the dogs or walked on hard trails all but a thirty-nine-mile-long stretch of incredibly slick ice on the Rohn and Kuskokwim Rivers

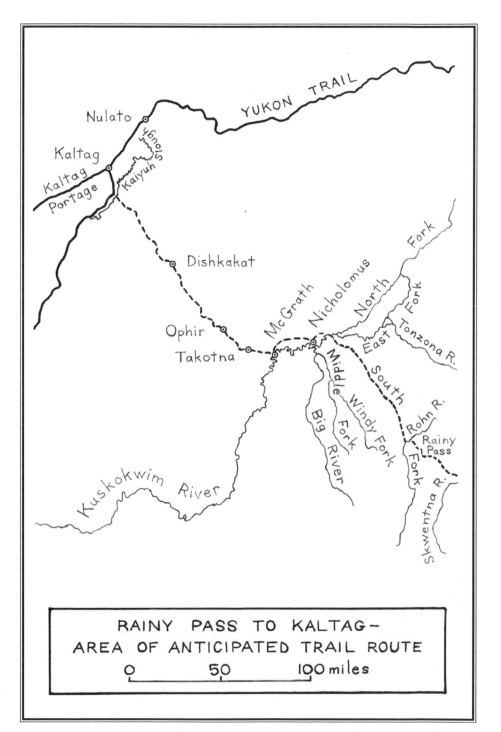

RAINY PASS TO KALTAG —
AREA OF ANTICIPATED TRAIL ROUTE
0   50   100 miles

where they had been able to sit atop the loads.

It had been a veritable beeline. The distance, Seward to Kaltag, Goodwin very roughly measured as 564 miles.

Later, when more accurately measured, it would turn out to be slightly longer. But it was still shorter than originally estimated and certainly far shorter than the winter route in common use. Valdez through Fairbanks to Kaltag was roughly one thousand miles.

Pulham and Jackson parted with the expedition at Kaltag. As they took on provisions and repacked their sled, Goodwin and Kinney heard that the trail was obliterated ahead. So resting their dogs, the men followed the common practice of the day: they awaited arrival of the mail carrier to let him break trail. On March 22, they left for Unalakleet behind the mail team. The age-old Kaltag Native Portage had seen very heavy traffic for the decade of the Nome Rush and its ensuing taper-down. Even so, to Goodwin it looked to be so hard to find in the bad weather, with so many twists and turns that needed to be eliminated, and over so much open, windswept, unmarked country, that had they not been following the mail carrier and his dogs, who knew the way intimately, they would have experienced great difficulty keeping the trail.

From Unalakleet, the two men followed the coast north and west to Nome. They assessed the condition of the Overland Mail Trail, constructed off the ocean to accommodate travel before freeze-up and after ice-out.

Goodwin and Kinney drove their dogs into Nome April 5, completing the "Winter Reconnaissance of 1908." It had been sixty-six days since they had left Seward. By the pathfinders' estimate, the entire Seward-Nome distance was about 865 miles.

In his summary report, Walter Goodwin evaluated the condition of the route as they had found it from Seward to Girdwood and the way over Crow Creek Pass as entirely infeasible for a mail route. He stated, however, that the route would become very practicable to put in and maintain if and when the railroad were constructed as far as the head of Knik Arm. That would not only advance the trailhead from Seward to the area of the future site of Wasilla, 160 miles closer to Nome, but bypass crossing of the Chugach Mountains and its passes, Crow or Indian.

Goodwin further concluded that there was just not enough demand for such a Seward–Nome route yet. While a path put in the way he had looked over would indeed result in a fine trail, he said the effort and expense of cutting a ten-foot-wide swath hundreds of miles through trees and brush, building log bridges, erecting thousands of tripods to mark treeless stretches and accomplishing other construction would just not be worth it at the time.

Goodwin wrote, *"**It would take infinitely more travel than is in sight at present** to break a fast or feasible trail over the route, even were a trail cut through the timber the entire distance, and unless the new Innoko District shows up well, **or some big strike is made along the route**, it would be entirely impracticable to send Nome mail by this route, as roadhouses would have to be built and maintained and **the entire route is entirely too far from the line of travel** under present conditions."*

Rod Perry: *As has been continually emphasized so it is understood very clearly by now, "the line of travel" Goodwin refers to is none other than the dominant traffic pattern of the day which ran between Nome and Fairbanks, and to a lesser degree by that time, on to Dawson and Whitehorse. In that day everyone familiar with Alaska understood that reference and Goodwin knew it needed no further explanation. Kaltag to Susitna Station and on to Seward was an out-of-the-way direction taking a route that few travelers found attractive. Therefore, what he was stating was that there would not be enough use to keep the trail broken and if not continually broken it would not be fast, and if the going was not fast, it would not be feasible as a mail route.*

No doubt, the Goodwin survey excited Nome. But to those who would evaluate the situation objectively, the reconnaissance only bore out the pros and cons road builders had probably already analyzed and discussed over and over before the trip: Fairbanks, by then the commercial and governmental center of Alaska, and Dawson, declining but still an important town farther up the Yukon, attracted a lot of summer shipping. The steamboat traffic not only caused villages along the great interior waterway to grow and thrive, but the steamers easily and inexpensively supplied the length of the Yukon River Trail. And the Valdez Trail was supplied from both ends by horse-drawn sleighs and wagons. That readied the way for winter service by busy dog-team traffic. The well-supplied infrastructure explains a great deal about why government road builders had kept Nome looking east up the Yukon for its winter connection to the outside world.

At the same time, when the Alaska Central railroad went broke in 1907 and construction crews left, the combined populations of Seward and the rest of the Cook Inlet region had bottomed out. The economy was a far cry from that found north in the relatively bustling heartland of the Yukon Basin. And how could a remote trail through hundreds of miles of the desolate, unpopulated wilderness Goodwin's crew had just traversed ever duplicate the infrastructure of the Yukon River Trail?

Obviously, the Alaska Road Commission would not have sent Goodwin had they not at least entertained possibilities of building a trail connecting Seward with Kaltag if his reconnaissance proved it immediately practicable. ("If" and "practicable" were obviously the operative words.) However, with a sizeable workload already, once Goodwin's assessment opined that rationale against the undertaking outweighed rationale for it, it is doubtful the ARC would ever have begun work on the project without some major shift.

Little could anyone guess in those days following Goodwin's passage that the very shift that would break things loose was already beginning. Decisions and actions of two men were setting in motion exploration which would lead to one of the greatest events in Northland history.

———————————

As the snows of the winter of Walter Goodwin's passage melt into summer and his ARC report is filed, by one venerable old-timer's testimony a solitary trapper working during his off-season in country so remote he has never seen another soul there, is bent over a small creek where he has trapped otters. Slowly swirling and tipping his frying pan, he washes out a scoop of streambed gravel.

Only a little over 100 miles straight as the raven flies from where the fabled trapper is swirling his pan, but many hundreds of miles away by the indirect, sinuous courses of the Innoko river and its main tributary, partners John Beaton and William A. Dikeman are prospecting the Inland Empire around the Ganes Creek discovery. The two are not altogether satisfied; they remain open and alert to better prospects. Along with their nonprospecting partner, Merton "Mike" Marston, who works any odd town job he can find to gather money for their ventures the trio lays plans for the following winter.

In Nome summer passes into fall. The once hopeful citizens see that not only is their pet trail project no closer to becoming reality, for all they know possibilities have all but disappeared since Goodwin turned in his assessment.

Back on the Innoko, through careful business dealings, John Beaton and William Dikeman have been able to buy the *K.P.M.,* a small steam launch. Having motored the hundreds of miles down the twisting course of the Innoko, the major Yukon tributary on the lower river, the prospectors drop on down to the Yukon River village of Holy Cross. Beaton and Dikeman load winter supplies and wheeling about, motor back up the great flow, returning to the Innoko. The partners head the *K.P.M.* upstream, apparently intending to resume work around Ganes Creek.

Rod Perry: *Stu Ramstad, commercial pilot, lodge owner, big game guide and outfitter, and stepgrandson of John Beaton, was only a small youngster when his stepgrandfather died. However, the story of how the Iditarod discovery came about was well told within the family. Stu's mother and grandmother were familiar with the particulars. Another who was said to be intimate with the story was the Beaton family's old friend, Tony Gularte. As a young boy recently orphaned, Tony came to Iditarod country in 1915 to live with his uncle, a storekeeper. He dwelt around the miners of Iditarod and Flat most of his life. Tony Gularte last related his unique recollections of the discovery story to Stu*

Ramstad as they talked following the wake at the passing of Stu's mother Jean, stepdaughter of John Beaton.

— ◆ —

Tony Gularte: "John and Bill were making the several-hundred-mile-long passage from the Yukon back up the Innoko with a haul of winter provisions. At the confluence of the biggest tributary which flowed in from the south, they happened on a lone man resting on the bank. Pulling the *K.P.M.* up near him, they learned he had just descended this small river from his faraway base camp up on the headwaters. This surprised them. That country was so remote, as far as John and Bill had been aware, no white man had ever ascended the tributary river; they had always thought of its far reaches as untraveled and unknown. Now those ideas were unraveled—here was a man who had indeed traveled it. This really perked their interest, so they asked him about the country up there.

"The man was a trapper. He said if you ascend this tributary river far enough back you'll reach where it drains the west flank of the Kuskokwim Mountains. He told them he'd first come into the headwaters from the other side, the Kuskokwim side. He'd gone up Crooked Creek, which flows into the Kusko from the north. Crooked Creek headwaters interlock with small streams draining into this major Innoko tributary the man had just drifted down.

"It seems the man thought he'd been the victim of a bad grubstake. He was racked with steadily worsening stomach miseries. The trapping season was coming up. Right then, he should have been back up in his haunts busy with getting ready. But there he was, headed out of the country. Now, paddling his tiny rat boat, he was descending to the Yukon. At the mission at Holy Cross, he hoped to get emergency treatment. From there, he figured to catch a steamboat up to the hospital in Fairbanks. Or maybe he'd head on down to St. Michael, where he could board a steamship south to the States.

"Then the trapper dropped them a real nugget of information. It would not only change the fortunes of John and Bill, it would change Alaska. There was a tributary way up by the mountains. He called it

Otter Creek because he'd trapped otters there. He reported to John and Bill he'd poked around a little in it, washed out a few scoops of its gravels in his frying pan, and found colors. They naturally asked him for his opinion on how far up he thought this river of his ran deep enough to navigate the *K.P.M.* He figured they could make it almost all the way up to Otter.

"Beaton and Dikeman had their outfits on board ready for winter. The tributary did look navigable. So they turned the *K.P.M.*'s bow upstream and began to churn toward Otter Creek."

Rod Perry: *Though there is dispute in some quarters regarding the validity of Gularte's injection of the trapper and his tip into the discovery story, we do know that Beaton and Dikeman had winter outfits aboard the K.P.M. and have left the Innoko, turning up its tributary.*

Beaton and Dikeman motor their way up that tortuously serpentining Innoko tributary. The little river endlessly flexes and contorts and coils back on itself. That late in fall, water levels are dropping. Whenever the boat grounds the men have to either laboriously work her back off or grind her on across the shallows into deeper water.

Rod Perry: *As an accountant, Joel Ramstad served John Beaton at Flat and the Olson Brothers at their platinum mines at Goodnews Bay. Ramstad and John Beaton's stepdaughter Eunice May ("Jean") married. Two of the couple's children were Phil and Stuart ("Stu") Ramstad. Phil, a commercial contractor who among other notable construction achievements built numerous airport runways across Alaska, partnered with the rest of the family in their Yukon Mining Company. Phil remembers his father relating how his stepgrandfather came to give the Iditarod River its name.*

Phil Ramstad: "First, we need some background. When he landed in Alaska, John Beaton worked as a hard-rock miner around Juneau. For miners who drill by hand following gold-bearing quartz veins, each foot of tunnel is terribly hard won. A full day's work yields little apparent progress, but extending the tunnel a few feet is all the condition of the rock and the manual drilling method allow. John said the miners' standard goal was making at least one length of a measuring rod (6 feet) a day. By the end of his shift, to another miner's inquiry about how he did that day, he wants to be able to answer, 'I did a rod.'

"Now back to the river naming. John and William have been making their way far upriver. One particular night they shut the engine down and tie up. It's been an annoying day of hard going. The river has constantly doubled back on itself in endless horseshoe and hairpin turns. John looks over the low bank, sees a downstream loop of the river, and, to his surprise and frustration, recognizes that they are virtually within spitting distance of the very place they tied up the previous night!

"The similarities to his Juneau hard-rock days come to mind: tough conditions, hard day of work, short measure of progress.

"So as a woeful commentary on their taxing day of inching their boat up the confused, twisting, turning bows of this river and only having a scant few yards to show for it, John looks over at their yesterday's anchorage, then looks at William. Laughing and shaking his head, in his heavy Nova Scotia-Scottish brogue he utters, 'I did a rod.'

"They're frustrated by the meanders. They need to call the river something. They see that nothing more appropriately characterizes the stream than the many bows. And nothing so characterizes their slow headway up its sinuously convoluting course than John's phrase 'I did a rod.'"

———◆———◆———

Rod Perry: *A common version ascribing naming of the river to John Beaton has him sounding from the bow of the* K.P.M. *with a measuring rod, trying to find water deep enough to proceed. In this version, he calls back to Dikeman, who is running the boat, "I did a rod."*

Joel Ramstad's rendition seems to me much more logical. It would attribute ascribing of the name as being due to influence of a prolonged, day-after-day experience. That would leave a more impactful impression than the mere momentary measuring of depth, common during progress on any river. Using "I did a rod" as a name commenting on the convoluted character of the course is also consistent with the naming by local Athapascans, one meaning of their "Haiditarod" said to be, "crooked river."

Certainly, coming by way of Beaton's son-in-law, who spent considerable time in company with John Beaton himself, Joel Ramstad's testimony should be respected and given major weight as a possibility.

———— • ——— • • ————

John Beaton and William Dikeman follow their I-did-a-rod as far toward the headwaters as they think practicable. Beaching their boat (about eight or nine miles below the future site of the town of Iditarod) they secure it for the season against the coming ice. The men build a small cabin on skids, thinking that they might need to move it later. Ready for winter, they shoulder heavy packs of camp gear and supplies, and picks, shovels, and pans, leave the cabin, and prospect their way southeast toward the unknown Kuskokwim Mountains.

While Beaton and Dikeman prospect during that early winter of 1908–1909 and snows again whiten the land and deepen, the part of Colonel Goodwin's reconnoitered route between McGrath's and Susitna Station lies dormant except for the occasional prospector possessed of some powerful need to dare the passage and take on the cruel vicissitudes. Out on that desolate stretch, nothing has changed. As far as anyone knows, nothing will.

But Beaton and Dikeman are sinking test hole after test hole. They thaw what they can of the frozen muck and gravel with all-night fires, then dig a little farther down by day. The man at the bottom of the 2½-by-6-foot hole picks, shovels, and fills buckets. The man at the top winds the load up with their spruce-log windlass, dumps it on the pile, and sends the empty back down. Backbreaking, miserable, cold work, day after day. And so, the two probe the unknown country for the yellow lure. November passes into December. Ten test holes . . . fifteen test holes . . . twenty test holes . . . twenty-five test holes, twenty-six . . .

And now the two partners begin to argue. Here they are with several days invested. Nightly, another ten inches are won by fire. Daily, with all the might and main they can muster against the rock-hard frozen ground, they are able to chip their way down only six more inches. So averaging about the usual combined sixteen inches each day on this twenty-seventh test hole, they have about a week into it. And it is looking to John Beaton like a waste of time and energy.

Stu Ramstad: "They've reached a layer of granite sand and it doesn't look like it's running out. Common thinking among miners was that granite sand's too light to carry gold. So John argues to quit the hole and start somewhere else. But William counters that bedrock must be close. Might as well finish the test. Back and forth the opposing reasoning goes."

The work is terribly taxing. Christmas approaches. Should they step back, give it a rest, and take the day off to celebrate in some simple way?

That Christmas Eve, as the men cuss and discuss that twenty-seventh test hole, almost 500 miles to the northwest, in the Nome office of the Alaska Road Commission, the entire written substance of Colonel Walter Goodwin's reconnaissance might well remain as it stands: just fourteen pages consisting of his expedition report and negative needs assessment, perhaps gathering dust in a file under some such heading as, "Ideas Investigated and Found Wanting."

Then it happens!

Chapter 31

———◆———

Iditarod Gold!

WILLIAM DIKEMAN'S GERMAN STUBBORNNESS wins out.

So there in the distant recesses of the remote, unknown Kuskokwim foothills, far back near the headwaters of Otter Creek, as the winter sun at its zenith barely peeks above the southern horizon to dimly light his work twelve feet down, John Beaton keeps swinging the pick, chipping at the frozen ground, slowly winning enough icy granite sand and gravel to load the bucket. And bucket after bucket, William Dikeman continues to crank on the windlass. He winds those buckets up, takes a few steps over to the dump and adds to the pile. There is little need for conversation and talk is sparse.

Then from the depths of that twenty-seventh test hole, on Christmas Day, 1908, John Beaton, cries up to William Dikeman, "GOLD!"

In Alaska, a land of fabulous paystreaks, the find will turn out to be the widest paystreak ever discovered.

The find of high-grade paydirt is in such remote surroundings that the country remains silent; nothing whatsoever is known about it because the men don't leave the uninhabited discovery area for some months. They prospect further, thawing and sinking test holes upstream and downstream in an effort to locate the richest concentrations. Between their Christmas Day strike and ice-out departure the men have staked close to a mile of Otter Creek alternating with each other claim by claim, staking, as John Beaton would put it, "For ourselves and a few of our friends." Of course, included is their supporting partner laboring back in town, Merton "Mike" Marston.

———◆———

Rod Perry: *John Miscovitch, born in 1918 in Flat into the large family of venerable miner Pete Miscivitch, grew up in the area of the Iditarod strike and mined around there most of his life.*

John Miscovitch: "Beaton and Dikeman's K.P.M. Association claims were staked as fast as mining law allowed. Monthly, each man was limited to staking two of his own and two for others by power of attorney. So they staked their way along Otter Creek, two claims wide by four claims long totaling eight claims a month. Those K.P.M. Association claims would be the only claims ever formally surveyed along Otter Creek."

Finally, spring frees their boat and the river clears of ice. Off Beaton and Dikeman head, down their meandering river. Reaching the confluence, they turn the *K.P.M.* up the Innoko, which they will ascend to Ophir, and there record their claims.

According to linguists, their little river is called in Athapaskan, "Haiditarod," said to mean in that tongue, variously, "distant place," "clear water," or "crooked river."

John Miscovitch: "All the Shageluk and Holicachuck Natives that I knew called it Haiditrarod, meaning 'crooked river.'"

Miners will call it by the name John Beaton insisted he gave it as he exclaimed in his heavy Nova Scotian Scotch accent to Dikeman, "I did a rod."

Rod Perry: *Trying to sort out the true source for the name Iditarod, one sees a "discrepancy within a confusion wrapped in a controversy."*

With three so very different Athapascan meanings attributed to, "Haiditarod"—distant place, clear water, and crooked river—there is still agreement among those who speak the local Shageluk and Holicachuk dialect as well as with Athapascan orthographers that Haiditarod is, and was, their name for the river.

Putting two and two together from this poor vantage point separated by a century from the event, it seems logical to believe that before he traveled there, Beaton had heard the winding river referred to by its Athapascan name. Passage by whites up and down the Innoko had been going on since the 1906 Ganes Creek discovery. Though reportedly no one had ascended the branch river, it is inconceivable that river men and exploring prospectors passing its mouth would not have wondered about this tributary that was obviously the Innoko's largest feeder. Questions could well have been asked of the Native inhabitants. There was frequent contact with the local villagers who market-hunted, sledding in game meat to the early miners. Or perhaps the fabled otter trapper told John and William. However he may have come by it, I am convinced John Beaton foreknew the Athapascan name for the river. How else would he have named the stream something sounding so all but identical?

Area Native Teams and Drivers at Iditarod

Claude Shea Collection, Roy J. Moyer, UAF-1988-156-16, Archives and Manuscripts, Alaska and Polar Regions Collections, University of Alaska Fairbanks

John Beaton was a man who in his lifetime was universally respected for his class and integrity. Not boastful in the least nor given to personal aggrandizement, he never climbed atop a pedestal or beat a drum about the subject of the river's naming. It was never to gain credit that he even repeated the details; it was just among friends and relatives as he afterward related the story of the gold discovery that the particulars of the naming came up. From what we know of the man, it seems entirely out of character for him to have claimed coining Iditarod unless he indeed had.

I'm betting that to John himself, the Indian's Haiditarod and his Iditarod had a clear connection. My guess is that this literate man of quick mind and sunny disposition simply gave the local Native name a slight, humorous twist with a nifty play on words when, working so hard to ascend the twisting river, he "did his rod."

Putting it all together—and this is only my own reasoning—it seems logical that the local Athapascan language provided the root, but it was John Beaton who gave us the derivation by which the famous river, gold strike, town, trail, and race would afterwards be internationally known.

———————

Somewhere during the hundreds of miles of winding down the unending bends of the Iditarod River and snaking up the equally tortuous Innoko, Beaton and Dikeman encounter another steamboat with prospectors aboard. True to the miners' code, the partners freely tip off the others.

Even after that, due to the isolation of the area, Iditarod country still holds tidings of the strike close to the vest. Word spreads slowly, apparently kept almost entirely within the remote community of prospectors already working the country of the Inland Empire.

Trailing Beaton and Dikeman's recording of their claims, later that summer of 1909 a few score prospectors make it into Iditarod country. Quickly, they stake the remaining ground on Otter Creek and its tributaries. Following those stakings, more gold is discovered on nearby Flat Creek.

Following hard in the prospectors' wake the second group of arrivals blow in: saloon keepers, gamblers, swindlers, con men, pimps, prostitutes, and their parasitic ilk. Soon after come the first merchants and other purveyors of upstanding business. Miners, bottom-feeders and honorable business entrepreneurs alike join to set up a camp on Otter Creek, seven miles east of its junction with the Iditarod River. They first call it Flat City. It soon becomes, simply, Flat. It is the first town established in the Iditarod Mining District. The miners, hurried with more pressing concerns, never stop to plat the ground. In their haste they throw Flat up right atop mining claims. That probably contravenes the law as far as legally establishing Flat's existence as a legitimately recognized town, but the place grows up despite the omission. With dollar signs dancing before their eyes, inhabitants don't really care to fuss about such details.

As remote as the new discovery is, with this much activity building, by the fall of 1909 word riding the winds regarding the size and richness of the strike gains full force outside the district. At last the clarion cry rings out widely across the North: GOLD! The rumors are true: It's a great new Alaska strike and stampede!

And so, the better part of a year after the Christmas Day find, confirmed tidings of the great scope and opulence of the new discovery first hit Nome. By a stretch one can imagine, in the holiday vacation silence of Nome's empty Alaska Road Commission office, Walter Goodwin's feasibility report becoming animated, commencing to shake in its folder, struggling to free itself from the ARC file, and the words, "or some big strike is made along the route" take on red underlining then begin trying to jump off the page and shout.

The exciting news hits Fairbanks, as well. The Seward Phoenix reports: *The people of Fairbanks are simply wild over the reports recently from the Iditarod . . . the scene of the latest stampede. The steamer* Martha Clow *is billed to leave tomorrow and will be the last boat of the season. Miners and others are so anxious to engage passage that they are simply fighting for the right to be taken on board.*

As winter freezes the waterways, some continue to venture in overland from the Yukon River Trail. However, most of the would-be stampeders choose to wait until the following spring to head for the new diggings by water.

Rod Perry: *If winter conditions so held up the thousands of stampeders who were desperate to enter the gold country over the much shorter and far less difficult trail from the populated side—the Yukon Trail side— how much more was immigration into Iditarod virtually stopped from coming in over the much longer and infinitely more difficult, sparsely populated side—the Seward-Su Station side. Only a trickle used that route in the winter of 1909–1910.*

When the rivers opened to navigation in the spring of 1910, two thousand souls were ready to stampede immediately. And so, the major part of the rush was on! Hordes by the hopeful thousands charged into some of the most remote real estate in Alaska, bound for Iditarod country.

In May 1910, almost one and one-half years after the discovery, thousands boarded steamboats bound for the remote goldfields. Some followed outgoing ice down from Fairbanks. The first craft, the steamboat *Tanana* arrived June 1 with others hard in its wake. The *Tanana* progressed as far as it could upriver, reaching a point eight miles west of Flat. There, where it off-loaded its cargo, the town of Iditarod sprang up.

The rush to Iditarod would turn out to be the last, great, hell-bent-for-leather, devil-take-the-hindmost gold rush on the North American continent. Some reports stated that as many as ten thousand had rushed to Flat by the summer of 1910. Conservatively, the number reached at least four or five thousand.

Iditarod was unique compared to the other blockbuster strikes of the North. In the rushes to the Klondike, Nome, and Fairbanks the claims fell to many newcomers. But in Iditarod it was estimated that up to ninety per cent went to veterans of those prior big discoveries of a decade before. Iditarod pulled men from the regions around Dawson, Forty Mile, Circle, Fairbanks, Nome and points in between, men who had been searching and waiting for the next strike. With so few cheechakos, Iditarod was largely a community of sourdoughs.

Besides Iditarod and Flat, Willow Creek, Discovery Otter, and Dikeman sprang up in nearby locations around the mining district. To

GREAT RUSH TO IDITAROD

Ten Thousand Gold Seekers Arrive and Confusion is Great.

Special to the New York Times

TACOMA, Wash., June 26...In the last week 10,000 goldseekers have been landed by steamers at the mouth of Otter Creek, on the Iditarod River, the scene of the latest Alaska gold stampede. Between 3,000 and 5,000 more are on the way. The landing of the thousands of newcomers with their baggage and thousands of tons of freight in the Iditarod wilderness has created confusion surpassing anything Alaska had previously experienced.

Several thousand "sourdoughs" who have mined in the Klondike and Alaska camps know exactly what to do. They are spreading out on Otter, Flat, Willow and other gold-bearing creeks. Merchants from Nome and Fairbanks are erecting temporary buildings and starting business. The best of order is being preserved by Deputy United States Marshals Wiseman of Koyukuk and Sheppard of Ophir. These were sent to Iditarod by Marshal Crossly of Fairbanks on his own initiative. Otter City, at the mouth of Otter Creek, the metropolis of Iditarod, is being surveyed.

The New York Times
Published June 27, 1910

build the towns, all lumber had to be brought in by boat. By August 1910, 3,000 people lived at Flat. Soon the communities of Flat and Iditarod were joined by a tramway.

The district went through a period of hardship before mining began to reap its bounty. During the winter of 1910–1911 a reported one thousand men were said to be getting by on one meal a day. The *Nome Nugget* would report, "Iditarod may be somewhat short of solids, but there is a large promise of no shortage of liquid."

As soon as the miners could mine enough gold to pay, there would be no lack of supplies.

John Miscovitch: "The Iditarod River, though small and twisting, usually ran enough water to navigate with even large steamers. Eventually the region was served by the Day Navigation Company with seven boats. They could get a 200 ton barge all the way to Iditarod. They were stopped from getting as far as Otter Creek only by a substantial riffle about midway between Iditarod and the Otter Creek mouth."

Initial shortages notwithstanding, within one year Iditarod grew to become, briefly, Alaska's biggest city. Built with foundations resting

IDITAROD GOLD FIELDS

upon mud laying atop the ice of permafrost, it boasted banks, news-papers, a theater, hotels, a ballroom, law firms, electricity, general and specialty stores, a slaughterhouse, telephones, automobiles, and, of course, the usual boom-town establishments crawling with practi-tioners of iniquity plying their specialties, saloons populated with gamblers and confidence men and houses of ill fame where ladies of the evening plied "the world's oldest profession."

In Iditarod's heyday, a singular event that took place yearly was the grand "Pretzell Ball" thrown by the ladies of "the Row." These occasions were well attended as were, year round, the individual cabins of the hostesses. It was said that veritable mountains of bottles stood behind those cabins, the height of each mountain serving as an accurate gauge to the popularity of the inhabitant.

With so much gold about, and so many bottom-feeders, it is almost a foregone conclusion that someone would attempt a heist. Indeed one was tried. A gold shipment from Flat headed for the concrete vault of the Miners and Merchants Bank at Iditarod was held up as it was being drawn by mules over the tram. The hue and cry went up so quickly, the thieves were speedily nabbed. The gold was soon recovered from where the culprits had thrown it down on the tundra in their panicked flight.

One outcome of the Iditarod Gold Rush was that it brought in-creased attention to the woeful lack of adequate government in the Last Frontier. As a result, in 1912, Congress elevated Alaska to full territorial status. Obviously, the gold strike of John Beaton and William Dikeman gave Alaska a most significant push toward statehood.

Chapter 32

———◆———

Constructing the Iditarod Trail,
Winter of 1910–1911

THE ALASKA ROAD COMMISSION QUICKLY ACCEPTED that the trail feasibility qualifier Goodwin had mentioned in his report, " . . . **or some big strike is made along the route** . . . " had become reality. And then some! The strike was not exactly right along the originally intended line of the Seward-Nome mail route, but it was close enough.

During ice-free months, steamboats served Iditarod by churning up the Yukon, turning up the serpentine Innoko, then winding up the tortuously twisting Iditarod River to the city located at the extreme end of high-water steamboat navigation. Though not all that far in a straight line, Iditarod lay the better part of a thousand river miles from the Bering Sea.

No other way than by water was practical in summer.

The beeline overland was too obstructed by streams, shallow ponds and lakes and passed over swampy, tussock-ridden muskegs spread over permafrost that would have quickly turned into an impassible quagmire once summer use destroyed the vegetative cover providing the thin layer of insulation.

Once winter set in, though, the freeze that stopped steamboat traffic not only left overland freighting and travel the only way possible, it also made it practical. However, there were yet no direct, high-quality winter trails to take advantage of the beeline possibilities to the Yukon, west to Anvik or north to Kaltag. Road Commission wheels began to turn.

In June 1910, trail work began because some work could be more effectively done in summer. The greater part of trail construction, however, would have to wait until after freeze-up. A few months later, early in the winter of 1910–11, the ARC again sent Colonel Walter

Goodwin out. This time his marching orders were to build what they officially labeled *The Rainy Pass–Kaltag Trail.* It would lead from Kaltag by way of Rainy Pass to Susitna Station. From there they were to continue to Seward over the existing trail and railroad bed.

Rod Perry: *Notice carefully that the colonel's project had not been called "the Rainy Pass–Nome Trail." To reiterate and add emphasis, the trail between Nome and Kaltag had been in and very heavily trafficked for many years before the Iditarod Strike. Again, the three giant gold rushes preceding Iditarod were connected by the Yukon River Trail and its branches. At their very peaks, the Klondike rush brought as many as 50,000 to the region around Dawson, the rush to Nome attracted about 30,000 to the Seward Peninsula, and Fairbanks lured masses in the many thousands to its expansive mining district. During their peaks, not only did hordes of gold seekers rushing from one great strike to the other flow back and forth over the winter trail, the way was kept beaten by the flow of general personal travel, commerce, and mail.*

After the last of the three great turn-of-the-century rushes— Fairbanks—settled down following Pedro's 1902 discovery and its booming aftermath, until the winter of 1910–1911 (the year the Iditarod Trail was built) you had the towns of Dawson, Nome, and Fairbanks, reduced far below the multitudes of their stampede years, but stable as they extracted the gold. Trade, transportation, travelers, and com- munication still flowed steadily between the three towns over the age-old trails. Although no figures exist, it is safe to say—because of the incredible numbers of stampeders who took part—that in the years of the three blockbuster gold rushes and the ten-to-twelve-year post- stampede aftermath, the Coastal Trail out of Nome, the Kaltag Portage, and the Yukon River Trail saw many times more pass over their miles than ever traveled the Iditarod Trail in all its glory years combined.

It is so often misstated that the Iditarod Trail extended from Seward to Nome. Or wrongfully worded that Goodwin built the trail through to Nome in 1910–1911. This is a good time to set the record straight. There was no need for Goodwin to build what was already built. Not that the Iditarod Trail should be demeaned as unimportant, because it was indeed important. But Goodwin, in just getting from Nome to Kaltag to start his main work, would travel those preexisting trails that had already far exceeded in importance the trail which he had been sent out to construct. He would perform upgrades on the way, but he would begin building the Iditarod (the Rainy Pass-Kaltag Trail) as he branched off from the Yukon River Trail at Kaltag.

Al Preston: "Between Colonel Goodwin's two expeditions, the emphasis had changed as far as where the main route was to be located as it passed through the area of the Inland Empire. No longer was the priority making a trail that would most expeditiously carry mail straight through between Seward and Nome by the shortest route. The main objective had become building a trail primarily for the purpose of best serving Iditarod and secondarily serving Nome. Remember that were it not for Iditarod, the Alaska Road Commission had scrapped the idea of a mail trail for Nome from Seward. Remember also that, for a brief time, Iditarod and Flat together were bigger than Nome. Creation of a straight beeline between Kaltag and McGrath's would have to wait. So Colonel Goodwin was directed to work on the trail by way of Iditarod. Therefore he would work on a long side-swing west from the straight line of the anticipated mail route that he had looked over three winters before.

"I want to clarify an important point to us Nome miners. The historically correct orientation, that of Colonel Goodwin and everyone else in our day, was that what would eventually become known as the Iditarod Trail was properly limited to the new route only, the route that branched from the long established Yukon Trail at Kaltag. Of course, everyone called the side loop to the west through Iditarod the Iditarod Trail. Some called the route going straight through from Kaltag to McGrath the "Mail Trail," some the "Seward Trail," and some just lumped everything with the side loop and called it the Iditarod, too. Absolutely everyone called the long trail from McGrath over to Su Station and on to Seward either the Seward Trail or the Iditarod Trail.

"But get this straight: *none* of us old trail hands, not one that I ever heard of, called the old trail between Nome and Kaltag the Seward Trail or the Iditarod. For heaven's sake, everyone had been calling the Nome-to-Unalakleet stretch by their old names, the Coastal Trail or the Overland Trail for more than a dozen years since the beginning of the Nome Rush. And the Kaltag Portage had been the Kaltag Portage for who knows how long before Nome became Nome.

"To read what some so-called historians write about it, you'd think that Nome had no trail, no one traveled in or out, and we got no winter freight or mail before Goodwin built the Iditarod (or Seward) Trail. What ignorance for people supposedly writing history to be oblivious that over the years since the Nome strike thousands upon thousands of trips had been taken over the route connecting us with the Yukon River Trail at Kaltag.

"And as far as the trail names, the beaten thoroughfare between Nome and Kaltag had been known so well by the old names that I tell you, it never so much as entered the mind of anybody I ever heard of to put new names on the whole doggoned way from Nome to Kaltag.

"Now, Rod, standing on your brake in Nome with your dogs yapping and ramming into their collars anxious to get going, you might say you were *headed for* the Iditarod Trail. But no one on the trail right out of Nome said they were *on* the Iditarod. Not yet. Naturally, we Nomites were attached and had a pride in our old trails in use long before that upstart strike at Iditarod. No, we didn't consider that we'd reached the Iditarod Trail until we'd first mushed three hundred miles over the old trails to Kaltag.

"That applied both directions. Travelers going northwest toward Nome through McGrath's or Iditarod thought of the part of their trip using the newer Iditarod Trail as having come to the end when they reached its junction with the old Yukon River Trail.

"So everyone understood that when people talked about establishing a Seward-to-Nome mail trail, that meant putting in a trail out in the middle. Out in the middle to connect the existing trail already heading Nome's way out of Seward that went as far as Susitna Station. Connect that Seward-Su Station trail with the long-established trails southeast from Nome that already headed in the direction of Seward. No matter how well founded the old trails were heading out of the two towns toward each other, their ends looked across hundreds of miles of a great wilderness at each other. Unless they were joined with a connector through that howling wilderness, there could be no Seward–Nome Mail Trail. I know I'm belaboring, but am I making it clear, Rod? The Nome–Seward, or the Seward–Nome Trail was made up of definite sections old and new and the Iditarod Trail was just a part.

"So Goodwin and other travelers of the day who were familiar with the Territory flat-out did not think of the Iditarod Trail as connecting Nome to Seward, but only Kaltag to Seward. Or even perhaps more accurately, a route through Rainy Pass to Susitna Station from Kaltag. After all, look at the name they gave the project: The official, government name was the Rainy Pass–Kaltag Trail."

<hr/>

From Dishkaket, Goodman's orders were to depart from the originally intended Seward mail line, that southeast-heading main line that went straight to McGrath's. They were to work on a new, high-quality trail sixty-seven miles south to Dikeman, the head of Iditarod River low-water navigation. His party would then continue south the remaining forty miles to Iditarod over the already heavily traveled, well-placed and marked trail along the east side of the river. From Iditarod they were to travel the ten miles through Flat to Discovery Otter, then turn east seventy-four miles to rejoin the Kaltag–McGrath trail at Takotna.

As stated, in the overall scope of the general project planning for the Seward-to-Nome Mail Trail, this out-of-the-way loop of about 192 miles to better connect Iditarod with the Yukon Trail, Nome and Seward had grown to take on even more importance than that of shortening the mail route to Nome. Evidence for the relative priority lies in the fact that following directions Goodwin would leave bypassed the formerly anticipated straightening and marking of the seventy-eight-mile stretch from Dishkaket to Takotna on the direct Seward–Nome line. When the focus of so much of the personal travel and mail delivery was the new gold-rush town and the bulk of the traffic took the long Iditarod side loop, it is easy to see why the route from Seward to Kaltag became known so widely as the Iditarod Trail.

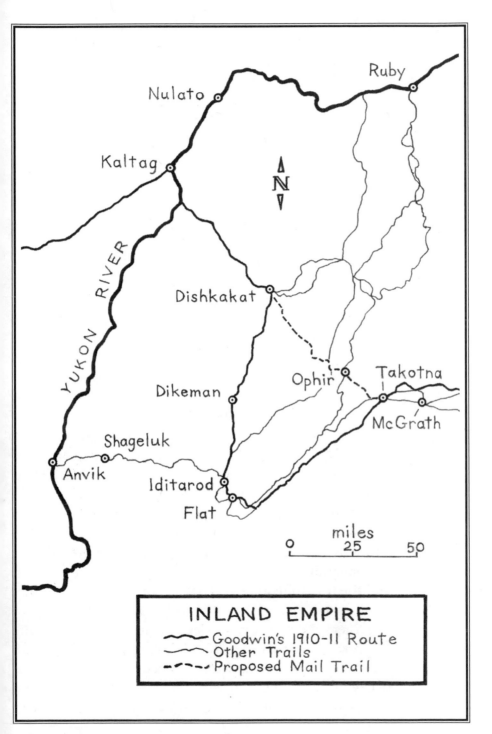

Ruby

Nulato

Kaltag

N

YUKON RIVER

Dishkakat

Ophir

Takotna

Dikeman

McGrath

Shageluk

Anvik

Iditarod

Flat

miles
0   25   50

INLAND EMPIRE
Goodwin's 1910-11 Route
Other Trails
Proposed Mail Trail

Pulling out of Nome on November 9, 1910, a nine-man construction crew and forty-two dogs divided into six 7-dog teams accompanied Goodwin. Stage one involved three weeks of trail work on the established Overland Trail between Nome and Unalakleet. They measured distances with a cyclometer, a measuring wheel attached to the rear of one of the sleds. They started with two, but one broke off and was lost on Thanksgiving Day. The remaining device had been tested for accuracy over the 47.2-mile-long surveyed road leaving Nome. It had checked out perfectly, and would function well the entire trip. On November 30 the group reached Unalakleet. The route taken measured 206.8 miles, correcting the 222 miles claimed for years.

From Unalakleet on the Bering Sea, the second stage was over the well traveled portage to Kaltag. Colonel Goodwin, remembered that during his passage two years before he would have been unlikely to have been able keep to the old trail had he not followed hard behind the mail carrier. He saw the historic Native trade route as typical of trails that were never carefully cut out, but merely beat in, its twists and turns taking the meandering path of least resistance. In one well-invested week the crew greatly upgraded and clearly marked a path that had remained crooked and indistinct for perhaps thousands of years. Arriving on December 7 at the Yukon River village, Goodwin recorded their newly straightened trail as a significantly shortened 73.9 miles. Nome to Kaltag was henceforth known to be 281 miles when the Overland Trail was taken.

The third stage began when they crossed Yukon ice and started over the newly straightened Kaltag-to-Dishkaket leg of the proposed Seward mail trail. A Foreman Giddings had done extensive work on the stretch, possibly during labor beginning the previous summer. Goodwin found the trail to require almost no work and reported that it was the best-marked trail he had ever traversed in Alaska.

Giddings' marker tripod design particularly impressed Goodwin. The colonel adopted the model. It featured two eight-foot poles with the third pole, one of ten or eleven feet, fastened so that the longest leg extended beyond the others at the top. The tripod's long end extended directly over the trail. The men placed such tripods close enough together across all treeless expanses that, even in a blinding blizzard, a driver could see the next marker.

One unique and important feature between Kaltag and Dishkaket was the windlasses and ropes that had to be established at several trail crossings of the Kaiyuh Slough.

The high banks were too steep to either take a laden sled down safely or for the dogs to pull it back up on the far side. Therefore Goodwin and his crew set up mechanical means to lower sleds into the gulch and raise them out.

———————

Rod Perry: *I've heard that another place the ARC installed windlasses was at what today's Iditarod racers know as the Happy River Steps. And at Ninemile Hill out of Knik, early trail-clearing crews working on the first Iditarod Race reported seeing remains of one of these mechanisms dangling from the trunk of an aged tree. The anchoring wrap had become buried deeply into the girth under the annual growth of decades.*

———————

Three days out from Kaltag the ten men and their teams finished the leg to Dishkaket, and none too soon. The bottom fell out of the thermometer. After a four-day layover, the mercury rose to a balmy thirty-six degrees below zero, so on December 14 they moved out. On December 20, they reached Dikeman, having marked the sixty-seven miles with more than 1,300 Giddings-model tripods.

The way from Dikeman to Iditarod required no work. It was the only well-broken length of trail encountered on the entire expedition. The work crew took two days to make Iditarod over the easy stretch, and again, arrived at shelter just ahead of a plunging thermometer. From December 22 through 27 they holed up while temperatures plunged to between sixty and seventy degrees below zero.

On December 28 they hit the trail by way of the mining creeks and smaller settlements and during the following few days accomplished trail work the next eighty-four miles to Takotna.

At Takotna they rejoined the direct Seward–Nome route. The long-dreamed-of through route to Nome, the direct Mail Trail, if all eventually went as planned and it was ever put in, would make its way straight from Dishkaket through Ophir to Takotna. That distance was but seventy-eight miles, 114 miles shorter than going around the side loop Goodwin had just traveled through the Iditarod district.

From Takotna the trail builders revamped the way to the mouth of Big River on the Kuskokwim River. Widening, marking, and straightening it, they saved three and one-half miles.

Beyond Big River, the fourth stage began and the complexion of the trip changed. All the way from Nome they had been either doing touchup work or relocation work on well-established trails. From Big River on to Hayes River, their way would be over sparsely traveled country with, but for a scant five miles, no cut or marked trail. This stage actually fell into two parts: first, a cut-off they would laboriously build from scratch from Big River to Mount Farewell, and, second, from Mount Farewell on over the divide to Hayes River.

From Big River, on February 21 the men began cutting a seven- to ten-foot-wide trail through trees and brush.

———◆———

Al Preston: "That country usually gets lighter snow than any other section on the whole way to Seward. Being close behind the inland side of the Alaska Range away from saturated ocean clouds, it's in what they call a rain shadow. What I don't know, and I never thought to ask Walter Goodwin is whether he directed the men to shovel down to ground level to make their cuts. I think he must have, or they would have been putting in a trail useless except in midwinter. Sleds just have an eight- or nine-inch clearance under the cross bents. No one would attempt to use the route in early fall and late spring if there was an impassable sea of harness-tangling, sled-wrecking stumps in their way.

"Of course, it would have added greatly to the work to make ground-level cuts and you can imagine what must have been going through Colonel Goodwin's head: *Should I add to the complexity of such an already time-consuming task? Especially when time itself adds to the complexity because of the increased provisions consumed by men and dogs that have to be hauled? Or should I leave the stumps, depending upon the ARC to either send out a crew later or contract with someone from the area to clean up our work during snow-free months?"*

After the first five miles out of Big River, Walter Goodwin kept to the single tangent he had noted as the best way on his 1908 passage, with slight modifications in places where the most direct line would not make the best trail. The cut-off took twenty-one days to clear through woods and willows, and to mark with tripods across open flats, but when they had finished, they had created a fifty-six-mile-long straight shot with all the advantages of an overland trail. The old way that followed the bends of the Kuskokwim had been 108 miles, Big River to Farewell.

Along the entire way game had been plentiful. The party added spruce grouse, sharp-tailed grouse and ruffed grouse, ptarmigan, snowshoe hares, and caribou to their fare whenever they came by them, but they seldom could afford taking time to hunt.

Provisions dwindled by the time they reached Farewell Mountain. During a halt to wait out a blizzard, weather notwithstanding, two men set out to hunt moose. It took but two hours to down a huge animal, a godsend for both men and dogs.

From Farewell Mountain they reversed the course of the 1908 reconnaissance to Susitna Station. On that stretch they did not stop to do substantial trail work except across one very notable area: They set tripods over the treeless twelve-mile expanse from the end of timber on the Dalzell River over Rainy Pass to timberline on the Pass Creek side.

Although Goodwin did not elaborate, the distance poles must have been hauled across long, open expanses from the sources of timber draws one to the conclusion that marking the treeless stretch must have occupied the trail builders for several very hard days.

If the men placed markers at the same interval they had over the Dishkaket-to-Dikeman stretch, almost 200 tripods per mile, locating and cutting and limbing the 7,200 individual poles (3 poles/tripod x

200 x 12 miles) carrying each pole by snowshoe from the stump over to the trail to stage them for pickup, then freighting them uphill with the teams would have been no light work. Then there was the joinery. The two eight-foot poles were cut at about sixty-five-degree angles at their top end so that when standing spread-out they could interface the eleven-foot pole sandwiched between them with fairly long, flat surfaces. All three poles were drilled with a brace and bit and a long, two-inch spruce dowel tapped through the holes to join them.

———✦——✦———

Rod Perry: *Today, the last known remaining tripod from this part of the trail hangs in Rainy Pass Lodge near the old trail route. The relic provides a study in construction of Goodwin's tripods.*

———✦——✦———

The cyclometer declared the distance from Nome through Iditarod to the summit of Rainy Pass to be 669 miles.

As Goodwin snowshoed his way down the Happy and Skwentna rivers, he again scrutinized the country with a view to creating an overland trail pursuant to the anticipated act of Congress appropriating $50,000 for work to begin the following winter.

A new ARC cut-off beginning 6.5 miles below Hayes River and leading straight cross-country to Susitna Station appears on the map showing their trip route. That trail project—somewhat equal in difficulty to Goodwin's Big River-to-Farewell work—had previously been built by another work party sent out from Seward. Under the direction of Anton Eide, that crew had performed upgrades and construction all the way to the Alaska Range.

Between Goodwin's two treks, the Alaska Central Railroad had been reorganized. The new operation was called the Alaska Northern Railway. Construction crews had extended work much farther along Turnagain Arm, opening access to Indian Pass. Winter sled and foot traffic had increased. These developments created not only a longer passage suitable for sled travel, but the increased use kept the trail broken better. Therefore, the party could pass over the country much more quickly than Goodwin had before.

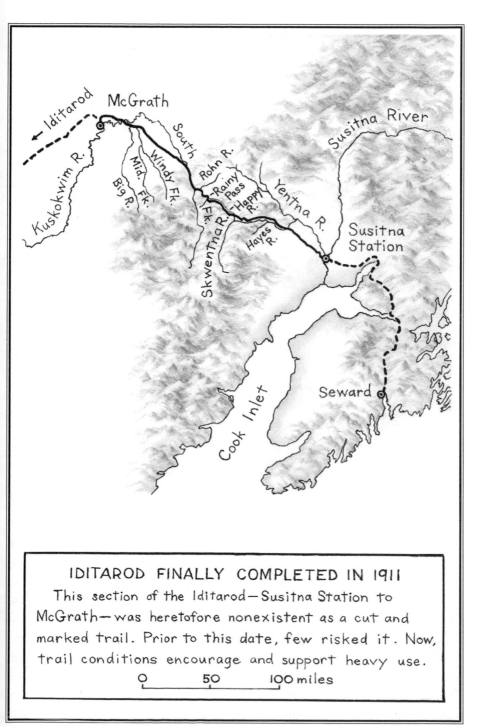

IDITAROD FINALLY COMPLETED IN 1911

This section of the Iditarod—Susitna Station to McGrath—was heretofore nonexistent as a cut and marked trail. Prior to this date, few risked it. Now, trail conditions encourage and support heavy use.

0   50   100 miles

The colonel was no doubt happy not to have to cross Crow Creek Pass. He found that terrible climb had been made unnecessary with the option of a much gentler route over Indian Pass that dog-team travel was taking. Even counting a one-day holdup at Glacier Creek (Girdwood) to wait out a blizzard, they required but nine days to cover the last leg of the trip, Susitna Station to Seward.

On February 25, 1911 they arrived at Resurrection Bay.

To the great pride of the expedition members, all forty-two of their sled dogs trotted into Seward in prime condition. Walter Goodwin's cyclometer had measured the route as 958 miles. Actually, 957.95 to be exact.

———————

Rod Perry: *Most writing about the old trail has been poorly researched, if researched at all. As a result, there is so much absolute hooey out there that is commonly repeated about the state of the Iditarod Trail and about its use prior to Goodwin's work. As previously mentioned, many writers today have made it sound like some thoroughfare existed and traffic simply whizzed back and forth over it since antiquity. Again, even after the 1906–1907 Inland Empire strikes, very few headed for the Interior from Susitna Station. In fact, Colonel Goodwin himself commented that the entire use of the route was limited to only about twenty travelers, total, the winter of his reconnaissance, 1907–08. Correctly speaking, it was not until Walter Goodwin's construction trip the winter of 1910–11 that there was truly an Iditarod Trail,—if one's definition of a trail is a definite path that may be followed fairly precisely. And it wasn't until the winter of 1911–1912, when a full complement of roadhouses was first in place that all the conditions were finally combined that allowed the way to become well-trafficked.*

Let's go over it again to clarify the chronology. It should be abundantly clear that until word of the Iditarod strike became known and the trail froze up the last couple of months of 1909, there had not been much reason to head over the route. The draw of the small midway strikes apparently wasn't that compelling. Only a few going between Cook Inlet and those minor diggings around Ophir had been risking the passage. Even after the big strike at Iditarod, even with an increase in numbers that wanted to get there, there wasn't much travel the winter of 1909–

1910. Even the winter of 1910–1911, the winter Goodwin cut and marked the trail, there wasn't heavy use of the trail because he didn't finish the work until most of that winter was over. And trail or no trail, because there were yet no resupply points mushers still had to mound their sleds with enormous loads, everything they would need to take them all the way through. It wasn't until the winter of 1911–1912 that enough of a trail infrastructure was in place in the way of a roadhouse system offering shelter and food for man and beast that significant travel commenced.

Because of the sheer mountain of erroneous thinking and writing out there, I feel compelled to pound it home one more time: Let it be firmly reiterated that it was not until the fall following Colonel Walter Goodwin's trail work, the fall of 1911, that the Iditarod Trail truly had its beginning as a real trail, a cut and marked path, not merely a general, barely known and hardly traveled route over deep, unbroken snow. Most emphatically, it was not until that fall of 1911—with the roadhouse system newly established—that use turned *from* risky and occasional *to* sure and heavy.

Chapter 33

---◆---

Use of the New Trail Skyrockets

ALASKA ROAD COMMISSIONERS HAD GIVEN Walter Goodwin the additional directive to locate advantageous sites for roadhouses along his way. Because stretches of trail between locations varied in difficulty, which affected traveling speed, the most important criterion was that they be spaced a typical day's foot travel apart. His usual spacing was about twenty miles between sites.

Enterprising folk who ventured into even the most remote locations to set up places of food and lodging jump-started heavy use of the trail. In anticipation of the traffic to come, a few would-be purveyors of shelter, sustenance, and supply followed hard on Colonel Goodwin's heels. They hardly allowed his trail to set up, using prime spring freighting conditions during the tail end of the 1910–11 winter to reach and claim their site before breakup and take in tools, building materials, and supplies to begin work. Others intending to locate near a navigable waterway probably awaited the opening of the river transport season to move what they needed as close to their little piece of heaven as possible. Some of the new businessmen spreading over the trail built on Goodwin's sites, some set up shop at locations they thought were better. Pat O'Cotter reported in the July 1911 edition of Alaska-Yukon Magazine that by the time of his writing (four months after Goodwin finished his trip) roadhouses were already spread all along the trail, one-half to one day's travel apart. Hikers covering twenty miles a day would not only be able to buy meals—for 50 cents to $1.50—and sleep in beds—50 cents to $1.00—each night, but they would also often be able to stop midway between for lunch.

Once the roadhouses were built and supplied, the terribly back-breaking and inhibiting do-it-all-yourself, make-it-clear-through-or-die nature of the former primitive passage was but a memory. The route was tamed. Now in place was the trail triumvirate of a defined, beaten trail, resupply waypoints, and shelter reachable daily. Whenever travelers found that combination—trail, resupply, and shelter —they could go fast and more lightly loaded, not having to carry much in the way of dog and human food and camp gear. That made all the difference. Now not just personal travel, but for the first time, commercial use of the trail was possible. Now that loads did not have to be entirely taken up with the stuff of sheer survival, commercial haulers were left sled capacity to transport mail or freight.

The rivers had hardly frozen the next fall when teams by the hundreds began pouring over Colonel Walter Goodwin's trail. During one week alone in November of 1911, some 120 teams pulled out of Knik bound for the goldfields of the Interior.

Because of the constant traffic it began to receive, the fall of 1911 also marked the first time a traveler could count on finding a trail with a hard base. Beginning then, even if it had snowed in or blown over in a storm, the dog driver or hiker could be assured that, at some distance below the soft surface lay a packed foundation. No longer would man and dogs have to wallow through tractionless depths. It was the cutting and marking of the way, the establishment of a set-up trail base and the rest and resupply points every twenty miles or so that jump-started trail use, turning the Iditarod into the thoroughfare of gold-rush renown and legend.

Rod Perry: *Only a dog driver who has struggled with a sled straining under many hundreds of pounds of cargo, floundering for days stretching into weeks through a ground-to-surface accumulation of unbroken snow can truly, thoroughly appreciate the value of a hard trail bottom!*

About the time Goodwin's party passed through in 1910–11, prospectors found more gold in the country between Ophir and the new Yukon River village of Ruby. Quickly, new settlements of Long,

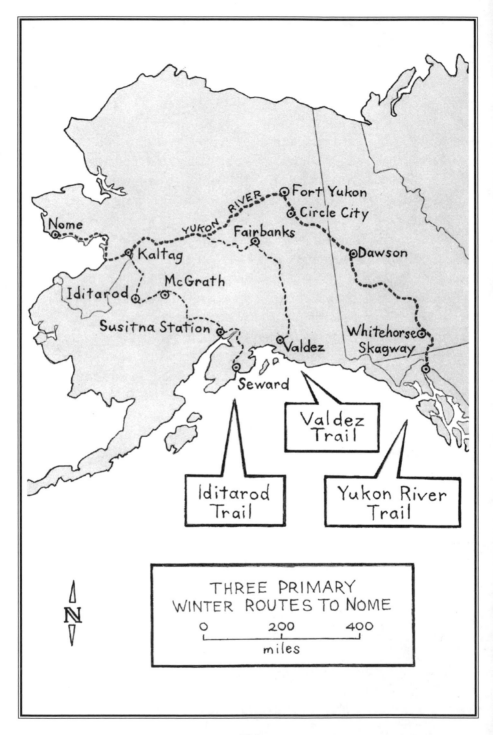

Nome

YUKON RIVER

Fort Yukon

Circle City

Fairbanks

Dawson

Kaltag

Iditarod

McGrath

Susitna Station

Valdez

Whitehorse
Skagway

Seward

Valdez
Trail

Iditarod
Trail

Yukon River
Trail

THREE PRIMARY
WINTER ROUTES TO NOME

0   200   400
miles

N

Poorman, and Cripple Landing sprang up. The finds not only added to numbers traveling the trail, but the new finds necessitated the building of several branch trails connecting Goodwin's trail with the new settlements.

Trappers—termed "cat stranglers" by the miners—made up another sizeable group who used the new trail. It gave them a beaten path and supply support leading deep into territory that previously had been too logistically difficult to effectively work. They quickly established a myriad of side trails of up to fifty or more miles in length, opening up thousands of square miles to the fur industry which ranked in importance only behind gold and fisheries in the territory.

The anticipated Mail Trail, planned to take the most direct Seward-to-Nome route, had not been finished. That was because the Takotna-to-Dishkaket leg had not, so far, been relocated to take a straighter line. Also, until 1914 the U.S. Mail contract still ran through Fairbanks. Therefore, most traffic heading north out of Seward and south from Kaltag was not traveling Seward to Nome or Nome to Seward, but bound for the new gold finds of the Inland Empire and Iditarod, chiefly the latter. Again, no wonder that the route between Seward and the Yukon quickly became known as the "Iditarod Trail."

Chapter 34

———◆———

Dog Days: Trail Life in its Heyday

ANYONE CONTEMPLATING A JOURNEY BY DOG TEAM from Seward over the trail to Iditarod country planned on a trip of two to three weeks; all the way to Nome could take four to five weeks. Travelers were of a wide description: freighters, miners, mail carriers, Natives, trappers, business people, and gamblers, to name a sample.

Those who wanted to travel as passengers could do so if they had a deep enough pocket. They usually went with the freight teams and hardly ever got to add their weight to the already heavily packed sleds. Not only did they have to walk most of the way, they were usually expected to help muscle the sled through tough passages. Passengers paid about $1,500 to go clear through to Nome and $275 was standard fare, Knik to McGrath.

A would-be driver could rent a team complete with a sled, towline and harness setup. Even individual dogs could be rented. Standard rates were in the vicinity of $200 for a team of five dogs (presumably all the way through to Nome), five dollars per harness (though they might be able to be used for multiple rentals, there was a good chance of the dogs chewing them—or completely devouring them), and $120 for a sled. Average feed costs ran about fifty cents per dog per day.

For most travelers, such rentals were cost-prohibitive so they walked. A few pulled burdened hand sleds. Some skied. On some sections of wind-blown ice or even where the trail was packed rock hard from constant traffic a pair of ice skates could gain a traveler many miles for the few who carried them.

Anyone taking a horse over trails created for dogs would immediately find dog drivers devising his slow, tortured death and fervently dreaming of converting his hay burner to dog food. Horse

The Dogs Were Big! Alma with friends.

hooves punched the trail with crippling holes that could quickly wipe out the shoulders, hips, hocks, and wrists of sled dogs.

Rod Perry: *Dogs of the day were large. My old sourdough friend, the late Carl Clark of Hope, used to freight for the trader at Tanana, where that great river joins the Yukon. The trader had two teams, Carl told me, the "little yappers," eighty- to ninety-pound native huskies used for lighter loads and faster going, and the heavy freight team of 120- to 140-pound Mackenzie River Huskies.*

The true origin of the fabled Mackenzie River husky is—arguably—lost to time, retelling, and lack of actual records many can agree with. Most agree that the breed was the creation, long before the Klondike Rush, of dogs from villages throughout the great Mackenzie River basin, with differences in characteristics developed by widely separated native populations. Some have said that early Hudson's Bay Company freighters in the Canadian Arctic around the Mackenzie delta developed a cross of these large, Native huskies with the Saint Bernard or some other giant working breed, and with perhaps a touch of wolf blood added. The genetic mix that made up the breed draws heated argument today. Whatever they were, they were not fast, but at their pace they could really yank the slack out of a towline.

Today, it is not uncommon to encounter an Alaskan who claims that his dog is a MacKenzie River Husky. Maybe it is, but if so, it may well be something substantially different from dogs of that designation during gold rush times. A man who claimed to know the old breed well was the late Raymond Thompson. Inventor of the famous Thompson locking steel snare, he trapped in the Athabaska country of the Canadian subarctic as a young man in the early years of the twentieth century. As an elderly gentleman, he wrote the "Sled Dog Trails" column in the *Alaska Sportsman Magazine*. Raymond Thompson once spent an entire summer in the 1960s traveling the Yukon and Northwest Territories searching to see if any of the breed still existed in a form he recognized. He found not one.

Freighting over the Iditarod Trail, most of the large dogs, when pulling substantial loads, traveled at about four and one-half miles per hour, an annoying, "too fast to walk, too slow to trot," in-between pace for a man.

By the time of the Iditarod Rush, dog-team gear, sleds, hookups, and methods had evolved substantially from what had been used far to the east along the Upper Yukon in the years leading up to and immediately following the Klondike strike. When thousands from the Interior migrated to the Arctic west coast during the Nome Rush, Russian and Eskimo dog-driving methods and gear began to exert a strong influence.

Just in front of the sled were the wheel dogs, or wheelers. These were often the biggest, strongest dogs in the team because from the position they not only had to pull, but had to counter the influence of the towline and sled. If, say, the majority of the team ahead had already gone around a hard bend to the left, the towline would be pulling with great force left across the turn before the last dogs and sled had yet reached it. The left wheeler would jump over the towline to the right side to help counteract the rest of the team's pull to the left at the same time the driver would be doing all he could to "run the sled out" by running and vigorously shoving the sled to reach the corner before the power from the towline pulling left could haul it off the trail over the inside of the curve.

Not only rounding sharp curves but just the common meandering of the sled over the usual unevenness of the trail continually jostled the wheelers. They had to be nimble because good wheeler work on a winding trail required that they continually had to jump the towline to pull from the opposite side in their effort to keep from being swept from the trail by the towline cutting a corner. Obviously, a dog of level disposition fit the job description best. It helped to rotate wheelers to give them periodic breaks.

Between the wheelers and the front of the team were "team dogs," the common working animals. The two just behind the leader were "swing dogs." Swing dogs were usually some of the fastest, most spirited animals on the team. A team somehow receives its pace signal from the dogs up front so speedy swing dogs helped keep the team moving faster. Most swing dogs knew the driver's commands to the leader, and were often themselves backup leaders or young leaders in training.

At the head of the team was the very extension of the driver himself, his leader or leaders. A well-trained lead dog could follow commands to start, stop, accelerate, and decelerate the team, steer it left and right, and turn back to reverse direction, as well as smoothly pass other teams without interference. Besides those things that lead dogs learned from their drivers, some possessed unique natural abilities, some of them downright uncanny and amazing.

Togo, the great lead dog of the immortal driver Leonard Seppala, hero of the world-famous 1925 dog team relay to race diphtheria serum to epidemic-stricken Nome, led his team across the sea ice of Norton Bay in the black of night during a raging blizzard on their leg of the life-saving dash. Seppala felt secure in entrusting his own life as well as the fate of Nome to Togo's uncanny ability to hold unerringly to an absolutely straight line of travel once he had been put on course.

———————

Rod Perry: *Following Togo's death from old age, Seppala had a taxidermist mount him. The mount may be viewed at the Iditarod Trail headquarters building on Knik Road out of Wasilla, Alaska.*

Some lead dogs could sense thin ice and turn the team to avoid the danger. The late Lester Bugsby, who seemed to strike it rich wherever he turned, be it in gold, salmon, or land, told me that with a newly purchased team and a young leader hauling a big sled weighted with his entire winter supply, he pulled out from the trading post at Tanana just after freeze-up, bound for his diggings on the Koyukuk.

———————

Lester Bugsby: "Rod, I'll tell you about the value of a leader. Heading out of the Tanana mouth onto Yukon ice, I come to a place where maybe the mixing of the two currents is causing some extra turbulence that slows ice formation. Whatever's going on under the ice, it makes for a thin spot.

"With no warning, the sled breaks through! The load weighs hundreds of pounds so it goes down like so much stone. As the current starts to suck me under with it, I have barely an instant to kick off from the cargo and reach the edge of the hole. I just manage to get my arms over the edge to hang on. The sinking sled is caught by the strong current. It drags the poor dogs backwards. They're desperately scratching and clawing, resisting for everything they're worth, but with all their power they're nothing compared to the current's drag on that huge, sinking load. I'm having all I can do to hang on and not be pulled under. I can't come close to getting to my knife or moving over to cut the towline. So they just disappear pair after pair into the hole and under the ice.

"I'm getting more and more numbed and can't hang on much longer. The tug of the current is terrible. When I'm just about to go the way of the dogs, an Indian man shows up. He'd been traveling with his family and they'd seen us break through. They live there and know the ice. He leaves his wife and kids back and drives his team and empty sled up as close as he dares. He moves fast, lines his team out away from the hole with his leader facing back toward his wife. He walks carefully closer with a line attaching him to his sled so the team can pull him out if he breaks through. He throws me another rope with a couple of loops at the end so I have something to grab. A real smart fellow and a quick thinker. I owe that man my life.

"Fifteen minutes later, old John, the trading-post owner, and Carl, his freighter, are mighty surprised to see me stumble through the door. My rescuer's helping me in. I'm half frozen and caked with ice. They get me in dry clothes, and sit me almost on top of the roaring barrel stove. They put hot water bags next to my back and belly, between my thighs and over my head. I'm halfway to my knees in a tub of hot water. They keep hot blankets coming to throw over me. As soon as I can, they get me to start swallowing hot soup.

"As soon as he thinks I'll be OK he tells me to just gather up a whole new outfit from his shelves and warehouse as soon as I'm ready. He loans me one of his big sleds. Then he sends Carl around the village to buy dogs from various owners and put together a whole new team. That's the old-time Alaska way; he trusts me to settle up when I can.

"Rod, we were talking about lead dogs and their talents. With my old leader, the breakthrough would have never happened. I could trust that savvy old river dog to sense thin ice. I don't know how he picked it up, but he had a real fear of it and he'd steer me well away. It was an uncanny ability the new leader lacked."

———◆———

Little wonder that drivers valued top lead dogs like gold, and drivers and their leaders grew especially close. Roadhouse operators commonly allowed drivers to bring their leaders in to sleep beside them. Some of the greatest lead dogs gained fame that spread throughout the North. One such dog, a huge, handsome animal owned by enthusiastic young dog driver, army lieutenant Billy Mitchell, became the envy of the Upper Yukon.

Valued lead dogs that grew too old for hard duty in harness but were still able to trot along sometimes had their careers extended as "loose leaders," trotting free in front of the team.

The great gold stampedes created a huge demand for dogs. It was said that no large dog wandering the streets of San Francisco, Portland, or Seattle was safe. Many were snatched up and brought north. With such a premium on large dogs, many of the working and guarding breeds that were fierce defenders of herd and home came into common use and often mixed their genes with some of the large native dogs that fought at the slightest provocation.

———◆———

Rod Perry: *The late Native leader and sagacious dog man Fred Stickman told me that his people along the Yukon sometimes mixed some wolf blood into their working dogs, but most selectively, only if they could catch a wolf with just the right rather streamlined build. Some famous sourdoughs such as Slim Williams and Frank Glazier— the latter of whom I enjoyed lengthy visits—bred teams of half, or even three-quarters wolf blood.*

My old pal, Ron Aldrich, the only man to run both the first Iditarod Trail Sled Dog Race and the First Yukon Quest race from Fairbanks to

Whitehorse, once asked tough old-time miner and freighter, the late Rocky Cummings, "Rocky, back in the old days when so many men drove teams of big fighting dogs, did you ever have any problems on the trail around other teams?"

Rocky Cummings: "One time I'm freighting out near McDougal, north of Su Station. While coming down a steep hill, the dogs prick up their ears and step up the pace. A moose or another team has to be close ahead. Immediately, we see a team coming up toward us. The trail's narrow, with room for only one of us. The downhill driver has the right of way because he has less control. The guy's not making any move to give me the trail. So I look for a trailside tree to snub off on to give him time to move his dogs and sled off. I can't figure him out, he doesn't do anything. He just brakes to a halt and stands perched there on the back of his sled motionless as an owl on a tombstone.

"My team's surging. I have all my weight on the brake. But with my heavy load and the power of my dogs dragging me down the slope I can't hold them back. As we try to pass, things happen just like I expected; a huge battle blows up.

"I yell to the guy to grab his dogs and help me bust up the fight. He just stands there, looking dumb. I get out my heavy shot whip (leather sewn in a long, tapering tube filled with number-eight lead bird shot) and go through his team. I use the butt like a blackjack to tap his dogs out. When all of them are lying there unconscious I straighten out my team—some of them are pretty chewed up—and get them going.

"The guy had never done one single thing to help and I'm boiling mad. As I pass by I swing from my heels. I land the nastiest, hardest right-cross you ever saw square on his temple and drop him like a bad habit!"

"You ask me what happened to him? I don't know, Ron. There's a big open flat starting at the bottom of the hill. When I get to the far end, I turn and look back. He's still lying there."

Drivers carried a whip and used it the way teamsters did while driving teams of horses and mules, almost invariably using it exclusively to crack for noise to reinforce voice commands. They had to keep absolute discipline and order. Sled dogs naturally take eagerly to trail work like a Labrador retriever takes to water; neither has to be forced to perform. Dog mushers of that day understood that happy dogs performed enthusiastically and energetically, but whipped dogs grew discouraged, even to the point of lying down. Almost ironically, using a whip like Rocky did to break up a fight was humane. It was better than allowing the animals to maim or even kill one another.

Almost everyone streaming north into Gold Rush Alaska came either from farm and ranch backgrounds or cities where most transportation was still horse-drawn. Naturally, sled-dog harness construction drew heavily from horse and mule harness design. Work dogs leaned into neck encircling, leather collars filled with hair or other padding. Singletrees (spreader bars) behind the tail allowed the pulling force to be transferred to the tug lines while keeping the dog's legs free of inward pressure from the traces that would otherwise interfere with movement.

Unlike far to the east in the Canadian north, where dogs were earlier lined up single file, later Alaska dog teams were usually lined up in pairs. From the sled bridle forward to the leader(s) a towline stretching the length of the team ran up the middle between the dogs in each pair. Three-foot-long tuglines connected the towline to each dog's singletree. Coming off the towline beside each pair's heads, footlong neck lines connected the main line to the pairs' collars. Each pair of dogs took up six feet of towline length. That gave them room to work and maneuver, yet kept the overall towline length as compact as possible. Old-time teamsters calculated "draft," figuring that the closer they could keep the load to the power source, the more efficiently the load could be drawn.

Freight sleds typically had basket lengths of ten to fourteen feet and usually measured twenty-four to twenty-eight inches wide, outside to outside of the runners. Runners were usually shod with steel, the harder the better, with band-saw steel being best. New steel ran relatively slickly but should the runners be dragged over a bare gravel bar such as was common on the upper Kuskokwim, the steel would be scored and thereafter pull harder, cutting the freighter's speed and unduly tiring the dogs. The colder the weather, the harder the steel dragged. Dog manure dropped on the run froze instantly to the steel when run over, creating a drag.

Some drivers built their own sleds during the off-season, but, as few had access to carpentry shops, many were built commercially, either Outside or in Alaska. Shops often turned out many sleds of stock design but would build to custom specifications. Designs varied widely depending upon their intended use, the conditions of the country, and the biases of the driver.

Though sleds built by Natives and some old sourdoughs were often constructed of native white birch, most sleds were built of much stronger and more long-lasting hickory, white oak or ash. At the turn of the twentieth century, eastern hardwood forests still held many old-growth trees, tall and straight with boles reaching far above ground to the first limbs. Long, quarter-sawn boards of straight-grained, knot-free sapwood (live, outer wood is more flexible than heartwood) were commonly available by order from Outside suppliers or from the stacks stocked by every general store and trading post in the territory.

The mark of a cheechako (newcomer, ignorant to the ways of the North) sled builder, especially if he was an advanced carpenter who took pride in his work, was that his joinery would be too tight and he would use bolts, screws, and nails to put his entire sled together. Such a sled had no give to it over uneven trails. When wood and steel became brittle in the intense cold, his sled would break apart. Sound basket-sled construction required joints featuring an "engineered sloppiness," not poor joinery, but a sizing of the parts with enough ease to allow movement in those mortise-and-tenon joints that needed to flex. All but the very few nonflexing parts were lashed together with babiche—long, rawhide laces cut from moose, caribou, or seal hide.

Cargo sleds commonly came with plow handles, most useful but nefarious features, extensions of the top rails that the driver could grab to help manhandle the load from the rear of the sled. Nothing worked quite as well for helping work a heavy cargo from the tail end, but, as they pointed directly at the driver's abdomen or groin when he leaned to the side to muscle them, should the sled hit anything and

Common Team Configuration and Harness Setup.
Sled Features Plow Handles.

Alaska State Library Historical Collections,
Alfred G. Simmer Photographs, ASL-P137-078

suddenly stop, the man could be badly injured. Or worse. A driver
was killed in such an accident while freighting near Lake Clark.

It was extremely hard to influence sled direction from the rear of
the sled, even with a load much lighter than the freighters usually
carried. In contrast, steering even the heaviest load could be done
with relative ease levering from the front of the sled with a gee pole.
When gee-poling the driver most often trotted in front of the sled,
straddling the towline. Traversing level ground or uphills this posed
no problem, but on steep downhills that was impossible for a lone
driver. The steeper the incline, the more the heavy sled would tend to
pick up speed and overrun the man and team ahead. On downhills,
someone needed to hold the sled back by standing on the big hinged
brake at the rear of the sled. Therefore, heavy freighting often
required two men, one on the gee pole, the other back on the plow
handles and brake. At the brink of extremely steep pitches, freighters
often stopped to roughlock the runners, that is, wrapping them with
dog tie-out chains. And up the climbs or down the drop-offs that were
impossibly steep for huge loads, such as up or down the benches of

the Happy River Canyon, drivers used the windlasses installed by the Alaska Road Commission.

In smooth going, when the effect on the team was judged negligible, the gee poler often attached a pair of short skis or a short toboggan called an *Ouija* ("o'wee-gee") board to the towline and rode as he steered. Rarely, the driver got to ride as well, though runner tails of that day usually extended behind the rear stanchions only far enough to accommodate the front half of a man's mukluk.

Another piece of specialized equipment found on many large sleds was a slew brake. Sleds slinging around corners on fast going, sleds encountering glaciering (seepage from underground springs that built up a thick layer of ice over the trail) that formed side slopes or sleds struck by side winds on slick ice tended to slew sideways. To keep them tracking straight in the direction of travel, the slew brake, consisting of a single or double blade mounted to straddle a runner tail for side support, was depressed. Like an ice-skate blade, it offered almost no resistance in a forward direction, but carved and greatly resisted sideways movement.

Alaska Road Commission Driver Steers While Riding Short Skis.

Walter W. Hodge Papers, UAF-2003-63-273, Archives and Manuscripts, Alaska and Polar Regions Collections, University of Alaska Fairbanks

Freighting With Tandem Sleds.

Alaska State Library Historical Collections, Alexander Malcolm Smith
Photographic Collection, ASL-PCA-136

On western Alaska trails, just as in earlier freighting on the upper Yukon as described by the Goin Kid, when freighting an extra-heavy cargo, two or even three sleds were drawn one behind another "cross-lashed" to keep the whole train tracking as true as possible. When managing such a procession, the gee pole man still worked right behind the dogs and the brakeman moved to the rear sled, treating the two (or three) sleds as if they were one.

Multiple sleds had several advantages: They reduced the risk of sled breakage under extremely heavy loads. They spread the load out to lower the center of gravity. Items that did not have to be unloaded until reaching their destination could be packed once and the lashings left alone except on one of the sleds. And the sleds could be detached to singly negotiate steep climbs and downhills and other difficult passages.

Cargo of every conceivable description—anything that could be piled onto a sled and for which someone was willing to pay a dollar per pound to be delivered, was hauled over the trail. In 1910, Bob Griffis—a former Black Hills stage coach driver and a respected mail carrier serving Nome—received a contract from the Miners and Merchants Bank of Iditarod to transport much of the season's gold out to Seward. On November 10 (one day after the Alaska Road Commission's Colonel Walter Goodwin and his work party left Nome to improve and mark the trail), Griffis began his trek over the raw, unmarked route to Susitna Station. More than five laborious weeks after pulling out of Iditarod with over 700 pounds of gold [then] worth a quarter-million dollars (today worth well over $10 million) secured under the canvas on the bed of his sled, he arrived in Seward, mission accomplished.

Having seen that such a haul could be successfully completed even over the primitive, uncut, unmarked, unbroken route, the bank felt even more secure after Goodwin's trail construction resulted in heavy traffic that kept the way broken. For the following eight years, Griffis' gold convoys became an annual institution, and some years he conducted more than one "gold train."

In 1912, four teams delivered 2,600 pounds of gold.

On December 31, 1916, the Griffis caravan came into Knik carrying 3,400 pounds of gold behind 46 dogs. (Those sleds resting outside of the roadhouse at Knik carried about $61 million in Year 2012 dollars on their beds! For another perspective, the dollar back then could buy about twenty times more than in 2012.)

O. G. Herning, proprietor of general stores at Knik and Susitna Station, reported a shipment of bullion coming through on November 25, 1921 with 1,500 pounds hauled by one dog team.

In addition to shipments of the Miners and Merchants Bank being freighted out bound for Wells Fargo, it was not unusual for individuals to mush production of their own out for shipment south. For instance, Herning recorded that on November 30, 1919 a team brought 100 pounds over the trail from the driver's own mine at Discovery. It should be remembered that general laborers of that day were making only a couple of dollars a day in the States. Even at the standard going rate in those years of $20.67 an ounce, this miner's sled toted over $33,000.

Only one major robbery ever took place on the Iditarod Trail. In 1922, the owner of Schermeyer's Halfway Roadhouse plotted with a shady denizen of Iditarod's red-light district to relieve a mail carrier,

"Old Charlie froze to death." Cargos of every
conceivable description were transported.

Alaska State Library-Claude Hobart Photographic Collection, ASL-P425-6-25

who was attracted to her favors, of his burden—$30,000 in payroll cash. After being tracked down and found hiding in California two years later, Schermeyer confessed. Also brought to justice was his partner in the crime, professionally known as the *Black Bear*. Acquitted in 1927 at her second trial in Fairbanks, she afterward married the dog driver she had allegedly helped rob.

The U.S. Post Office was a major player in the establishment (and, finally, abandonment) of thousands of miles of winter trails criss-crossing Alaska Territory. The late Iditarod racer Don Bowers well described some of the gold rush mail service history and the mail carrier's importance.

———————

Don Bowers: "The U.S. Post Office . . . contracted for its first regular long-distance Alaskan mail route in 1895 with the son of the chief of the Taku Tlingit tribe, Jimmie Jackson.

"He received seven hundred dollars plus a dollar per letter to deliver the mail from Juneau to the goldfields on the upper Yukon River near Circle. He and two Tlingit friends went up the Stikine River in a canoe as far as they could and then went by dogsled the rest of the way to Circle, more than a thousand miles. The Indian mail carriers delivered mail year-round on the Juneau–Circle route, receiving six hundred dollars per trip, until the completion of the White Pass and Yukon Railway from Skagway to Carcross, British Columbia, in 1899.

"From the other end of the Yukon, in the winter of 1897–98 Jack Carr carried the mail from St. Michael on the Bering Sea, up the Yukon to Dawson, and over the Chilkoot Trail to Dyea. He arrived in Dyea after eighty-two days on the trail, covering more than two thousand miles.

"Jimmie Jackson was the first of Alaska's legendary mail drivers, starting a tradition of 'Contract Star Route Carriers' that endured for decades. (The last dogsled mail delivery in Alaska was in the 1960s by Chester Noongwook to Savoonga on St. Lawrence Island, which until then was one of the few remaining Alaska communities without a suitable airstrip.)"

By the early 1900s the mail driver reigned as king of the winter trail. Don Bowers helps us understand the circumstances of such travel, explaining how, " . . . winter traffic along the trails had a well-established hierarchy. At the top were the mail drivers, the parka-clad Pony Express riders of the north. They ran on schedules and usually had the biggest, fastest, best-trained teams, sometimes more than twenty dogs. They were highly respected, often opening trails after storms and pushing through hazardous conditions. More than a few mail drivers died when their sleds went through the ice or they were caught in avalanches or became trapped in blizzards.

"By law, mail teams had the right of way on all trails. The drivers always received the best seats at roadhouse dinner tables, the first servings at meals, and the best bunks. In addition to the mail, they hauled some freight and passengers, and kept their loads to about fifty pounds per dog. For the most part, mail by dog team was limited to first class, meaning letters and small packages. Like most mushers of the day, they often spent more time walking or running alongside the sled than riding it, but mail drivers were usually able to ride the runners much more frequently than other teams on the trail."

Rod Perry: *The stature of the drivers and the vital nature of their deliveries cannot be overstated. In the wonderful book by Jim Reardon about the life and times of venerable Native leader, Sidney Huntington,* Shadows on the Koyukuk, *painted this picture of the Koyukuk mail run from Tanana to Wiseman, which lasted from 1906 until 1931.*

"The monthly mail run was the sole contact with the outside world for miners and prospectors who lived in the Koyukuk in the early 1900s. There were no airplanes. Dog teams carried everything in winter . . . Letters from loved ones, magazines, and newspapers were treasures beyond value for these isolated men. In remote villages and mining camps, I've seen magazines with loose pages, the print worn from handling, treated as if they were valuable documents, as they

George Adams with U.S. Mail Team

were handed from man to man. Small wonder that mail drivers were considered special."

————◆————

Alma Preston: "Some of our drivers had some, umm—let's just call them "unusual" experiences while on their mail runs. See this snapshot here of George Adams with his team? I don't know whether his or Al Ferrin's experience was the most unusual but I'll start with George's, just the way he told it to me."

————◆————

George Adams: "The Iditarod Trail wasn't just used to go straight through, but, also, to get to where we could branch off to run the mail into places off the main trunk. Like Hope.

"I pulled into Hope one day and if a bunch of the bystanders hadn't rushed out to help control the team by grabbing my dog's collars,

445

I hate to think what would've happened. Right there in the middle of the main street was a man on his sled. And what should be pulling it by a chain from the sled to his collar but a two-year-old grizzly! I don't know whether the man was in town on serious business, maybe to pick up supplies, or on a bet, or just to create a sensation. But there he was.

"I found out more about the man and his bear later. Seems he was Nate White, a miner from Sunrise, six miles away. That fall he'd loaded his belongings on a big sled to move his family over to Hope for the winter so the kids could go to school. The wife and kids were perched up on top of the load.

"Now I don't know whether she was fortifying herself for an expected famine or laying on a thick layer of insulation against a long, arctic winter but the wife was quite a load all by herself. And disposition? Sour as spoiled milk, and a nasty temper she had, too.

"Here they come approaching Hope, the dogs really leaning into it to pull all that tonnage. From ten feet of chain attached to the rear bent, the grizzly's trotting along behind the sled as nice as you please. Well, when they reach the edge of town, every malamute in Hope cuts loose in an excited din.

"That bear just panics. As strong as the team is and as heavy the load, that durned grizzly drags them backwards to a big cottonwood. He's still young enough he can climb and he goes up 'til he has the back of the sled leaning up the tree way off the ground. The kids bail off and think it's high, good fun. But the round lady rolls down the load 'til she whacks her noggin and bloodies her nose on the headboard, and lands all tangled with the wheelers.

"While she's flopping and thrashing around like some beluga gone dry on a sandbar, just bellowing and cussing, all scrambled up in the tug lines, the terrified dogs start to fight. In the melee one of 'em musta mistook her wallowing posterior for his enemy. He champs his perlies right into some of that bacon. She squeals like a stuck pig. Her husband's been there from the start trying to get her free of the bedlam, if she'd only let him. When she's finally unwound and picks herself up, she's blubbering and swearing at the bear and her husband. And then she lights into her kids and the village onlookers who think it's one of the best shows they've ever seen. Alma, you couldn't stage or buy entertainment like that!

"Well, they get settled into their cabin and start village life. Now that they're living in the big city they can't just let a grizzly go wandering around wherever his bear desires would take him. So he's kept on his chain that can slide along a cable running between the cabin and the outhouse. The doggoned bear's eyelids are getting pretty droopy; it's that time of year. The critter doesn't think very highly of the digs under the outhouse so the only other natural place he can reach to den up is beneath the cabin. He burrows under, curls up and snoozes off.

"You'd think everything would be fine 'til spring, but if you do, you haven't counted on the creativity of the hefty lady to find something to get herself all worked-up about. From down below the floor comes this slow snoring. The husband and kids think it's kind of nice. It reassures them their friend is contentedly doing what snug bears do. But the old lady builds up a good rage. She just keeps jerking the poor critter awake by his chain, pulling him out and making him drink coffee strong enough to float Elisha's axe head.

"Well now, Alma, my lass, I don't know about the effect on a grizzly bear if he's awash in caffeine in the best of times during summer. But while the lady's screaming at him to guzzle concentrated brew, everything in this bear is screaming sleep. He's getting as irritated as she is. It's plain the critter's sense of humor is totally used up. One day when the husband's off on some errand, the bear gives his tormentor a cuff and sends her rolling halfway across the yard. She's got plenty of padding so just picks herself up. But then she takes one look at the mad animal and scampers for cover. She barely reaches the outhouse a half step ahead of the grizzly. Every time she tries to escape back to the cabin, the bear rushes at her and it's nip and tuck to make it back to the outhouse and slam the door. By the time her husband returns, she's been trapped for two or three hours. She's shaking cold and so mad she's spitting nails. Well, that spells doom for the bear; she shrieks that it's either the bear or her.

"That wouldn't have been much of a choice for me, but the husband was a better man than I am."

447

May 1917
Hope, Alaska

Sled Grizzly

Alma Preston: "You couldn't make up stories as crazy and bizarre as some that actually took place. Al Ferrin, told me about this one."

Rod Perry: *Examination of the sign over the business establishment in the background of the grizzly and sled photo shows Ferrin as one of the owners.*

Al Ferrin: "I was on the Hope run. On the trail down Sixmile Creek I stopped at one of the trailside cabins to deliver mail to the old miner and get a cup of coffee like I always did. Ol' Anthony was nowhere to be seen, no smoke coming up from the chimney, no answer to my halloo, nothing. Long story short, I found him dead around behind the cabin. He'd obviously had a heart attack while splitting kindling. He'd just sunk down on his knees, leaned over with his chest on the chopping block and arms hanging down and died. It had been near zero for days and he was frozen solid.

I had quite a time wrestling the body around the cabin and was wondering about the best way to load it when it occurred to me he was frozen into a perfect sitting position. I just rearranged some of my mail and sat him up on one of the bags like he was a proper passenger. The only posture that looked much different was his arms reaching out. I got the axe knocked out of one hand, but in his other was the chunk of spruce he'd been splitting from. It was frozen so tight seized in his grip I couldn't work it out.

"We must have been a sight to behold coming into Hope, Ol' Anthony sitting there big as life atop the load, face looking like the frost king, with both arms reaching out, one with that hanged chunk of split spruce clutched in it.

"I suppose it might've even been humorous, in a morbid sort of way, if we all weren't such good friends of Ol' Anthony. At the roadhouse they helped me off-load and carry him around back to a shed. We hung him from the rafters up where nothing could gnaw on him until the marshal could get there, maybe a week or two. I went on to the post office to make my delivery and get the dogs fed and settled in for the night.

"From a ways off as I walked back to the roadhouse I could hear quite a hullabaloo going on inside. You know what a bunch of Anthony's old miner friends had done? They'd gone back and brought him out of the shed and into the roadhouse. There at the bar on a stool sat Ol' Anthony with his arms outstretched like he was reaching out to the bar tender for something. They'd tapped with the back of a boy's ax on the end of the chunk until they got it driven out from his grasp. In its place they put a glass and filled it with whisky. Those crazy miners!

"Well, as you know, Alma, we mail drivers were never supposed to drink when we're working. But I figured this occasion called for at least a small shot. Maybe a couple. Well OK, several, I guess.

We told our favorite stories about the deceased. Then someone brought out a mouth harp and another guy went and got a fiddle. We gathered around Ol' Anthony, sang every song we thought he'd enjoy and just gave him the best sendoff we knew how. It went on through the night 'til he commenced to slump. We sure laughed a lot, and I guess we shed a tear at the end. But all in all we thought we did Ol' Anthony proud."

Alaska Commercial Company became Northern Commercial Company (N.C.) and operated the most prominent system of general stores and warehouses throughout the Territory. N.C. won the biggest postal contract, the Yukon River Trail mail run. During a thirty-one-year span they won contracts to deliver mail over thousands of miles of trails elsewhere in Alaska as well.

The company prided itself on the professionalism of its drivers and its well-trained and cared-for teams. N.C. mail drivers and teams comprised most of the men and dogs that in 1925 became international heroes in one of the most famous dramas in the history of the North. As the very world held its breath, not over the Iditarod Trail, but over the Tanana Trail to the Yukon, down the Yukon Trail to Kaltag, over the Kaltag Portage to the Bering Sea, and up the coast to Nome they ran legs of a dog team relay of life-saving serum, battling through blinding blizzards and temperatures down to forty degrees below zero to rescue epidemic-stricken Nome from diphtheria.

Rod Perry: *In 1969 my father (whose picture graces the cover of this book) and I worked on the brickwork of the final, major N.C. store construction in Alaska. It now houses Nordstrom on Sixth Avenue in Anchorage.*

Besides the freighters and mail drivers, individual travelers in great numbers used the Iditarod. Some of them drove full teams, some used just a dog or two to help pull a Yukon sled as they walked, and many walked carrying backpacks, some accompanied by pack dogs carrying loaded panniers.

———————

Al Preston: "Rod, people of all descriptions used the trails. This is a rare one. A veteran dog driver, Will Fentress, told me this bizarre tale. I never knew of him to exactly lie, but Ol' Will had an obvious flair for a story, and he could sure color it up.

———————

Will Fentress: "Al, I know you might find this account hard to believe but I'll tell about an encounter with the strangest trail user I ever saw or heard of. I was freighting with my team of big, hundred-pound, mixed-breed malamutes. I really had to lean hard on them whenever we passed another team to keep them from picking a fight. What I'm stressing is that bunch of dogs didn't back down from anybody.

"Way out along a remote stretch, I was crossing a long, open flat when my dogs began to act queerly, kind of fearfully. Then they all but stopped working. As I halted the team, all eyes turned toward the far side where the trail came emerged from the timber.

"Out of the trees appeared a big team, long sled, and a driver traveling at a fast pace. The closer they came, the more upset my dogs got. Once, the oncoming driver cracked a long, blacksnake whip above his team. He was still 200 yards off but it was like a rifle shot, and my dogs jumped. Other than that, he stood stock-still on the runner tails.

"As that team drew closer, I just stared in amazement at those swift, lean, striders. They all stood a full half foot taller than my own big freight dogs and every one a matched jet black. The animals looked like huge, gaunt wolves, yet not quite like wolves either. I've simply never seen their like. The contents of the long sled they pulled were shrouded by a black canvas.

"I'd been working my sled off the trail. As I got my dogs off to the side to let the oncoming team by those warriors of mine laid their ears back and began to whimper.

"As remarkable as the black team looked, they couldn't compare to the appearance of their driver. He was a giant of a man clad in a full-length black wolf-fur parka. He wore a huge Cossack hat of black bear fur pulled low over his ears. His face was real swarthy and his great, black, full beard framed it. Heavy black eyebrows accented the giant's dark, grim visage.

"As the black team passed, some of my dogs tried to bolt away farther out into the deep snow. But they couldn't because of the anchor of the others that froze there cringing on the ground, just cowering pitifully. The black dogs hardly looked right or left. They payed almost no attention to my groveling team.

"Now came the strangest part of all. I tentatively raised a hand in greeting. Though we two were alone miles from the nearest other person, and though the grim traveler passed within three feet, the giant in black glared straight ahead.

"Al, his expression was so cold and foreboding it still chills me to think about it! He never so much as acknowledged my presence, like I wasn't even there.

"I just stood there with my hair on end and goose pimples all over me, kind of dumbstruck. My dogs and I followed the forms of that mysterious train as the dogs, sled, and driver grew smaller in the distance. We watched until they vanished from the flat into the far timber. I'll tell you, Al, I couldn't have felt weirder if I'd seen the very hounds of Hades pulling the death sled driven by the Grim Reaper himself. Shoot, for all I know, that's who it might have been. Maybe hell-bent on his way to collect on a debt!

"My terrified dogs simply couldn't pry their eyes from the point where those hellhounds had vanished into the woods. Minutes later, we heard the far distant, rifle-shot crack of the blacksnake."

———————

With the likes of the Dark Rider possibly abroad, neither Will Fentress nor his team would have wanted to bed down alone by the trail that moonless night. But if they could not have made it to the sanctuary of a roadhouse before dark they might have had to do just that. Before the advent of flashlights, there wasn't a lot of travel on moonless nights. Most travelers put in at a roadhouse until daylight.

Dogs were either chained out singly or, at the more developed roadhouses, sheltered in dog barns sectioned off in individual cubicles. A few better-constructed barns featured openings on both ends. Drivers could direct big teams in under cover, stop, and unharness. Then each dog's hay-filled stall was only a step away. Drivers could leave the towline and harnesses strung out in front of the dogs, but out of their reach. In the morning it was easy to harness up and drive out the open door at the far end.

Often, when fast-moving teams reported that slower travelers had been passed on the way, the roadhouse owner hung a "widow's lamp" out where it could be seen from as far away as possible. It only came down when the last traveler had arrived safely.

Salmon fishermen along the rivers did a brisk business supplying dog drivers with dried salmon. The premium product and most coveted were Yukon chums (dog salmon) and kings (Chinook) caught below the mouth of the Anvik River. Since salmon cease feeding once they enter freshwater, the Yukon fish that were bound for the upper river had to carry tremendous energy reserves to fuel their 1,000- or even almost-2,000-mile-long fight against the current. A practiced eye grew able to tell which fish were going farthest. Such fish, when caught on the lower river, were not "used up" like fish caught upriver near their spawning beds. Dog men knew the rich nutrients translated into performance, for "it can't come out through the feet unless it first goes in through the mouth."

During the off season many dog drivers left their teams to be boarded, freeing them to go about their summer work such as prospecting. Commonly, dog-boarding operations were run by the same fishermen who supplied the driver with winter dog food. As they caught and dried their catch, they fed the boarded dogs part of the resource.

Rod Perry: *In the area of dog care, a need then as now was worming. With no commercial chemical wormers available, drivers used the age-old methods of the Natives, which those close observers of nature may*

At Bird Creek Roadhouse, Salmon Swam Right to the Door.

well have picked up by observing the scat of wolves. Periodically, sections of moose and caribou hide, hair on, were fed. Or ptarmigan were tossed to the dogs, "guts, feathers, and all." Enough of the dog's tape and round worms at their mature stage became entangled in the hair or feathers and passed for the host to gain some relief from the continually ongoing infestation.

Many roadhouse owners, freighters, mail contractors, a few forward-thinking individual dog team travelers as well as the many trappers who used the Iditarod to reach the points where their trapline trails branched off, contracted with salmon fishermen to have the dried bales delivered to roadhouse locations. They were stored high above the ground in dry, bear- (and loose dog-) proof caches.

More than a few of the initial roadhouses began as mere heated tents, others as small log hovels. Some of them survived, many went quickly out of business. Some that died out had set up in poor locations, perhaps out of sync with the regular Twenty-mile day's-travel spacing. Others earned negative reputations. These were weeded out by natural economic elimination. An operator who turned a profit and saw a future in the business usually invested in better and more permanent structures and stayed in business as long as there was enough traffic to provide a good income.

Most of the roadhouses provided welcome havens and some gained widely recognized reputations for the quality of their accommodations and service. Cox's Roadhouse at Poorman featured a 22 by-30-foot central building with a lean-to kitchen attached. It boasted a dining room plus running water and an "outside white porcelain bathtub." Both a cache and an outhouse stood nearby. For the entertainment of patrons, the roadhouse had a pool table, card tables, and a phonograph "with forty records." The nine single beds were topped by springs and mattresses. Henry Cox took pride in his establishment as a resting place of comfort and leisure.

Famous church leader and intrepid dog team traveler, the Archdeacon Hudson Stuck, claimed that the finest roadhouse on the Iditarod Trail was the Bonanza Creek Roadhouse near Iditarod, praising the fresh meat and roomy bunks as luxuries.

Anyone familiar with Stuck's adventures and writings will vouch that the Archdeacon was no whiner. So when we read that he stopped at a filth-ridden, low-ceilinged roadhouse at Shaktoolik where he disgustingly noted that the inhospitable proprietor went on with his card game, ignoring his patrons, we know it was far below even the rough standards of a long, exhausting trail dotted with rugged outposts frequented by hard men.

However, it seems that Stuck's record of the lack of a quality reception at that coastal village roadhouse expressed a mere annoyance. His experience there could not hold a candle in shock value to accounts of some of the other encounters that have come down to us through the pens of travelers of northern trails who, though taken aback, had no choice but to endure whatever conditions they found where they stopped at day's end.

*Most trail users walked. Roadhouses often had bare-bones
beginnings. Once a beaten trail and roadhouse system
were in place, travelers could progress at a good
pace, only needing to carry a light pack.*

Alaska State Library Historical Collections, Papers from the Klondike
and Alaska, Fred W. Best, ASL-MS13-4b-22-12

Al Preston: "One trail waypoint was described by an old friend as run
by two 'low-lifes' who were indescribably despicable. Their scraggly
hair and filthy beards looked like they had never been cut, combed,
or washed. Their mouths were ringed with grease. Their yellow teeth
were so coated they appeared to be growing sweaters. They must've
had a severe case of the 'zacklys.' That is, their breath smelled 'zackly'
like the bottom of the henhouse!

"The only thing shiny about those guys was their too-short
mackinaws that shone with impregnated grime and let their bellies
hang out.

"When they'd go outside to scoop up buckets of snow to melt for
water, they took no care to watch what they were dragging off the
ground. It was a toss-up if you got sicker from the water or from

looking into the bucket. The contents usually could be counted on to include sawdust, rabbit droppings, urination (animal? human?), and maybe more.

"My friend said they carved moose meat off a carcass lying right on the floor. When you went near it the shrews gnawing on it scattered in all directions. It was so old, it was black. As the steaks bubbled in old bear grease that had been used over and over, in a pan that had possibly never been washed, you could see dirt coating them. Anyone starved enough to eat them had to be careful not to break a tooth on the gravel from the floor imbedded in the meat. This whole insult cost my friend a buck fifty and he felt lucky to survive.

"I know that was on the farthest low end of bottom-of-the-barrel waypoint stopovers. The worst of the lot were always dirty and you didn't know what kind of vermin might lurk there. You got soaked a couple bucks a night even if you didn't get a bunk and had to bed down on the floor with the rodents. The grub? It could be anything from red squirrel tasting like spruce pitch to scrawny rabbits, greasy beaver, grizzly that was half-raw, or tough old bull caribou shot during the rut with a taste and odor that would make a starving dog run and hide. Breakfasts often ran toward flapjacks that maybe had been cooked the week before and recycled from other guests who had pushed them away. The coffee might be nearly cold and taste like poison. And you didn't even want to consider eating the dark-looking, foul-smelling eggs. Or maybe I should have said, 'fowl'-smelling because some were fertile with baby chicks rotting in the yolks. Their canned goods were usually just left to the elements so the cans were rusted and bulged from being continually frozen and thawed with the contents turned to mush.

"The proprietor of one roadhouse I stopped at kept picking tobacco out of his rotten teeth with a fork, then he'd use the fork to stir his cooking. I'll tell you, you might pull into a place like that hungry and you didn't even have to eat; just one look at the cook, his habits and what he called food was all it took to take care of your appetite! You'd just lie in your bunk praying for the hours to fly by so you could get up and make a run for it. We used to joke that some of those operators had to post an armed guard to make sure no one escaped before morning."

Alma Preston: "During the very peak years of the Iditarod boom, the Iditarod Trail route couldn't wrest the mail contract away from the old Valdez–Fairbanks–Yukon River Trail route. At first, mail bound for Iditarod came down the old Yukon River Trail then took a branch trail south to Iditarod. And mail bound for Nome kept on over the old, traditional route over the Kaltag Portage and Coastal trails. But finally, in 1914 we won the contract, or I should say, my boss did. But the "colonel"—he was known far and wide by that name but he actually held no official rank—made us feel like family so I say we. Here's a picture of him taking a picture of me, and here's another one of him with his favorite mail sled and lead dog. I used to ask Colonel Revell questions about his early days in Alaska and life on the trail, which I seldom got to see since I was so busy tending his dog operation along the railroad between Moose Pass and Spencer Glacier."

"Colonel" Harry Revell: "I stampeded into Cook Inlet country back in '96 looking for gold. Instead I found a wife, Eva. She was the daughter of Frank Lowell who was the real pioneer of Seward. Eva and I married in 1903 in Seward.

"Beginning in 1905, my brother-in-law Alfred Lowell and I had the winter contract to run mail to Hope and Sunrise, Girdwood, Old Knik (Eklutna), New Knik (Knik), and Susitna Station. As soon as Walter Goodwin cleared the trail in 1910-11 and roadhouse operators rushed in to set up shop, I began thinking about going after the big contact to Iditarod and Nome. I'd already been running up to Su Station for several years so I knew the first 200 miles out of Seward. I used make that run when it was really tough. We had to start all the way back in Seward; there was that horrible Crow Pass climb and descent, not much in the way of shelters along the way, and very little traffic, so we were always breaking trail.

"But things were getting better. A huge improvement happened in the fall of 1908 following Goodwin's scouting trip of the winter before. They started building trail from Girdwood around toward Bird Creek.

"Colonel" Harry Revell

Then the next year while the railroad was being reorganized they did some work and pushed the grade and a construction trail farther around Turnagain Arm. Whether roadbed or trail, the upshot was that we gained the use of Indian Pass. What a breakthrough! After that we didn't have to use Crow Pass, which had been close to impossible.

"Let me stop and tell you about that. When you climbed Rainy Pass, you were crossing the height of land over the greatest mountain range in all of North America. You started slowly gaining elevation maybe a hundred miles before you got there. The last thirty miles, you started picking up height a little faster. Then at the last, you had a steeper climb to the summit, but it wasn't bad at all.

"But when you tackled Crow Pass you had to start at sea level, and in a scant handful of miles climb 150 feet higher than Rainy Pass! The whole ascent was torture enough. But right at the last it was nearly impossible. For the last third of a mile, the climb was forty-five degrees. Even with a hard-packed trail and perfect footing, no dog team ever born can pull even a light sled straight up an angle like that. Well, if you know that country around Girdwood, you know it is a deep-snow area, always snowing. That usually meant that every time you got there, you couldn't find any trace of a trail from the last traveler before you. We had to do things like go up and shovel out switchbacks the day before and let them set up overnight and break down the load at the bottom of the final pitch and make several trips. Going down the other side you could wrap tie-out chains around the runners to roughlock them and still not be able to keep the sled from overrunning the dogs. So we usually did things like drag the sled down on its side. And Crow just brimmed with avalanche danger.

"But when we got started using Indian Pass, we found a nice, long ramp to the summit and the pass itself was 1,200 feet lower than Crow Pass. No one who hasn't hauled heavy loads with dogs can imagine the difference that change made.

"Another thing which started making the trail better was an increase in traffic into the Susitna Valley. In 1905 there was a small rush into a strike on the Yentna. A pretty sizable community sprang up around the Alaska Commercial store at Susitna Station. I think they counted about 200 men living there at least part-time, and enough families with kids they built a school. Then another community began up the Yentna. Several men established roadhouses along the trail from Knik all the way past Su Station to the Yentna. The increased traffic meant the trail got broken out ahead of us more often and we didn't always have to do it. And the roadhouse operators made some trail improvements.

"When they struck gold at Iditarod, the first winter after word of the discovery went out—that would be in '09–10—a few more people *wanted* to go over the range from our side. But that didn't mean they did. As much as the Iditarod strike built up desire for trail use beyond Su Station, not many tried it because, gold strike or no gold strike, the trip was still just barely doable, just as bad as before.

"Most kept going into Iditarod from Nome and Fairbanks and the Yukon River Trail, because that's where the population and good trail were. That continued the next year, too, the winter of 1910–11. Nothing changed that winter, even after Goodwin and Eide went through, cutting and marking the way. Oh, a few went through on their new trail in the last of February and March before all the snow was gone. But not many because a musher would still have to carry the same old mountainous load to make it all the way on his own.

"But then, at the tail end of that Goodwin-Eide winter and on through the spring and summer, businessmen hurried out there and worked like madmen to get roadhouses ready by the next fall. Then, with the first snows in the fall of 1911, the floodgates burst open and the trail almost melted down from the traffic. We figured we were already hauling mail to Su Station, so why not go after the Iditarod and Nome contract?

"At that point, I started to prepare bids to try to win the mail contract. But no matter how I sharpened my pencil, I just couldn't compete with the beautiful trail-and-roadhouse system and the slick operation and might of the N.C. Company, who seemed to have a lock on the contract. It might have been a lot longer distance to go from Valdez to Fairbanks and down the Tanana and Yukon River Trails, but they had it easy compared to us. There was so much traffic over their trail the way was being rebroken every time you turned around. Harder trail means easier, faster going which equals less overhead.

U.S. Mail teams come through at Mile 54

And remember, by 1913 the trail had been improved to the point that the first motor vehicles made the Valdez–Fairbanks run. Of course, they couldn't do it in winter, but the point is, it had gone from just a trail to a road.

"Then you consider the overhead of the roadhouses, and how that affects their fees and the quality of their service. Up on the Yukon and Tanana steamboats pull right up and off-load. Even between Valdez and Fairbanks they could haul in a ton or more at a time by horse-drawn wagons in summer and sledges in winter. Compare the economy of that to a lot of the roadhouses on the Iditarod, where you had to wait for winter and stock them piecemeal, long distance, one sledload at a time.

"Now consider something like dried salmon for the dogs. The best feed in the world is Yukon fish that are selected by their fat layer. Those rich salmon swim right up to the dog lots of those Yukon Trail mushers. That means a lot of them don't even have to buy them. That reduces their overhead.

"Now compare that with a remote roadhouse on the Iditarod Trail route. Those proprietors have to buy them from a commercial operation, then transport them hundreds of miles, maybe the last leg by dogsled. By the time they get there, and you buy them, you wonder if they're made of gold. Just buy Kuskokwim fish close to our trail? If you don't have anything else, they're OK, but think about it: they're pretty close to their spawning beds, and can't compare with the Yukon fish to fuel your dogs.

"For three years I tried to outbid the N.C. system working the Yukon River Trail. The thing that kept edging me closer to the advantage I needed was when the federal government bought out the old railroad interests, set up a new headquarters at Ship Creek (now Anchorage), and employed thousands to really get construction rolling. As construction moved north, my trailhead moved with it, Anchorage, Wasilla, Nancy, and so forth. That kept making things easier and easier on my end as it cut down the length of my haul by dog team. Shorter trips cut our expenses and made us more and more competitive. Finally, expensive as our route was per mile compared to the route up north, when our way shortened enough to cut out enough miles it tipped the scales in my favor. We won the contract and ran the Iditarod and Nome mail for four winters, 1914 through 1918.

"But you know what? Those years we missed, 1910 through 1913, turned out to be the biggest years of Iditarod and the most profitable for a mail contractor. By the time I was able to win the contract, Iditarod was starting to slide. That meant three things: First, as traffic tailed off, it made it harder for the roadhouses to stay profitable. Second, we had a tougher time with the trail because it didn't stay as constantly broken. Third, with the population dropping, there wasn't as much mail.

"Funny thing, the straight trail running from McGrath (in 1910, the Post Office dropped the 's' from Mc Grath's) straight through Ophir and Dishkaket to Kaltag, the way the people of Nome had dreamed of, and the path of the route that Goodwin and the ARC first intended to cut, well, that never did become the most heavily used way for the Nome mail. Instead of that straight shot to Kaltag, some of our mail routes went west and others east of it. We went west around the big side loop to Iditarod. East, we took mail through the other new Inland Empire communities that had sprung up with discoveries that followed hard on the heels of the Iditarod strike: Poorman, Long and Ruby. And some freight dropoff points on the Innoko like Cripple Landing. So when our drivers got to Takotna, the Nome-and-way-points mail bags left on a spur that went through all those new mining settlements and connected with the Yukon River Trail at Ruby. From there it went on down the Yukon Trail through Nulato to Kaltag, then on to Nome.

"Finally, our mail runs just got overly hard. There simply wasn't enough traffic anymore. That often left us too much trail to break. We had a contract schedule to meet and that kept a lot of pressure on the drivers to push through no matter how snotty the trail was. The measures we had to take to keep to the schedule got more laborious. The drivers got sick and tired of it. Conditions working against us eroded the profit margin. The mail contract that had been such a lucrative opportunity was, for me, golden no more. I could see that all the factors chewing into the profitability were only going to get worse.

"By the time Alaska Railroad construction had pushed north far enough to get through the Alaska Range to Kobe, use of our section of the trail had pretty much dried up anyway as far as mail traffic. So even if Iditarod had kept going as a big population center, our part of the trail was as good as dead to the mail contract. Anyway, the contract went back to the boys up north."

Chapter 35

———◆———

Decline and Death of the Old Iditarod Trail

THE SINGULAR ENDING SENTENCE distinguishing the winding down of every great placer gold rush invariably begins with, "And so, when the last of the easy gold was mined . . ."

Gold in the Iditarod Mining District lay both fairly rich and shallow. Not only was that a perfect combination for poor placer miners to gain quick returns working only simple, affordable methods, but a perfect combination, as well, for dredging. Therefore, it was no surprise when the Guggenheims sent in their mining experts to evaluate the claims. In 1911 they followed initial surface investigations by taking options on virtually every Flat Creek claim. They then spent $50,000 dredge prospecting with their diamond drills, thoroughly crosscutting each claim. Subsequently, the "Googs" threw up all those options. In their evaluation, the ground was not rich enough to justify the high prices claim holders were asking.

By 1912 however, the miners of Iditarod country, having generally gone through the shallowest, most easily extracted placer deposits, reduced what they deemed their claims were worth. So when the Guggenheims returned they were able to buy or lease at prices they felt were justifiable. When Googs moved in and with their resources began to mine deeper, harder-to-reach gold with bigger machinery, particularly their huge, floating dredges, they spelled the swift population decline of Iditarod area towns. One dredge was able to replace one or two hundred men. Not only did the out-of-work miners move on, so did the support industries. A dredge does not have to be fed, clothed, supplied, housed, or cared for with other services so a dredge could not substitute for the men it replaced as far as supporting towns the size Iditarod and Flat had grown to be in the height of labor-intensive placer diggings. In the summer of 1913, not only miners and laborers, but tradesmen and merchants exited Iditarod country like rats off a sinking ship. With freight rates so high, everything that could be sold was sold for pennies on the dollar to those who stayed on.

The Iditarod boom hit its peak from 1910 to 1912, after which gold production began to taper off. Iditarod faded until neighboring Flat was left the bigger town. By 1920 Iditarod had but fifty residents. Many buildings and even Iditarod's telephone system were moved to Flat.

A flood in 1922 delivered the final blow, cutting a new channel that left Iditarod marooned on an isolated, shallow side slough. The once booming town saw its post office close in 1929, and in 1931 the town became disincorporated.

By 1930 the population of Flat had fallen to 124. The Post Office continued to deliver there until 2000.

Peter Miscovitch Sr., an almost unschooled Croatian immigrant who had arrived penniless in the great Iditarod rush, married, raised a large family at Flat, and through shrewd analysis and business management ended up with most of the claims. Pete was quite an innovator and inventor. His use of new machinery and methods allowed Miscovitch and Sons to profitably mine for decades ground that had already been turned over—and sometimes twice and thrice turned over. But it was primarily limited to a Miscovitch family show.

During Iditarod's peak, one giddy Chamber of Commerce type enthusiastically promoted Iditarod as Alaska's thriving new commercial hub. A natural destination for a railroad, he expounded. But his designation of the boom town as a hub was only true in the abstract, spatially. It was certainly not rooted in economic practicality. To anyone who would step back and carefully consider, history had shown that the easy gold in all placer discoveries is soon played out. Then the town must have some other reason for existence. Iditarod's single-product limitation coupled with its remoteness and *location so separated from the principal lines of travel* would leave it no reason once the easily extracted gold was largely gone. With Seward southeast, said to be 489 miles away, Fairbanks separated northeast by 499, and Nome distanced northwest 484, it was centrally located, alright. However, far from that providing strategic central location for a thriving commercial hub, Iditarod was more realistically just separated by 500 miles from anywhere in all directions. Iditarod redefined the phrase, "middle of nowhere."

Rod Perry: *Remember Goodwin's phrase, "out of the line of travel?" For all of Nome's early hopes and dreams for its own, shorter mail route to the sea, even after they got their trail pushed through to Seward, most of the mail kept flowing the old way from Valdez through Fairbanks and down the Tanana and Yukon. Remember, in the Alaska Road Commission's evaluation, justification for putting in such a trail depended upon creation of sizable business out in the middle between Susitna Station and the Yukon River Trail. The strike at Iditarod provided that volume of business, but it was momentary. As the Iditarod and Flat area population crashed, the level of justification faded nearly back to the lack Walter Goodwin had pointed out in his initial reconnaissance report.*

It must be pointed out that even at Iditarod's very peak, the dominant Fairbanks route and Yukon River Trail with all of its well-developed resources and smoothly working systems, carried most of the mail and freight into Iditarod and Nome. Even when several thousand inhabited Iditarod and Flat and tons of mail flowed in and out each winter, maximizing Goodwin's required justification, even then during the pinnacle of the Iditarod boom the U.S. Postal Service continued to deliver Iditarod and Nome mail via the Valdez–Fairbanks and Yukon River Trail route. Iditarod and Nome only got their winter mail via the trail from Seward during those four short years of Colonel Revell's contract, which came after Iditarod's population had fallen to a fraction of its former swarming hordes.

As the Alaska Railroad extended its rails northward, the trailhead for Iditarod-bound traffic moved along with construction. Eventual extension of steel through the Alaska Range eliminated the reason for the old route over Rainy Pass, for there no longer remained any need for dog teams to laboriously climb over the mountains to reach the Interior. In 1922, dog drivers switched to a route to Iditarod that left the railroad at the Kobe Section and paralleled the north flank of the Alaska Range. Running over relatively flat country the northern trail proceeded through Lake Minchumina to connect with the former trail near McGrath.

Most of the few remaining roadhouses on the old Knik–Rainy Pass–McGrath route that had managed to stay open for the already dwindling traffic shut down. As roadhouse proprietors quit their operations, the government established a system of shelter cabins in the Inland Empire area. Although those cabins did not provide nearly the level of support service the roadhouses had, the unmanned, unsupplied shelters at least supported travelers to some

"New Iditarod Trail" Over Flat Country North of the Alaska Range. Mail carrier Bill Burke's outfit: 21 dogs, 3 sleds, 7 drivers and passengers.

Anchorage Museum at Rasmuson Center, CHIS Coghill Collection,
Bill Burke, AMRC-b57-2-17

extent. To enhance safety, the cabins featured a sign-in-and-sign-out system to track travelers. It is likely that the flow of traffic the shelters kept going, though reduced, allowed the last of the die-hard roadhouses to stay in business as long as they did.

On February 21, 1924, Fred Milligan, a dog driver on the northern route, heard the distant drone of an approaching engine. At first, he may have been puzzled as to the source so deep in remote wilderness. However, it must not have taken him long to deduce that it must be emanating from an aircraft. In a few minutes he watched the plane pass almost directly overhead. It was legendary pioneer aviator Carl Ben Eielson flying a government-owned, ski-equipped de Havilland DH-4BM, following the dog team trail on a historic flight, the first delivery of the U.S. mail by air in Alaska.

Eielson had contracted to conduct ten Fairbanks–McGrath flights to test the feasibility of mail delivery by air in Alaska. He flew one way in two hours, forty-nine minutes, and after laying over several hours, had time to make it back to Fairbanks by dark. It was the first time McGrath residents could get mail originating in Fairbanks and return an answer the same day. The Nenana-to-McGrath round trip by dog team took ten days to two weeks. The two dollar per pound rate by air was half the dog team rate. Though the Postal Service canceled the contract after eight flights gave them all the information they needed (they could see there was potential but did not think Alaska was quite ready) Eielson's successful Fairbanks-to-McGrath delivery ushered in one new age and signaled the beginning of the demise of another.

Interestingly, in the evolutionary progression from ancient to modern transportation systems, from simple trails traveled by foot and beasts of burden to air transport, Alaska was—and is—unique. It skipped the usual step of covering the country with a well-developed web of highways and rails. Alaska went from the dog team directly into the air age.

The coming of the airplane brought down the curtain on most of the old trail and roadhouse systems that had catered to dog-team travel. So ended the most picturesque period of Alaska's history, that which begun with the great gold rushes.

469

As the old trail fell into disuse, the undisturbed, cleared swath provided a perfect environment for seeds to sprout and trees and brush to spring up. Only a few stretches near villages and remote hunting lodges continued to be kept open by use. Year by year, more of the marker tripods rotted, fell and returned to the soil. The roadhouses succumbed as well. Those built with sod roofs went first. Then, one by one, even those structured with more lasting roof construction had their covering cave in, leaving walls, floors and the rest of the once snug havens to be obliterated by nature. And so, just as the great dogs and grizzled travelers who had frequented its miles waned in vitality and disappeared over the final Great Divide, the last great gold rush trail in North America faded into silent memory.

Chapter 36

———◆———

John Beaton, Discoverer of Iditarod Gold and Builder of Alaska

OF THE PRIMARY DISCOVERERS OF GOLD in the Yukon Territory and Alaska, one stands apart. He is unique as the only member of that select fraternity who both remained in the North for life and invested his wealth wisely, not only for himself and his family, but for the general enhancement of the North Country. John Beaton, the man who uttered the Christmas Day, 1908 cry, "Gold!" from the bottom of the test hole on Otter Creek, setting off the Iditarod Rush, was not only an astute businessman, he was a quiet, but enthusiastically active builder and promoter of Alaska.

Born in Rear Little Judique (later Saint Ninian), Nova Scotia, in 1875 of Scotch highlander Catholic stock, Beaton had come north in 1899, magnetized by the Yukon and Alaska gold strikes that had inflamed the continent. Through the worked-out placers of British Columbia to the already-claimed Klondike he ventured, and considered the recent rush to Nome. Obviously, he was late. Chances for rich diggings greatly multiplied for the prospector positioned among the first arrivals at a new strike. But holding the prevalent faith among gold hunters that Yukon Territory and Alaska held major wealth yet to be discovered, John dedicated himself to searching the North.

Beaton's next few years appear sketchy. Early on, he is said to have made a grubstake working the great hard-rock mines of Juneau. It may have been wages carefully saved from this Juneau employment that gave him his grubstake to move about Alaska on his search. He is thought to have prospected around Fairbanks.

What we do know is that somewhere during his searches he acquired that resource almost all far north prospectors found indispensable to a successful venture: a hard-working, trustworthy, and compatible partner. John, in fact, found two. The trio worked out an arrangement: Merton "Mike" Marston would labor at any town job he could secure to keep Beaton and William Dikeman supplied and afield prospecting. (Later, John Beaton would comment that during his prospecting years he must have eaten "a ton of beans.") The men focused on the area of fairly new discoveries around Ganes Creek and Ophir on the upper Innoko River.

John Beaton

Along the way, the team made a noteworthy purchase which would not only prove to be a key to their Iditarod discovery, but served as evidence of the partners' business perspicacity. Somehow they either saved or otherwise raised sufficient money to buy a small motorized launch of their own, the *K.P.M.* Such a craft was not a trivial purchase for a couple of wandering miners.

The partners' greatly enhanced mobility allowed them to leave whatever prospects they may have had going around Ganes Creek, navigate the better part of a thousand miles to resupply, explore, and reach—with a full load of gear and supplies—distant, unprospected gravels on headwaters prohibitive for them to have accessed without their power launch.

That competitive edge afforded by the *K.P.M.* took them into country far beyond the common reach of other prospectors. So positioned, when they made their huge discovery at Iditarod, their strike owned a very singular characteristic that was absolutely monumental: the find was in country so distant and remote, so far separated from other prospecting activity, that they had no competition whatsoever. Without the pressure of having others engaged with them in a pell-mell race to stake claims followed by a sprint to reach the recording office, they were free to remain in the area as long as they wished and methodically claim the country as they desired. Throughout the North, no other discoverers of the great strikes were able to—uncontested—stake, record and keep so many claims for themselves as well as those for whom they staked by proxy.

After recording in Ophir and getting things settled enough on his new claims to feel he could break away, John immediately took up another stampede. Rushing back to Iverness County, Nova Scotia, near his former home, he married Florence MacLennon of Dunvegan. The two dashed back to John's diggings where Florence became the first white woman to live in Discovery Camp on Otter Creek.

William Dikeman, after extracting some of the most easily mined gold, decided to sell out. Reportedly the partnership of Riley and Marston bought his claims for $250,000. That was a fortune hard to turn down at a time when a worker out in the States averaged about three dollars a day.

———◆———

Rod Perry: *One unconfirmed report is that Dikeman may have invested proceeds of his gold claims in oil, particularly in the rich Teapot Dome and Signal Hill fields.*

———◆———

Beaton, though, bemoaned that his friend "Willy" sold out. Canny Scot that he was, John resisted the quick windfall. Then, by a succession of shrewd moves he reaped many times the quick harvest of his former partner.

After mining some of his own ground, Beaton optioned rights to the Guggenheims to mine a single time through his Otter Creek claims. Pocketing their $250,000 option, he watched developments. The Gugs, with their almost unlimited capitol, were able to move expensive drilling outfits onto Beaton's sites and employ that sophisticated technology to extensively core drill his properties. Following their comprehensive assessment, they decided not to mine.

John, having gained their expensively won subsurface drill data free, had much of the guesswork removed as to what his ground held at depth. He then used the empirical findings to attract various miners to work his claims on a once-over basis. Royalties paid by these operators added to Beaton's coffers. And when they had finished, the property was still Beaton's to work and rework. From them, he and his future partnerships would take fortunes by dredging.

Flourishing with his mining, John Beaton invested with businessman Harry Donnelly in the Miners and Merchants Bank of Iditarod. It was Miners and Merchants (possibly in concert with Wells Fargo) which contracted with colorful Nome freighter and mail carrier, (former Black Hills stage coach driver) Bob Griffis, to conduct his famous "gold trains." Each winter Griffis hauled sledloads of ingots valued in the millions of dollars out to Seward by dog team. From Seward Iditarod gold was shipped south to Wells Fargo vaults.

———————

Rod Perry: *Gold constituted an extremely heavy cargo which was not only terribly laborious to freight by dog team, but ran the risk of breaking through river ice during winter shipment. Just why it was not simply and easily floated downstream by steamboat to ocean shipping during summer is a matter of curiosity. They obviously had their very sound reasons, easily explained if we could bring back banker Harry Donnelly, miner John Beaton, or freighter Bob Griffis. But though it seems so singular, I have not questioned any old-time authority able to provide the reasoning.*

———————

Beaton also forged a very successful mining partnership with Gilbert ("Gilly") and William Bates of Seattle and with Harry Donnelly. In 1916–17 they shipped components in by river for building a dredge. Assembled on Black Creek, where some ground they worked is said to have run as high as an ounce to the pan, the Donnelly-Beaton dredge very successfully mined much of the Iditarod discovery.

———————

Stu Ramstad: "My father, who was grandfather's accountant, told me that the dredge (which cost forty thousand dollars) paid for itself within the first forty-eight hours of operation. Remember, that was at seventeen dollars an ounce."

———◆———◆———

Just when things seemingly couldn't go better in the life of John Beaton, tragedy struck. On October 25, 1918, after grounding on Vanderbilt Reef in Lynn Canal near Juneau, the ship *Princess Sophia* sank with all 343 passengers. Florence, pregnant and accompanied by the couple's two children, Loretta, age six and John Neil, age four, were among the lost.

———◆———◆———

Rod Perry: *Much of the season's Iditarod gold production went down with the Princess Sophia. Of course that was trivial compared to the human tragedy. In the worst maritime disaster in Alaska history, the passenger manifest included many notable Alaskans. It was widely stated that the ship "took the North down with her." One was Walter Harper, who perished with his wife. Youngest son of legendary pioneer prospector Arthur Harper and his wife Jenny, Walter had been first to stand on the summit of Mount McKinley.*

———◆———◆———

Heartbroken, John left the active working of his ground to others. Perhaps for recovery as much as anything else, he bought a farm near Vavenby in British Columbia's Blue River country. Further diversifying, he constructed—possibly in concert with the Bates Brothers of his mining partnership—the old Strand Theater in Seattle. During this period he continued drawing income from his mining property.

Several years passed. Then during travels in the States, John met Mary "Mae" Grant. She was a young widow with a daughter, Eunice May ("Jean"). Conversation led to their discovery that Mae, a Scot whose maiden name was MacDonald, and John had grown up near one another in Nova Scotia. Mae became Mrs. John Beaton on February 12, 1924. Although John never formally adopted Jean, the two always looked upon one another lovingly as father and daughter.

Beaton returned full time to Alaska and his mining. In 1926 John, Mae, and Jean, as well as a new addition to the family, son Neil Daniel Beaton, began residing in Anchorage. In 1927 he sold the British Columbia farm.

***

Rod Perry: *Neil Daniel would become the father of Pencia, Loretta, and their brother, John Beaton. Neil Beaton cut his teeth working big equipment such as drag lines in his father's mining operations, beginning at age nine. He is remembered to this day by numerous old steelworkers as the incredibly talented heavy equipment operator hand picked from the ranks of Anchorage's Operating Engineers Local 302 to work the giant cranes that set in position and helped assemble the first offshore drilling platforms in Cook Inlet.*

***

Pencia Beaton: "Grandpa's house stood on the present site of the Boney Courthouse. John Beaton was such an important pioneer and contributor to Alaska, it's tragic—actually it seems almost criminal—that his house could not have been preserved and moved somewhere. Nearby their house, they planted a crab apple tree given them by their friend James Delaney, one of Anchorage's first mayors. The old tree still stands beside Third Avenue between I and K Streets."

***

In many small communities, particularly in such competitive environments as mining, rivalries and factions often develop. In Flat, John separated himself from sinking into slander, jealousies, and cliquishnesss, thereby retaining universal respect. Being the objective of such broad high regard, he paralleled the legendary pioneer of the Upper Yukon known as "Father of the Country," Jack McQuesten. Also like McQuesten, John Beaton was known for his open-handed help to numerous miners trying hard to get a start.

Although John Beaton never set out to become an aviation industry founder, he became one, playing a prominent part in Alaska's transition into the air age. Because they had the money, heavy equipment, and abundance of mine tailings for material, and because their remote, multimillion-dollar operations needed ready access to air transport, the miners of Flat built a superb gravel airstrip.

Wealthy, and a staunch believer in the future of air delivery of mail, freight, and passengers in Alaska, Beaton provided major backing in the developing and solidifying of Star Air Service, which grew into Alaska Airlines. He also provided key early money in the development of Bethel Airways.

An important air pioneer who grew to be a powerful airlines business figure, the late Ray Petersen, was acknowledged as an Alaskan aviation industry historian. Petersen flatly stated, "He [John Beaton] started both those airlines (Star and Bethel Air). Back then he was the only one who could have."

Rod Perry: *Bethel Airways went out of business when the last two of their planes crashed. To replace Bethel Airways, in 1936, Ray Petersen, a young pilot with Star Air, began Ray Petersen Flying Service. He later merged it with several other Western Alaska air services to form Northern Consolidated Airlines. When Northern Consolidated finally merged with Wien Airlines, the second oldest airline in the United States, the merged airline became Wien Consolidated Airlines. Petersen finished out his long career in the industry as C. E. O. of Wien. At one time, as a major airline with jet service ranging from Point Barrow to many western cities as far south as Oakland, Denver, and Phoenix, Wien flew to more destinations in the world than any other airlines but Russia's Aeroflot.*

Ray Petersen was certainly more qualified to render irrefutable testimony regarding the importance of John Beaton's airlines founding contributions than those historians who have let him go unmentioned.

Stu Ramstad: "The two airlines were "started" (originated) by others. What Ray Petersen was saying was that it was John Beaton who solidified them near their beginnings to make sure they stayed started. It was Grandpa's injection of aircraft and capital that put those airlines on the strong foundation they needed to survive and thrive.

"Back then in those early days of air transport, to an established miner who was located in remote country it was of great benefit to have air services at their disposal. Fully functional air services they could count on. Some of the bigger miners bought planes and leased them to the air services. That gave them leverage. They sat atop the air service's priority list. They could call for a flight any time they had need. John bought several airplanes and placed them with air services under such arrangement."

———————

Phil Ramstad: "Those early aircraft were constantly crashing. Bankers wouldn't often chance loans to the pilots and air services. But John needed their service so it was to his benefit to see them grow. He put up a lot of behind-the-scenes money to build up outfits like Star and Bethel Air."

———————

From time to time visitors dropped in on John at the mine. One dropping in unannounced dropped a little too hard. He was world famous pioneer aviator, Wiley Post, in the midst of attempting to set the speed record for around-the-world flight.

It was July 20, 1933. He had left Khabarovok, Siberia over twenty-two hours before. Needing to land, he spotted the runway at Flat through a hole in the clouds. His faulty landing in a crosswind resulted in running off the right-hand edge of the strip and damaging his famed craft, the *Winnie Mae*. It was looking like his quest was over. But Post hadn't counted on the can-do spirit and capabilities of the Flat miners. The bent prop was hurriedly flown to Fairbanks for straightening. Fortunately, a new one happened to be available, saving time. Legendary bush pilot Joe Crossan rushed it to Flat.

While the prop remedy was underway, John and the rest of the area inhabitants rigged an A-frame with blocks and tackle and worked the Lockheed Vega 5B up onto the strip. Their on-site machine shop speedily repaired the right landing gear. As soon as the new prop was installed, Post winged away in time to set the world record of seven days, nineteen hours.

John Beaton continued to work his claims. Long after the Guggenheims had given the country the once-over and pulled out, Beaton's North American Dredging Company, working the Beaton and Donnelly dredge, kept going.

By 1937 Otter Creek had been gone over hard for almost thirty years. John Beaton's dredge manager, Hugh Matheison, somehow convinced his boss that the ground was played out and he should look elsewhere for fresh diggings. As a result, Beaton sold out major ownership to Matheison. Fortunately, he retained an interest. It turned out that Otter Creek still held ground rich enough that another fortune was taken out with the Beaton-Donnelly dredge.

The old dredge would work the Flat area until the late 1950s.

Stu and Phil Ramstad: "Our grandfather became active in the buying and selling of mining properties. At one time he held as many as sixteen scattered around Alaska.

"After serving as Grandpa's accountant and having married Grandpa's stepdaughter Jean, our father, Joel Ramstad, turned to mining. He started Yukon Mining Company and owned the Ganes Creek dredge. On the Lower Yukon Grandpa Johnny owned property on Kako Creek north of Russian Mission. The two worked a swap. That's how our company came into its Kako operation. And that's the way Grandpa and his partner A. A. Shonbeck—an old Klondike miner and grandpa's friend of 1910 mining days in Flat—began mining Ganes Creek.

"One investor in the Ganes Creek operation was E. A. Rasmuson. He had been a pioneer Swedish Evangelical Covenant Church missionary teacher who later became an innovative, forward-thinking banker."

Rod Perry: *The connection of the Rasmuson family to that of John Beaton and his family as well as to the continuing legacy of Iditarod is close, ongoing, and active. At the time E. A. Rasmuson was investing with Beaton and Shonbeck in their Ganes Creek mining venture, his son, the late Elmer Rasmuson, was well into a career in accounting and* banking. That career would eventually see him grow E. A.'s bank into one of the nation's foremost family-owned banks, National Bank of Alaska. In addition, Elmer would go on to become mayor of Anchorage and Alaska's most generous philanthropist, dedicating more than any other person in history to benefit the state and its citizens.

In 1940, while E. A. Rasmuson partnered with John Beaton and A. A. Shonbeck in their mining venture, his grandson—Elmer's son— Edward was born. That same year John Beaton's stepgrandson Stuart Ramstad was born. The two boys would grow up inseparable friends.

Edward—at the close of his own very successful banking career that began in 1964—in 2000 merged National Bank of Alaska assets into Wells Fargo Bank. In doing so, he merged into the very institution with which—during the glory years of the Iditarod Gold Rush— John Beaton's Miners and Merchants Bank of Iditarod had a close working relationship.

Between 1910 and 1918, Wells Fargo's northern venture in essence exchanged stage coaches for dogsleds. They established some forty offices across Alaska. It was to Wells Fargo vaults that John Beaton and Harry Donnelly sent out their famous yearly "gold train." Transported by dog teams, millions of dollars in bullion from their Miners and Merchants Bank annually came out over the old Iditarod Trail.

To those in the know enough to connect the historic dots, Miners and Merchants and Wells Fargo banks enjoy an ongoing celebration of their Alaska frontier relationship with every running of the Iditarod.

Today, Wells Fargo, of which Edward Rasmuson is a major stockholder, keeps up its close ties to Iditarod by providing one of the major sponsorships of the Iditarod Trail Sled Dog Race.

Outside of banking connections and the past Rasmuson-Beaton mining industry association of the 1940s, the two prestigious Alaska pioneer families enjoy third-generation camaraderie. Ed Rasmuson and Stu Ramstad remain inseparable friends. Not only do they hunt, fish, fly, and enjoy other experiences together, they, like their forebears, share a deep interest in preserving Alaska's history and promoting Alaska's future.

Managing and investing his money wisely, John Beaton continued to have other significant impacts in the building of the new territory. Along with his mining partner A. A. Shonbeck he entered several ventures in Anchorage and the Matanuska Valley.

————•————•————

Pencia Beaton: "A. A. Shonbeck and my grandfather sent a sampling of lush Matanuska Valley produce to Washington D.C. They wanted to convince the federal government that the land was capable of sustaining a government-sponsored colonization that was under discussion."

————•————•————

Stu Ramstad: "Another of my stepgrandfather's projects with A. A. Shonbeck (who held the Standard Oil and Ford distributorships in Anchorage as well as other business holdings) was to team with him when Shonbeck headed up action to create an airstrip for Anchorage. They went to work clearing the forest and leveling the ground and got the citizens to pitch in. The field they built is now known as the Delaney Park Strip between Ninth and Tenth Avenues. They play softball, soccer and other sports there now. Grandpa used to enjoy golfing on it."

————•————•————

When Shonbeck founded Anchorage Air Transport and hired Russell Merrill as pilot, Beaton lent enthusiastic support. (Anchorage's Merrill Field—which handles more takeoffs and landings each day than does New York's LaGuardia Field—was named for the young aviator, as was Merrill Pass through the Alaska Range.)

————•————•————

Pencia Beaton: "John Beaton was such devout Catholic. When the Sisters of Providence pushed to build their Hospital at Ninth and L Street, Grandfather supported their effort. He stayed in the background, but if you research back you see Grandmother's name on documents and in the news having to do with the founding.

"Amazingly, grandfather has been left out of Anchorage history. Although place names around Anchorage abound for a lot of people who did far less for the city and Alaska, not one thing in Alaska's biggest city is named for John Beaton."

———————

Phil Ramstad: "A tiny tributary to Coal Creek just east of Woodchopper along the Yukon River is named *Beaton Pup.*"

———————

During their travels, John and Mae especially enjoyed crossing Canada by rail to visit the place of their childhood, Nova Scotia. They stayed in nice hotels, dressed stylishly, and, though not spendthrifts, it would not have been hard, seeing them on the street, to guess they had money. But out on his mining operation, John, clad in bib overalls and pulling on his corn-cob pipe, looked like just another of his hired help.

John was happiest when mining. Upon acquiring the Ganes Creek dredge with A. A. Shonbeck, (and with E. A. Rasmuson an investor) the partners began working ground near where he and William Dikeman had been looking back in 1908 right before they first headed into Iditarod country.

"Double A" and John mined Ganes Creek until World War II shut down gold mining as a non-essential industry. But following the war, in late June of 1945, the two journeyed back to their holdings, probably with a view to opening back up. Driving on a mining road with trapper Cashmere Naudts catching a lift in the pickup bed, it was reported that Shonbeck, who was at the wheel, may have suffered a fatal heart attack. The pickup plunged from a bridge abutment into Ganes Creek. Miners who rushed to the scene were said to have found the doors jammed, preventing Beaton's escape.

Kindly, cheerful, optimistic, wise, and generous, John Beaton was also characterized as small, quiet, and calm. That might be surprising to someone expecting a frontiersman of such larger-than-life reputation to be of imposing stature, rough, impulsive, and dominating. But his exterior spare stature, considerate manner, and good humor belied that he had been a man of on-the-edge adventure.

Since losing his first family, those around him knew he held a deep-seated fear of drowning. So it is ironic that he should be taken that way.

In his passing he joined his old partner, William Dikeman, who had died in a horseback riding accident.

John Beaton has indeed been largely overlooked by historians. Prior to Iditarod, the United States' most northern possession had been classed as a mere civil and judicial district. It is widely held that it was attention generated by the Iditarod Rush that in 1912 spurred Congress to elevate Alaska to full territorial status. That constituted a big step toward statehood. However, even though it was Beaton and Dikeman's gold strike that spurred the transition the two were left out of the common historical discussion regarding statehood during Alaska's 2007 fiftieth-anniversary celebration.

Although no less an authority as the late Ray Petersen, certainly positioned to be in the know, vouched that it was Beaton's money and infusion of aircraft that did more to solidly Star Airlines (which became Alaska Star which became Alaska Airlines) than any other factor, he was not mentioned in the Alaska Airlines publication celebrating their seventy-fifth anniversary.

Such oversights do not seem fair, but perhaps it is the way this quiet man would have wished. His investments and loans were without fanfare, quietly done to boost Alaska and Alaskans.

There is the inscribed marble marking John Beaton's grave in Anchorage Memorial Park Cemetery. The crab apple tree still grows at Third and I Street. The multibillion dollar airline business that he helped start thrives in its eighth decade. The area of his great Iditarod discovery has produced some 1,320,000 ounces of gold and is still being mined. All of these serve as monuments to this prominent Alaskan, at least to those who know of his connections.

It could be contended, however, that John Beaton's greatest living monument is that it was his and William A. Dikeman's gold strike which necessitated building North America's last great gold rush trail, the Iditarod Trail. The old path oozes history and legend from its every twist, adventure and excitement from its every turn. No less magnificent a relic than this internationally famous trail could so marvelously serve as a platform over which to run the annual event which yearly turns the eyes of the world upon Alaska: the Iditarod Trail Sled Dog Race, "The Last Great Race on Earth.®"

It may be that if the race continues to grow and thrive, that its tangible and intangible value to Alaska at large will someday exceed that of all the gold ever sluiced and dredged out of Iditarod. Indeed, market analysts count the Iditarod Trail Sled Dog Race as one of Alaska's most marketable products and the word *Iditarod* the state's most marketable single word.

It may also be argued—backing up his own, long-held testimony—that it was none other than John Beaton himself who coined this world-famous Alaskan word (or at least coined the popular derivation from the Athapascan root word) when in the autumn of 1908, far up an unknown river, from their little power launch *K.P.M.,* in his pronounced Nova Scotia-Scottish accent Beaton exclaimed to William Dikeman, "I did a rod."

Today, personal memory of John Beaton is kept alive especially by the Anchorage Beaton, Ramstad, and Szymanski families that remember him fondly as, variously, "Grandfather," "Grandpa," or "Grandpa Johnny."

<hr />

Rosie Szymanski: "In my hometown of Seward at the Iditarod Trail's Mile One monument I attended the 2008 ceremony commemorating the centennial of the Iditarod gold strike and creation of the Iditarod Trail. Governor Sarah Palin read her proclamation and delivered a short talk. Then, she and I spoke briefly as I introduced myself as John Beaton's granddaughter.

"As attendees mixed, visiting in the aftermath, I heard little if any talk about my grandpa and his discovery. Really, there was not all that much even about the trail as a historic trail. As usual, whenever the word Iditarod comes up, most attention turns to today's modern race.

"Now that can be frustrating to a granddaughter of John Beaton. After all, without his discovery, there would have been no Iditarod gold rush or Iditarod Trail. And with no trail, Joe Redington would have never come up with the idea of a thousand-mile race.

"However, that said, I know if it had not been for Joe and his race-founding group coming up with the idea and crusading for inclusion of the Iditarod in the system of National Historic Trails, it would have never come about. Then the trail and my grandfather's gold discovery would be all but forgotten except by a handful of relatives and historians.

"So all in all, the greater the race becomes, the more magnificent the memorial to John Beaton, even if not one in a thousand race fans makes the connection. My grandfather was a humble, quiet man. He wasn't the type to go around seeking attention and demanding his due. He was all about building Alaska. Were John Beaton alive to see this race and what it has done to enhance and energize Alaska, he'd be more than happy to sit in the background. He'd watch from afar, revel in the event and its wonderful contributions, and cheer its new heroes."

⸻ ◆ ◆ ⸻

The idea to stage "The Last Great Race®" over its course would never have entered the fertile mind of founder Joe Redington, had there not first dwelt within him a deep yearning to relive something of the old trail's romantic past. His race is, in part, an Old North reenactment. It takes us back to the times when Iditarod country boomed, gold flowed, its trail pulsed, and humble Scot, John Beaton, stood atop— and at the bottom of it all.

Old Iditarod

---◆---

Reuben Gaines,
Former Alaska Poet Laureate

The Old Trail, the Crooked Trail, to Old Iditarod,
The pioneers who laid it down, the very first who trod
The muskeg of the creekbeds, in search for yellow stuff,
Are now no more, but then it does seem sensible enough,
To think that from positive digging, far off in the blue,
They're laying down their picks, to watch
the mushers coming through.

The Old Trail, the Winding Trail, to Old Iditarod,
It took a certain type of man to stand the gaff by God,
Whatever misery you wanted, scurvy, bitter cold,
Mosquitoes, they were there abundantly, in the days of old.
Well, men lived them out and those succumbed, quite a few,
Will settle back today and watch
the mushers coming through!

The Old Trail, the Devil's Trail, to Old Iditarod,
Was walked by men in stages, careful, rod by rod,
A miner with a lick of sense was not a fool for haste
For passing paystreaks by and letting labor go to waste.
But things are more demanding now for men who earn their due,
The ghosts take their ease today to watch
the mushers coming through.

Chapter 37

---◆---

The Final Curtain Call

THE IDITAROD GOLD RUSH was the final, great, old-fashioned, hell-bent-for-leather, devil-take-the-hindmost gold stampede. Even as it was happening, advancements in transportation, communications, and other technology were coming to the North so fast they were removing any possibility that late-1800s and early-1900s circumstances characterizing the grand adventure could be repeated. There could never be a replay.

The fabulous turn-of-the-century gold rushes to the Upper Yukon and Alaska were the final expression of "westering," going on since Europeans began settling North America's Eastern seaboard. There was land to be claimed west of the frontier; freedom, adventure, and opportunity lay in that direction. The admonition, "Go west, young man!" reverberated throughout our young republic, energizing us and forming part of our spirit, character, and identity. Our intrepid explorers and pioneers were opening a continent and the rest enthusiastically followed their heroics, cheering them on.

The California gold rush and wagon train migrations of the mid-1800s began populating western regions in earnest. Then, completion of the transcontinental railway in 1869 joined the settled East with the Wild West and the swift spreading of branch railroads and wagon roads accelerated claiming and taming of the west. And so, by the 1890s the curtain came down on almost three centuries of westering. We had run out of continent. Eyes looking farther west saw only sea. In the part of the national consciousness that had so long been occupied by exploring untamed lands and claiming their bounty, a void and longing was felt.

Just as a nation habituated to look only west for wild adventure and raw opportunity thought it had seen the last act and was resigning itself to a more staid existence, just then, from a different direction and out of a far country rang the turn-of-the-century cry, "Gold!"

The continent was electrified. Thousands rushed north. In Yukon Territory and Alaska, free for the taking was a grand supply of unknown spaces to explore, resources of yet more continent to personally claim, and unfettered life to live. Westering had returned for a dramatic encore. Crossing the stage came the Klondike, Nome, and Fairbanks, as well as the many other lesser rushes to noteworthy finds. And then came Iditarod.

Iditarod was the last curtain call. As the final major gold rush, Iditarod could be considered the final great expression of the laissez-faire individualism that had so colored our first three hundred years of European presence in North America. Today, living amid mass conformity and increasing regimentation and social restriction many moderns look back at Old North gold rush times with the feeling of Paradise Lost.

Growing urbanization and advanced technology have removed us far from the land, insulating and isolating us from the natural world in which, for millennia, we had been so inseparably interwoven. No wonder there still resides within the human spirit a nostalgic desire for a simpler, less fettered way of life more closely joined to the Creation.

No wonder that many who are interested in the North are drawn to stories and images of the gold rush era. Walls of Alaska and Yukon Territory museums, art stores, businesses and homes are hung with pictures that evoke a longing. Canvasses depict familiar Yukon and Alaskan icons: intrepid old sourdough miners, hunters, and trappers in their solitary pursuits; the lonely cabins and caches these colorful men erected (needing no one's permission) beside pristine rivers flowing out of unpeopled valleys nestled between unnamed mountains...and dog drivers going about their self-directed endeavors, their laden sleds pulled by the great dogs of the North.

———————

Rod Perry: *No wonder that millions are captivated by the Iditarod Trail Sled Dog Race! With an international following of untold millions ranging from highly interested through hopelessly captivated to wildly* *fanatical, the event owes its attraction to a number of magnificent intangibles. One of them is the powerful magnetism of the trail's gold rush history. It simply reaches out and irresistibly pulls us in, arousing in our emotions nostalgia for a romantic era in our pioneering past.*

Because the trail—the most prominent surviving physical relic and foremost symbol of the Iditarod Gold Rush—provides its platform, the event joins itself to that symbol of the final expression of westering individualism with its all of its accompanying nostalgia and images.

In part, our race may be thought of as an expression and commemoration of our more free and adventurous pioneering roots. In the here and now of our present event we may watch, touch, and participate in a living symbol of the Yukon and Alaska gold rush era.

Old North

———◆———

WHEN AN ALASKAN DOG MAN LIKE ME is old—and I will not see 87 again—it is pleasant to rock gently by the firelight and dream, dream of the bygone days, the glory days, of the old Iditarod Trail. My grandsons tell me to rest that I may gather vigor and stamina for the day I asked them to arrange for me. They say that added rest will give me strength to journey back to visit one last time the legendary trace, the path leading to the site of the world's last great gold rush. But then in my ninth decade, what else is there to do but rest? The boys need not fear—I will be ready.

Tomorrow, I will be flown over the old route. As we fly toward the Range, and I look down at the land passing by—the miles from Knik to Susitna Station and far beyond to where Anderson's Road house once stood up near the Rainy Pass summit—the distance will fall behind in minutes that once took us days to cover. I am hopeful the years will seem to fall away as well, for I yearn, in the time while they leave me alone, to reunite with the, oh, so familiar trail of my prime.

They say the mighty freight dogs that opened and developed the North are gone now, vanished with hardly a trace. The great native breeds that existed for millennia, and the large mixes produced to meet the needs of the gold rush, shoved aside by machines, and all within a few short years. Yes, I know there are much smaller racing dogs, light-boned speedsters only half the size. But, beyond a few scattered individuals, the old breeds are no more. With no hunters, trappers, wood, freight, and mail to haul and their usefulness past they have gone the way of the freight-collar-and-single-tree harness and gee pole. At least that's what I am told.

Now the ear-splitting whine of engines has replaced the almost silent swish of babiche on snow, the passage of webs driven by legs of steel in our long, swinging strides that broke our trails. Machines make it easier now and allow soft muscles to do the same work. So, too, they accomplish the tasks done for so long by the draft dogs. It seems to me that when machines took their place, the steely sourdoughs and old breeds departed, taking with them the Old North. That, I think, is a pity. But then, perhaps, I am too archaic and sentimental and what do I know? Maybe I view things only by dim lamplight, things which younger men might see better by the hard glare of modern lighting.

A rumor reached me that a homesteader named Redington—they say he treasures the old trail and its memories like I do—I'm told he plans to commemorate the old days with a great sled dog race over the route. It sounds too wonderful to hope for. And I think too big to pull off. But I pray he succeeds. I'd like to meet the man.

Well, the old dogs are gone, and the old trailsmen, but at least, they say, vestiges of the old trail remain. Tomorrow I will go back to reminisce. Out on the trail of my youth, I think the old life will come back to me as yesterday. My hope is that, as I stand out there, my last sixty years will seem to slip away as the miles once slipped away beneath our runners.

—Levi Hoyt, March 5, 1973

From the Sled:
End of the Trail Overview and Epilogue

———•———•———

C.K. SNOW OF RUBY, ALASKA, who during 1915–18 represented the Fourth District in the Territorial House of Representatives, offered this perspective from the end of the trail in Seward, February 15, 1919: "If you love the grandeur of nature—its canyons, its mountains, and its mightiness, and love to feel the thrill of their presence—then take the trip by all means; you will not be disappointed. But if you wish to travel on 'flowery beds of ease' and wish to snooze and dream that you are a special product of higher civilization too finely adjusted for this strenuous life, then don't. But may God pity you, for you will lose one thing worth living for if you have the opportunity to make this trip and fail to do so."

Well, my friend, after just having completed a journey several times the distance of that of Snow's, we couldn't agree with him more. Together, and with the help of my old sourdough friends Al and Alma Preston, we've traveled the trail of McQuesten and Harper, Henderson and Carmack, the Three Lucky Swedes, Pedro and finally, the trail of Beaton and Dikeman. Now you know why this trail of ours had to start so long before and so far away from Iditarod. You've examined, firsthand and in-depth, the meanders of the greatest of the gold rush trails, how one flowed into another, and now you can comprehend how vital the transportation corridors were to the birthing and life of the Far North. Covering the thousands of miles behind our tireless team, you got to briefly look into how Old Ben Atwater, the Goin' Kid and the rest of the old ones traveled and moved loads.

On our way, many's the night under the glittering stars that our malamute chorus serenaded us, lifting their heads and pouring out their souls, perhaps compelled by an ancient urging to respond to the plaintive, drawn-out howl of a distant wolf. Through it all, the trail took us onward, ever onward . . . to Iditarod.

I couldn't have asked for a better traveling companion.

You never complained, you kept your sense of humor in the heaviest going and always pulled more than your weight with the camp chores and dog care. I'll never forget you—it's tough right now to bid you farewell. Before you go, will you help me put away the dogs and sled? Just go up and unharness old Baldy there and then . . .

Wait! . . .

Shhhh . . .

Look . . . do you see him?

Close your eyes. . . . Now do you see what I see . . .?

It is March 6, 1973. Old Levi Hoyt, slightly bent from his eighty-seven winters, stands alone in the vastness of the northern wilderness. The old-style, pull-over, knee-length, ticking parka, recently taken from a trunk in his attic, keeps the cold at bay. He surveys the surroundings hopefully. Towering above him rise the shimmering white peaks of the Alaska Range. The stark beauty is as he recalls it, but the landscape appears lifeless. Not so much as a passing raven does he see. The thick silence begins to disappoint him. This is not the uplifting return he anticipated. Maybe Thomas Wolfe was right, "You can't go home again." Maybe he was foolish to think otherwise. He wonders if the old trail, which seems so devoid of life, is truly dead. Or might it be only dormant, like nearby Pass Creek hibernating under its winter encasement of ice and snow?

Dead or dormant, this is not at all like the bustling trail he knew. He closes his eyes and remembers. In a clip from an old movie that has replayed so many times, yet again his mind's eye sees a man trotting up the trail toward him. Clouds of blowing snow somewhat obscure the image, but the man is obviously in the full vigor of youth, ramrod straight and strong, clad in a parka identical to the one the old onlooker now wears. Stretching out in front of the young man is a long team, eleven pairs of mighty draught dogs following an old loose leader. Heads and tails are low, ears laid back, they are digging hard to pull their heavy load toward the pass. The man's mittened right hand reefs on the spruce gee pole that steers a big sled, its 14-foot-long basket heavily laden with freight. Coupled to the rear of his sled trails another of like length, similarly loaded. Behind the rear sled jogs a venerable sourdough, seemingly as aged as the mountains themselves. Every exhalation adds to the icicle buildup on the weathered old driver's long, gray beard. As the team trots by and the young man draws close, he turns to stare straight into the eyes of the trailside observer.

The old, familiar vignette has played so many times before, but this time, out beside the very trail, it seems so real. The old man at trailside wants so badly to connect to the two, engage them in trail talk, anything, just to bridge the gap. As the drivers and team draw away and a strong gust sends a dense cloud that begins to hide the image, the old man reflexively reaches out to them and opens his mouth to bid them stop.

That he went so far as to almost actually call out jolts him back to reality. Feeling foolish for allowing himself to enter so fully into a fantasy, he jerks himself out of his reverie and sees that, of course, the drivers and team are not there, not so much as an apparition. He grows angry at his lack of good sense, cursing the notions that brought him here. It was nothing but pure, unadulterated, ill-conceived idiocy for him to have expected anything uplifting to reward him for the trouble and expense of all it took to make it back here to reminisce.

He closes his eyes again as dull disappointment deepens and a heavy sense of melancholy weighs upon him. No use to indulge in imaginations, they are vain. The old trail is dead. And it won't be long before he, too, crosses that last great divide.

But wait! Something begins to register on his consciousness, this time on his hearing. He catches his breath to hear more clearly. Is it? Could it be? It indeed sounds like the banging of the front end of a swiftly moving sled as it bumps over trail moguls. Now comes to his ears the unmistakable, approaching, quick panting of a working dog team . . . The old man fears that the sensory treat will fade if he opens his eyes. Yet the old familiar sounds seem so real. And they are growing closer. Then he hears the driver whistle to his team and the old man's eyes fly open.

Bursting into view from around a bend surges a fast-moving, gray-brown leader. He and the team that follows are certainly no phantoms.

Here he comes, the spirited animal driving his team hard, his ground-eating strides closing the distance toward the old man.

"Hotfoot! On by!" The long striding husky leads his team on by and the old man's attention switches to the driver. He sees a young stranger, perhaps somewhere in his late twenties. There is a friendly, but determined glint in his eye. The old man and the young driver lock gazes, wave and connect for a moment.

"Who are you, son?" cries out old Levi to the receding man on the sled. As his team disappears behind a low hill, the driver turns slightly on his runner tails. Over his shoulder he cups a gloved hand to his mouth and calls back, "Wilmarth!"

———————◆—————◆———————

The Iditarod lives! Behind the unquenchable faith and relentless drive of Joe Redington, a simple, yet remarkable country visionary, the old trail has been reborn, raised to new vitality, glory and fame. A race for the ages is on! The trail-breaking running of the Iditarod Trail International Championship Sled Dog Race is underway, and intrepid men, including gold miner, trapper, and bush pilot Dick Wilmarth of Red Devil, Alaska, with his great Lime Village leader, Hotfoot, are on the trail in quest of adventure and $50,000 in prize money.

———————◆—————◆———————

Rod Perry: *That no road was ever built over the old trail's route and that the country it traverses remains largely raw wilderness has preserved its primitive character and colorful gold-rush luster through the decades of abandonment as if the trail has had an appointment with destiny.*

To the trail's romantic allure may be attributed one of the main reasons the Iditarod would one day live again. A half century after heavy trail use died out, in a "man-and-team-against-the-wilderness" setting, the old path experiences a glorious rebirth. From its long slumber it awakes to hear the barely audible hiss of runners and the creaking of sled joints, it feels the staccato footfall and listens to the panting of trotting huskies. The most wondrous sled dog race of all time, a fabulous contest of unprecedented proportions, is being held over its spectacular course, capturing international attention.

In future years, Ian Woolridge of the London Daily Mail will coin the phrase to describe the event, "The Last Great Race on Earth®." Nothing else will so universally be acclaimed to epitomize the Spirit of Alaska. It will gain such international recognition that if questioned, "What comes to mind first when you think of Alaska?" more people around the world would answer, "The Iditarod!" than anything else. The direct and indirect economic benefits of the Iditarod Race to Alaskans, not to mention the surpassing value of its intangibles, is beyond immeasurable.

———————

So, trailmate, not so fast with unharnessing our animals. My zest for the trail is undiminished. I still hunger for the view over the next ridge and exult in the feel of the team's power coming back to me through the sled. The dogs are hitting their tugs, anxious to be gone. The pull of the trail is just too magnetic to resist. I need a traveling companion . . .

Old friend, will you come?

Levi Hoyt travels back and forth between the gold-rush-era Iditarod and its glittering resurrection as a spectacular modern race. And so can you by reading both volumes of *TRAILBREAKERS Pioneering Alaska's Iditarod.*

The Iditarod
bursts upon the north, a path to riches
North America's last great gold rush trail

It pulses with energy and adventure, then fades out
For a half-century it sleeps—then

The Iditarod
is gloriously reawakened, stage for
The Last Great Race On Earth®

Rod Perry writes
TRAILBREAKERS Pioneering Alaska's Iditarod
as a two-volume work.

You've just read Volume I,
Blazing the Last Great Gold Rush Trail
in North America 1840-1930

You've just learned how, a century ago
the Legendary Trail Itself was birthed in the Gold Rush

Now Journey Ahead
to the Do-or-Die Winter of 1972-1973
When Daunting Obstacles Loomed and

the Iditarod's Very Fate
Hung in the Balance

Learn about how the great sled dog race that runs
over the famous Iditarod Trail was born

Read Volume II, The Most Daring
Iditarod Adventure of All Time
Founding the Last Great Race on Earth®

The Other End of the Trail

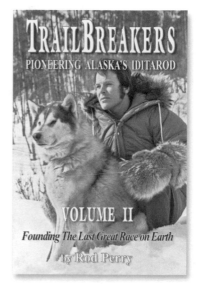

THE IDITAROD TRAIL SLED DOG RACE has ascended to such world fame, that one would probably have to dwell in a realm featuring mail delivery beyond Planet Earth not to know the event is a spectacular challenge in which intrepid men and women and their magnificent dog teams pit themselves against a thousand miles of untamed Alaska wilderness, battling all that nature can throw against them, dueling one another in quest of riches, adventure, and glory.

If you are reading these lines, chances are good that you are familiar enough with the renowned event that you think you have a good idea about how it all started. You may even be so immersed in Iditarod culture that its founding seems old hat to you.

But—Do you really know?

Not many were privy to the inside story even back then when the very fate of The Last Great Race On Earth® teetered on the brink.

Would it ascend to heights of glorious success and international renown?

Or would it go down to the grave in ignominious death, beyond all possibility of resurrecting, never to be heard of again?

Today, not one in a million race fans and even few of the racers themselves are knowledgeable of the actual story, of how, between October, 1972 and April, 1973, all the race has ever been—all it is today—all it will ever be, wobbled so precariously as it struggled to the starting line and battled and straggled its way over the long, blizzard-lashed trail, that it could have easily gone crashing down at many points and they would have never thrilled to the word, "Iditarod."

So, think you know all about those fateful times when the event desperately fought for birth and its first breath? Think you have the straight scoop about how it all began?

Only a small handful really knows.
For the first time, the amazing inside story is told.

"It's about time someone wrote it this way! If you are jolted when parts of this story differ from commonly accepted renditions, you may be sure that Rod's version is accurate. Unlike most other writers, he was there close to us. From his experiential, insider's viewpoint, Rod writes about how The Last Great Race® was begun as it should be: carefully researched and artfully, factually—and humorously—described."

—Gleo Huyck, Cofounder, Iditarod Trail Sled Dog Race

"Rod's got his facts down. Dad would be proud of this book."

—Joee and Raymie Redington, sons of the late
Joe Redington Sr., "Father of the Iditarod"

What a bold, risky, and wild experiment! Hands down that trail-blazing run ranks as the greatest Iditarod adventure of all time; no other comes even close. Joe Redington Sr. of Knik, Alaska was the man who set the grand odyssey in motion and thereby became a legend. The contest he concocted was so grandiose, extravagant, and spectacular in all of its facets that few believed it possible. *Part I* (of *Volume II*) tells of his struggles amidst apathy, skepticism, ridicule, and open opposition, to found the most captivating, most famous event in northern sports history.

Part I goes behind the scenes and exposes the mountain of resistance thrown up by the established sled dog racing community, the relentless dogging of the media, the doubt of the business community, and the part an illegal lottery tangled in scam and theft played in thwarting Joe's plans. It also relates the vital help of a radical group of oft-naked hippies, the indispensable part played by a drunken newscaster, the desperately needed money that saved the race from infamy secretly gained as hush money (through blackmail of a prominent Alaskan!), and how Alaska's commanding U.S. Army general got the race off and running when he threw the might of the 172nd Airborne Division against the Alaskan wilderness.

Worked into the prerace telling are a number of anecdotes concerning my own preparations:

- Tutored in the fine points of sled design by a friendly old sourdough, I am surprised by the later revelation that my mentor is none other than the fabled bush rat who had "dispatched" his first wife, cremated her body in the cabin stove, then disposed of her ashes down a hole in the ice of Lake Louise, one of the most famous murders in the annals of the North.

- Requested to haul a rented Santa by dog team to visit a local grade school, I pick him up smelling fresh in his regulation red, white, and black—and deliver him, in odor and appearance like I had taken a side swing by the sewage treatment plant and had him dipped.

- On a final training run at under forty below, beneath the brilliant moon and shimmering aurora lighting the polar sky, I stop to kindle a bonfire, oblivious that a man is freezing to death not far from where I soak up life-saving heat.

That first Iditarod was such a plunge into the unknown for administrators and mushers alike! Joe Redington sought men to fill his field who neither needed nor expected much support, men so steeped in bush skills that were they to be thrown naked and alone into the depths of a subarctic wilderness winter, they could be expected to emerge in spring ten pounds heavier sporting a new set of fur clothes. And that's just who signed up. Gold miners. Trappers. Big game guides. Homesteaders. White adventurers. Indians and Eskimos from remote subarctic and Arctic villages. Trail-hardened men with seasoned, working dog teams. Every one of them, tough to kill.

Come, look on with me from where the race leaves the road system: Two wives stand sobbing as dog teams disappear into the birch forest at the end of Knik Lake. It is as if wild Alaska, crouching jaws open, has just devoured their husbands. Each fear they will never again see them alive. Out on the cruel trail, raw nature throws everything it has at the trail-breaking pioneers—blinding blizzards, fifty-below cold, the greatest snowstorm in race history. The racers must—simply must—make it through; the entire future of the event depends upon them and their heroic dogs. As if on a reconnaissance, scouting the way for all races and racers to follow, the forerunners experience incredible adventures:

- Two men lose the trail, then, on starvation rations, take more than a week to snowshoe ahead of their dogs more than a hundred miles back out to civilization—and all the while, race officials are not even aware the men have left the race and are somewhere out amidst the great wilderness on their own!

- One member of a two-man team (tandems are welcomed this first race) is too badly injured to transport on a sled. As he is abandoned by the last drivers and left alone for days, his fate depends upon end-of-pack mushers making it almost a hundred miles to where they hope to find primitive communications to summon help. Again, race officials are unaware any such emergency is transpiring.

- An official and two competitors are drunk most of the way.

- A competitor is racing who had slipped into the field without it being noticed that he had neither paid an entry fee, nor sent out supplies. He now makes his way along the course by helping himself to the food drops of other racers—mainly mine!

Race fans acquainted with today's well-funded, highly structured, and slickly organized event can hardly imagine the rag-tag disorganization and craziness of that preposterously wild and wooly, flat-broke-but-go-anyhow first test drive of Joe Redington's audacious creation.

Part II chronicles as well the saga of gold miner, bush pilot and former trapper Dick Wilmarth, who comes out of nowhere to win the first race with his collection of Native trapline dogs gathered from the far reaches of the remote upper Kuskokwim.

So journey back with me. Relive that time decades ago when everything the Iditarod has been over the decades and all it will become—EVERYTHING!—depended upon the desperate drive between October and April of that do-or-die winter to bring off one of the most daring, most stupendous sporting events ever conceived. Join some of us who are in the know—Tom Johnson, Gleo Huyck, Dick Mackey, Dan Seavy, the Redingtons, Ron Aldrich, Dave Olson, a few others and me—as we stare analytically at the realities. What we plainly see and foresee is this: The Iditarod's foundations are so wobbly, its credibility so close to nonexistent, that should the haphazard, seat-of-the-pants attempt die this winter—this particular winter of 1972–73 and no other—resultant humiliation and loss of already thin repute will be so utter, and defeat will be so final, that it will render resurrection altogether impossible. Our view into the future shows a possible birthing of an amazing phenomenon of vast international renown. But it also shows that to realize that possibility we must not fail. As it struggles for birth and its first breath that winter, we must assure that it lives or the Iditarod miracle will never see the light of day.

And we do not let it die; our trial run succeeds brilliantly! Breaking trail for all Iditarod races to follow our pioneering passage blazes a path across the North like a dazzling comet, spreading new luster to the state's image, adding to Alaska a novel, internationally famous identity. In the minds and hearts of the world, one symbol rises to eclipse all others to epitomize the very Spirit of Alaska: the Iditarod, The Last Great Race On Earth®.

Come with me as I spin the tale.

Books by Rod Perry may be purchased at
www.rodperry.com

More About the Author

GROWING UP ON THE OREGON COAST, Rod had a father whose compelling descriptions summed with his avid reading about the North to inspire his enthusiasm for life in Alaska. In 1963, just five years after the territory became the forty-ninth state, he first came to southeastern Alaska to work with the Alaska Department of Fish and Game. After returning to Oregon State University to finish a bachelor of science degree in wildlife management, Rod and his brother, Alan, moved to Alaska permanently.

During his first years in Alaska, he helped coach the wrestling team at Dimond High School in Anchorage with Larry Kaniut, who would go on to become the well-known author of *Alaska Bear Tales*, *More Alaska Bear Tales*, *Some Bears Kill*, *Bear Tales for the Ages*,

Danger Stalks the Land and other popular books. Rod and Alan both won Alaska freestyle (Olympic-style) wrestling championships in their respective weight classes in 1968 and 1969.

On the Kenai Peninsula, fabled then as supporting one of the greatest moose populations in the North, Rod served for a time on a moose research project. Though he was highly interested in the work, his creative nature, thirst for adventure and bent toward independence made agency work too confining. Additionally, a big part of his reason for moving north had been his vision to produce his own outdoor adventure motion pictures.

In 1969 Rod began assembling footage that would become part of his major motion picture, *Sourdough*. It depicts the story of a venerable old prospector and trapper, a member of a vanishing breed attempting to carry on a traditional northern wilderness lifestyle amidst a passing old-time Alaska. Rod's father, Gilbert Perry (pictured on the cover of this book), starred as the old sourdough. With final production help from Bob Pendleton, George Lukens, and Martin Spinelli of Anchorage's Pendleton Productions plus Hollywood's Albert S. Ruddy Corp. (which produced *The Godfather* and *The Longest Yard*, among others) *Sourdough* swept around the globe in 1977–78. To this day more viewers worldwide have seen it than any other motion picture ever filmed in Alaska, including features made in Alaska by major Hollywood companies.

During the years of filming *Sourdough* Rod took time out each season to guide sheep hunters in the Wrangell Mountains with master guide, Keith Johnson. He also managed to work in a lot of his own hunting. On one memorable marathon, Rod, his brother, Alan, and their friend John Lindeman made a 120-mile-long backpack hunt for sheep. That same fall he continued to take friends in quest of moose until he and six others had their winter meat supply.

Needing a dog team as part of his motion picture cast led Rod to assemble a few huskies, which he boarded with friends Mike and Carolyn Lee. On one fateful weekend driving dogs at the Lees, Rod met dog musher Joe Redington. The man set Rod's imagination afire. Joe said he was planning a sled-dog race of epic proportions to be named The Iditarod Trail International Championship Sled Dog Race.

Rod did not see how he could prepare and compete while in the thick of filming *Sourdough* but somehow, some way, he just had to go.

The idea of staging an event of such a size, cost, and difficulty drew endless public ridicule and scorn, especially from Anchorage-area sprint mushers. As a result, although the Anchorage bowl held half of the state's total population, only one local driver—Rod—was interested enough or had enough faith in the Iditarod to compete in the first race.

The media, therefore, focused more attention on him than might be expected for a seventeenth-place finisher. Drawing even more of the hometown air time and ink than Rod, however, was his big malamute-Siberian lead dog, a real character named Fat Albert. Anchorage media soon made the colorful dog a local celebrity.

After completing the historic first Iditarod in 1973, and with the snows hardly melting from the trail, Rod chronicled his and Fat Albert's wild, primitive, trail-breaking experiences for *Alaska Magazine* in what editor Ed Fortier said was the longest two-part article ever to appear in that publication. The article was otherwise historic in that it was the first-ever feature-length piece on the Iditarod Trail Race to hit the international periodical press. One result was that Fat Albert's celebrity status began to spread beyond Alaska's border.

The following year, the *National Observer* (a publication noted for journalistic excellence and a readership among the country's moneyed intelligentsia) ran twelve straight weeks of Fat Albert and Rod Perry news. The *Observer* was the weekly news magazine companion to the *Wall Street Journal*, and several weeks, the *Journal* itself printed the coverage. That put the race before the eyes of the nation's foremost business and political leaders. It was reported that over 160 newspapers around the country ran some, if not all of the articles. The *Observer* staff stated that the series drew more reader response than anything else in the history of their publication, including their coverage of the Kennedy assassination and Watergate.

By the third year of the contest, *Sports Illustrated* took the race to its millions. Associate editor Coles Phinizy opined that in the short history of the Iditarod, the event had already established its Babe Ruth—but that the figure was not a man, but a dog named Fat Albert. Phinizy devoted a significant share of the feature to Rod's big leader.

Reader's Digest picked up the *Sports Illustrated* article, further extending the legacy of Fat Albert.

With all of the vast coverage, Fat Albert became the best-known sled dog since Balto, the lead dog famed for the 1925 Nome Serum Run. Fat Albert publicity on the pages of some of the most widely read newspapers and magazines in the United States played a significant part in jump-starting the Iditarod in the international consciousness.

Then Cecil Andrus, Secretary of the Interior under President Jimmy Carter, appointed Rod to the original Iditarod National Historic Trail Advisory Council. In 1980, personally worried that the new agency trail administrators might not be "doggy" enough, Rod outfitted and led the top three local officials to McGrath by dog team.

Rod and his brother, Alan, ran the first six races, three apiece, placing in the money each time. Rod has often lamented that his two biggest undertakings, *Sourdough* and the Iditarod, overlapped. *Sourdough* would have been better without the Iditarod to divert his energies and vise versa. But Rod states emphatically that he would not have given up either for the world.

Away from the spotlight, usually on his own, Rod has promoted the race in every way he could. As an example, he designed and produced the large and colorful Anchorage–Nome Iditarod Mushers patch. It is one of the world's most famous, exclusive and coveted patches, and one that, properly, may be worn only by drivers who have officially completed the great race. Using a picture taken of him and his team approaching Nome on the first Iditarod for a model, Rod became "the musher on the patch."

In order to run the 1977 Iditarod, it was necessary for Rod to drive his team some 175 miles through largely trackless wilderness from his training headquarters at remote Lake Minchumina. On the way out he encountered trapper Leroy Shank, beginning a long friendship. As Rod's party stayed at Leroy's remote cabin overnight, a dream was kindled within the trapper to run his trapline by dog team. Driving dogs on his trapline led Leroy to driving dogs on the Iditarod, which finally led to him spawning the idea for the North's other epic sled dog race, the Yukon Quest. That race runs a thousand miles between Fairbanks, Alaska and Whitehorse, Yukon Territory.

Leroy invited Rod to stay at his Fairbanks home the winter of 1983–84 and help him, his friend, Roger Williams and the support group they had assembled get the Yukon Quest off the ground. Leroy, Roger and Rod worked sixteen-hour days, seven days a week, all winter long on the project. Early on, the three added Bud Smythe to form a quartet to drive to Whitehorse. There they spent four days breaking the news of Leroy's plan to Canadian mushers, government officials and the public, convincing them of the Yukon Quest's tremendous potential and helping them get an official structure started.

On their journey to Whitehorse and back the four discussed and argued race philosophies and rules. A number of the rules that became Yukon Quest cornerstones and characterize the race, particularly during its early years, were either of Rod's creation or carried his input.

Following his early Iditarod years, Rod fished commercially for everything from razor clams, shrimp, and king crab to herring, halibut, and salmon. Most prominently, he owned and operated a Bristol Bay salmon drift gillnet business for many years with his partner, Reverend Keith Lauwers, one of Alaska's best-known and beloved ministers.

Besides big-game guiding, working on moose research, commercial fishing, and running the Iditarod, Rod humorously supposes that he can lay claim to having done just about everything else on the classic Real Alaskan list. He has survived several bear charges, his closest call being the encounter at three paces in a dense thicket with a snarling sow with cubs guarding a kill. He has lived in the Alaska Bush, some of that time in Eskimo villages where he was honored with an Eskimo given name, Bopik. Rod even developed a taste for Native delicacies such as muktuk (whale skin with blubber attached) and oshock (walrus flipper buried in the frozen ground for a year to ferment.) Rod helped build three log cabins. He served nearly two decades with the Alaska Department of Fish and Game.

While Rod does lack a couple of musts on most people's short list of necessary Real Alaskan accomplishments, he laughingly boasts others that, though unusual and bizarre, should more than make up for the omissions. For instance, Rod has never been a bush pilot. But how many bush pilots can truthfully claim to have ridden a wild moose?

(Brother Alan, later rode one, too.) Nor has he climbed Mount McKinley (although, with their dog teams, Rod and his old pal Ron Aldrich helped veteran freighter Dennis Kogl haul a climbing team's gear and supplies for a Mount McKinley assent through McGonnigal Pass to a high ridge above the Muldrow Glacier.) On the other hand, how many McKinley climbers can truthfully boast to have sucked milk straight from a moose's udder? Rod has done that, not once, but twice! (He says the first time was spurred by curiosity, the second by hunger.)

For some twenty-five years Rod's old wrestling-coach friend, author Larry Kaniut, prodded him to write a book. His knowledge of gold-rush history and intimate familiarity with the details of the founding of the Iditarod Trail Sled Dog Race made producing this two-volume work second nature to Rod. How the original gold rush trail came to be—*Volume I*, and how the modern race was established—*Volume II*, came as readily as driving his dog team over a well-broken trail.

Rod and his wife, Karen, have raised and home-schooled a family of five children, Jordan, Ethan, Levi, Laura and Gabriel. They live in Chugiak, Alaska.

Resources and Recommended Readings

Captain Jack McQuesten, Father of the Yukon by Jim McQuiston

Israel C. Russell, National Geographic Society

An Informal Background of Mushing in Alaska, the Alaska Trail System, and the Iditarod Trail by Don Bowers

Shadows on the Koyukuk by Sydney Huntington as told to Jim Reardon

Two years in the Klondike and Alaskan Gold-fields by William B. Haskell

Alaska Department of Natural Resources, Division of Parks and Outdoor Recreation. Alaska State Trails Program. Online at http://dnr.alaska.gov/parks/aktrails/ats/idita/iditarod2.htm

Bowers, Don. *An Informal Background of Mushing in Alaska, the Alaska Trail System, and the Iditarod Trail.* Mike Zaidlicz, Bureau of Land Management, and Joan Dale and Rolfe Buzzelle, Alaska Office of History and Archaeology, contributers. Online at http://backstage-iditarod.blogspot. com/2008/06/don-bowers-history-of-iditarod-trail.html

Brooks, Alfred Hulse. *Blazing Alaska's Trails.* Fairbanks: University of Alaska Press, 1953 (2nd Ed. 1973).

Forselles, Charles. Edward Pratt, ed. *Count of Alaska: A Stirring Saga of the Great Alaskan Gold Rush: A Biography.* Anchorage, AK: Alaskakrafts Publishing, 1993.

Hamilton, W. R. *The Yukon Story.* Vancouver, B.C., Canada: Mitchell Press, 1967.

Haskell, William B. *Two Years in the Klondike and Alaska Gold Fields.* Hartford, Connecticut: Harford Publishing Co., 1898.

Heller, Herbert L., ed. *Sourdough Sagas.* Cleveland, Ohio: World Publishing, 1966.

Huntington, Sidney. Jim Reardon, trans. *Shadows on the Koyukuk: An Alaskan Native's Life along the River as told to Jim Reardon.* Anchorage, AK, and Portland, OR: Alaska Northwest Books, 1993.

Iditarod National Historic Trail Alliance. *Iditarod National Historic Trail.* Online at www.iditarodnationalhistorictrail.org.

Martinsen, Ella Lung with Edward Burchall Lung. *Black Sand and Gold.* Portland, OR: Binford & Mort Publishing, 1976.

Minter, Roy. *The White Pass Gateway to the Klondike.* Anchorage, AK: University of Alaska Press, 1987.

Russell, Israel C. "Timberlines." *National Geographic Magazine 14 (February 1903).* 80–81

Russell, Israel C. "An Expedition to Mount St. Elias, Alaska." *National Geographic Magazine 3 (May 1891).* 55–204.

Russell, Israel C. "Second Expedition to Mount Saint Elias, in 1891." *Thirteenth Annual Report of the United States Geological Survey 1891–'92.* Washington, D.C. : Government Printing Office, 1893.

Russell, Israel C. "A Journey up the Yukon River." *Bulletin of the American Geological Society 27, No.2 (1895).* 143–160.

Russell, Israel C. *North America.* New York and London: D. Appleton and Company, 1904.

Herbert L. Heller, editor *Sourdough Sagas.* Cleveland World Publishing Company, 1966 U.S. Dept. of the Interior, Bureau of Land Management. Iditarod National Historic Trail. Online at http://www.blm.gov/ak/st/en/prog/sa/iditarod.html.

Walden, Arthur T, [Treadwell]. *A Dog Puncher on the Yukon.* Rpt. Wolf Creek Books, Inc., 2005; Houghton Mifflin, 1928.

Wright, Allen A. *Prelude to Bonanza : The Discovery and Exploration of the Yukon.* Sidney, B.C., Canada: Gray's Publishing, 1976.

Gates, Michael. *Gold at Fortymile Creek: Early Days on the Yukon.* UBC Press, 1994

Bronson, William with Reinhardt, Richard. *The Last Grand Adventure.* McGraw-Hill Book Company, 1977

Web, Melody. *Yukon: The Last Frontier.*

Ogilvie, William. *Early Days on the Yukon; And the Story of its Gold Finds.*

McQuiston, James A. *Captain Jack: Father of the Yukon.*

McQuesten, Leroy N. *Recollections of Leroy N. McQuesten: Life in the Yukon 1871-1885.* Dawson City Yukon Order of Pioneers

Mercier, Francois. *Recollections of the Youcon, Memories from the Years 1868-1885.* Alaska Historical Society. Translated by Linda Yarborough, Alaska Historical Commission, Studies in History No. 188, 1986

Also, be sure to visit the Anchorage Field Office of the Alaska Bureau of Land Management's Iditarod National Historic Trail. It's a trip well worth making.

Golden Time Line

1868—Francios Xavier Mercier begins building trading posts on the Yukon River

1873—Jack McQuesten, Alfred Mayo, Arthur Harper arrive on Upper Yukon, begin establishing supply system to attract and sustain prospectors

1873-75—George Holt becomes first white prospector to find and cross Chilkoot Pass, begins era of seasonal prospecting expeditions in from Alaska Coast

1882—Prospectors begin to stay year-around on upper Yukon, increasing gold finds

1886—First large gold strike and in 1893 the second, result in first towns on upper Yukon, respectively Forty Mile, Yukon District and Circle City, Alaska

1896—Klondike Gold discovered, late August. Nearby miners stampede, stake all of Bonanza Creek and El Dorado Creek bottoms within days

1897—Rush to the Klondike begins seven months after main creek bottoms taken

1898—Great Klondike Gold Rush: major part occurs almost two years after strike

1898—Nome Gold Strike: discovery of upland placers

1898—White Pass and Yukon Railroad (WP&YR) begins at Skagway

1899—WP&YR broaches mountains, establishes railhead in Interior

1899—Golden Sands of Nome discovered

1899—U.S. Mail contracts with dog drivers to send winter mail to Nome over WP&YR and down Yukon River Trail

1900—WP&YR finishes railroad to Whitehorse, Yukon Territory

1902—Fairbanks Gold Strike

1902—WP&YR builds Overland Trail, Whitehorse to Dawson

1902–3—Fairbanks develops connecting trail to Gakona to join Valdez-Eagle Trail. U.S. Mail contract for Nome's winter mail soon switches to this "All American" route

1903—Alaska Central Railroad construction begins in Seward, bound for Fairbanks

1904—Abraham Appel establishes post on Kuskokwim at Takotna River mouth

1905—Alfred Lowell and brother-in-law "Colonel" Harry Revell contract to carry U.S. Mail by dog team to communities around east side of Cook Inlet and Susitna Valley

1906—Ganes Creek gold strike begins several years of Inland Empire discoveries

1907—Alaska Central Railroad goes bankrupt with 52 miles of track, 72 miles of roadbed and approximately 150 miles of surveyor's pack trail completed

1907—Major Wilds Richardson of Alaska Road Commission (ARC) upgrades Valdez–Fairbanks dog-team and pack trail to winter-sledge and summer-wagon road

1907—20 miners from McGrath area travel over trailless wilderness, averaging a month to reach Susitna Station. All straggle in, their condition described as "pitiful"

1908—Colonel Walter Goodwin of ARC with a crew of four scout feasibility of proposed Seward-to-Nome Mail Trail early in year. Becomes first to travel entire route.

1908—Girdwood-to-Bird Creek Trail: mid-year construction effort to replace Crow Pass with easier, safer trails toward Upper Cook Inlet

1908—Iditarod Gold Strike, Christmas Day. No word of late '08 discovery gets out as miners remain in remote location until ice-out

1909—Iditarod Gold Rush finally begins in mid '09 when, one-half year after discovery, miners leave site to record claims

1909—Alaska Central Railroad, during reorganization becomes Alaska Northern Railway. Under receivership, extends rails to Girdwood and construction trail farther, allowing access to Indian Pass

1909—Even after Iditarod Gold Rush creates powerful attraction, lack of trail and absence of resupply from Su Station to McGrath keeps travel perilous and infrequent over future route of Iditarod Trail

1909—U.S. Mail reaching Iditarod and Nome comes through Fairbanks until 1914

1910—Bob Griffis contracts to bring 700 pounds of gold out of Iditarod. With no trail yet from McGrath to Susitna Station, struggles more than five weeks to reach Seward

1910—Still no trail from Susitna Station over desolate Alaska Range stretch of future Iditarod Trail, route still hardly traveled even with great gold rush at peak

1910–11—Walter Goodwin from Nome with nine men, 42 dogs, and Anton Eide, from Seward with similar crew, construct Iditarod trail, first-ever defined trail over route

1911—(late winter-spring)—Still no great use of new Su Station-McGrath stretch. It's cut, but daunting. Mushers still must carry everything to supply trip, start to finish

Final U.S. Mail by Dog Team Leaves Anchorage, March 28, 1917

1911—(late winter-spring)—Entrepreneurs hurry to use last of winter trail, then summer building conditions to establish roadhouses Susitna Station to Iditarod; finally everything in place for traffic

1911—(fall)—Iditarod Trail really begins to be Iditarod Trail as most think of it. Dog team and foot travel extremely heavy

1914—"Colonel" Harry Revell captures contract to take Iditarod and Nome mail from Seward

1915—U.S. government takes over building railroad, Anchorage becomes construction headquarters. Mail drivers pick up mail farther inland from trains carrying it from Seward

1917—Last-ever dog-team mail delivery out of Anchorage leaves in late March

1918—Iditarod traffic and mail decrease to point Colonel Revell gives up that mail contract.

1922—Alaska Railroad reaches Alaska Interior, rendering need to cross Alaska Range by dog team obsolete. Use of old route to Iditarod via Rainy Pass largely ceases. North of Range, new trailhead established. Trail leads through Lake Minchumina to reach McGrath

1924—Pioneer aviator Carl Ben Eielson, makes first mail run by air in Alaska

Late 1920s—Dog-team mail along Iditarod Trail phases out. Teams continue to be heavily used across Alaska Bush for travel, transport, trapping, hunting, and racing

Location of Photographs

Merrill and Alma Leonhardt visit Anchorage, 1918